Assassins

Our morality is completely subordinated to the interests of the class struggle of the proletariat.

Lenin

Nothing in the underworld of the intelligence past can be known with complete assurance or certainty.

Angus S. C. Mitchell

Assassins

The KGB's Poison Factory
Ten Years On

Boris Volodarsky

FRONTLINE BOOKS

An imprint of
Pen & Sword Books Ltd
Yorkshire – Philadelphia

First published in Great Britain in 2019 by
Frontline Books
An imprint of
Pen & Sword Books Ltd
Yorkshire – Philadelphia

Copyright © Boris Volodarsky 2019

ISBN 978 1 52673 392 4

Printed and bound in the UK by TJ International Ltd,
Padstow, Cornwall.

Pen & Sword Books Limited incorporates the imprints of Atlas,
Archaeology, Aviation, Discovery, Family History, Fiction, History,
Maritime, Military, Military Classics, Politics, Select, Transport,
True Crime, Air World, Frontline Publishing, Leo Cooper, Remember
When, Seaforth Publishing, The Praetorian Press, Wharncliffe
Local History, Wharncliffe Transport, Wharncliffe True Crime
and White Owl.

For a complete list of Pen & Sword titles please contact

PEN & SWORD BOOKS LIMITED
47 Church Street, Barnsley, South Yorkshire, S70 2AS, England
E-mail: enquiries@pen-and-sword.co.uk
Website: www.pen-and-sword.co.uk

Or

PEN AND SWORD BOOKS
1950 Lawrence Rd, Havertown, PA 19083, USA
E-mail: Uspen-and-sword@casematepublishers.com
Website: www.penandswordbooks.com

For Valentina and Dennis, without whose support this would have been so much harder, if at all possible.

Contents

Acknowledgements

I am indebted to many people who helped in this project. I thank all of them, but first of all, I thank my wife, Valentina. She was, as always, the first reader and gave daily encouragement as well as valuable ideas and comments. Without her and our son's understanding and support the task would have been so much more difficult.

My first British publisher, Frontline Books, an imprint of Pen & Sword, entrusted me with this project ten years ago and were patient and understanding as it progressed resulting in *The KGB's Poison Factory: From Lenin to Litvinenko*, which came out in 2009. Shortly following this and the US edition, other international publishers succumbed to the wiles of Paula Hurst and published the book in several other countries and languages. Martin Mace, a military historian and author, appointed the publisher for Frontline Books in September 2014, was very enthusiastic about bringing out the present work, a sequel to the previous book and, in fact, its second volume. Thank you very much, Martin. I also want to put on record my thanks to Lisa Hooson for her understanding and much-needed help. Thank you, Lisa, and many thanks to Tara Moran, Pen & Sword's marketing executive. Finally, I must thank Kate Baker for her painstaking and insightful reading and editing of the text. I have benefited a lot from her perceptive comments.

While working on *The Poison Factory*, I met the former chief of the British Secret Intelligence Service (SIS or MI6), Sir Richard Dearlove, and his American colleague, James Pavitt, former Deputy Director of Operations (DDO) of the CIA, with both of whom at different times and in different parts of Europe I had a chance to discuss several problems relating to the subject matter of this book and whose opinions were important for the better understanding of many processes behind the scenes.

On Christmas Eve 2013, my very good old friend Tennent H. 'Pete' Bagley, one of the most respected experts on Soviet espionage, sent me his last book, *Spymaster*, containing 'some stories from places and times we've known', as Pete wrote in his inscription. After only a few weeks, his daughter called me to say that Pete had passed away. Former deputy chief of the CIA's Soviet Bloc Division, Pete, as all his friends knew him, had spent a lot of time and effort reading and correcting my texts and advising on the most important and crucial issues of intelligence history. My gratitude to him is profound, while any errors that remain are exclusively my fault.

Two people very close to Alexander 'Sasha' Litvinenko later taking an active part in the police investigation following his death, and in the inquest-come-public inquiry proceedings – his wife Marina and his associate Alex Goldfarb – devoted considerable time discussing with me various aspects of the Litvinenko case. Despite several disagreements, I am grateful to both of them for their time and effort. I am also very grateful to Professor John Harrison of Oxford Brookes University and Public Health England for sending me his research paper (written together with his colleagues) on the polonium-210 (^{210}Po) poisoning of Alexander Litvinenko, which became a basic scientific document for the public inquiry on the case.

Two American journalists and authors, Steve LeVine and Pete Earley, also provided some help before and after *The Poison Factory* was published. After our rendezvous in London, Steve returned to Washington and wrote his account of meetings with Soviet defectors Nikolai Khokhlov and Oleg Gordievsky – an excellent book that I was happy to use as one of the important and reliable sources for my own narrative that follows. Pete, in his turn, also published two important books (mentioned in the bibliography) and arranged contact with Sergey Tretyakov, another KGB officer who defected to the United States in 2000. Unfortunately, soon after I started communicating with Pete, Tretyakov unexpectedly died aged 54. There's still a mystery surrounding his strange demise although in a letter to me in February 2018, Pete categorically denied any foul play.

A prominent Italian politician, journalist and author, Paolo Guzzanti, former president of the Mitrokhin Commission of the Italian Parliament, helped in unlocking many doors to allow a better understanding of the Italian part of the Litvinenko story and the people involved. Paolo remains a good friend to this day. He published his own version of events called *Il mio agente Sasha* (2009) claiming that Litvinenko was killed because he had worked for the Mitrokhin Commission, which was, without doubt, one of the reasons.

Several librarians, archivists and filmmakers also rendered considerable assistance during my research. The National Archives in Kew, Richmond, England, became an invaluable source of information for this and other research projects as well as the CIA, FBI and NSA FOIA files, the German Federal Archives (Bundesarchiv in Koblenz), the Office of the Federal Commissioner for the Records of the State Security Service of the former German Democratic Republic, and the newly opened archives of the Ukrainian Security Service, SBU. Max Fisher of Windfall Films, London, kindly gave me video material covering the Markov case in its modern perspective. I also used the latest German documentary directed by Klaus Dexel *Silenced: Georgi Markov and the Umbrella Murder* (2012), which led me to Markov's suspected assassin. All in all, I have used over two dozen documentaries that helped a lot, and myself took part in a few of them, but the most revealing was the film by Andrei Nekrasov called *The Magnitsky Act: Behind the Scenes* (2016).

I must make particular mention of two historians, both from the former Soviet Union: Dr Nikita Petrov, Deputy Chairman of the Council of the Scientific and Educational Center of the Society 'Memorial', and Serhii Plokhy, Professor of Ukrainian History and Director of Ukrainian Research Institute, Harvard University, who have helped find important archival documents and references pertinent to this work. In the course of preparing a chapter on Ukraine, I have also had the good fortune to rely on the advice of Dr Taras Kuzio, a British academic and expert on Ukrainian political and economic affairs at the Canadian Institute of Ukrainian Studies in Toronto. I have benefited too from the very helpful comments of Father Peter Baulk, Archpriest and former Deputy Rector of the Cathedral of the Dormition, Russian Orthodox Church in Chiswick, London, who has contributed to both the first and second volumes.

Throughout the writing of this book, as with my other works in the past, I have had the good fortune of being able to discuss various matters with my teacher at the London School of Economics Professor Paul Preston – the world's foremost historian of twentieth-century Spain. I am deeply grateful to him for his friendship and for sharing with me his encyclopaedic knowledge. In June I was happy to learn that Paul had been knighted in the 2018 Queen's Birthday Honours. I must also thank Christopher Andrew, the former Official Historian of the British Security Service MI5 and convenor of the Cambridge Intelligence Seminar, and Ángel Viñas, both eminent academics and experts.

My travails were made especially rewarding thanks to the efforts and unstinting assistance of these men and women. Without them, I could not have done it while, as always, my family have been and remain my greatest inspiration.

Boris B. Volodarsky,
London-Vienna, 2019

Preface

Regarding the Fourth World War (after the Third, Cold War, was over and the 'hot peace' was established), I agree it would have been a rather grave mistake. No, not mine. But, thank God, it hasn't happened yet and what a consolation to know it is not going to be my fault should it ever occur.

In my life, I only took part in three major coups worth mentioning here. One was to meet and marry a girl who after four decades is still my wife, and I am more than happy about it. We have raised a fine son while so far enjoying robust good health, for which I am deeply grateful though I not know exactly to whom: fate, fortune, parents or deity.

As you have probably realised, I've just finished reading *The Outsider* by Frederick Forsyth and thought it was his last one. But no, here the best-selling novelist famous for his realistic spy stories comes again with *The Fox* – a race-against-time thriller, as his marketing people advertise it. And, ironically, it is about a principally new weapon – a human brain. An interesting coincidence. But I am getting ahead of myself.

The second coup was to become a student of the London School of Economics at the age of 50. Not that it is something extraordinary, but there I met Paul Preston, which was yet another piece of good fortune. My dictionary explains 'fortune' as chance or luck and the way it affects your life. One could not dream of a better teacher. Paul – or I should say Sir Paul because Professor Preston was been knighted in the 2018 Queen's Birthday Honours – is a widely celebrated historian and academic whose books are translated into several world languages and have a significant impact on many people including professional historians and statesmen. I am extremely grateful and proud to be his pupil and even to be mentioned in the acknowledgements to his 2012 masterpiece *The Spanish Holocaust*, although my contribution to Paul's great work was very minimal.

The third coup was to get acquainted with Oleg Gordievsky, a double agent who had worked for British intelligence for over a decade and who was exfiltrated from Russia by MI6 in a brilliant rescue operation in 1985. We had been corresponding for many years, but I only met Oleg in person in 2005, when I visited him in his Surrey home. Interesting people are always great to talk to and Gordievsky, with his life story, seemed very interesting. Soon after, I moved into a small hotel nearby, largely because he needed my help: a young man who we both knew by the name of Sasha Litvinenko had just been poisoned, and the full-scale investigation was still unfolding. SIS, the overseas intelligence organisation and Gordievsky's minders, were only watching and assessing while MI5, the security service who guarded him in London when he was spying in the Soviet Embassy, was in full control of the Litvinenko investigation carried out by SO15, the Counter Terrorism Command within London's Metropolitan Police Service. I was on the way to London when Sasha died in terrible torment in University College of London Hospital (UCLH). The world's media had gone crazy trying to learn any tiny detail that could be reported on the front pages or in the prime-time news, so Oleg was in great demand.

The hotel was freshly refurbished and positioned on the lake near his house, and although I was quite busy travelling often to London, having been contracted by BBC's *Panorama* programme, we met every evening to discuss the situation and exchange the news. One day, Oleg announced that the SO15 detectives would be coming to talk to us and, indeed, in the afternoon two pleasant-looking young officers, who introduced themselves as Michael Hoban and Lisa Harman, quite certainly their operational aliases, arrived at his house.

As they were mostly interested in the operational methods of the KGB, Oleg spoke first. When he finished, I took his place. We told them that without doubt Sasha's death was the result of a well-planned joint clandestine operation of Russian intelligence services and this only became known because polonium-210 was, quite by chance, found in Sasha's body. It was not too different from the operation against Georgi Markov almost 30 years earlier. At the time, I did not know that Francesco Gullino, a Bulgarian agent strongly suspected of murdering Markov, had moved to Austria and was residing in a place not far from where my family lived. After our interview, Michael and Lisa gave me their mobile numbers and I continued to meet them from time to time while the investigation continued.

During that year, I got to know plenty of very interesting, sometimes quite extraordinary people like Cambridge Professor Christopher Andrew – the world's leading authority on intelligence history. I also met Boris Berezovsky, an academic and a Russian business tycoon who was by then a political exile and a declared Enemy No. 1 of the Kremlin, duplicating the fate of Trotsky. Berezovsky, a kind and clever man and a shrewd politician, died in the English home of his former wife under extremely suspicious circumstances so that even the inquest coroner recorded an open verdict. Ahmed Zakayev, another political exile in London and Sasha's friend, who a year later became prime minister of the unrecognised Chechen Republic of Ichkeria, was also one of those who came my way that year, as well as Marina Litvinenko and Paolo Guzzanti.

Paolo, an Italian journalist and politician, then a senator and former president of the Mitrokhin Commission of the Italian Parliament, became a very good friend for many years. His daughter, Sabina Guzzanti, a tremendously popular Italian actress and satirist, who I also met, became known in the British media as 'the scourge of Berlusconi', thanks to her film *Viva Zapatero!*, which was a protest against the lack of political freedoms in Italy under Berlusconi (the former Italian prime minister and a friend of Putin). Shortly before leaving for London, I met Dmitry Peskov, President Putin's press secretary and deputy chief of staff, at the Diplomatic Academy of Vienna. Peskov has served as Putin's spokesperson since April 2000, and certainly played a very big role in the propaganda campaign covering Russian assassinations that have taken place under the presidentship of his boss.

I was also very lucky to meet two lords. The first was Nicolas Rea, a British doctor and politician who achieved his medical diplomas at UCLH and was one of the ninety elected hereditary peers to remain in the House of Lords after the House of Lords Act of 1999. When there, he sits on the Labour benches. Another was Hugh Thomas, Baron Thomas of Swynnerton, a prominent English historian, writer and life peer. He was born in Windsor, studied at Queen's College, Cambridge, and the Sorbonne in Paris, and became world famous for his 1961 book *The Spanish Civil War*, reissued so many times that half a century after its first publication he signed for me its latest edition. Hugh Thomas, a very generous and nice man and a good friend, died in May 2017. His last work was a short introduction to my book *Between Stalin and Franco*, which is currently being prepared for publication.

Gordievsky was not the only Soviet defector that I knew. Forsyth, who visited him while working on *Icon* (1996), noted in one of his books that quite a few defectors changed sides for genuine 'conscience' reasons, but most spies who turn on their own country 'do so because they share a quite monstrous vanity, a conviction that they are truly important in the scheme of things'.

Nikolai Khokhlov, a Soviet assassin who defected to the West and later became a professor of psychology at the California State University, was one of the real victims of a sophisticated Russian poisoning plot. He was also one of the first Western scientists who established without doubt that the Soviets had long been working on a super-weapon. Khokhlov, like a number of researchers in secret laboratories before and after him, came to the conclusion that the most dangerous weapon in the world may be not a nuclear or hydrogen bomb, or a clever missile, and not even a computer virus that can cause data loss or system crash. No, murder by malware is child's play for teenagers like Luke Jennings, 'The Fox' in Forsyth's new book.

'The development of weaponry based on new physics principles: direct-energy weapons, geophysical weapons, wave-energy weapons, genetic weapons, psychotronic weapons, etc., is part of the state arms procurement program for 2011–2020,' the Russian defence minister reported to President Putin in March 2012. For the layman, uninformed of secret military research, this sounds like science fiction. But it is not fiction.

Chapter 1

Prologue

Classified cables sent to the White House in Washington, DC were leaked to the media. The documents revealed that Russian undercover agents hounded staff working at the British Embassy in Moscow and that Russian espionage activities continued to exist in Britain – surprise, surprise – following the fatal poisoning of Alexander Litvinenko in London in November 2006.

One of the cables stated that, according to the British diplomats, Her Majesty's Government (HMG) had good reasons to refuse many Russian visa requests. HMG officials, it said, see a real 'intelligence threat' from Russia and regret a 'missed opportunity in the late 1990s and early 2000s to assess these intelligence threats'. Michael Davenport MBE, now British ambassador to Kuwait and then the FCO's head of the Russia, South Caucasus and Central Asia Directorate, reportedly admitted that there was a divide within the government over how to deal with Russia. There still is.

In spite of their good, solid education and considerable life experience, the diplomats are usually rather naïve. In the Russian capital, behind the glittering facades of the Kremlin, whose magnificent imperial halls are now restored and used for state and diplomatic receptions, there is a heavily guarded three-storey building known as the Senate Palace. Inside, is the dark, wood-panelled, very covert working office of the President of Russia.

During his rule in the Kremlin, Stalin was known as the Master of the House and the communist regime under his leadership was responsible for millions of victims both inside and outside the country, well exceeding those of Hitler and Pol Pot. It seems as though a kind of a 'Kill List' has been on the agenda of every Russian ruler, be it Ivan 'the Terrible', Peter 'the Great' or Nikita Khrushchev, 'the Corn Man'. Since Lenin moved to the Kremlin in 1918, the list has been permanently expanding, almost never shrinking. Like a universe. Naïve Western politicians and diplomats believe that with the end of Stalin's reign it was all over, that 25 or 30 million people, for whose deaths this 'effective manager' was responsible, is a big enough figure to stop killing. This is OLDTHINK. Ideas inspired by events or memories of times prior to Putin's Revolution. In short, PR. The second longest-serving master of the house recently declared that he simply does not need the rest of the world without Russia. In other words, in the language that he well understands – *Russland über alles*. For those who still remember the original text – *uber alles in der Welt*. The new Song of the Russians! And, as usual in the West, there is still a divide on how to deal with it.

When I was writing *The KGB's Poison Factory* a decade ago, it was more or less clear – Alexander 'Sasha' Litvinenko was murdered in London by a nano-nuclear device, a complex compound based on radioactive polonium-210, and the culprit was Russia. The British public inquiry named the Russian president as 'probably' responsible for ordering this murder and the assassins sent by the Kremlin as probably those who carried out the killing. However, 'The odds of getting someone to face trial at the Old Bailey are somewhere between slim and none,' concluded a senior police source, and that was it.

In the first volume, which has the subtitle *From Lenin to Litvinenko*, I wanted to show the Litvinenko operation in every detail, as I had personally investigated it in London, starting with my article in *The Wall Street Journal* published one day *before* Sasha died at University College Hospital. In the article, I suggested it was a radioactive substance that was killing him, and, indeed, traces of polonium-210 were subsequently found in Sasha's body. My reconstruction of the Litvinenko operation – how I understood it as a former Soviet special operations officer and at the same time a British intelligence historian and academic – was based on similar cases of poisonings that happened during more than 70 years of Bolshevik rule. In the book, I demonstrate that the Litvinenko poisoning is just one of many similar murders and that practically all of them have been carried out according to more or less the same pattern. In other words, by the book. Some of the cases that I showed were already known. Others were revealed for the first time.

Before his death, Litvinenko had said: 'You may succeed in silencing one man, but the howl of protest from around the world, Mr Putin, will reverberate in your ears for the rest of your life.' I am pretty convinced this is going to happen one day. But there's still a long way to go. And the Kremlin kill list, as the world has seen, exists and expands as before. In this second volume, *Assassins*, I give a new fresh catalogue of the victims, many of whom were murdered after Litvinenko. Among them are 96 people on board Polish Air Force One[1], including President Lech Kaczyński; then in Chechnya Natalia Estemirova; in England Alexander Perepilichny and Boris Berezovsky; in

---

[1] The Polish Defence Minister publicly accused Putin of orchestrating the destruction of Polish Air Force One, see https://www.independent.co.uk/news/world/europe/vladimir-putin-polish-president-lech-kaczynski-plane-crash-russia-poland-defence-minister-antoni-a8111831.html

Moscow Boris Nemtsov; in Kiev Pavel Sheremet, Denis Voronenkov and Maxim Shapoval; and in March 2018, the poisoning of Sergei Skripal and his daughter in Salisbury, Wiltshire. This is only a 'short list'.

I remember the story told by a Russian official about Yevgeny Murov and Victor Zolotov, one head of the Federal Protective Service and another of the most secret and powerful Presidential Security Service of Russia – both especially close to Putin. According to the source, Murov and Zolotov 'decided to make a list of politicians and other influential Moscovites whom they would need to assassinate to give Putin unchecked power. After the two men finished their list, Zolotov announced, "There are too many. It's too many to kill – even for us."'[2] Zolotov, who figures prominently in my *Poison Factory* book, had headed the Presidential Security Service (SBP) for 13 years from the day when Putin first came to power. Zolotov was already his bodyguard back in St Petersburg where the future Russian president was a bureaucrat at the mayor's office. Since that time, Zolotov has progressed from colonel to colonel general and recently to General of the Army, member of the Security Council of Russia, and 'Director' or commander-in-chief of the Russian National Guard, the elite special forces, which is more than 340,000 personnel-strong and directly subordinated to Putin.

The name of the high Russian official who told this story about the two highest-ranking Federal Protection Service (FSO) officers and described their meeting in New York to prepare Putin's visit is Sergei Tretyakov. Tretyakov, a full colonel of the Foreign Intelligence Service (SVR) and deputy head of station under the diplomatic cover of First Secretary of the Russian UN Mission in New York, spied for the CIA and FBI. He defected in October 2000. Ten years after changing sides, Tretyakov died at his home aged only 53.

In the meantime, most of the British and American media have an ongoing problem with the various bodies of the Russian intelligence community, typified, as a master of the genre has put it, by a seeming inability to work out which is which.

There are five main services. The least known is, ironically, the biggest. This is the National Guard, or Rosgvardiya, which reports directly to Vladimir Putin. The National Guard is separated from the Russian Armed Forces. It was established in 2016 by an executive order signed by the president. Rosgvardiya consolidated all Special Forces of Russia into one Service. This is at the same time Putin's personal army and Praetorian Guard, and they have even more powers than the Federal Security Service (FSB).

---

[2] See Pete Earley, *Comrade J: The Untold Secrets of Russia's Master Spy in America After the End of the Cold War* (New York: G.P. Putnam's Sons, 2007), 298–9.

The FSB is often – even inside Russia – regarded as the direct successor of the old and much-feared Soviet KGB, which is not right. It is true the FSB headquarters occupy several imposing buildings on Lubyanka Square (until 1990 better known as Dzerzhinsky Square) previously belonging to the KGB, but the similarities almost end here.

The FSB is the principal security agency of the country. With regards to the inheritance of structures, contrary to what is stated in Wikipedia, this service is the main successor of only the Second Chief Directorate of the KGB. It is Russia's domestic counterintelligence and security agency and like MI5 in the UK, or the FBI in the USA, is part of the country's secret services machinery. Alongside the FSB, Russian special services also include the Foreign Intelligence Service (SVR), the Main Directorate of the General Staff of the Russian Armed Forces (GRU), the Federal Protection Service (FSO) and the most secretive Presidential Security Service (SBP).

The FSB is directed to protect Russian economic interests, to conduct counter-terrorism and espionage activities within the territory of the Russian Federation and carry out serious crime investigations. For some time, it also incorporated the Border Service and the major part of the FAPSI or Federal Agency of Government Communications and Information as well as Drugs Control. The Service has regional offices across the country and is headed by a director who reports to the president. The current director (since 2008) is General of the Army Alexander Bortnikov, and the current President of Russia served as the FSB Director for one year from July 1998 to August 1999. What is said here of the inheritance of structures, traditions and personnel is also true with regard to the inheritance of the specific KGB mentality. The majority of FSB officers are the same as, and in most cases even much worse than, the old KGB secret police. Back in the USSR, I dealt several times with KGB staffers of different ranks and positions, and their major flaws were usually despicable careerism, corruption, excessive womanising and drinking. Now, I've heard, they are also very greedy for money. And money is king in modern Russia. In England, it is different.

There is no equivalent of the Secret Intelligence Service, which is widely regarded as a glamorous agency, not only due to Ian Fleming's James Bond but also because it employs the crème de la crème of British society and very often members of the nobility. Its chiefs are traditionally knighted and become 'sirs', and even rank-and-file officers can sometimes be granted titles of peers of the realm, not to mention that automatically they are all members of HM Foreign Service.

In Russia, the one regarded as the genuinely elite foreign intelligence agency is the GRU. It is also much bigger than the SVR, its 'civil' intelligence 'neighbour'. In reality, SVR officers only look and behave like civil servants, while all intelligence personnel are commissioned officers and have military ranks. The 'illegals', however, can be civilians and even foreigners.

Unlike the FSB, so often mentioned in the reports of Western correspondents, the SVR is the overseas intelligence organisation. The task of SVR officers is foreign information gathering and its presence is truly worldwide. I remember one of the KGB or SVR chiefs saying that there is no place in the world where there is not at least one KGB/SVR officer or agent. Indeed, SVR (and, for that matter, also GRU) stations or *rezidenturas* (residencies) are in all Russian diplomatic missions operating from the so-called 'legal positions'. That means they are 'covered' by their official status of diplomats, trade representatives, journalists, bankers or airline/railway/shipping company officers that are seconded to the embassy. In the cities like Vienna, Geneva or New York, Russian intelligence officers under diplomatic and non-diplomatic cover are placed in every possible slot of the UN or other international organisation. Their life is often miserable, but any position abroad is always better and by far more prestigious than in Russia. Today, many of those who have managed to make any decent money at home have moved their families to Europe, which is much more convenient than America, Canada or Australia, because the rest of Europe is nearby. Once there was a case when the family of a serving SVR officer settled in America and, after a while, he also moved there. As a result, a network of Russian spies was apprehended by the FBI.

Large, diverse and complex Russian communities in Britain, Germany or Israel provide a good natural cover for the agents. SVR and GRU illegals may be of two types – those who operate using a foreign identity, name and biography (known as a 'legend') different to their own, or those who use their own name and a biography that is 'tailored' for the assignment. That means that an illegal can, for example, get married or marry a foreign subject in order to obtain a new legal name and passport, or acquire a profession useful for the job. An excellent example of this kind of undercover operation is what became known as 'Illegals Program', which describes a network of Russian non-official cover agents operating in the USA.

Since September 2016, the Chief of the SVR, whose official rank is director, has been Sergei Naryshkin, formerly head of the Presidential Administration. The Service is based in Yasenevo, south-west of Moscow. Officers are brought there in the morning by a special bus from the capital and come back home in the evening. The Director resides in Yasenevo.

The Federal Protection Service (FSO) is similar to the US Secret Service. It is a government agency concerned with close protection, a euphemism for bodyguarding the high and mighty, as well as their residences that officially belong to the state. The Patriarch of Moscow and All Russia also belongs to such VIPs. Traditionally, since the Bolshevik Revolution, all primates of the Russian Orthodox Church and many priests have closely collaborated with Russian secret services. Those rare ones who have not – like Father Pavel Florensky, for example – were arrested, exiled or executed. Although during its long history the Protection Service had many names, among insiders it is still known as *devyatka*, the good old 9th Department of the KGB. The former head of the Presidential Security Service, General Dmitry Kochnev, now heads the FSO.

Since Putin became president and brought Victor Zolotov to the Kremlin as his personal bodyguard and the most trusted person of all, the Presidential Security Service (SBP) under him was quickly transformed into a very special agency. It now has roughly two to three thousand personnel and the very best equipment that is available from any supplier. With Zolotov as its CO, the Service can operate anywhere in the world. They even had, perhaps still have, their own intelligence branch, the so-called Psychological Security Department. This brought together the best experts from the SVR, GRU and FSB and could use for its operations any specialists, including officers from the 1st, 2nd and 8th departments of the SVR Directorate S as well as the very shadowy Zaslon ('Screen' or 'Barrier') unit, which was created within the Service in 1998 to carry out most sensitive operations abroad. Officially, they are not supposed to exist. This was the most dangerous private army. For over a decade they had been known as 'Men in Black'.

Of course, nothing of the sort was thinkable when Lenin moved to the Kremlin in 1918. Then, he used talented and ruthless individuals to murder his enemies for him. They were Russian and foreign communists who dreamed about the world revolution. Stalin also used talented individuals alongside sheer fanatics who dreamed and cared about nothing. After Stalin, there were ups and downs but never a stop. When Putin came to power in 2000, the new century began: the time of the assassins.

Chapter 2

The Last Farewell

Oleg, his life companion Maureen and I got out of the cab at the designated place on Swain's Lane by the entrance to Highgate Cemetery West, which was surrounded by hundreds of television cameras and photographers who were being kept at a distance by the police. We moved forward, crossed the courtyard and were greeted by a solemn and rather small group of mourners gathered under the roof of the retaining wall, anticipating rain. I thought, most people become celebrities because of their extraordinary lives. Sasha Litvinenko became a celebrity because of his extraordinary death.

The group included: Berezovsky and Zakayev, both of whom I met in person, rather than in the news, for the first time; Alex Goldfarb who, together with Litvinenko, came to see me at the Connaught a year earlier to discuss a business project; Marina Litvinenko (Sasha's widow); Boris's gorgeous girlfriend Elena Gorbunova, mother of his two children; Walter and Maxim Litvinenko, Sasha's father and his younger half-brother, who had just arrived from Italy; and as Andrei Nekrasov, a good-looking film producer, who I immediately liked and who would soon become famous for his documentaries about his friend's life and death. I did not notice then that Vladimir Bukovsky, a prominent figure in the Soviet dissident movement of the 1970s, was also there. Like Andrei Illarionov, Putin's former economic policy adviser, Bukovsky is a senior fellow at the Cato Institute in Washington, DC, a public policy research organisation and a think tank dedicated, according to its website, to the principles of individual liberty, limited government, free markets and peace. It turned out he was there with Pavel Stroilov, who introduced himself as Bukovsky's personal aide, and Gerard Batten, then a UKIP member of the European Parliament. They were in the company of Litvinenko's first wife and her two children. Later I learned that there were also two Norwegians – Maria Fuglevaag Warsinski, a documentary filmmaker from Oslo, and Ivar Amundsen, a Norwegian investment banker and businessman also serving as the Honorary Consul of the Chechen Republic of Ichkeria in his country and Director of the Chechnya Peace Forum in London.

Not surprisingly, given the occasion and the ill-assorted group of people gathered on that tragic day at the cemetery, a political discussion broke out and was only interrupted by a signal that the burial was about to start. It was already raining heavily when we entered a muddy road to accompany Sasha Litvinenko to his final destination. But the real storm would begin later.

When we all gathered around the grave, Walter Litvinenko said in barely audible Russian: 'Sasha was killed for telling the truth by those who are afraid of what he had to say.' These words were somehow recorded by *The Telegraph* correspondent, reproduced in his report from the funeral and would be used by the Russian propaganda machine a decade later.

Sasha Litvinenko was laid to rest among the Victorian ivy-clad monuments near the poet Christina Rossetti, scientist Michael Faraday and the graves of Mary Anne Evans, better known by her pen name George Eliot, and at the opposite, eastern side, Karl Marx. After it was all over, we were all given small white security passes and transported to Lauderdale House in Highgate, where an elabroate memorial service had been arranged.

As soon as the choir finished the first song (*There is a green hill far away* by Pitts), Boris Berezovsky made the opening address. I remember he was very articulate and an excellent speaker. Boris was aware of his authority and strength, especially in this company and situation. Bukovsky, Zakayev, Amundsen, Goldfarb, and Sasha's good friend David Kudykov all spoke, but none as well or with as much feeling and emotion as Berezovsky.

After the ceremony, we were seated in waiting buses and taken to the Italian restaurant Santini on Ebury Street in Belgravia, where dinner was served, and everyone remembered Sasha. Though it was both the wrong place and the wrong time, I used the opportunity to speak to Boris and Marina and got their agreement to be interviewed for the BBC programme. I also managed to discuss some details with Kudykov, who appeared to be very garrulous and who immediately gave me his business card with private numbers. Later, Lord Rea appeared at the party and apologised that he had not been able to attend the funeral. We all ate, drank and talked a lot, and I had a strange feeling that this evening symbolised the beginning rather than the end of something. I could not imagine how right I was.

In late October 2005, Andrei Lugovoy, a former major in the *devyatka*, 9th KGB Department (later to become the Federal Protection Service, headed by Murov and Zolotov), made a telephone call to one of Sasha's mobile phones suggesting a meeting. Lugovoy knew Litvinenko because they had both worked and moonlighted for Berezovsky when the tycoon lived in Moscow.

Like Lev Davidovich Bronstein (Trotsky), Boris Abramovich Berezovsky (Elenin) had not always been a political exile and critic of the regime. In the 1990s, he was one of the richest and quite certainly the most influential man in the country, deputy secretary of Russia's Security Council, friend and adviser of Yeltsin's younger daughter Tatyana and her husband Valentin

Yumashev, and a prominent member of the president's inner circle. Besides, Berezovsky controlled such important assets as LogoVaz, Russia's leading car dealership; the national airline Aeroflot; and the Siberian oil company Sibneft. He also had a 49 per cent stake in the main television channel ORT (now Channel One). In 1997, three years before he had to leave Russia, *Forbes* estimated Berezovsky's wealth at roughly 3 billion US dollars.

Litvinenko picked up the phone and was happy to hear a familiar voice from Russia. He was well aware that Lugovoy used to serve as head of the ORT security detail and was detained in connection with the alleged escape attempt of Nikolai Glushkov, who headed the management team that Berezovsky had placed at the helm of Aeroflot hoping to privatise it eventually. In February 1996, Glushkov, deputy general manager of the company, discovered that all heads of the Aeroflot offices abroad were either GRU or SVR, two Russian foreign intelligence agencies. Besides, about 30 per cent of the whole staff were somehow connected to secret services. In December 2000, Glushkov was arrested on trumped-up charges of siphoning hundreds of millions of dollars of Aeroflot money through Berezovsky's company Andava, registered in Lausanne, Switzerland. (When I went to Lausanne, sometime before those events, my friend, the general manager of the prestigious Lausanne Palace hotel, proudly showed me a suite on the first floor that used to be Berezovsky's permanent residence when he came to the town.)

In April 2001, Nikolai Glushkov, officially in custody, was hospitalised for a minor treatment. One evening, when he was, as usual, leaving the hospital wearing his gown and slippers to spend the night at home, he was arrested by the FSB and charged with attempted escape from custody. Berezovsky was in France when word came from the Kremlin that the price of Glushkov's freedom would be 49 per cent of Boris's ownership of ORT. He duly sold his shares at the price offered by the Kremlin (Roman Abramovich was dispatched as the negotiator), but Glushkov remained under arrest.

In March 2004, after three years in jail, Glushkov was brought to trial, cleared of charges of fraud (but found guilty of attempted escape from custody) and released from Lefortovo. Lugovoy was convicted of allegedly assisting him to escape and sentenced to a prison term of fourteen months, but was released because they said he had already spent this time in detention awaiting trial. After his release, Lugovoy went to London to see Berezovsky. The formal pretext for the trip was a football match between the Russian Army Central Sports Club (TsSKA) and Chelsea on 20 October. During that visit, Lugovoy also met Litvinenko in London for the first time.

Back in Moscow, Lugovoy found himself a modest job in the private company Lentus LLP, which still exists, specialising in the production and installation of acrylic coatings for tennis courts. Very soon, however, he moved to the now-bankrupt Moscow commercial bank Metropol as head of security. It was from there that he telephoned Litvinenko in November 2005 to arrange a meeting.

Lugovoy arrived in the British capital later that month on a multiple entry tourist visa. Litvinenko immediately took him to RISC Management, a private security and intelligence company controlled by former Metropolitan police officer Keith Hunter and established earlier that year from the London branch of ISC Global. There they met its Operations Director, Garym Evans, who now works at Vanguard.

Berezovsky, one of the important clients of ISC Global, had first introduced Litvinenko to Hunter back in 2001, and Sasha quickly learned that working for such private firms could bring really good money. His problem was that he did not speak, let alone write, English, had no useful contacts in Russia and no idea how to do this job, so he badly needed a professional partner. In mid-2005, Evans was appointed as Litvinenko's account manager. Over the previous few months, he and Evans had met at the RISC offices seven or eight times but never for business, because Sasha was simply unable to do investigations and make reports. To be engaged in this work with Lugovoy, who Litvinenko knew well enough and trusted absolutely, seemed an ideal solution. Besides, Sasha had a hidden agenda to use Lugovoy in his work with MI6 and the Security Service.

RISC Management's predecessor company, ISC Global, was founded in 2000 by Stephen Curtis, a lawyer whose contacts in Russia included Boris Berezovsky and Mikhail Khodorkovsky, the CEO of the Yukos Oil Company, one of the world's largest private oil companies. Curtis brought together former Metropolitan Police detectives Nigel Brown and Keith Hunter, who had been working as private investigators, because he needed a company that would carry out security, risk management and due diligence on behalf of the oligarchs. The company went on to recruit several more leading detectives such as Anthony Brightwell.

Curtis died in a helicopter crash close to his palatial home in Dorset in March 2004 – a fortnight after he had gone to Scotland Yard saying that he had received death threats and feared that a hit team had been sent from Moscow to assassinate him. 'If anything untoward happens to me, it will not be an accident,' were his words. But the police investigation decided it *was* an accident.

After Curtis died, there was a falling out between Brown and Hunter. Nigel took over the Israel-based operations, renamed GSS Global Security, and Keith retained control of the London team. He named the new group RISC, with RISC Management being the lead company based at 1 Cavendish Place from October 2005 onwards. Clifford 'Cliff' Knuckey was appointed managing director, Garym Evans Operations Director and Anthony Brightwell soon left the company, which including administrative staff employed twenty people.

In 2006, Keith Hunter was implicated in a corruption case involving the Metropolitan Police. The case began when the Met's anti-corruption squad received a dossier from someone within the company when it was still ISC Global. The dossier detailed payments of £20,000 to a police officer codenamed NOAH in exchange for confidential information concerning Russia's attempts to extradite one of the company's important clients, Boris Berezovsky. Eventually, the case was closed and no charges were pressed.[1]

Earlier that year, the Metropolitan Police had launched an inquiry into potentially explosive claims that peerages had been 'sold' by political parties to their wealthy owners. The Met's Intelligence Development Group (IDG), a covert arm of the anti-corruption squad, feared that RISC Management, for whatever reason, was 'corrupt[ing]' officers as part of attempts to seek information about the investigation. According to an article in *The Telegraph* in October 2016, the secret operation launched by IDG (codenamed BARTONIA) was 'concerned with the suspected leakage of information from the cash for honours enquiry to an employee of RISC'. The decision by the Crown Prosecution Service not to charge anyone was announced in July 2007 on the grounds of insufficient evidence against any individual. Nevertheless, the operation lasted until RISC went into administration in January 2014.

Knuckey first met Litvinenko in late October 2004, when he conducted an investigation into the firebombing attack on the houses of Litvinenko and Zakayev in Muswell Hill. In the early hours of Friday 15 October, Molotov cocktails were thrown into both houses. Contrary to what was claimed in the media, it was the work of two Chechens, who demanded money from Berezovsky while Litvinenko was trying to mediate on Berezovsky's behalf. At that time, both Zakayev and Litvinenko claimed it was the work of the Russian secret services.

On 23 January 2006, Lugovoy was among the numerous guests who Berezovsky invited to celebrate his 60th birthday, an extravagant and very formal black-tie event. Together with the others coming from Russia, he arrived in a specially rented private jet. During the reception, Lugovoy

---

[1] For details, see https://www.telegraph.co.uk/news/2016/10/06/scotland-yard-corruption-scandal-met-police.

sat at the same table as Sasha and Marina. Unbeknownst to them all, the preparation of Stage Two of what I call Operation VLADIMIR – the murder of Litvinenko – started on that very night.

The last ten months of his short life, from January to the end of October 2006, was perhaps the most difficult and the most fruitful period for Alexander Litvinenko. In February, he went to Italy where, with the help of Mario Scaramella, he recorded a sensational video testimony openly accusing Romano Prodi (who would soon be the prime minister again after defeating Silvio Berlusconi in the April election) of being 'a KGB man'. This was the last opportunity for Sasha to help the Mitrokhin Commission, because at the end of March its mandate expired. In January 2007, after Mario was arrested, both the BBC and ITV broadcast programmes showing video footage of Litvinenko making the claim against Prodi.[2] This followed a meeting at ITV headquarters between Deborah Turness, then Editor of ITV News, Bill Neely, who later became Chief Global Correspondent for NBC News, and a friend of Scaramella. When Scaramella made his allegations public, Prodi threatened to sue but named no one in particular.

Litvinenko's articles for the Chechen press became fierce and crushing, copying the style of Anna Politkovskaya, who he greatly respected and sympathised with. Politkovskaya would be shot dead in Moscow on 7 October 2006, Putin's birthday. I heard the news at the Vienna international airport upon arriving from London. Pete Earley later recalled in his book about Tretyakov, the SVR colonel who defected in New York, what Sergei had told him about Murov and Zolotov, two chiefs of Putin's 'Men in Black', his Praetorian Guard. 'They are common thugs,' Tretyakov's friend from Moscow, an FSO officer who knew the whole story, told Sergei and Sergei related to Earley. He explained that Putin wanted to get rid of Alexander Voloshin, head of the Presidential Administration under Yeltsin, who was still fulfilling this role when Putin was officially inaugurated as president.[3]

The Presidential Administration of Russia is somewhat similar to but at the same time different from the Executive Office of the President of the United States, which is a group of offices and agencies at the centre of the executive branch of the federal government. Likewise, in Russia, the Presidential Administration, All the King's Men, is a special institution that supports the work of the president. The chief of the Presidential Administration, who oversees its work, his deputies, heads of main directorates and services and their deputies are appointed and serve at the pleasure of the president who can

---

[2] See, for example, https://www.ft.com/content/c1eb2990-8158-11db-864e-0000779e2340
[3] Pete Earley, *Comrade J* (New York: G.P. Putnam's Sons, 2007), 298-9.

dismiss them at will without anybody's approval. Other staff are appointed by the chief of the administration, who is a senior Kremlin figure. The current chief of staff is Anton Vaino, the grandson of the former First Secretary of the Communist Party of Estonia. In today's Russia, the Presidential Administration controls everything – from the secret services to freemasons, whose Grand Master, the chairman of the Communist Party of Social Justice Andrei Bogdanov, was a candidate for the 2008 presidential election.

Due to political reasons, Putin could not fire Voloshin, so Murov and Zolotov were discussing ways to murder him. One idea was to use Chechen terrorists.[4] In the end, Voloshin survived and was succeeded as head of administration by Dmitry Medvedev. But Politkovskaya and, later, Boris Nemtsov were assassinated precisely according to this scheme, that is, in central Moscow by Chechen gunmen. Russian media reported that all suspects in these two cases were members of the Russian special services.

In 2006, Sasha's work for the Chechen commission preparing evidence for the International Criminal Court in the Netherlands became more organised and systematic. He had already visited Georgia using his new British identity in an attempt to find the key witness of the 1999 Russian apartment bombings and was now actively assisting security services and law enforcement agencies in Europe and Israel to arrest Russian gang bosses, many of whom, he knew, were tightly linked to the SVR and FSB.

Some months before, in a sweeping police operation codenamed AVISPA, which involved 400 officers from the Costa del Sol and elsewhere in Spain, twenty-eight alleged 'Russian Mafia' members were arrested, many of them high-level capos, according to the Spanish police. The operation involved the national police forces of six countries. In the weekend raids, carried out mostly in the Costa del Sol, Catalonia and Alicante, police searched 41 homes or premises, froze 800 bank accounts at multiple banks and seized 42 high-end vehicles, according to the *Costa del Sol News*. The authorities said the mobsters, mostly from former Soviet Bloc republics, brought criminally acquired money from their home countries to launder it in Spain via commercial or financial entities created for the purpose. Among the many properties held by the gang were a number of luxury chalets, some with high-security 'safe rooms', as well as a 16,621-square-metre property in Benalmádena on which the mobsters planned to build a 38-house development called Los Eucaliptus.[5] This demonstration of unprecedented police competence and expertise in dealing with serious Russian organised

---

[4] Ibid.

[5] See Oliver McIntyre, 'Major "Russian Mafia" Ring Busted', *Costa del Sol News*, (June, week 23–29), 2005.

crime was only the beginning – the first experience of the Spanish police that would culminate in Operation TROIKA two years after Sasha's death. At the time, the responsible agencies were the National Anti-Terrorism Coordination Centre (CNCA) and the Intelligence Centre against Organized Crime (CICO), both under the Secretary of State for Security. They would later be united into one intelligence organisation.

At about this time, Sasha told Goldfarb that he had been consulting MI6 on Russia's organised crime in Europe and was travelling on their behalf to various countries in the EU assisting local law enforcement. He also showed Goldfarb his British passport issued by the Service on his alias identity 'Edwin Carter'.

However, Litvinenko and his handlers could have never expected that within the Spanish intelligence service CNI, Spanish partners of SIS, there would be a mole working for the Russians. Roberto Flórez García had been betraying all his service's secrets to his SVR controller between 2001 and 2004. Petr Yakovlevich Melnikov, posing as Counsellor of the Russian Embassy in Madrid,[6] was quite certainly head of Line VKR (former KR, counterintelligence) at the residency and Roberto's case officer. As soon as Litvinenko started collaborating with the Spanish authorities, his name was leaked to the CNI and from there to Moscow. Sometime later, in 2004, Flórez García also betrayed Sergei Skripal, a Russian GRU colonel working for MI6. At the time of Skripal's poisoning, in March–April 2018, I worked with three separate reporter teams from *The Times*, British commercial news channel *ITV News* and the American edition of the international men's magazine *GQ* to try to find out what really happened. We examined every place in Salisbury that Skripal and his daughter visited or could have visited on the day when they were attacked. The results of my investigation are in Chapter 11, but what I have said already and want to repeat is this: 'The biggest fear of all [for any intelligence operator] is not that you have run out of tradecraft or luck, but that far away … some bastard has betrayed you.' This is from Forsyth, of course. Spanish media reported that Flórez had handed over the identities of dozens of agents.

In early 2006, Goldfarb discussed with Litvinenko his financial situation concerning the funds that Sasha was receiving from the Berezovsky's foundation IFCL. Berezovsky asked Goldfarb, the IFCL director, to review the budget for 2006. Litvinenko admitted that he was receiving 'some money' from the secret services but 'that was not enough to live on' so could not

---

[6] As reported by the two leading Spanish newspapers, *El Mundo* (11 Feb 2010) and *ABC* (13 March 2018).

forgo Berezovsky's support altogether. As a result, Sasha's support from the IFCL was reduced by half – from about $60,000 a year to $30,000, which was a very considerable reduction indeed bearing in mind the exchange rate. That meant instead of approximately £3,400 a month, Litvinenko now received from Berezovsky about £1,380. However, the two men did not fall out, as confirmed by Berezovsky's aide Misha Cotlick, who I also met, with Berezovsky's continuing to pay Litvinenko's son's tuition fees and the family's accommodation rent in London.

When Garym Evans left RISC in February 2006, he passed the management of Litvinenko to Daniel Quirke, another staff investigator. Mr Quirke also gave evidence to the inquiry. '[Mr Litvinenko] was trying to establish a business,' he said. 'He was working hard. I think he was short of money. I think monies that he'd previously got from – as like a retainer from Mr Berezovsky had ceased and that left a hole in his finances.'

In April 2006, Lugovoy was again in London, one of a dozen visits over the course of a year. Along with an interpreter, Lugovoy and Litvinenko went to a meeting at the RISC offices in Cavendish Place. Altogether they were there five or six times, but the first business took place in the early months of 2006. RISC was engaged in a complex investigation on behalf of Stolichnaya vodka against the Russian government. The client was the SPI Group (formerly known as SoyuzPlodoImport) owned by Yuri Shefler. This case is well-known from the media. 'The task that Mr Litvinenko was given, apparently by Mr Knuckey,' Dan Quirke said to the coroner, 'was to make enquiries into the Russian agriculture minister, named Mr Gordeyev.'

Naturally, Litvinenko could not do even this comparatively simple research and enlisted the assistance of Lugovoy. Actually, their *modus operandi* had been: Sasha finds customers in London interested in the Russian market, for which he gets a commission of 20 per cent, and Lugovoy carries out the research and compiles the report in English. Thus, the SVR and FSB were immediately aware of what interested their adversaries, not only in the UK but in other parts of the world too, while being able to feed them any information or misinformation they wanted. Very convenient.

In April, when Litvinenko and Lugovoy presented their report, both gentlemen from RISC were unimpressed. They thought, and their boss agreed, that all information had probably been culled from Russian websites. Nevertheless, Lugovoy demanded $10,000 – a disproportionately large fee – and they settled on $7,500, to be transferred to a bank account in Cyprus because Berezovsky, Sasha's mentor, was a very important customer plus, they say, they 'wanted to cultivate this relationship'. That is, to have a well-connected informer, as they thought, inside Russia.

In the course of a public enquiry, it also became known that the other two London private security companies with which Litvinenko had been involved, though not actively before he met Lugovoy, were linked to each other and shared a suite of offices in Mayfair. Titon International was established in 2004 by two co-founders: John Holmes, ex–SAS, and Dean Attew, ex-investigator at Bernard Charles 'Bernie' Ecclestone's Formula One Management. At the time, Titon's headquarters were located at 25 Grosvenor Street in premises rented from Berezovsky. As soon as the company was established, Attew got acquainted with Litvinenko, who had worked for but had never been employed by Boris. They even became friends of sorts, meeting from time to time but not working together until May 2006. According to the company's brochure, its work covers business intelligence, asset tracing and investigation, fraud detection and prevention, counter-intrusion consultancy and training, telecommunications security and electronic countermeasures.

Major General John Holmes was actually the former commanding officer of the active-service 22nd SAS (as opposed to the part-time 23rd SAS), and between 1999 and 2001, Director Special Forces. To make it clear, officially the Special Air Service regiment has nothing to do with the SIS. The DSF comes under the Director of Military Operations who reports to the Chief of General Staff. But because members of the two secret services have much in common, the SIS and SAS know each other and sometimes cooperate on joint operations or sensitive missions. They also sometimes meet at the private Special Forces Club in Knightsbridge and this is where I saw General Holmes during my Litvinenko lecture there in 2008.

The second company, Erinys (UK) Limited, also incorporated in 2004 and based at the same address as Titon, is part of a large security company, Erinys International, registered in South Africa. It was founded by two former British Army officers and specialises in providing security guards in conflict zones including armed personnel. General Holmes, part of the company's management, is also director of Erinys UK. His assistant there was Tim Reilly, also a former officer. The major business of Erinys was the provision of physical security services to the oil industry.

Tim Reilly joined Erinys in April 2006 and the company was pleased to get him as their employee considering him 'the greatest new addition to the Erinys rooster'. Tim had worked with Exxon and Shell and, being fluent in Russian, specialised in the CIS markets. Sasha was very happy when he learnt about it and dropped by for a chat whenever he could. In his testimony for the Litvinenko inquiry, Mr Reilly estimated that within only a few months in 2006, he saw Sasha between 20 and 30 times. In June or early July, Litvinenko brought with him Lugovoy, introducing him as a good friend from Russia who might be able to help arrange the right contacts in the Russian oil and gas industry. Lugovoy obviously played his role well and made it clear he could also facilitate communication with the security department of Gazprom.

In July, Yuri Shvets called Litvinenko from Washington, where he had lived ever since he moved to the United States in 1994, and asked whether Litvinenko could help him with getting commissions from London to produce due diligence reports on the Russian officials. Shvets was a former KGB major who was stationed in Washington, DC, under the cover of a TASS correspondent in 1985. His tour of duty in the US capital had lasted only two years. Back in the USA a decade later, Shvets published a book *Washington Station: My Life as a KGB Spy in America* (1995), about which *Publishers Weekly* wrote: 'His shallow, inflated, clunkily translated memoir is worth reading if only for its exposure of obtuse and counterproductive KGB policies and of the schemes that led Shvets to resign in 1990 and seek asylum in the US. The most arresting aspect of the book is his argument – regrettably undeveloped – that spying in general is a waste of effort and that the profession should be eliminated.'[7] Litvinenko and Shvets had met and became friends in 2002 when, on the orders of Berezovsky, they were involved in what became known as the 'Kuchmagate' scandal in Ukraine, which I describe in detail in *Poison Factory*.

The first opportunity with Titon came in August, when Dean Attew, the Chief Operating Officer, got a commission related to Russia. Among other things, he needed some insider information on Victor Petrovich Ivanov (born 12 May 1950), a former KGB officer who had served in the KGB Directorate for Leningrad and Leningrad province under Oleg Kalugin, among other chiefs, also spending a year in Afghanistan during the Soviet invasion. After Putin's rise to power, Ivanov was appointed deputy head of the presidential staff for HR and later chairman of the board of directors of the state-owned Almaz (from June 2002, Almaz-Antey) – a company producing air defence systems. Since November 2004, Ivanov had also served as chairman of Aeroflot.

To show that he would be able to cope with the task, Sasha invited his friend Dean to Heathrow, where he introduced him to Lugovoy. Mr Attew says he did not like the Russian but placed an order anyway.

As expected, Litvinenko asked Lugovoy to draft a report, which was almost an impossible task because Ivanov had been an old friend of Putin and a high-ranking government official. Accordingly, no one dared to give

---

[7] See https://www.publishersweekly.com/978-0-671-88397-3

any information about him or even concoct something not known from the official media, leaving Lugovoy no choice. He emailed to Sasha less than half a page based on what was written about Ivanov on the Russian Wikipedia site. Under the circumstances, Litvinenko had no option but to ask Shvets to write a report adding some facts that had become known to him from the Kuchma tapes. Those facts, however, had nothing to do with Ivanov. The report compiled by Shvets was ready on 19 September and was very well received by Titon. In the view of Dean Attew and others, this and other reports that Shvets provided were of very high quality, so Shvets and Litvinenko were, according to Holmes, handsomely remunerated.

Meanwhile, Litvinenko was also collecting some money from Spanish intelligence. In September, he told Berezovsky that he had helped them to arrest a Russian crime lord operating in Spain, Zakhary Kalashov (aka 'Shakro Molodoy'). According to the US authorities, Kalashov was a key member of the criminal syndicate known as 'the Brothers' Circle'.[8] In June 2005, as a result of Operation AVISPA, which targeted 30 members of this syndicate in Spain, Kalashov fled to the United Arab Emirates where he was soon arrested and, in 2006, extradited to Spain. He returned to Moscow in October 2014 a free man.

On Friday 13 October, Sasha and Marina attended their citizenship ceremony, making an oath of allegiance and a pledge promising to respect the rights, freedoms and laws of the UK. At the end of the ceremony they were presented with their certificates of British citizenship and a welcome pack, and Sasha was quick to inform everyone about it. But, ironically, because he was inventing and fantasising so much, few people believed him. Shortly after he had been naturalised as a UK national – and in the days that followed the murder of Politkovskaya – the 'executive phase' of the Litvinenko operation began. Sasha and Marina's British passports arrived in December.

On 16 October, the commercial Transaero flight from Moscow landed on schedule at London Gatwick. Two Russian passengers in economy class proceeded to the immigration hall to join the crowd waiting in line for passport control. The Russians, Andrey Lugovoy and Dmitry Kovtun, caused some suspicion and were stopped and questioned by Detective Constable Spencer Scott but were allowed to proceed and soon came out through the 'Nothing to Declare Green Channel'. They were followed but noticed nothing. This surveillance was conducted by friendly agents from

---

[8] See US Department of the Treasury designation of 20 December 2012.

Moscow. From the airport, Lugovoy telephoned Litvinenko to say he had successfully arrived and that their meeting should follow as planned.

About an hour later, Lugovoy and Kovtun checked into the four-star Best Western Premier Shaftesbury Piccadilly hotel in Soho. Just around the corner were Piccadilly Circus, where Sasha always arranged his meetings, and Leicester Square, the heart of London's West End. Although the property advertised itself as 'a boutique hotel that embodies a haven where you can be sure of warm traditional hospitality', neither of the two rooms that they had booked was available for the guests when they arrived. Soon, Room 107 was ready for Lugovoy, so they left their luggage in this room and rushed to the meeting at the entrance to the Nike shop on Oxford Street.

It has not been established how they reached London or who they met on the way or near the hotel shortly before Lugovoy's room was ready for them. But there is absolutely no doubt that somewhere between Gatwick and the Shaftesbury hotel they received a container with the poison, opened it in Lugovoy's hotel room and were contaminated, having no idea about what had happened. It is also clear to me that it was Kovtun who had dealt with an open radioactive source without any protective clothing, safety glasses or even latex gloves and that a major spill had occurred contaminating his skin and everything around him.

Sasha did not expect to see Lugovoy with anybody else but was not suspicious when Lugovoy introduced his companion as Dmitry Kovtun, a businessman who had recently joined his company. They studied at the same military command academy in Moscow and had been friends since childhood, Andrei explained. Unlike Lugovoy, Kovtun had never served in the KGB or any other intelligence service but was a former army officer stationed in Germany before the collapse of the USSR and disappearance of the DDR. Kovtun was also neither GRU nor Spetsnaz, as claimed by many news media. In the army, he was just an ordinary drill sergeant.

Litvinenko was satisfied. After a meeting with Tim Reilly in a rather cramped fourth-floor boardroom of the familiar offices of Erinys at 25 Grosvenor Street, where Kovtun did not say a single word, Sasha invited his guests to the Itsu on Piccadilly. It was his favourite Japanese eatery. At about 5 p.m. they split up – Litvinenko went home to Muswell Hill, while Lugovoy and Kovtun remained in central London. In the evening, the two Russians had a late dinner at the Italian restaurant Pescatori in Dover Street in the company of another Russian by the name of Dr Alexander Shadrin. The bill for dinner was paid using Lugovoy's credit card.

Dr Shadrin was registered as a director of four companies: Ecological Finance BV; Eco 3 Capital Limited; Innovation Admin Limited; and Continental

Petroleum Limited (CPL). All four were located at 58 Grosvenor Street conveniently opposite number 25. Continental Petroleum was incorporated in June 2005 and officially registered in Esher, Surrey, until 2009, when it was frozen and then dissolved in May 2012. Its name was strangely similar (with just one letter different) to a real business named Continental Petroleums Ltd., a listed company at the Mumbai Stock Exchange, founded in 1986. CPL was a typical shell company with nominee directors, like Charles Balfour (who figures in The Litvinenko Enquiry Report as 'the Chairman of CPL'), company secretaries and shareholders. For some time, Eco 3 Capital and Continental Petroleum (CPL) played the role of Lugovoy and Kovtun's business partners. That Lugovoy paid for their meal that night would be rather unusual under normal circumstances. But no one paid any attention.

After dinner, Lugovoy and Kovtun went on to a bar near their hotel named Dar Marrakesh, a Moroccan restaurant and shisha lounge on Rupert Street, just off Shaftesbury Avenue, where they had a shisha pipe and then mooched around Soho.

The following day, 17 October, Lugovoy and Kovtun checked out of the Shaftesbury Hotel without asking for a refund for the second night that had been booked but not used, and moved into the upmarket Parkes Hotel, a luxury establishment located in a tree-lined cul-de-sac in Beaufort Gardens in Knightsbridge, just a short stroll from Harrods. No doubt by pure coincidence their elegant new lodgings were conveniently placed near the Lanesborough Hotel, Berezovsky's favourite meeting place.

Parkes, which had come top of TripAdvisor's pick of London hotels, was quite certainly too good for Lugovoy and Kovtun, with its oak-panelled reception area, Parisian-chic rooms, king-sized beds and marble bathrooms at about £300 per room per night. Remarkably, the booking was made by email at approximately the time – 3:00 p.m. – when Lugovoy, Kovtun and Litvinenko were meeting Mr Reilly at Erinys. The rooms were reserved online, allegedly by Tatiana, Lugovoy's daughter. She was not interviewed and no one investigated such a minor detail. The two men checked into the Parkes Hotel at about 2:00 p.m. on Tuesday 17 October, staying in rooms 23 and 25. An hour later, they arrived at the offices of Mr Shadrin vis-à-vis Erinys, where they remained until 5:30 p.m.

Says Lugovoy: 'On 17 October, we met again with Litvinenko in the afternoon. We went together to a meeting at another security firm. After the meeting, we went back to the hotel where I had a meeting with an old acquaintance while Litvinenko waited for us downstairs. Then we went for dinner with him in Chinatown.' This was reported by Mark Franchetti of *The Sunday Times* in December 2006, long before the inquiry. Indeed, together with Litvinenko, Lugovoy and Kovtun visited Keith Hunter's RISC Management at 1 Cavendish Place in Mayfair, where they met Dan Quirke. The meeting took less than an hour. The man whom Lugovoy was meeting at the hotel was identified by the police and interviewed, but not investigated. That is, the veracity of his statement was not established.

Litvinenko felt quite at ease. From the elegant Beaufort Gardens area, he and his visitors returned to Soho, the right place for them to be, and had late dinner at the Golden Dragon in Gerrard Street, a popular Cantonese and Peking restaurant. Again, Lugovoy paid the bill. From there they moved on to a modest bistro named Café Boheme in Old Compton Street – Litvinenko did not like the place, left them there and went home by bus. Later in the evening, Lugovoy and Kovtun, who drank sake in Chinatown, proceeded to the Hey Jo 'erotic nightclub' in fashionable Jermyn Street, a recently opened establishment much favoured by the 'new Russians', where they stayed until early hours, coming back to the Parkes after 3:00 a.m. The late Dave West, the notorious owner of Hey Jo, who also opened an adjoining 150-seater Russian-themed restaurant called Abracadabra (a reviewer wrote that dining at Abracadabra was like eating in 'an overpriced McDonald's in a brothel') later claimed that Litvinenko was also there that night, which was a pure lie.

On Wednesday 18 October, Lugovoy and Kovtun went back to Moscow on Transaero, landing at the airport of Domodedovo. They were duly met, and reports collected from both at once.

Lugovoy was suddenly back in London on 25 October. According to the Litvinenko inquiry report:

6.152 A week after he and Mr Kovtun had flown back to Moscow, Mr Lugovoy returned to London. He arrived on an evening flight on Wednesday 25 October 2006. On this occasion, he was not accompanied by Mr Kovtun. In further contrast to the earlier trip, the evidence is that Mr Lugovoy's travel on this occasion was hastily arranged. Whereas the arrangements for the first trip (including, it appears, obtaining a visa for Mr Kovtun) had been several weeks in the planning, the evidence was that on this occasion Mr Lugovoy's flight and hotel bookings had been made only the day before he travelled, on Tuesday 24 October 2006. In the interim, Mr Litvinenko had made his speech at the Frontline Club about Anna Politkovskaya's death, publicly attributing the blame for her murder to President Putin.

This time, the British Airways machine from Moscow flew into Heathrow. All passengers who were not catching a connecting flight proceeded to the immigration hall for the passport control. There were two queues – one for European Union, European Economic Area, British and Swiss nationals, and a second for all other nationalities. Above this large space and to one side, a mirrored wall contained a two-way mirror and a room behind it. Matthew Butterworth, Intelligence Manager with Heathrow Airport Police in charge of the airport security, known to his friends simply as Matt, stood in that room looking down at the crowd. He saw Lugovoy and decided the guy must be either from the army or the Home Office. This time the Russian did not cause any suspicion and was soon on his way to central London. There he checked into the Sheraton Park Lane Hotel in Piccadilly, a celebrated art deco property, where he was given Room 848. Because it was rather late, he probably went straight to bed.

The next morning, a limousine picked him up and he went to visit Badri Patarkatsishvili at his spacious house near Leatherhead in Surrey. Badri told the police that he had known Lugovoy since about 1993, when the latter had been the head of security at ORT, the Russian television channel that Patarkatsishvili and Berezovsky had run together. This date is wrong because until the end of 1996 Lugovoy served as a commissioned officer of the FSO, the successor of the KGB's 9th Directorate. More recently, he said, Lugovoy organised his security in Georgia, visiting him there every two months. Patarkatsishvili recalled the meeting at his house in Surrey in October 2006. He said that in addition to himself and Andrei Lugovoy, the meeting had been attended by Vladimir Voronoff and a man named Marti Pompadour [*sic*]. 'He said,' the Litvinenko inquiry report states, 'that the purpose of the meeting was to discuss outdoor advertising in Moscow. There is no reason to think that this was anything other than a genuine business meeting.'

While Marty Pompadur (the correct spelling) may be a genuine figure – no one actually investigated, but according to official reports, he joined News Corporation in June 1998 as executive vice president and held some important positions there until 2008 – it may be a different story with 'Mr Voronoff'.

Vladimir Voronov had been posted to the Russian Embassy in London in July 1991, serving there 'in an official diplomatic capacity', according to his own words, until 1 October 1993. About two weeks later, on 18 October, he was already appointed director of Vantix Ltd. Since then, he has served as the director of various companies in London, including Stargate Management Ltd from 11 September 1995 and Raven Management Ltd from 21 November 1995. Additionally, as he informed Ben Emmerson QC representing Marina Litvinenko, he was president of a big holding company based in Moscow called News Media. Although oil production, trade and any other oil-related businesses have never been Mr Voronov/Voronoff's speciality fields, he was appointed director of Continental Oil Limited in May 2006 and T-Oil Exploration Limited in November 2007. It was Mr Voronov/Voronoff who recommended that Lugovoy provide security services for CPL. However, Alexander Shadrin, CPL's acting director at the time, told the inquiry he had threatened to resign if the company used Lugovoy's services ... And at the end of 2006, outdoor advertising was of rather doubtful priority for Badri who at that time started to be actively involved in Georgian politics, began financing opposition parties and finally founded his own Our Georgia political party.

The investigation documents show that on 27 October, Lugovoy visited CPL offices arriving there at 11:30 a.m., but no one was able to comment on this for the protocol. For two days, 26 and 27 October, Lugovoy met Litvinenko in the evening at the Sheraton bar, the same place that Sasha had been discussing ways of helping the English banker, Peter Shaw, with Martin Flint, then one of the directors of Risk Analysis (UK) Ltd. A coincidence, perhaps.

On Thursday, 28 October, Lugovoy left for Moscow. The plane took off at 9:10 a.m. In the course of the frenzied preparations for the operation, Kovtun flew to Hamburg on that same day, 28 October, by Aeroflot. A day before, a ticket was purchased for him for a flight from London to Moscow on 3 November. His short visit to Germany seems to have been a clumsy attempt to mislead the investigation that everyone knew would almost certainly follow and at the same time to renew his residence permit for Germany. Kovtun, who operated completely 'in the dark', was advised to visit his former family with whom he maintained good relations. His Russian/German ex-wife Marina Wall picked him up from the airport in a BMW and drove to the multi-family building at Erzberger Strasse 4 in Hamburg's Ottensen neighbourhood, where she shared an apartment with her partner and their children. Kovtun, who, apart from his ex-wife's residence, owned yet another apartment in the same building, which had been rented to other tenants, then went to town to do some shopping and spent the night on the sofa.

On Sunday, 29 October, he booked an early-morning flight to London for 1 November, paying with the credit card of his ex-wife's partner because he did not have his own. In the afternoon, his ex-mother-in-law, Dr Eleonora Wall, a neurologist, picked him up and drove him to her house in Haselau outside Hamburg, where he spent the night. Kovtun returned to his ex-wife's apartment on 31 October after spending the previous night at his friend's home. It was his old pal, an Italian, with whom he had worked as a waiter in Il Porto restaurant in the harbour area of Hamburg.

On the morning of 31 October, Tatiana Lugovaya, 20, and her boyfriend Maxim flew from Moscow to London. The rest of the family – Svetlana, Lugovoy's wife, their daughter Galina, 19, and their son Igor, 8, accompanied by Vyacheslav Sokolenko, an old friend of the family – caught an afternoon flight. With the exception of Maxim, they all stayed at the Millennium Hotel in Grosvenor Square, having arrived there in the evening. The girls stayed in Room 101, Sokolenko was placed in 382 and Lugovoy with his wife and son were allocated Room 441. Shortly after 9:00 p.m. that evening, Litvinenko called Lugovoy (and not vice versa, as Judge Owen states in his inquiry report). The call lasted slightly over six minutes. They agreed to meet on the next day. Forty-five minutes later, Lugovoy called his daughter Tatiana. It took him only 1 minute 19 seconds to say what he wanted to say.

Kovtun spent his last night in Hamburg drinking and talking with his ex-wife and her new family until the early hours. On 1 November a taxi took him to the airport for a 6:40 a.m. Germanwings flight to London. His presence in the old Hansa town on the River Elbe might have passed unnoticed if one early December morning a postman had not put a thick copy of *Der Spiegel* in the post box of the Hamburg police headquarters. Its front cover and the article 'Todesurteil aus Moskau' immediately attracted attention. The story occupied half of the magazine and mentioned Dmitry Kovtun by name, saying that he came from Hamburg. Even before the MLAT request for legal assistance came from the UK and Stuart Goodwin from Scotland Yard arrived in Hamburg, the Hamburg Police called on the unit responsible for the defence against nuclear hazards, known by the German abbreviation ZUB. The ZUB is a combined emergency force of the Federal Office for Radiation Protection (BfS), the Federal Police and the Federal Criminal Police Office, also receiving assistance from the Federal Central Support Unit.

The CID officer who took over the case was Thomas Menzel, Director of the Hamburg LKA Organised Crime Unit. Alan Cowell, a *New York Times* correspondent who had met Menzel while researching a book on Litvinenko, noted that he was tall and slender, a 30-year veteran of the police force who wore his greying hair swept back and who worked out of an office at the Polizeipräsidium in the picturesque Winterhude area of Hamburg-Nord. Menzel codenamed the Kovtun operation THE THIRD MAN, after the Orson Welles film, and used the signature tune – the Harry Lime Theme – as a ring tone on his cell phone. In December, Menzel also met officials from the US Consulate General in Hamburg. While the Federal Criminal Police Office (BKA) and various German agencies were involved in the investigation, he told them Hamburg was leading the inquiry.

The investigation's main focus was to check every place Kovtun had stayed between 28 October and 1 November, find contaminated areas and monitor all those who were in contact with him for potential radiation exposure. Both field and laboratory techniques were used to evaluate the measurements.

The Hamburg police began by searching the apartments where Kovtun had stayed and followed the trail from there. They did not have to wait long for results: a pale lilac glow of polonium-210 lit up across the city. The operation became a major police action. Some 600 officers were drafted on to the case. The apartment building where Kovtun spent the night on his ex-wife's sofa was evacuated and its residents hospitalised and tested for radiation. Altogether, 53 people were checked.

Kovtun left polonium traces on almost everything he touched – vehicles, objects, clothes, furniture and people. Marina Wall's apartment tested positive for secondary polonium contamination. Both the Haselau residence and the BMW were contaminated. It was established that the highest radiation dose was received by Marina's toddler. Remarkably, German investigators concluded Kovtun did not have polonium traces on his skin or clothes – polonium was literally pouring out of his body. Experts from the BfS decided he became contaminated with polonium-210 *before* his visit to Hamburg in October 2006. The authorities also wanted to test the Aeroflot aircraft that flew Kovtun to Germany – somehow the Russians must have found out about these plans because 'at the last minute' Aeroflot swapped planes.

That Wednesday, 1 November 2006, began at 08:22:53 a.m. London Time with Andrei Lugovoy calling his friend Vladimir Valuyev. The call lasted 2 minutes and 7 seconds. It is possible that Lugovoy made an early report that he and his team had arrived, and all was going as planned.

Valuyev was born on 22 April 1965 and went to the same military command academy as Lugovoy, Kovtun and Sokolenko. Like Lugovoy and Sokolenko, Valuyev had served in the Chief Directorate for Protection charged with protecting the nation's leaders and physical security of government buildings. The Service was a successor to the 9th Department of the KGB (close protection, government bodyguards) and existed until August 1996, when the FSO was established. Valuyev also later worked in the same private security companies as Lugovoy and Sokolenko. His role has not been established, but it is possible that he and his son Alexey were part of the operation against Litvinenko and that he – wittingly or unwittingly – was used as a contact point in Moscow, because a call to an old friend and colleague can always be justified. Only the timing of Lugovoy's calls to Valuyev looks strange.

Dmitry Kovtun arrived at the Millennium Hotel in Grosvenor Square shortly after 8:30 a.m. but did not check in, as he had no reservation. Instead, he went to Sokolenko's room – Room 382 – which they subsequently shared for the two days and two nights that they were in London taking part in the operation. All three buddies, Lugovoy, Kovtun and Sokolenko, knew each other rather well from their younger years. Like Lugovoy, Sokolenko had been invited and accepted to serve in the KGB's 9th Department, which he left a year before it became FSO. After a sleepless night, a lot of booze and an early flight, Kovtun immediately went to bed and took a nap. The taxi that had brought him from the airport was later found to be contaminated with polonium-210.

At about ten o'clock that morning, Lugovoy called his daughter Tatiana in her hotel room and about half an hour later called Shadrin, director of Continental Petroleum. At 10:57:59 a.m. he telephoned Kovtun to wake him up, and Kovtun responded immediately with a return call. They did not talk. The whole of Lugovoy's family then went down to eat their breakfast with Sokolenko joining them. The plan was to go shopping and sightseeing and Sokolenko seemed ready to accompany the family. No one knew, of course, that he had a very special mission of his own. After a series of calls the previous day, Sokolenko started calling Risk Advisory Group PLC again at 10:09:35 a.m. Altogether during that day he made 21 telephone calls to their number, never speaking for one second. With this in mind, it must be concluded that no one picked up the phone.

Sasha Litvinenko switched on his mobile phone at 08:53 a.m. near his home at 140 Osier Crescent. At about 11:00 a.m. Marina was ready to leave. That day was their sixth anniversary in London. It was agreed that they both had a lot to do and they would celebrate in the evening. Sasha wished her a good day and Marina left. She later claimed that Sasha stayed at home a little longer and then dashed off to town without breakfast. He never ate his breakfast alone, Marina said. In mid-December, while on location preparing to shoot the *Panorama* episode featuring John Sweeney's interview with Marina, Marina and I tried to recount the events of that morning down to the smallest detail.

According to the schedule of Litvinenko's movements based on CCTV footage, mobile phone data and witness statements, codenamed Operation AVOCET, Litvinenko had a light breakfast at home at 11:00 a.m. and left at 12:15 p.m. According to Sir Robert's report, which, like the above-mentioned schedule, is somewhat inaccurate, as shall be seen, Litvinenko left home at about 12:30 p.m., arriving at Oxford Circus shortly after 1:30 p.m. This is hardly possible. The police report presented by Detective Inspector (DI) Craig Mascall claims that Litvinenko made two telephone calls, at 11:41:14 a.m. to Lugovoy (4 min 46 sec) and on the way to Zakayev at 12:23:00 p.m. (17 sec), after which, according to Litvinenko's oyster card, he took bus 234 on Wilton Road at 12:29 p.m. He also made a call to Marina at 12:35:11 p.m. (1 min 30 sec), then Dan Quirke at 1:06:34 p.m. (48 sec) and Dean Attew at 1:07:55 p.m. (37 sec), entering East Finchley underground station Northern line at 1:10 p.m. One cannot get directly to Oxford Circus from the Northern line, so in order to travel there, he had to change at Warren Street or Tottenham Court Road or get out and walk. But the schedule produced by the police states that 'Litvinenko entered East Finchley tube' again (?) at 1:34 p.m., according to his oyster card. Did he change trains or exit at Tottenham Court Road at this time or change at Warren Street for the Victoria line, arriving at Oxford Circus a little later than 1:30 p.m.?

At 1:41:05 p.m. Litvinenko called Zakayev (1 min 10 sec) and sometime later David Kudykov, his friend. For whatever reason, this call is not registered.

David lives in London. Originally from Riga, Latvia, he is a partner in a shipping company. As usual, he answered his friend's call at once. At the time, he was abroad taking care of one of their cargo vessels in the Netherlands but was already on his way to Berlin from where he would return to London. David listened to Sasha attentively and then asked several questions. As he later told the police, he didn't like what he heard. I have found neither his statement among the available documents of the inquiry nor his name in the list of witnesses.

About the time of his call to David, Litvinenko was having a meeting with Lugovoy and another man at the Millennium Hotel in Mayfair – this is what David told me and he repeated on camera to the BBC team in my presence. John O'Mahony was filming. It never appeared anywhere. From Goldfarb's witness statement to the police on 26 November 2006: 'I then asked Litvinenko and he confirmed that the meeting took place in the Millennium Hotel. There were two Russians, Andre [*sic*] Lugovoy and another man unknown to Litvinenko who he called Vladimir. To my recollection, he said the meeting was *before* the meeting with the Italian Scaramella, but I am not certain of this.'

Litvinenko entered the room where Lugovoy introduced him to a new man. Sasha was not surprised or suspicious because his good friend Lugovoy had introduced Kovtun, some two weeks before, in exactly the same fashion (in this operation Kovtun obviously played the role of 'the Third Man'). Regarding 'Vladimir', Lugovoy said he was another powerful businessman from their Global Project business, the president of an oil company with good connections. The man did not speak much and Lugovoy was doing most of the talking. He explained that this project was about to open incredible new business opportunities to them all. It involved liquefied natural gas (LNG) and copper. Major international oil companies such as Royal Dutch Shell, BP and other giants were active players. With the help of their new friend, they would export to Latin America because he would guarantee competitive prices. The shipment must be by sea via Latvia, and specially constructed vessels to ship around the world would be necessary. Did Sasha have anybody in this business in Riga?

Sasha had, so he called his friend David. Kudykov quickly realised that those people in the room were ill-prepared for discussing business details. They did not know elementary terms, were confused about prices and could not tell CIF from FOB. David told Litvinenko that the deal looked unrealistic and advised against it.

But Sasha was overexcited. Millions, man, damn millions! He would be rich and would not have to bother about stupid and complicated due diligence reports for which he was not qualified. Money makes the world go round, so he would make the world go round!

Litvinenko finished his tea, quietly served from the hotel teapot by their new friend, and said he needed to go because he had a meeting with his Italian contact.

A security guard at 7 Down Street, the offices of Boris Berezovsky, misleadingly told the police that Sasha was there between 1:00 p.m. and 2:30 p.m., so it was decided that he was there at approximately 1:40 p.m. In reality, between about 1:45 p.m. and 2:30 p.m. Litvinenko seems to have been in a totally different place.

Some time later, *The Daily Telegraph* reported that a senior government source who was aware of the discussions of the cabinet's emergency committee, COBRA, said: 'Clear traces of the radiation were found on the floor in a room, thought to be in the Millennium Hotel in central London, as well as on a light switch in the same room. The traces were so strong that they indicated the actual source of the radiation was present, not a secondary source such as excretions from Mr Litvinenko's contaminated body.'[9]

Now it is known that the reference was to Room 382 shared by Sokolenko and Kovtun. The highest readings were found in the bathroom and the peak of those in a sediment trap below the plughole. The expert evidence was that these readings were only consistent with primary contamination. And there were indeed some polonium traces on the wall near the light switch measured at 590 cps (counts per second), which is high enough. Based on the measurements, the coroner concluded that the radioactive poison in one form or another had been poured down the plughole. Remarkably, in Room 441,

[9] Ben Fenton, John Steele, Roger Highfield and Duncan Gardham, 'Net tightens on the amateur assassins', *The Telegraph*, 1 December 2006.

shared by Lugovoy, his wife and young son, only secondary contamination was found.

Sir Robert claims that at about noon, Lugovoy and Kovtun were at 58 Grosvenor Street visiting Eco 3 Capital together with Continental Petroleum (CPL), staying there for several hours:

> 6.253 It is quite clear that Mr Lugovoy and Mr Kovtun did attend the CPL offices at some point on the morning of 1 November. I have already referred to the evidence of the Visitors' Book and the cell siting. The Visitors' Book does not record a time of arrival. Mrs Davison's evidence was that the two men arrived between 11.00 a.m. and noon, which is broadly consistent with DI Mascall's understanding of the cell site evidence. [This is not correct.]

> 6.254 I heard evidence from three individuals who were present at the CPL offices that day and who recalled meeting Mr Lugovoy and Mr Kovtun. They were Dr Shadrin himself, his assistant Mrs Davison and Mr Gorokov [*sic*], a colleague of his. Mr Gorokov was confused over dates, but it is clear that the events he was describing took place on 1 November ...

> 6.257 Dr Shadrin recalled that there had been a meeting on that day and that he had had some general discussions with Mr Lugovoy and Mr Kovtun about possible new projects, but his main memory appears to have been of Mr Lugovoy and Mr Kovtun discussing the football with Mrs Davison and Mr Gorokov. He said: 'Frankly I don't remember that we actually discussed anything ...' When asked whether he remembered Mr Kovtun being present, Dr Shadrin said: 'I don't remember, actually. Probably he was. But effectively they were talking more about football, and openly I just quitted the meeting, because I think that was probably early – it was midday/early afternoon, because obviously everyone was going to ... attend the match.'

On 24 February 2015, *The Guardian* reported: 'Alexander Shadrin, CPL's acting CEO, told the inquiry he had threatened to resign if the company used Lugovoi's security firm ... Shadrin told the court that although he had not used Lugovoi's security services and had only commissioned a report from him, he paid him $200,000 (£129,000) because while "he couldn't actually help us a lot, probably he could make our situation worse".'

Ben Emmerson QC also interviewed Dariya Davison, who described her position as 'executive assistant to Dr Shadrin in Eco 3 Capital Limited'. She also did 'some paperwork' for Continental Petroleum, altogether being employed 'about a year and a half, from September 2005 to February or

March 2007'. The names Lugovoy and Kovtun were entered in the visitors record book for 31 October, but 'as a matter of interpretation, that would appear to relate to 1 November'. Remarkably, the time in and time out were not specified in the visitor book. Anyway, shortly before noon, visitors were still not in the CPL/Eco3 offices, according to the book. And Shadrin had just left by this time, as he testified.

During the interview with Dariya it was established that at lunchtime and after 5:30 p.m. the visitors record book was left open for everyone who cared to sign in. So as a matter of fact, an entry for 31 October 'with an interpretation of 1 November' could have been done in the late afternoon by anybody. Mrs Davison could not even know who among those two was Lugovoy and who was Kovtun and thought it was Kovtun who had two grown-up daughters with him in London.

To cut a long story short:

Q: 'How good is your memory of these events, Mrs Davison, eight years on without your statement?'

A: 'Bad.'

On the next day, one of the two visited the CPL office again. The time of the visit was not recorded.

The third 'witness' of Sir Robert, Nikolai Gorokhov (correct spelling), is a professional nominee. As usual in such cases, he is from time to time appointed to shell companies and then his 'appointment' is automatically terminated, for which he is paid. Thus, apart from Eco 3, he also served as 'economist' in Innovation Admin Limited, registered at the same address (Shadrin was also there as CFO), and 'project manager' at Tumsky Petroleum Limited at 11 Oldfield Mews. All those companies are Russian-owned, of course.

It is probably be safe to conclude that statements of all three of the above individuals regarding Lugovoy and Kovtun's afternoon visit to the CPL offices on 1 November 2006 are unreliable. The CCTV camera footage shows Lugovoy and Kovtun entering the lobby of the Millennium Hotel at 3:30 p.m. Judge Robert Owen believes they had spent over three hours at CPL.

According to the inquest report, at about 2:00 p.m. Sasha, for whatever reason, visited Titon International at 25 Grosvenor Street, right opposite number 58 where Lugovoy and Kovtun were allegedly sitting at that time. Litvinenko, the report claims, paid a short visit to Dean Attew, leaving him about half an hour later – that is, about 2:30 p.m. At 2:32:20 p.m., however, Sasha was already making a telephone call from Bruton Place, and this must be believed because for the call times and positioning we have Calling Line

Identity (CLI) localisation from the mobile phone tracking data, which must be accurate. He was calling Lugovoy to say that they should, by all means, meet again later that day, but the telephone was silent. After that Litvinenko called Zakayev at 2:35:43 p.m. (25 sec), 2:40:24 p.m. (18 sec) and 2:45:09 p.m. (4 sec).

DI Mascall claims that Litvinenko then visited 'Sasha Piccadilly', about whom we shall hear later, at St James' Churchyard, Piccadilly, at approximately 2:40 p.m. But in reality, at 2:41 p.m. he was caught on CCTV in Cork Street. Whatever he did, he was in Piccadilly Circus at 3:03 p.m., approximately a seven-minute-walk away.

Mario Scaramella arrived at Piccadilly Circus much earlier. He was impatiently waiting for his Russian friend because he had very important news to share. At the same time, in the Pizza Hut restaurant where he was sitting, Mario was charging his mobile phone, just in case.

Sasha was only a few minutes late and as usual, arrived unnoticed. Later, Mario showed me the exact place they met on that day – right in front of Eros's statue in Piccadilly Circus – and described every detail, including the time of the meeting. He also showed and explained everything to DS Steven Walker of the Metropolitan Police and repeated the same in his witness statement. Mario and Sasha greeted each other in a friendly way and Scaramella kissed Litvinenko twice in the Italian fashion saying, 'In Italy, we give two'.

Litvinenko was very relaxed and looked casual. He was wearing blue jeans and a denim jacket, a khaki T-shirt matching his shoulder bag, and he was hungry. Sasha said in his broken English: 'Mario, there is a good restaurant. They have very good fish at a very low price, let's go there.' So, they went the whole way back along Piccadilly and CCTV captured them at 3:10 p.m. walking towards Itsu.

Not to lose time, because both were quite busy, they talked on the way and Sasha explained his new project, adding that he had just completed a copper deal. 'Millions, Mario, millions!' he shouted. He explained that in Russia, secret services were gaining complete power over companies that were exporting oil, gas, metals and other commodities, and the companies would do as they were told. 'I have a friend in the secret services,' Sasha said, 'who knows a president of one such company and for whom goods will be offered at very special prices.'

When they finally settled at a table on the lower-ground floor of Itsu, it was Mario's turn. He showed Litvinenko an email with threats to Berezovsky, Guzzanti, Mario and Sasha, but because it was in English Litvinenko was not able to understand it properly. He, however, knew the sender and dismissed all threats as 'bullshit', promising Mario that he would check with his Moscow sources (meaning Lugovoy). After about twenty minutes they parted. Litvinenko never saw his Italian friend again. Itsu was the first place where Litvinenko, during their late afternoon meeting, left polonium traces. Starting from this moment, he was leaving them everywhere.

On the opposite side of Piccadilly, vis-à-vis Itsu, near the entrance to the sumptuous carpeted Burlington Arcade, Sasha made a telephone call to Lugovoy at 3:35:15 p.m. and left a voice message, which Lugovoy received. Three minutes later, he called again (39 sec). He then made several other calls while walking along Grosvenor Street (CCTV) in the direction of the Millennium Hotel at 44 Grosvenor Square in Mayfair.

Before entering the hotel lobby at 3:58 p.m., Sasha managed to call Berezovsky and then from the lobby Lugovoy (3:59:04 p.m., 3 sec). The line was busy. Records show that at 3:58:27 p.m., Lugovoy called his Moscow office (1 min 51 sec). Litvinenko repeated this call 24 seconds later. Interestingly, before leaving the bar to meet Sasha, Lugovoy called Vladimir Voronov/ Voronoff, one of the nominee directors of CPL (according to the witness testimony of Dariya Davison, she saw him in the company three or four times during the whole period of her employment) who Lugovoy had last met at the house of Badri Patarkatsishvili. Although Lugovoy knew that Litvinenko was waiting in the lobby, the call with Voronoff lasted for almost six minutes. That means that Litvinenko and Lugovoy spent a maximum of 20 minutes or less in the bar together.

There is no video footage of the meeting because, as stated in the inquiry report, there were no CCTV cameras in the Pine Bar in 2006. There are only two testimonies, and both belong to the eyewitnesses who were direct participants of the events. One is Norberto Andrade, the head barman of the Pine Bar who served that afternoon, and another is Alexander Litvinenko, the victim.

Andrade was sure that he had served the men – he explained that the bill bore the name of a different member of staff because he had been using someone else's log-on card that day. This was not investigated. It is obvious from the bill that the guests had made many different orders during the time they were in the bar, but strangely Andrade did not enter the details into the computer at the time the orders were made. So, no one actually knows what had been ordered, when, or by whom and whether Lugovoy and Co. really had ordered and consumed what was later reflected in the bill. Judge Owen stated that he had heard evidence from Mr Andrade and vouched that the barman had a good memory of serving the three men that afternoon. So far, it is all correct.

This is what Mr Andrade, at the time 67 and having worked at the hotel for almost three decades, said in an interview to *The Sunday Telegraph* published on 15 July 2007, some eight months after the meeting in the bar. 'When I was delivering gin and tonic to the table,' he explained, 'I was obstructed. I couldn't see what was happening, but it seemed very deliberate to create a distraction ... I think the polonium was sprayed into the teapot. There was contamination found on the picture above where Mr Litvinenko had been sitting and all over the table, chair and floor, so it must have been a spray.'

The Italian barkeeper also revealed that he used to serve Albert R. 'Cubby' Broccoli, the late producer of James Bond films, as well as Sean Connery and George Lazenby, who both played 007 (quite symbolically, Connery played in the first five Bond films including *From Russia with Love*, 1963, and Lazenby after him in *On Her Majesty's Secret Service*, 1969).

According to the inquiry report:

6.302 It was apparent from Mr Andrade's evidence that at the time in question, he was busy serving a number of customers. Understandably, he paid only limited attention to the group at Mr Lugovoy's table. He said that the men were 'very well behaved and well dressed'. He did not overhear anything that the men said and did not remember anything unusual about the way they acted. In particular, he did not notice anything unusual about the tea or the way that it had been drunk. He said, 'It was as normal as any other table or any other time'. He disassociated himself entirely from various sensational accounts that had been attributed to him in the press.

On the bill were three teas, three Gordon's gins, three tonics, one very fine Cuban cigar (Romeo y Julieta Romeo No. 1), one champagne-cocktail plus one Gordon's gin without tonic. That means there were most probably three 'well-dressed' people in the bar *before* Litvinenko came there because, in his worn jeans and khaki T-shirt, he was not 'well-dressed' to say the least. Before he appeared in the lobby, Lugovoy and Kovtun were marching in front of the CCTV cameras while the third man remained at the table unnoticed, because there were no cameras in the bar. Of course, all participants of the operation knew about it and Lugovoy's remark about how many security cameras there was nothing but sarcasm, a form of wit intended to show what he thought about their security. Then shortly before Litvinenko came to the hotel, and they knew he was on the way because he called three times, first at 3:38:53 p.m., Kovtun quietly disappeared and Lugovoy was in the bar *with another man*, who Litvinenko called 'Vladimir' in his later statements to Goldfarb and police. 'Lugovoy was with another Russian, Sasha said, whom Sasha had not met before. "He had the eyes of a killer," he said. He knew the type,' Goldfarb recalled of his discussion with Litvinenko at Barnet Hospital in mid-November. And this was not Dmitry Kovtun, who Litvinenko called Dima and who he knew from their previous meetings only two weeks before.[10]

It is almost certain that Kovtun was not even present during Litvinenko's 'last supper' at the Pine Bar. This KGB ruse is known as substitution. I have described it in detail in *Poison Factory* in relation to the Artamonov case in Vienna. There were three people at the table all right, but Kovtun was not among them. The three men were Andrei, Vladimir and Sasha.

Later, discussing the case with Jay and Colin, Marina's liaison officers from Scotland Yard, Goldfarb asked why British authorities demanded the extradition of only Lugovoy in connection with the murder of Litvinenko while Kovtun's name was noticeably absent from the extradition request. He was told the prosecutors concluded that the evidence they had was good enough to convict Lugovoy but not necessarily Kovtun. (The extradition of Kovtun was demanded five years later, in February 2012.)

Lugovoy went out to the lobby and invited Litvinenko to the bar at about 4:10 p.m., according to the inquiry documents. Andrei briefly introduced his companion and explained that they were leaving for the football match shortly, so there were no more than 10–15 minutes to have a quick chat to discuss plans for the next day. He asked Sasha if he wanted to eat or drink anything and Sasha refused. Nevertheless, the barman brought a clean teacup. According to Litvinenko, there was only a little tea left at the bottom of the teapot on the table, and it made just half a cup. 'Maybe about 50 grams,' he said. 'It was green tea with no sugar, and it was already cold.' Mr Andrade recalled that 'this was, in fact, an order for green tea with lemon and honey'. Both the lemon and honey were served separately, not the Russian way. Sasha didn't like it because 'it was almost cold with no sugar' and he 'only swallowed maybe three or four times'.

Describing the end of the meeting, Litvinenko testified: 'In the end [Lugovoy] looked at his watch; he said his wife was about to come. There in the hall, Andrei's wife turned up. She was waving her hand and he said, "That's it, let's go". So Volodya [shortened version of Vladimir] and I stayed, the two of us, and he stood up, approached his wife, Andrei, and then he brought his son, eight years old. He is such a boy, eight years old, wearing a

---

[10] In his 'Witness Statement' to the police of 26 November 2006, Lextranet reference INQ003010-INQ003019, Goldfarb testified about Litvinenko: 'He was a very intelligent man with a photographic memory.'

jacket. He said, "This is Uncle Sasha, shake his hand." We shook hands, and he went (INAUDIBLE). So, then we came out.'

Here, Litvinenko missed one crucial detail – at one moment Lugovoy went out of the bar and at 4:26:12 p.m. called Vladimir Valuyev again. As before, the call was very short, only 1 minute and 08 seconds. Its tracking details have not been disclosed.

During his interviews at the hospital with police officers Detective Inspector (DI) Brent Hyatt and Detective Sergeant (DS) Chris Hoar, Sasha could not remember the name of the company they had been dealing with calling it 'Global Risk' (it was, in fact, RISC Management). He also incorrectly described the teapot in which tea had been served in the Pine Bar (it was not silver metal, as he said, but white porcelain). When police finally came to talk to him, Litvinenko was in a rather critical state. Nevertheless, the *Guardian* journalist Luke Harding was right when he reported that Sasha helped to investigate his own murder.

At 4:40:16 p.m., Sokolenko called the same telephone number for Risk Advisory Group PLC that he had called before, but again no one answered. The last call was at 5:01:23 p.m., and altogether during that day he called them, as already mentioned, 21 times with short intervals. The inquiry material gives no explanation for this.

Risk Advisory looks like a traditional business intelligence company similar to Risk Analysis or RISC Management or Control Risks, and, indeed, it declares it is doing exactly the same except that it was founded (under a different name) in 1997 by two Russians: Oleg Babinov and Evgeny Tarasov. Both are still directors and members of the Management Board (but, remarkably, not of the Board of Directors, which is well-represented by exclusively non-Russian names), and both are responsible for Russia, Eastern Europe and Eurasia. Tarasov succeeded Babinov as head of the Moscow Office in 2004, but that was the only change. Both have been fully controlling Russian operations for all those years. The company's London office is at 3 More London Riverside, SE1, and besides London and Moscow, the company also has offices in Washington, Beirut, Dubai and Hong Kong. However, probably following the good old tradition that gentlemen do not read each other's mail, no one dared or wished to investigate the investigators, and Risk Advisory has not aroused any interest of Scotland Yard detectives.

After he left the Millennium Hotel, a CCTV camera caught Litvinenko calling Ahmed Zakayev while moving towards Audley Square and then further to Berezovsky's office in Down Street. He was seen there at about 5:00 p.m., copying the emails that Scaramella had brought to their meeting.

Sasha wanted, by all means, to give them to Boris who, on that day, was leaving for Israel. At 5:40 p.m. Zakayev, together with his personal assistant 'Yasha' (Yaragi Abdulayev), picked up Litvinenko to drive him home to Muswell Hill, where they were neighbours. Yasha told me later that all was nice except that several weeks later, investigators found polonium traces in their car. This would not have been possible if Sasha had been poisoned in the bar, as generally assumed, because not enough time had passed.

By about 7:00 p.m., Litvinenko was already at home calling Attew. The call was registered at 6:54:24 p.m. At 7:09:26 p.m. Marina called Sasha from their landline phone – she was probably in the kitchen preparing a festive evening meal while he was upstairs at his computer. Then Sasha called Attew again, and at 7:30 p.m. his favourite spicy chicken on a bottle was served. During the evening, at short intervals, he called Zakayev, Marina, Bukovsky (twice), and Shvets in the USA. His last call to his wife was at 10:37:36 p.m., which lasted for 51 seconds.

At about 11:10 p.m. Sasha Litvinenko began to die.

On 10 November Gordievsky called me saying that Litvinenko had been poisoned and was now in hospital and that he suspected the Italian, Scaramella. Oleg said he had already spoken to several Italian newspapers and they were publishing reports, and it was very good because this would mean the case would attract as much international attention as possible. I said I very much doubted that it was Scaramella. Sasha's story reminded me of the poisoning of Nikolai Khokhlov in Frankfurt in 1957. A year before Litvinenko's poisoning, I published a small book describing the Khoklov case, and Gordievsky wrote a foreword. When Michael Binyon from *The Times* called him, Gordievsky dictated another version of events. On 20 November Michael's article 'Kremlin gave orders to kill dissident and former spy, claims top defector' was published.

On 22 November my own article, 'Russian Venom', came out in *The Wall Street Journal*. In the article, I suggested it must be a radioactive substance that was killing Sasha. On the same day, a meeting between police officers, forensic experts, representatives of Public Health England and Defence Science and Technology Laboratory, both from Porton Down, as well as specialists from Atomic Weapons Establishment (AWE), was arranged and it was announced that polonium was present in Litvinenko's samples. It was discussed but thought that this reading was an anomaly, perhaps caused by the plastic bottle in which the sample had been stored.

In the early afternoon of 23 November, further testing was conducted at AWE. The results, which confirmed polonium-210 contamination, were communicated to the police between 3:00 and 5:00 p.m. But it was too late – at 9:21 p.m. Sasha Litvinenko was pronounced dead. Police officers came to Marina's home late at night to evacuate her and Tolik, their son. On the next day, I arrived in London to launch a private investigation that still continues.

Chapter 3

Kamera Never Dreams

In March 2005, Matthew Kaminsky, then working at the Brussels office of *The Wall Street Journal*, asked me to contribute an article about Soviet poisonings. I was happy to comply and on 7 April 'The KGB's Poison Factory' appeared in this highly respected newspaper. In the article's limited space, it was, of course, impossible to give a full exposé of the Russian poison-producing facilities and the history of its special laboratory that became known as Kamera (Russian for chamber). However, I briefly referred to the poisoning of the Ukrainian president Victor Yushchenko and several other cases that for some reason I was directly or indirectly involved with either as a writer, journalist, or a private investigator.

The first historically registered attempt on the life of the founder of the Soviet state is commonly regarded as having taken place on 30 August 1918. Shortly after Lenin concluded his short speech at the Mikhelson armaments factory with the words, 'There's only one issue – victory or death,' he was going back to his car parked in the courtyard. At this very moment, three shots were fired, hitting his left shoulder and the left side of his neck. The third bullet hit a female worker standing nearby. The vigilantes detained several suspects and immediately turned them over to the Cheka. Among this group was a Jewish woman who would become forever known as Fanya Kaplan, revolutionary pseudonym 'Dora'. Her full first name was probably Faiga or Feiga and her real family name remains unknown in spite of several published versions that give it as Reumann, Roidman, Roid, Roitman, Reutblatt and so on. Later that evening, the Soviet government was quick to place responsibility for the attack on the Socialist Revolutionary Party, of which she was a member, using this opportunity to not only drag through the mire their major political rival but also to announce it, during a show trial in 1922, responsible for the conspiracy to murder Lenin.

Kaplan was an unlikely assassin. She had suffered from periodic total loss of sight caused by an explosion in a hotel room in Kiev where she was assisting her anarchist friend when, as a result of careless handling, a homemade explosive device detonated, and she received several head injuries among others. The young woman, aged only 19 at the time, was arrested and put into prison. Three years later, in May 1909, a prison doctor diagnosed complete vision loss.

She was pardoned after ten years in jail and settled in Simferopol in the Crimea on the Black Sea. After successful surgery, her visual field partially returned with some blurring in both eyes. In the summer of 1918, she went to Moscow, where she had lived for a month after her penal servitude.

On that day, no one knew until the last moment when and where exactly Lenin was going to speak. A revolver, which Kaplan was allegedly shooting, was 'found' four days later, but it could not have fired the bullet extracted from Lenin's neck by a German doctor ... in April 1922. I saw this bullet proudly exhibited in the Lenin Museum in Moscow, now part of the State Historical Museum.

Kaplan told the Cheka nothing and was shot without any investigation or trial on 3 September on the personal orders of Jacob (Ya'aqov) Sverdlov, chairman of the highest legislative, administrative and revising body of the country. There's a rather plausible theory that Lenin's shooting was an attempted coup d'état organised by Sverdlov himself while Trotsky, Dzerzhinsky (Polish: Dzierżyński) and Stalin were away. Sverdlov suddenly died the following March.

After the leader of the world communist revolution and the first head of the Soviet state (who many serious researchers accuse of having been a German agent) recovered from his wounds three days later, the Cheka provided him with a full report on the incident. Three years later someone also suggested that the bullets were poisoned, an absurd theory readily picked up by Richard Pipes and several other historians without consulting any experts. It was said the poison was curare, a dark resinous extract obtained from several tropical American woody plants, especially *Chondrodendron tomentosum* or certain species of *Strychnos*. The actual name, curare, is a corruption of two Tupi Indian terms meaning 'bird' and 'to kill'. The curare vine is used by some South American Indians for poisoning arrowheads.

The Bolshevik leader with sadistic personality disorder was fascinated. Thus, in 1921 the first poison laboratory was established – right in Lenin's own secretariat, at that time called the 'Special Room' – under the leadership of Professor Ignaty Kazakov. From the very beginning, its 'products' were to be used against the 'enemies of the people'. That, of course, was a euphemism. What the Russian kingpins always meant was enemies of the Kremlin. To be more precise, enemies of the national leader himself, whatever his name.

Such a laboratory naturally became a top-secret institution. But during the near-chaos of the early 1990s, several researchers managed to obtain secret documents and testimonies that throw historical light on what *The Wall Street Journal* called 'The KGB's Poison Factory', which eventually, and quite unexpectedly, led to a book. In the book, I gave a full exposé of that secret laboratory, where the most sophisticated poisons for the Russian Intelligence Services (RIS) have been produced since Lenin's times.

American intelligence learned about the Kamera in February 1954. One year before the Soviet occupation of Vienna was over, a man in a Russian-made civil suit and carrying MGB (another earlier name of the KGB) credentials in his left breast pocket walked into the American barracks on Stiftgasse, opposite the large Herzmansky department store, now known as Gerngross. The man, who for several minutes was window-shopping before finally deciding to go ahead, introduced himself to the duty officer as Major Peter Sergeyevich Deriabin, a member of the Vienna MGB station and former officer of the elite Kremlin Guards Directorate. Soon, a Russian-speaking CIA official was called in and the new defector was driven to a safe house. Here the initial debriefing started.

Tennent H. ('Pete') Bagley, a 29-year-old CIA officer later to rise to deputy chief, counterintelligence, of the Soviet Bloc division at Langley, conducted the debriefing. Fifty years later, we met in Brussels. Pete still had a wonderfully clear memory and an impressive private archive covering half a century of Soviet espionage in Europe and the USA.

This is what Deriabin told the CIA during his debriefing:

As late as 1953, the interrogators were backed by terror devices, which would have done credit to the worst of the Gestapo professionals. From 1946 until that year, the state security maintained at its Moscow headquarters a quietly notorious laboratory called the 'Chamber' (Kamera). Its staff consisted of a medical director and several assistants, who performed experiments on living people – prisoners and persons about to be executed – to determine the effectiveness of various poisons and injections as well as the use of hypnotism and drugs in interrogation techniques. Only the Minister of State Security and four other high officers were allowed to enter.

The laboratory prospered. The 'doctor' in charge [Grigory Mairanovsky] was given a special degree of Doctor of Medical Science by Moscow University and nominated for a Stalin Prize for his 'researches'. The Soviet regime announced the Chamber's closing to a select group of State Security officials in October 1953, after blaming its existence on the Beria excesses. It has probably not been reactivated; but its researches continue to be exploited by selected personnel of the State Security.[1]

---

[1] Tennent H. Bagley's private archive. Deriabin later used this information in a book written with the American journalist and writer Frank Gibney.

Mairanovsky was arrested in 1951 and allegedly spent ten years in prison, later heading, as he almost certainly had done during his 'incarceration', a biochemical laboratory.

Deriabin was misled about the facility 'not being reactivated'. What happened is typically described in the professional jargon as double-compartmenting. That is, spoofing the original group who held the information into believing the operation has ended while it was simply moved to a new compartment. Indeed, after the laboratory was officially 'closed down', the deadly experiments continued as part of the Department of Operational Equipment (OOT). After Mairanovsky's arrest, it resurfaced as Laboratory No. 12 of the 5th Special Department. Its poisons continued to be successfully used for executions outside Russia.

In March 1953, days after Stalin's death, Minister of State Security Semyon Ignatyev reported to the new collective Soviet leadership of Malenkov, Molotov, Bulganin and Khrushchev:

> The execution of [Wolfgang] Salus – Trotsky's secretary in 1930 – was conducted with the help of an MGB agent, who gave him a special substance on 13 February 1953. The substance causes the death of a person in 10–12 days. After this, Salus got sick and died on 4 March in one of Munich's hospitals. Using different sources, it was ascertained that the poisoning of Salus did not cause any suspicion of the adversary. Doctors came to the conclusion that his death was a result of pneumonia.[2]

When I mentioned this episode in my article, a valuable tip-off came from a reader. The MGB agent who poisoned Salus in Munich was Otto Freitag. Indeed, according to the well-documented research paper published by the German author Hermann Bubke, the East German intelligence service sent Freitag on a secret mission to Munich in 1949. In 1951, he successfully infiltrated the Trotskyist movement, which was considered 'very dangerous', long after the murder of Trotsky himself by the paranoid Stalinist clique. In 1953, through his East Berlin masters, Freitag received Moscow's orders to 'liquidate' Trotsky's former secretary by poisoning him with a substance provided by the special lab. As can be seen from Minister Ignatyev's report, the operation went as planned.

A year later, in 1954, Freitag was assigned to prepare the kidnapping of General Reinhard Gehlen, then head of the Gehlen Organization, known as the 'Org', which became the West German intelligence/information service, BND (Bundesnachrichtendienst). The MGB had a top-ranking mole inside

---

[2] Ignatyev's report to the Politburo, no. 951/I of 8 March 1953.

the Org, Heinz Felfe (codenamed PAUL), who in 1953 moved from Münster to its Pullach Headquarters to oversee, first as deputy and from early 1957 as chief, the BND's whole counterintelligence effort against the Soviets, the so-called Referat 'Sowjetunion' of Abteilung IIIf. Before the Russians picked him up, Felfe had been working for the British SIS. Perhaps to avoid exposing their most valuable source in Germany, the kidnap operation was called off.

More than ten years after his undercover mission, Freitag returned to East Berlin to take part in the propaganda campaign against the West and further served as an 'officer in the special employment' (OibE) at the Stasi headquarters.

In the 1950s and 1960s, the 'products' of the Special Laboratory, now called Lab X in internal documents, were used against 'enemies of the people' who lived in exile in Europe. In February 1954, Nikolai Khokhlov was sent to Frankfurt am Main to organise the assassination of a prominent anti-Soviet activist by shooting him with a poisoned bullet from a gun concealed in a packet of cigarettes. In September 1957, Khokhlov, who had turned himself in and began working for the CIA, was himself poisoned while attending a conference in Frankfurt. A month later Lev Rebet, a Ukrainian immigrant was poisoned by Bogdan Stashinsky on Moscow's orders and died. In October 1959, one of the leaders of the Ukrainian anti-communist opposition, Stepan Bandera, was poisoned entering his house in Munich. Stashinsky subsequently defected to tell the West German authorities all about the Rebet and Bandera assassinations that he had carried out.

In 1963, 'direct actions', a euphemism used by the KGB to describe such questionable activities as shooting, poisoning, blowing up and subversion, were handed over to the newly formed Department T. Two years later, it was passed on to Department V ('V' for 'victory') of the First Chief Directorate (FCD) of the KGB, which had the capability to plan and mount special operations of a quasi-military nature.

In October 1964, a West German anti-bugging specialist, engineer Horst Schwinkmann, was sent to Moscow to discover and remove KGB bugging and recording devices planted in the West German Embassy. His techniques caused aural pain to those listening in, and this irritated the KGB. While Schwinkmann was admiring religious relics at the Troitse-Sergeyeva Lavra in Zagorsky Monastery, outside Moscow, he was shot in the buttocks with a nitrogen-based mustard gas capsule. The attack, though excruciatingly painful, apparently was not meant to kill but to punish Schwinkmann, so he survived – although, according to some accounts, he almost lost his leg. All this I mention in *The KGB's Poison Factory* book as historical background.

In 1978, Laboratory No. 12, which had hugely expanded, became the Central Scientific Research Institute for Special Technology attached to the Operational Technical Directorate (OTU) of the KGB. It was here in the OTU that the notorious umbrella that killed Georgi Markov was transformed into a gun and tested. The umbrella, by the way, was not Russian. A few pieces had been purchased by a KGB officer in Washington and sent to Moscow to work with.

However, in 1973, five years before the assassination of Markov in London and a year after the Soviet Union signed the Biological Weapons Convention, a quasi-civil entity was established. It became known as Biopreparat. Under the cover of a civilian pharmaceutical and vaccine company, Biopreparat was in fact in charge of biological weapons research and production, consisting of forty facilities that included a dozen major complexes. The staff was more or less evenly divided between the development of new weapons and work on cures and antidotes. Both the KGB and GRU (Russian military intelligence) were using the Biopreparat 'product' and contributing to its research requirements. Directorate 15 of the General Staff of the Soviet Army directed the military part of the operation.

According to Western sources, at one time the Soviet Union had the world's largest biological warfare programme with somewhere between 25,000 and 32,000 people employed in a network of 20 to 30 military and civilian laboratories and research institutions. An additional 10,000 or so worked in defence ministry bio weapons laboratories. Some commentators give a figure of at least 47 labs and test facilities scattered across Russia, employing more than 40,000 workers, 9,000 of whom were scientists. Between 1,000 and 2,000 of those scientists were experts on deadly pathogens.

In 1989, the first defector to emerge from Biopreparat, Vladimir Pasechnik, revealed that the Soviet biological warfare effort was ten times larger than estimated by US or British intelligence. And in 1992 Dr Kanatzhan 'Kanat' Alibekov (aka Kenneth 'Ken' Alibek) defected, providing new details of Moscow's extensive biological and toxicological weapons development programme. Dr Alibek, a naturalised US subject, who at the time of writing was listed as a Professor and Vice Dean of Nazarbayev University in Kazakhstan, wrote a highly classified study of the Soviet biological weapons programme for the US government and testified several times before the US congress. Other defectors have provided additional information to Western intelligence agencies.

On 20 September 1992, an article entitled 'Poisoned Policy' written by Dr Vil Mirzayanov and another chemist, Lev Fedorov, appeared in *The Moscow News*. Mirzayanov wrote: 'I decided to make another attempt to expose before the public eye the hypocrisy of the military-industrial complex, which, on the eve of the signing of a Government convention to ban chemical weapons, developed a new type of chemical weapon five to eight times stronger than all known weapons.'

The development of neurotoxic agents began in the Soviet Union in 1972 under the scientific supervision of Professor Peter Kirpichev of the Moscow State Scientific Research Institute of Organic Chemistry and Technology, where the first agent, A-230, was synthesised. The research programme, codenamed FOLIANT, was commissioned and controlled by the Ministry of Defence. The experimental laboratory was located in the Volsk branch of the institute in the village of Shikhany, a top-secret facility.

Neurologic agents, commonly known as 'nerve agents', belong to chemical warfare agents and have been of special interest due to their high lethality and stability. They are organophosphorus compounds that act by inhibiting the enzyme acetylcholinesterase, which is fundamental for the control of transmission of nervous impulses. According to the specialists, there are several ways of treating intoxication by organophosphorus compounds, but 'none of them is efficient against all the known neurotoxic agents or against all of their effects'.[3] One of the Soviet scientists who, under the supervision of Professor Kirpichev, was personally responsible for the synthesis of such neurotoxic agents (liquids) as A-232 and A-234 in 1976, which along with A-230 and later A-242 (solid) became known as the Novichok series, has stated in several interviews that there is no antidote to them.[4] Gary Aitkenhead, chief executive of the Defence Science and Technology Laboratory (Dstl) in Porton Down, Wiltshire, UK, confirmed to *Sky News* in April 2018 that there was no known antidote to Novichok. According to the latest research,[5] even the quick identification of a neurotoxic agent in order to choose the proper treatment is usually not fast enough to either save the life of the patient or to avoid serious permanent damages.

In 1993, Russian scientists Mirzayanov, Fedorov and Uglev tried to inform the West about new Russian chemical weapons. But, partly because the Organisation for the Prohibition of Chemical Weapons (OPCW) – the implementing intergovernmental body for the Chemical Weapons

---

[3] Reinaldo T. Delfino, Tatiana S. Ribeiro and José D. Figueroa-Villar, 'Organophosphorus Compounds as Chemical Warfare Agents: Review', *Journal of the Brazilian Chemical Society*, 20/3 (March 2009), 407.

[4] See, for example, Vladimir Uglev's interview with Svetlana Reiter and Nataliya Gevorkyan for *The Bell*, 20 March 2018. According to Dr Simon Cotton, Senior Lecturer in Chemistry, University of Birmingham, 'the effect of the nerve agent cannot be reversed'.

[5] Delfino, Ribeiro and Figueroa-Villar, 'Organophosphorus Compounds', 407.

Convention (CWC), which entered into force in April 1997 – did not exist at the time, and partly due to bureaucratic dithering, their calls were largely ignored.

After his article was published in the USA, Mirzayanov was arrested and placed in Lefortovo Prison. Referring to his trial, US ambassador Thomas Pickering said in Moscow that it seemed 'strange to us ... that someone could either be prosecuted or persecuted for telling the truth about an activity which is contrary to a treaty obligation of a foreign government'. On 11 March 1994, Russia's Prosecutor General dropped all charges against the scientist.

In February, after Mirzayanov's release from prison, General Nikolai Golushko, director of the Federal Counterintelligence Service, a 75,000-person agency that replaced the Second Chief Directorate (SCD) of the KGB and would soon become the FSB, answered a question about organisational changes in the Operational and Technology Directorate (formerly in charge of Lab X). He told the journalist Yevgenia Albats:

> We now have two such directorates. The scientific-technical directorate includes institutes for the design of special technology and intelligence equipment. The scientific-technological directorate, along with the designers and the institutes, numbers about ten thousand people. We also work for intelligence and help the Ministry of Internal Affairs. Through the second of these directorates, Operations and Technology, we carry out operational and technical activity with the sanctions of the procurator – and, today, in compliance with the new Constitution and the courts.[6]

These words should be remembered in connection with the Litvinenko case and the new law approved by the Russian Parliament in July 2006 that allows the Russian president to sanction operations, including assassinations on foreign soil, against the enemies of the regime. The question is, who decides that one is 'the enemy'? That must be Mister President himself.

Terminations, that is, eliminating enemies abroad, never stopped fascinating Soviet and Russian leaders from Lenin to Putin. Pavel Sudoplatov recalled what one KGB major general by the name of Vasili Shadrin told him in 1988 about Mikhail Gorbachev's interest in the special laboratory. The last Soviet president and the father of perestroika read an article by the former KGB chairman Vladimir Semichastny in the popular *Ogoniok* magazine. In it, Semichastny reported that the then future Soviet leader Leonid Brezhnev had hinted to him it would perhaps be easier to poison Khrushchev than

---

[6] Yevgenia Albats, *The State Within a State: The KGB and Its Hold on Russia – Past, Present and Future* (New York: Farrar, Straus & Giroux, 1994), 352.

oust him from power. Gorbachev's KGB chief, Victor Chebrikov, summoned Semichastny to his office and ordered him to report in writing on experiments with poisons and Brezhnev's alleged remarks. Semichastny, however, refused to provide any written statement. An old member of the Soviet nomenklatura, who rose through the ranks of the Communist Young League, Vladimir Yefimovich Semichastny quickly realised that it would be healthier for him to keep his mouth shut. And he was right.

Valery Butuzov hardly remembered the name of Semichastny. He was a career intelligence officer and a KGB colonel who in the early 1990s worked in Department 12 of Directorate S ('Illegals') at the Soviet and later Russian intelligence headquarters in Yasenevo. Colonel Butuzov was temporarily seconded to Biopreparat. Ken Alibek, at the time Kanatzhan Alibekov, who just succeeded General Anatoly Vorobiov as the deputy director of the establishment, recalled how Butuzov walked into his office seeking professional advice. 'I'm looking for something that will work with a gadget I've designed,' the KGB colonel said. 'Let's say we put this assembly into a tiny box, maybe an empty pack of Marlboro, and then find a way to put the pack under someone's desk, or in his trash basket. If we were then to set it in motion, the aerosol should do the job right away, wouldn't it?'[7]

When Alibekov replied that first of all it would depend on the substance used, Butuzov dutifully asked what would be the best substance to ensure a target came to a sticky end. Butuzov was thinking of 'something like Ebola', Alibek noted. (Ebola is the common term for a group of viruses and for the disease that they cause: Ebola hemorrhagic fever (EHF). Because Ebola is lethal and since no approved vaccine or treatment is available, Ebola is classified as a Category A bioterrorism agent.)

'That would work,' mused Alibekov, 'but you'd have a high probability of killing not just this person, but everyone around him.'

'That wouldn't matter', Butuzov said thoughtfully, upon which Alibekov asked whether this was merely a theoretical discussion or if his visitor had any particular person in mind.

'No one in particular,' the KGB man said. 'Well, maybe there is one person – Gamsakhurdia, for example.'[8] Like Vaclav Havel in Prague, Zviad Gamsakhurdia was a dissident, Shakespeare scholar and writer. He became the first democratically elected President of Georgia, winning more than 87 per cent of the votes. Gamsakhurdia had long opposed Moscow's policies

[7] Ken Alibek with Stephen Handelman, *Biohazard: The Chilling True Story of the Largest Covert Biological Weapons Program in the World – Told from the Inside by the Man Who Ran It* (London: Arrow, 2000), 174.
[8] Ibid, 175.

toward his country, pushed for independence and led a demonstration against the bloody Soviet repression in 1989 of a demonstration in Tbilisi that left nineteen people dead.

Several months later, Alibekov asked Butuzov what happened to that idea of his, the one about a pack of Marlboro and Gamsakhurdia.

'Oh, that,' Butuzov chuckled, 'well, to tell you the truth, it never really got anywhere. We had a plan prepared but the bosses finally turned it down. They said it wasn't the right time.'

On 22 December 1991, armed opposition launched a violent coup d'état that was, reportedly, secretly supported by the Russian special forces. A military junta took over the government and installed as its chairman Gamsakhurdia's old rival Eduard Shevardnadze (who until recently had served as Soviet foreign minister) ruling for the next four years without any elections. Gamsakhurdia managed to escape but returned to Georgia in September 1993 and started a successful civil war, until the Russian troops moved in to protect the ruling regime.

On New Year's Eve, Gamsakhurdia – formally still the legitimate President of Georgia – was found dead with a single bullet wound to his head. What happened to him remains unknown to this day. According to Alexander Kouzminov, a former KGB officer who had served for almost ten years with Butuzov in the same department, the colonel had been awarded the Order of the Red Banner for a 'clandestine combat operation'. It is, however, unusual that the Georgian president was shot rather than poisoned. Normally, poisoning leaves no traces and it is very difficult to point the finger at an interested party.

I recalled this episode when answering a question from the Georgian newspaper *Sakartvelos Respublika* in late August 2008, in the middle of the new Russo-Georgian crisis.

'Do you think that the same thing might happen to President Mikheil Saakashvili [who became the Georgian leader when Shevardnadze was ousted from power] as happened to the Ukrainian president Viktor Yushchenko and Alexander Litvinenko?'

My interviewer, Iya Merkviladze, had in mind an assassination attempt on the life of the then Ukrainian presidential candidate in 2004 that left him disfigured from dioxin poisoning and the murder of the former KGB/FSB officer with polonium-laced tea in 2006 in London. I answered, certainly, these are Moscow's methods and advised President Saakashvili to ask the British SAS or the French SPHP (Service de Protection des Hautes Personnalités) to protect him. The interview was published in the Georgian capital Tbilisi on 3 September.

There was a good reason to ask this question. After the Russo-Georgian war of August 2008, when Russian forces invaded Georgia granting independence to two of its rebel territories, Abkhazia and South Ossetia, Georgia broke diplomatic relations with its big neighbour. Naturally, the Kremlin intensified pressure against Saakashvili, openly supporting his opponents. On 5 May 2009, the BBC reported, quoting sources inside Georgia, that the Georgian 'troop rebellion' (an attempted mutiny at a military base) was over and that it was part of a Russia-linked coup attempt to kill President Saakashvili. For several years, relations between Moscow and Tbilisi had remained frosty and tense while the Russian mass media mocked and insulted the Georgian president. In October 2012, Saakashvili's party was defeated by the coalition led by the Moscow billionaire Boris (Bidzina) Ivanishvili. Saakashvili and his Dutch wife had to flee to Ukraine.

I forgot to tell Iya, the New York correspondent of *Sakartvelos Respublika*, that when Saakashvili came to power in Georgia after the November 2003 'Rose Revolution' and then became president in January, I wrote to Markus 'Misha' Wolf, the legendary former chief of the Stasi foreign intelligence service. I asked him about the Jenapharm company, which produced highly sophisticated pharmaceutical preparations not only for the needs of Wolf's directorate but also for the East German and Soviet sportsmen. A pill known as Oral Turinabol was given to the athletes to bolster their hormones. This Oral Turinabol, or O-T, was an anabolic steroid derived from testosterone. Produced by Jenapharm, it was given to the most promising Soviet athletes as part of the secret state programme. 'Iron Misha' leisurely and very politely responded in good English but never provided any information.[9] However, I was aware that in the DDR more than 3,000 Stasi moles within the sport system monitored scientists, coaches and athletes, secretly reporting every move they and their colleagues made. Even more snitches were in the Soviet sports organisations.

After almost a year of fruitless attempts, I stopped asking and bought Wolf's book. The former East German spymaster writes:

I knew … that even after Stalin's death, the Soviets still had a department that developed bizarre ways of killing enemies. Even within the KGB, the existence of this department was a closely guarded secret. In addition to murdering Bandera with a poisoned bullet [*sic*, it was a lethal gas], the KGB assassinated the defector Truchnovich [*sic*, Dr Alexander Trushnovich, and he was not a defector], the head of the Russian emigrant organization

---

[9] Correspondence with Markus Wolf covering the period from January to December 2004 in this writer's personal archive.

the National Workers Union [*sic*, it should be People's Labour Union], in Berlin, while attempting to kidnap him. One KGB man was dispatched to buyers throughout the Eastern bloc bearing wares such as untraceable nerve toxins and skin contact poisons to smear on doorknobs. The only thing I ever accepted from him was a sachet of 'truth drugs', which he touted as 'unbeatable' with the enthusiasm of a door-to-door salesman. For years they lay in my personal safe. One day, in a fit of curiosity, I asked our carefully vetted doctor to have them analysed for me. He came back shaking his head in horror. 'Use them without constant medical supervision and there is every chance that the fellow from whom you want the truth will be dead as a dodo in seconds,' he said. We never did use the 'truth drugs.'[10]

One needed to know General Wolf, who had a fascinating 33-year-long career in the intelligence service (1953–86), to understand that the above is a mixture of rumour, fantasy and exaggeration. The old spymaster had a wonderful sense of humour that, I guess, never left him. In reality, seen from the multiple documentary sources, defectors' testimonies and explanations of those who were directly involved in the programme, Russia's murder poisons have always been considered as an extremely dangerous and efficient weapon by Western experts. Suffice it to say that in November 2006, when Litvinenko was dying on his hospital bed, no one in Britain had the slightest idea of what was killing him. And until this day, there are plenty of questions regarding the Skripals' poisoning.

Obviously, there are conventional poisons like cyanide and many others that could easily be identified during an autopsy or even at a glance by a trained eye, whereas special poisons like ricin or abrin produced specifically for the army or intelligence services are very difficult or impossible to diagnose or detect.

During my training, I was given only a very general idea about poisons used in special operations. Mainly it was related to the poisoning of the Afghan president Hafizullah Amin in his recently refurbished Tajbeg Palace in Kabul in September 1979. A Soviet illegal, Lieutenant Colonel Mitalin Talybov (codenamed SABIR), served as Amin's cook and managed to add poison to the president's meal just before Operation STORM-333, the assault on the palace, took place. The Afghan president survived only to be shot during the attack. Almost all of the officers who conducted our training had recently returned from Afghanistan where they were part of the active-service 345 Special Airborne Regiment.

[10] Markus Wolf with Anne McElvoy, *Man Without a Face: The Memoirs of a Spymaster* (London: Jonathan Cape, 1997), 235.

The Russian Intelligence Services' choice of a particular type of substance always depends on the precise effect that is to be reached. Putting aside a strict scientific classification of the 'operational means', produced by the Russian secret laboratories, I propose for the sake of clarity to group them in two categories: 'soft' chemicals and deadly poisons.

'Soft' chemicals are not designed to kill. To this category belongs the serum that Markus Wolf described. It was almost certainly one of the SP varieties, a psychotropic drug that induces a person to share his most deeply hidden secrets with his interlocutor. It loosens the tongue and has no smell, taste or colour and no known side effects. In different publications, SP stands either for 'syvorotka pravdy' meaning 'truth serum', or 'spetspreparat', that is, 'special drug'. The Wikipedia article interprets truth serum as 'a colloquial name for any of a range of psychoactive drugs used in an effort to obtain information from subjects who are unable or unwilling to provide it otherwise. These include ethanol, scopolamine, 3-quinuclidinyl benzilate, midazolam, flunitrazepam, sodium thiopental, and amobarbital, among others.'[11] In Russia, 'truth drugs' such as SP-26, SP-108 and SP-117 have been documented. Kouzminov, a KGB/SVR officer who worked with SP-117, notes that a person exposed to it has no recollection of ever having had a 'heart-to-heart' talk. It is sometimes used during covert interrogations, like that of the double defector Vitaly Yurchenko, but more often to test illegals, especially when they return from the first overseas familiarisation trip. SP-117 may also be administered to field agents when they come home for furlough or a briefing. Kouzminov claims that he found evidence of the use of the 'truth drug' in almost all the operational files of illegals to which he had access in a period of eight years. This former officer of the Directorate S testifies in his book *Biological Espionage* (2005):

These operations were always held in conditions where there were no distractions. Department 12 carried them out in operational conspiracy apartments [*sic*, safe-houses] usually in Moscow or East Berlin. Officers of the department invited the Illegal or other agent for a friendly dinner 'among our own people' and a grandiose drinking of spirits. At a suitable moment, SP-17 [*sic*] was administered, mixed into the contents of one of the bottles. In order to avoid an accidental overdose, and to control the condition of the 'drunkard' (i.e. the secretly interrogated person), there was always – either in the adjacent room or among the actual 'warm, friendly company' – a medical doctor to neutralise the 'medicine' quickly.

---

[11] For the CIA interpretation, see George Bimmerle, '"Truth" Drugs in Interrogation', *Studies in Intelligence*, 5/2 (Spring 1961), A1–A19.

If, later on, the interrogated person still tried to recall why he so quickly became drunk, he was shown 'evidence' of the 'wild party' – empty bottles in profusion, sufficient to prove they were drunk all night. We found and used a few other situations in which we could secretly apply the drug – in the sauna, while picnicking, etc. – and, in those circumstances, the episode of 'sleepiness' could be explained as sunstroke, intoxication from the fumes, hot weather, fatigue, etc.[12]

I asked Kouzminov to provide more details, but he politely declined. When his book was published, the author served as a full-time senior environmental health science adviser (communicable disease and environmental health policy) at the Ministry of Health of New Zealand, later moving to private business.

In a way, a 'truth serum' is the legacy of Mairanovsky. For Mairanovsky had not simply worked out how to kill people quickly and without a trace, he had also noticed that when he administered the chemical mix he called 'Injection C', victims displayed a tendency to talk and answer questions during the twenty-four hours before they died. He noted, 'This led me to think that perhaps the mix could be used on suspects during the course of an investigation, to obtain what we call greater openness from suspects during interrogations. It could have been extremely useful ... with those prisoners who too energetically refused to admit their guilt.' Mairanovsky was denied the chance to test these theories fully. Other 'doctors' carried on the experiments.

'Soft' remedies are also used to frighten the victim, or to incapacitate him or her temporarily to prevent a particular activity. They may also be used as sleep-inducing agents, or in specific operational circumstances to simulate death. In his book, Kouzminov recalls an episode of using a malodorous preparation against an agent who was not willing to continue collaboration with his Moscow handlers after being deployed in the West.

In 2004, Anna Politkovskaya, a crusading Moscow journalist, was poisoned on her way to North Ossetia to report on the Beslan school siege. At the time of writing, many aspects of the hostage crisis are still in dispute, but this tragedy is well-documented. Armed Chechen rebels had kept 1,128 people, including 777 children, hostage for three days, demanding that President Putin put an end to the Second Chechen War. On the third day, the Russian special forces stormed the building using tanks, 'Bumblebee' rocket launchers with thermobaric and incendiary warheads, and other heavy weapons, leaving 186 children and 147 adults dead and 728 civilians wounded. Twelve men

---

[12] Alexander Kouzminov, *Biological Espionage* (London: Greenhill Books, 2005), 106–7.

from the special troops also perished during the storm. Chechen separatist warlord Shamil Basayev, who took responsibility for the hostage-taking, blamed the outcome on the Russian president.

Politkovskaya was hurrying to Beslan to stop the bloodshed. She wrote: 'It is the morning of September 1. Reports from North Ossetia are hard to believe: a school in Beslan has been seized. Half an hour to pack my things as my mind works furiously on how to get to the Caucasus. And another thought: to look for the Chechen separatist leader, Aslan Maskhadov, let him come out of hiding, let him go to the hostage takers, and then ask them to free the children.'

Next, she was in Moscow's Vnukovo Airport. Crowds of journalists were trying to get on a plane south while one flight after another was being postponed. Anna knew there were people who would like to delay the departure of journalists into the war area. 'I use my mobile and speak openly about the purpose of my flight: "Look for Maskhadov", "persuade Maskhadov",' Politkovskaya wrote in her article 'Poisoned by Putin' published by *The Guardian* days after the siege. Aslan Maskhadov was a leader of the Chechen independence movement and the third president of the Chechen Republic of Ichkeria. He was killed in Chechnya in March 2005. Shamil Basayev was a Chechen militant Islamist who briefly served as Deputy Prime Minister in Maskhadov's government. He was assassinated near the Chechen border in July 2006.

Anna was finally shot and murdered in her apartment block in Moscow in October 2006. The BBC comment on the 2009 trial said: 'The alleged killer was somehow tipped off and was able to flee the country. And it has never emerged why Anna Politkovskaya had been under surveillance by the FSB for at least two months before her murder. Very quickly, the investigation ground to a halt. As soon as it became clear that the FSB was involved, a veil of secrecy descended.' In December 2012, a former police officer was found guilty and sentenced to 11 years for the murder. In June 2014, five men were sentenced, two of them received life imprisonment. It was reported that the murder was ordered by a Russian politician who has never been identified. The day of the assassination was very special: Putin's birthday. Somebody had given VVP a birthday present.

On 24 November 2006, less than twenty-four hours after Litvinenko was pronounced dead, Yegor Gaidar, the former Acting Prime Minister of Russia (June–December 1992), was poisoned during his visit to Dublin.

'Doctors don't see a natural reason for the poisoning, and they have not been able to detect any natural substance known to them in Mr Gaidar's body,' said his spokesman.

'So obviously we're talking about poisoning [and] it was not natural poisoning,' his aide said in an interview to the Associated Press later that month. Back in Russia, Gaidar quickly recovered. Three years later he was found dead in his country house near Moscow. Ever since he was mysteriously poisoned at the conference in Ireland, he had been in poor health. He was 53.

There is little doubt that this well-known public figure was used as a pawn to divert initial attention from Litvinenko. Among the illegals this trick is known as *imitatsiya*, or diversion. Obviously no one was going to kill Gaidar, but I well remember the *Evening Standard* issue of the day with a banner headline on the front page, NEW RUSSIAN POISON VICTIM, bringing additional mystery to the case. As predicted, it did not last long as the former prime minister was not poisoned to die, just as Anna Politkovskaya was almost certainly not poisoned to die in 2004. In her case, she was incapacitated so as not to reach Beslan. Gaidar was poisoned to mislead the media and the public. As simple as that. Just to mention, for some time Andrey Lugovoy – the key suspect in the murder of Litvinenko – served as Gaidar's bodyguard.

The second big group of substances that are capable of causing the illness or death of a living organism when introduced or absorbed are deadly poisons with different toxicity ratings (almost always as high as five or six – the top marks).[13] They fall under three categories: chemical agents, biological agents and radiological weapons. This arsenal has continuously been refined over the years as advancing science opens new possibilities and as Kremlin leaders develop new requirements. Whenever a new type of poison is used, like the dioxin 2,3,7,8-TCDD-based preparation in the Ukrainian president Victor Yushchenko case or polonium-spiked jelly in the Litvinenko case, it is catalogued and studied by Western experts.

Whenever police investigate crimes where Moscow's hand can be traced or suspected, several 'signature indications' invariably bear the hallmark 'Made in Russia' at the crime scene. First of all, the substance used must make the victim's death or illness appear natural or at least produce symptoms that will baffle doctors and forensic investigators. To this end, the Kamera developed its defining speciality: combining known poisons into original and untraceable forms.

Second, the poisonous agent is always 'tailor-made', like a bespoke suit from London's famous Savile Row. They are first discussed in every detail

---

[13] For expert information on poisons in this chapter, if not referred to separately, I am using Serita Stevens and Anne Bannon's, *Book of Poisons* (Cincinnati, OH: Writer's Digest Books, 2007).

and then tailored for the specific target in a well-planned and oft-rehearsed environment.

Finally, the operation will always be carried out in such a way that the victim's self-defence instincts or vigilance will be minimised so that he will not be expecting treachery and may even not see or remember the poisoner. All cases described in this book follow this pattern.

In spite of the unprecedented publicity and speculation surrounding the Litvinenko story, in addition to the great number of available documents related to the investigation, such a fatal poisoning is a covert operation where a lot of things remain unknown or unclear to the investigation. It must be carried out clandestinely, without any public knowledge and preferably without any reaction to the sudden death of a victim. Better still, without any investigation and autopsy. It is never designed to demonstrate anything, only to kill the victim, quietly and unobtrusively. In all the cases of Russian poisonings that I have studied during many years, this was an unbreakable principle.

Occasionally, chance plays an important role in uncovering a crime and its perpetrator. Seventy years ago, a box of sweets found in an abandoned hotel room helped to reconstruct the murder of a Russian dissident.

As a rule, terminations fall into two categories. One is 'operational requirement' when, paraphrasing Forsyth, the person in the way has to be eased out of the way, fast and permanently. The other category is for those already on the execution list. This category, which might have contained the names of Boris Berezovsky, Akhmed Zakayev, Anna Politkovskaya and Boris Nemtsov, among many others, are those who are considered enemies of the Kremlin and consequently of Russia. Like, for example, Alexander Perepilichny, whose cause of death remains undetermined. Such people are 'wasted' when there is a chance but usually as a result of a complex, well-planned operation.

Modern chemical weapons fall under five classes: nerve agents, blistering agents (vesicants), cyanide, pulmonary agents and riot-control agents.

Most nerve agents are initially in a liquid form that subsequently evaporates and becomes gas and vapour. They can be inhaled, ingested or placed on the skin. The LD50 (median lethal dose, or dose of a poison that will kill 50 per cent of those exposed) is given in milligrams (mg) for a person weighing 140 pounds.

G-type nerve agents are clear, colourless liquids that are volatile at ambient temperature. They mix in water and most organic solvents and evaporate at the same rate as water. The odour, when there is one, does not provide adequate warning time. Effects and symptoms are much the same for all the agents. The severity depends on which gas was used, the density of the vapour or liquid, and the length of exposure. Muscle spasms followed by flaccid muscle paralysis are classic symptoms.

Nerve agents are generally absorbed by eye contact and inhalation, and produce rapid, systemic effects. The liquid is absorbed through the skin, but it may take several minutes for effects to appear. In severe attacks, the central nervous system collapses, causing violent seizures, confusion and coma.

Vesicants or blistering agents produce skin and mucous membrane irritation, blistering and then necrosis. In the arsenal of the Russian services, however, there are substances probably based on the venom of some jellyfish that cause severe chest and abdominal pain, difficulty swallowing, skin necrosis, and respiratory and cardiac depression leading to death. According to Oleg Kalugin, in the early 1970s a KGB agent rubbed a jelly on Alexander Solzhenitsyn in a store in Russia, making him violently ill. In that case, the author of *The Gulag Archipelago* survived.

Agatha Christie frequently killed off her victims with poisons, and cyanide was one of her favourites. In Russia, potassium cyanide is perhaps one of the best-known poisons. However, KGB assassins in the early 1920s and 1930s preferred to use prussic acid as it mimics heart attacks.

Pulmonary agents are used in military operations.

Riot-control agents also come under the heading of chemical warfare and include several types of tear gas.

Biological weapons use toxins from microorganisms, such as viruses or bacteria, to injure or incapacitate people. Odourless, tasteless and invisible to the naked eye, biological agents can be disseminated easily. There is also the potential for greater toxicity than with chemical weapons. This group includes anthrax, which became widely known in recent times after the terrorist attacks in the United States in 2001. In April 1979, in Sverdlovsk (now Yekaterinburg), weapons-grade anthrax was accidentally released into the air from a Soviet biological warfare facility. Reportedly, about 100 people died, although the exact number of victims remains unknown. One person died four days after the release, ten over an eight-day period at the peak of the deaths, and the last six weeks later. Immediately, the KGB was engaged in extensive cover-ups and the destruction of records, which continued for around fifteen years, until Russian president Boris Yeltsin admitted this accident and let a combined US-Russian team investigate what happened. According to some sources, to this day Western inspectors have not been allowed to visit this facility. In Yeltsin's memoirs, *Midnight Diaries* (2000), I have found no mention of the outbreak.

Other biological substances that can be used as weapons-grade agents are – just to mention a few – ricin, smallpox, tularaemia and Ebola.

An informed specialist could not miss the article written by a group of Russian scientists that was published on 30 April 1999 in *FEBS Letters*, a scientific journal covering all aspects of molecular biosciences and dealing with new achievements in highly specific research. Alexander I. Sotnichenko and his colleagues from the Moscow Research Institute of Medical Ecology had experimented with dioxin and fetal proteins, in particular with a- or alpha-fetoprotein (AFP), a molecule produced in the developing embryo. AFP levels decrease gradually after birth and it has no known function in normal adults. Except as material for quickly developing scientific research.

As a result of Russian experiments, a stable complex had been formed between 2,3,7,8-TCDD and AFP. It was observed that the solubility of this particular dioxin in water increased 105-fold, while its toxicity was similar to that of free TCDD administered in oil solutions. The death of experimental animals (mice) was followed up to day 45 after the injection, and the cytotoxicity of the TCDD:AFP complex, that is its toxicity to cells appeared to be much higher than that of free dioxin.

The fact that the Ukrainian presidential candidate Viktor Yushchenko was poisoned in September 2004, not just by 2,3,7,8-TCDD but by a much more complex agent, a product of a special laboratory, as confirmed by the British Defence Science and Technology Laboratory in Porton Down, clearly demonstrated that the murder attempt was a Russian operation.

During a period in Russian history that became known as *perestroika* (meaning 'reconstruction'), Soviet citizens were encouraged to discuss publicly the problems of their system and seek solutions. As a result of this policy of openness (*glasnost*), several scientific works and newspaper articles came out that threw light on the most secret, dangerous and 'mystical' weapon known to mankind: psychotronic weapons.

Plans to introduce new super-weapons were announced by the then Russian defence minister Anatoly Serdyukov in March 2012. He said: 'The development of weaponry based on new physics principles – direct-energy weapons, geophysical weapons, wave-energy weapons, genetic weapons, psychotronic weapons, and so on – is part of the state arms procurement programme for 2011–2020.'

Specific research activities denoted today as unconventional have been secretly carried out in Russia since the early 1920s. Precise details of and psychophysical principles behind these systems have been revealed in many academic publications in Russia and the West. These are related to the impact of weak and strong electromagnetic emission on biological objects, the effect of microwaves on internal organs, acoustic psycho-correction and others – a broad programme dealing with several boundary areas of psychology on the one side and theoretical physics on the other. The research has shown that low-frequency waves can affect brain cells, alter psychological states and make it possible to transmit commands directly into someone's mind. Directed microwaves can control behaviour and damage the functioning of internal organs. The former KGB-FSO major general Boris Ratnikov explained in an interview that the principle of the psychotronic generator's remote impact on a human is based on the resonance of the frequency characteristics of human organs – the heart, kidneys, liver, brain. Each human organ has its own frequency response, he said. And if it is influenced by electromagnetic radiation at the same frequency, which can be programmed on a particular individual, the organ enters into resonance, as a result of which acute heart failure, renal failure or inadequate behaviour occurs. As a rule, microwaves hit the most weakened, damaged parts of the human body. In some cases, a fatal outcome may also take place, or a victim can be driven to suicide.

All this comes to mind when analysing the sudden and unexplained death of Boris Berezovsky in Ascot, England. Thames Valley Police and the South East Counter Terrorism Unit carried out a thorough investigation and concluded that Berezovsky committed suicide. The investigation could find nothing to support the hypothesis of third-party involvement. This 'third-party involvement', however, was quite evident to everybody who knew Boris personally and, moreover, to an eminent German expert who concluded it must have been murder. How this murder was carried out should be a matter of a new investigation. Such things had happened before.

A radiological, or nuclear, weapon is defined as any weapon using a radioactive or radiation-emitting source as the primary source of destruction. Walter Litvinenko, Sasha's father, was absolutely right when he said that a minuscule nuclear bomb had killed his son. That was a proud product of Russian nanotechnology. Besides polonium-210, which gained worldwide infamy after the London poisoning in 2006, other radiological poisons may be built from harmful amounts of thallium-201, cesium-137 as well as from radioactive forms of plutonium, americium and curium. The death of Roman Tsepov in St Petersburg on 24 September 2004 was, without doubt, a result of radiological poisoning. No autopsy records have ever been released.

In November 2017, it was announced that levels of ruthenium-106 in atmosphere near the Urals were 986 times the norm. The Russian weather monitoring service released test data that showed levels were indeed much higher than normal, especially close to the Mayak Nuclear Production facility near Oziorsk, Chelyabinsk district. 'In 1957,' experts note, 'Mayak was the site of the Kyshtym disaster, one of the worst nuclear accidents in history.' A report from France's Institute for Radioprotection and Nuclear

Safety (IRSN) said traces of ruthenium-106 from Mayak had been detected in France too.

Symptoms of radiological poisoning depend, among other factors, on how much radiation is received and how one is exposed. Symptoms include nausea and vomiting, diarrhoea, weakness and fatigue, loss of appetite, fainting, dehydration, inflammation of tissues, bleeding from the nose, mouth, gums or rectum, low red blood cell count (anaemia), and hair loss. Large doses of radiation can cause extensive damage to the cells and result in cell death.

Evidently, the physicians in Barnet Hospital and University College London Hospital where Sasha had been treated did not read the right books. The cause of Alexander Litvinenko's illness was not diagnosed until after his death. Only in March 2017, a scientific report by Professor John Harrison and a group of his colleagues was published.[14] They concluded that the absorption to blood even of one-hundredth of that estimated for 1 November 2006 might have caused irreversible kidney damage.

In the summer of 2017, I contacted Professor Harrison, who very kindly sent me the full text of his report that had been given to the Litvinenko inquiry commission. After having studied the inquiry report and Dr Harrison's evidence, I had a lot of questions that I was eager to discuss with this prominent specialist. That led to the proposed chapter called *Litvinenko: The Final Analysis*. At the end of the day, I found out it could not be written – even ten years after Sasha's death, too many records and documents remain classified.

---

[14] See Dr Amit C. Nathwani, James F. Down, John Goldstone, James Yassin, Paul I Dargan, Andres Virchis, Nick Gent, David Lloyd, and John D. Harrison 'Polonium-210 poisoning: a first-hand account', *The Lancet*, 388/10049 (September 2016), 1075–1080; and John Harrison, Tim Fell, Rich Leggett, David Lloyd, Matthew Puncher, and Mike Youngman, 'The polonium-210 poisoning of Mr Alexander Litvinenko', *Journal of Radiological Protection*, 37/1 (March 2017), 266–78.

Chapter 4

A Murder in Coyoacán

I remembered this old case to draw a parallel to the recent death of Boris Berezovsky in London. And even to the poisoning of Alexander 'Sasha' Litvinenko which, at first glance, it seems to have nothing to do with. For a start, I have not the slightest doubt that in the case of Berezovsky – with whom, as with Sasha, I was personally acquainted – it was an assassination, a meticulously planned and perfectly executed crime. An impeccable murder by all standards. And although historically Trotsky and Berezovsky were not figures of the same calibre, they both managed to become Enemy Number One for the Kremlin. It took them both about ten years to climb on this pedestal before they were murdered.

Many years ago, a CIA analyst published an article about Trotsky in a classified CIA journal.[1] Since then it was declassified. The author claims that from the time of his involuntary exile from the USSR, Trotsky was extremely careless when it came to matters of his personal security and neglected plenty of warnings of the NKVD penetrating his close circle of friends and associates. Trotsky, it says, was engrossed in his attacks on Stalin's personal regime, 'but like so many other revolutionary leaders before him, he had no interest in collecting information on the plans and operations of hostile agents.' His papers show that apart from the newspaper clippings about the NKVD assassinations of his aides, there are no reports about the Russian Intelligence Services' operations against him or his movement. A variety of confusion techniques used by the NKVD with the help of their agents in Trotsky's entourage often made it impossible for him to distinguish between real threats and elaborate hoaxes. The CIA article concludes: 'The account of how the NKVD killed Trotsky reveals both the ruthless tenacity and skill of the Soviet [intelligence] service and Trotsky's own gullibility, arrogance, and waywardness. It's clear that the men in Moscow who drew up the blueprint for his murder understood his weaknesses and used them.'

As Benjamin Disraeli has put it, it is probably true that the secret of success in life is for a man to be ready for his opportunity when it comes. The man

---

[1] Rita T. Kronenbitter, 'Leon Trotsky, Dupe of the NKVD', 16/1, *Studied in Intelligence* (Special Edition 1972), 15–61.

in Moscow who drew up the blueprint for Trotsky's assassination was Pavel Sudoplatov and success attended him. After his return from Rotterdam, where he successfully blew up the leader of the Ukrainian nationalists, the 31-year-old NKVD officer returned to Moscow and was immediately promoted, at the same time acquiring a reputation as a first-rate demolition expert. In truth, he would be remembered as one of those unbending 'Knights of the Revolution' for whom the party's interests were more precious than human life. In March 1939, Sudoplatov received instructions personally from Stalin to liquidate Trotsky and on the same day was appointed deputy head of Soviet foreign intelligence.

He promptly moved into his new office, No. 735, on the top floor of the Lubyanka NKVD headquarters. Soon he introduced Nahum Eitingon, his former boss but now deputy, to the young new chief of Soviet foreign intelligence as an officer in charge of the operation against Trotsky. Only a day before, Eitingon returned from Paris, where he had moved after the defeat of the Republicans in Spain. Codenamed UTKA ('Duck'), this operation was given absolute priority over any other tasks by the *Instantsiya*, the highest authority similar to Orwell's Big Brother. The operational plan, typed personally by Sudoplatov in one copy only, would be ready by July and approved by Stalin in early August 1939. The operational budget was $31,000 for six months (in 2018 values, $545,875). By that time, preparations for the 'hit' were already in full swing.

In 1936, en route to Mexico, Trotsky wrote in his journal: 'Stalin conducts a struggle on a totally different plane. He seeks to strike not at the ideas of the opponent, but at his skull.' Much later, Sudoplatov recorded in his memoirs that 'during 1936–1939 in Spain there were, in effect, not one but two conflicts, both a matter of life and death'. In one, he wrote, the nationalist forces led by Franco and assisted by Hitler clashed with the Spanish Republicans helped by the Soviet Union. In another, a completely separate struggle was going on inside the Republican camp, where one side was represented by Stalin and the Soviet Union, and the other by Trotsky, who was in exile. Both parties wanted to appear before the world as rescuers and guarantors of the Republican cause, thereby placing themselves in the vanguard of the international communist movement. 'We sent to Spain our young, unskilled operatives and experienced instructors-professionals,' Sudoplatov explained. 'This country has become a kind of testing ground, where our future military and intelligence operations have been tried out.'[2] Thus, from the outset, the

---

[2] Pavel Sudoplatov, *Razvedka i Kreml: Zapiski nezhelatelnogo svidetelya* (Moscow, Geya, 1996), 38.

NKVD in Spain was engaged in a war on two fronts: against Trotskyists within the Republicans and the International Brigades, as well as against the nationalist forces. (Sudoplatov was exaggerating: the latter was a very limited engagement. Rather, it was a matter of developing the Red Army's own defensive and offensive potentials, testing and training her forces. This would become much more efficient if the vaunted Soviet war machine could test its combat tactics with her own capabilities. The NKVD had a different role to play in the Spanish war.) In one of the telegrams sent by the NKVD station in Madrid in October 1936, the centre was assured that 'the Trotskyist organization ... can be easily liquidated'. Two years later, it was the turn of Trotsky himself.

According to the official KGB version, already in April 1938 two reliable illegals codenamed FELIPE and MARIO, who also took part in the Spanish Civil War, arrived in New York on board a Soviet ship from Novorossiysk and quickly established contact with the New York NKVD station. This, of course, is pure fantasy because at that point nothing had been heard about a Soviet commercial fleet, let alone cruise or passenger ships sailings between New York and Novorossiysk. Besides, only diplomats were permitted to use direct routes while the illegals were obliged (and still follow this rule) to travel by complex roundabout ways before reaching their final destination. Indeed, both agents MARIO and FELIPE (the latter was Iosif Grigulevich, about whom we shall hear more) came to Mexico from New York. First, they took a train from Moscow to Paris and from there to Cherbourg, travelling to the New World by RMS *Queen Mary*, an ocean liner that sailed for the Cunard Line. In June, both were already in Mexico. But in November, two senior NKVD controllers who were in charge of the operation were arrested in Moscow. Accordingly, the agents were ordered to return to the United States, and while Grigulevich successfully landed there in July 1939, MARIO was detained on the border and after some time sent back to Mexico.

In January, Grigulevich/FELIPE briefly returned to Moscow to report and by mid-February was back in New York. He reappeared in Mexico City driving a 'luxurious, dark coloured car', as it was later described, and established his quarters in a nice house that he was renting from a rich landlord with a perfect reputation. Not by chance, the house was conveniently located in Acacias, close to Avenida Río Churubusco where Trotsky resided. The house is still there, now turned into a museum.

Soon Grig contacted Antonio Pujol Jiménez (codenamed JOSE), who he later described as 'very loyal, exceptionally reliable and quite bold'. Back in 1933, Pujol became a member of the League of the Revolutionary Writers and Artists and in 1936, together with celebrated Mexican painters David Alfaro

Siqueiros and Luis Arenal (brother of Angélica Arenal, the wife of Siqueiros), participated in the first Pan-American Congress of Artists against War and Fascism. Shortly after the congress, Pujol joined the International Brigades in Spain. There he was spotted by the NKVD and quickly agreed to help.

Among Grigulevich's other collaborators were his future wife – the Mexican communist Laura Araujo Aguilar (LUISA) – and two Arenal brothers, Luis (RAFAIL) and Leopoldo. In Coyoacán, one of the boroughs of Mexico where Trotsky and his entourage lived, Pujol used three communist girls, Julia Barradas Hernandez, Águeda Serna and Ana Maria López, to rent an apartment on Calle Viena that could be used to watch Trotsky's house and entertain police officers who were sent by the authorities to guard the famous Russian revolutionary. Not because he was a Russian or a revolutionary, which was not that important, but because he was under the patronage of President Cárdenas.

As usual, the assassins had two different plans of action. According to the first plan, which seemed almost perfect, the attack on the Trotsky's villa was to be led by a group of militants drawn from the veterans of the Spanish Civil War and headed by Siqueiros, a former lieutenant colonel of the Popular Army, with Pujol and David Serrano Andonegui (alias 'Miguel Julio Justo') acting as his second-in-command. Serrano had fought in Spain with the Republican forces and reportedly 'had been trained in Moscow and Spain in NKVD work for the preceding six years', as claimed by one reporter, though there is no way to prove it. Another report claims that Julia Barradas and Águeda Serna were both legitimate wives of David Serrano – one Mexican and the other Spanish. This group was controlled by Grigulevich, aged 27 at the time. The whole operation in Mexico City was supervised by Eitingon and in Moscow by Sudoplatov. Eitingon was also in charge of a small back-up unit that included the Spanish Communist Caridad Mercader, who was given a simple codename MOTHER, and her son Ramón with an equally uncomplicated codename RAYMOND.

Caridad was born on 31 March 1892 to a wealthy family in Santiago de Cuba as Eustacia María Caridad del Río Hernández. A mother of four, she had left her husband, the Spanish railroad magnate Pablo Mercader Marina, and fled to Paris. When the Spanish Civil War broke out, she was living in Barcelona and, together with the anarchists, successfully fought against the rebels. Her eldest son, Pablo, was killed in action. Ramón, Jaime Ramón Mercader del Río, her middle son, who was born in 1914, commanded a Republican army unit at the beginning of the war. The youngest son, Luis, and her beautiful daughter Montserrat came to Moscow in 1939 with other children of Spanish Republicans who fled from Franco.

According to the semi-official KGB history, Ramón was recruited in 1937 and, after some training in Moscow, sent to Paris on a doctored Belgian passport in the name of 'Jacques Mornard' to infiltrate the Trotskyists movement there. He was chosen for this mission because, among other things, the young lieutenant was good-looking and spoke fluent French, having grown up in France.

As part of a back-up plan, with the help of an American NKVD collaborator, Mercader got acquainted with Sylvia Ageloff, an American Trotskyist, who would play a key role in introducing him to Trotsky's inner circle. They both took part in the founding conference of the Fourth International in Périgny, France, in September 1938, which Trotsky was barred from attending.

Sylvia was a sister of Ruth Ageloff, Trotsky's secretary. Two years later, according to the notes of the police chief Leandro Sánchez Salazar, 'Sylvia herself had framed her role in Trotsky's assassination in terms of being used'. During interrogation, she broke down, cried and said: 'I am sure now that I served as the instrument by which Jacson [Mercader's new alias for this operation] got in touch with Trotsky so as to kill him. I can't offer any proof of what I say, but that is what I feel. There is no doubt that Jacson is a Stalinist and that behind him are other Stalinists whom I do not know. Stalin is the person who has the greatest reason to get rid of Trotsky. And it is I who have served as his tool.'[3]

From the end of 1939, Operation UTKA was simultaneously run out of the Soviet missions in Paris and New York. In Paris it was supported by Lev Vasilevsky (alias 'Tarasov'), who came here from Spain and was now using the cover of Consul General, and in New York the station was reinforced by a man named Grigory Rabinovich.

Rabinovich was a former Kremlin and Lubyanka physician sent on an intelligence mission posing as a representative of the Soviet Red Cross. It was decided that, as a Jew and a medical doctor, he was best suited to penetrate Trotsky's organisation. Much later, the CIA analyst writing the aforementioned article on Trotsky and the NKVD noticed that Trotsky 'paid no heed to the warnings from non-Jewish comrades in Berlin and Paris; yet all his aides who were subsequently discovered as GPU-NKVD penetration agents were of that category.' The article further states that 'there is no record in his or Sedov's files indicating that Jewish or Zionist comrades were investigated when joining the movement, whereas applicants of other racial stock were subject to suspicion as possible provocateurs'.

---

[3] Quoted in Eric M. Gurevitch, 'Thinking with Sylvia Ageloff', *Hypocrite Reader*, 55 (August 2015), 8–9.

At the Lubyanka headquarters, Rabinovich was given the codename LUCH ('Beam'), arriving for the first time in New York in September 1934. He was suddenly recalled to Moscow in 1936 or early 1937, only to be sent back to the United States in November. Now codenamed GARRI ('Harry'), Rabinovich started receiving information that finally helped to identify the Ageloff sisters Ruth, Hilda and Sylvia as reliable leads to Trotsky's household in Mexico. However, his Red Cross office was not the only base of an anti-Trotsky operation in the New York City area.

From the Soviet Consulate General, Pavel Pastelnyak was assigned to supervise the operation. Documented as 'Klarin' (codenamed LUKA), he was initially sent to New York as head of security of the Soviet pavilion at the New York World's Fair, where one of his assistants was a young officer by the name of Konstantin Chugunov (alias 'Shabanov', later codenamed SHAH). Suddenly recalled back to Moscow, the official Soviet delegation left the fair in early December, but Pastelnyak and Chugunov remained in the USA assigned to the local NKVD station.

Before moving to Mexico, Eitingon had spent three unhappy months in Paris preparing first to travel to the United States and finally getting his visa in September. It was a rather risky endeavour because his former boss in Spain Lev Nikolsky (alias 'Alexander Orlov'), having deserted his post in Barcelona, had already been in the USA for two years by that time and no one knew whether he started collaborating with the FBI or was keeping his promise not to betray anybody. It was probably judged that the risk was minimal. In mid-November, Eitingon was already in Mexico where he received a long-encrypted message from Moscow Centre, which read in part:

5. Continue your academic work ... Keep in mind that any scientific and economic activity, especially in agriculture, requires patience, thoughtfulness and ability to wait for the results. Making your harvest decision remember that the fruit should be fully ripe. Otherwise, it'll taste bad and your scientific work will not be accomplished. When there is no certainty, it is better to wait for the fruit to attain full maturity. To prevent the destruction of your plantation by a sudden storm, find or build a suitable and sustainable greenhouse, in which you may do research work. Avoid ill-conceived experiments, go for guaranteed results, and then you are sure to make a valuable contribution to science, but always act in such a way that your exercises do no harm to your health and that of your assistants.[4]

---

[4] Reproduced in L. Vorobyov, 'Operatsiya UTKA', *Ocherki*, 3/8, 97.

Ramón Mercader and his mother were also in Paris. Because for whatever reason the American Embassy was not quite satisfied with his Belgian documents and refused to grant him an entry visa, Moscow supplied Ramón with new Canadian papers identifying him as 'Frank Jacson' (with a traditional error in the family name spelling, typical to the NKVD forgers). In what concerned Operation UTKA, the Paris NKVD station was only active until the end of March 1940, when Ambassador Surits had to leave France declared persona non grata. An article in the *Times* alleged that Surits had sent Stalin a telegram *en clair* concerning the French position in the Finnish war, which had been intercepted by the censor and was regarded by the French government as interference in its domestic affairs. And although Vasilevsky, the NKVD resident, remained in Paris until June, New York and Mexico City became the two most important centres of the anti-Trotsky activity.

Six months were spent on preparations. On 21 May, Caridad suddenly came to New York from Cuba with a letter from Eitingon (TOM), in which he explained that she had been recognised in Mexico and had to leave urgently and that Ramón also didn't have much to boast and would soon follow his mother. It was clear that the agents failed to penetrate Trotsky's close circle of friends and assistants. What happened a few days later, New York and Moscow learned from the newspapers.

It is certainly wrong to think, as some do, that a key part of the initial assault plan was the infiltration of a young American 'agent', Robert Sheldon Harte (codenamed AMUR or CUPID), pretending to be a New York Trotskyist, as a volunteer guard at Trotsky's house. Harte's role was only to open the main gate of the guarded compound after the assault group staged its surprise attack at about 4 o'clock in the morning of 24 May. The American was young and naïve and, according to General Salazar, who headed the investigation, a devoted Stalinist, but quite surely not an agent. At about the same time that Sheldon left for Mexico City in April 1940, a real agent, Tom Black, was given money and told by his NKVD controller in New York to go to Mexico to spy on the Trotsky household but, he later told the FBI, he somehow managed to skip this assignment. A few months later, Trotsky was murdered.

One Nestor Sánchez, who became acquainted with Siqueiros in Paris at the time of the Spanish Civil War and who also took part in the attack on Trotsky's house, stated in his police testimony that 'Siqueiros had assured us that all would go well because one of Trotsky's guards had been purchased'. He added that he (Sheldon) 'had no doubt been bribed by the French Jew', which was how he described Grigulevich. Both Siqueiros and Grig decided not to brief Sheldon Harte on what would happen after he opened the gate.

This is indirect proof that he was not an agent as claimed in many published accounts, but a naïve collaborator who was kept in the dark about the whole affair. In his account of the attack written right after it, Trotsky reasonably argued that 'if Sheldon Harte were an agent of the GPU he could have killed me at night and gotten away without setting in motion 20 people, all of whom were subjected to a great risk'.[5]

An even more solid corroboration comes from the VENONA decrypts, where in a message from New York to Moscow (No. 1143-1144) Robert Sheldon Harte was named by his full name and some concern was expressed that a new investigation into Trotsky's murder was being demanded by Trotsky's widow. Mexican investigators found out that Robert had spent the night of 21 May, that is, three days before the attack on the villa, at the Hotel Europa with a prostitute who was soon found. She testified that Sheldon had a large sum of money on him and was a little drunk that night, without doubt after leaving the company of Grig.

KGB records identify Grigulevich as the leader of the assault on Trotsky's villa, which is obviously an exaggeration. The head of the Mexican secret police, General Leandro Sánchez Salazar, described him as 'undoubtedly an agent of the G.P.U. and the real instigator of the attack'. Like his key witnesses, the Mexican police chief believed Grigulevich to be 'a French Jew' partly as a result of discovering some of his underwear had 'bought on the Boulevard Saint Michel in Paris'. This is another indicator that Grigulevich indeed operated in Paris after his ten-month assignment in Spain, as Sudoplatov recalled. From there he and MARIO sailed to New York. The remaining 2,000 miles to Mexico they travelled by train.

At that stage, the role of Eitingon was that of a supervisor, while the whole organisation was given to Grigulevich and Siqueiros. A more senior and experienced operative, Eitingon remained in the shadow, virtually unknown to other participants. General (then Colonel) Salazar wrote that it seemed 'all the important agents of the G.P.U. [sic] use the simplest names (Pedro, Leopoldo, Felipe) and that their own collaborators do not know their real identity'. He identifies the Communist and Spanish Civil War veteran Juan Zúñiga Camacho as 'one of the three people who played an important role' in the May attack using the alias 'Pedro'. Remarkably, Eitingon's documented cover name in Spain was also 'Pedro' or 'Pierre' (while he signed his reports from Mexico as TOM). Thus, one may conclude that the Mexican police knew little about Eitingon or had been misled by the mixture of real and

---

[5] Trotsky, 'Stalin Seeks my Death', *The Fourth International*, 2/7 (August 1941), 201–7, written in Coyoacán on 8 June 1940.

invented names. In this game of pseudonyms and aliases, 'Leopoldo' was probably Leopoldo Arenal, 'Felipe' – Grigulevich, and 'Pedro' – Zúñiga.

Whoever planned this operation planned it rather well, in spite of its subsequent failure. In addition to a reliable and unsuspecting contact inside Trotsky's well-guarded villa (Sheldon Harte), and a large group of armed young people in military and police uniforms (many of them former Spanish fighters), three young and attractive women were employed to watch the villa and, if necessary, drop prejudices and seduce members of the police force assigned by the government to guard it. Julia, the former wife of David Serrano, his present wife Águeda, friendly and affectionate, and Ana Maria, a girlfriend of another member of the Siqueiros group by the name of Mariano Herrera Vasquez, rented apartments 11 and 13 in Abasolo Street, a few steps from where Trotsky and his entourage resided. They expertly combined duty and fun and by the end of May befriended many police officers. On the night of 23 to 24 May, the girls organised a big party with their uniformed wooers taking part. After hearing the first shots from the villa they disappeared.

Besides all of these measures, an extra facility was also rented in the village of Santa Rosa on the Desert of the Lions road (but actually about a mile off the road) on the top of the hill. It was a hut used as one of the external bases though many people including Grig, Siqueiros, his young wife Angélica Arenal, her two brothers Luis and Leopoldo, Antonio Pujol and a few others knew about it and either visited or stayed there for some time. This later allowed the police to find the house and learn about the fate of Robert Sheldon Harte.

Harte was visibly shocked by the attack. Eitingon testified during an interrogation in Moscow in March 1954, no doubt with his tongue in his cheek: 'Sheldon appeared to be a traitor and brought the attackers to the room where there was neither Trotsky nor his archive. As soon as they started shooting, he angrily told the assault group that being an American, had he known how they would behave, he would never have let them in.' He also said that Sheldon was murdered by the Mexicans. Sudoplatov, who was in charge of the whole operation, admitted, quite uninhibitedly, that Harte was taken away and shot because he knew Grigulevich and could expose him. 'And what else could we do with him!' exclaimed Grig when later asked for the reason young Sheldon was murdered. 'To hide him away and then illegally transport to Moscow would be too complicated,' as recalled by a former KGB colleague. Harte's corpse was found in a shallow well filled with lime in a garden near the hut. The house was rented by Luis Arenal, the brother-in-law of Siqueiros.

Regarding MARIO, whose role in this operation remains unclear, this was the NKVD codename for Vittorio Vidali. Under the pseudonym 'Carlos

Contreras', Vidali had played a crucial role in the founding of the famous Fifth Regiment during the civil war in Spain. Both Siqueiros and Grigulevich briefly served in the regiment, which later became the core of the Popular Army. Among the attackers, there were many veterans of the civil war, and it is reasonable to think that Vidali could have acted as a political instructor, while Siqueiros and Grigulevich were taking on the organisational chores. Vidali could have also served as a liaison to the Partido Comunista Mexicano (PCM, Mexican Communist Party), being one of the members of its Central Committee, because the operation required a lot of support from the PCM, including a considerable propaganda effort. Whatever his role, he managed to escape unscathed.

As described by Trotsky himself, the armed attack on his compound was a thoroughly professional operation. Before going to bed, he took some sleeping pills and at first could not understand what was going on when his wife woke him up and told him about the shooting in the courtyard. Crossfire was cutting through the windows and doors. Although some 200 bullets poured into the bedroom alone, at the end of the day the only casualty appeared to be Trotsky's grandson with a wound in his toe. In one of his last written accounts describing the assault on his villa in Mexico, Trotsky wrote: 'I know that Stalin often admitted that my deportation abroad was his great error. Only a terrorist act could correct that mistake.'

The failure of the first attack on Trotsky in May 1940, followed by the dispersal of Siqueiros's gunmen, led the second group of assassins (Eitingon, Caridad and Ramón Mercader) to start implementing the back-up plan. In due course, Siqueiros was tracked down and apprehended in the state of Jalisco. Grigulevich, however, remained unidentified by Mexican police and managed to smuggle himself, Pujol and Laura out of the country. They were assisted by the Chilean Consul General in Mexico and communist sympathiser, Pablo Neruda, who also arranged a Chilean visa for Siqueiros when the painter was released on bail. For a while, the trio settled in Montevideo, Uruguay, where Pujol took the name 'Abel Bertrán Bastar'. Together with his wife Ada, who he met during his forced exile, he returned to Mexico in 1960. Thanks to Neruda's help, Siqueiros and his family also left Mexico, although with some difficulty, and settled in Chile, where they stayed in Neruda's private residence. Another important accomplice, the aforementioned Juan Zúñiga Camacho, then about 28 years old, also escaped arrest.

The KGB account adds that, like the FELIPE group, Luis and Leopoldo Arenal also managed to escape. Later, Luis Arenal assisted Siqueiros in the creation of murals and lived in Mexico City until his death in May 1985.

Leopoldo Arenal and his second wife, Rose, using forged Cuban passports in the name of Francisco José Guillén y Fernández thanks to Neruda, quickly received Chilean visas and disappeared in Santiago de Chile. It is possible, though not certain, that Leopoldo Arenal later figured in the VENONA traffic as ALEXANDER. Remarkably, MARIO (who figures but is not identified either in the VENONA intercepts from New York or in the KGB history volume) never appeared in any document relating to this operation, including the award list that names all of its principal participants. It seems that the role attributed to Vidali in this particular case is greatly exaggerated in most of the published accounts, both in Russia and in the West.

Trotsky was deadly wounded by Ramón Mercader on 20 August 1940. The NKVD assassin, whose identity was a mystery until September 1950, served his full term in prison, spending 19 years, 8 months and 14 days of his life in the 'Black Palace of Lecumberri' (which now houses the Archivo General de la Nación) along with other criminals. On 6 June 1941, Beria wrote a memo to Stalin, and about a week later the Presidium of the Supreme Soviet of the USSR issued a decree that remained secret for more than half a century. According to the decree, a group of NKVD officers and agents who had committed themselves to serving the Soviet state by their 'exemplary performance of special tasks' would be recognised with awards.[6] In 1960, the assassin was awarded the golden star of the Hero of the Soviet Union. Naturally, his real name was not mentioned, even in a secret government decree. The award was given to Ramon Ivanovich Lopez. The same name is inscribed on his gravestone in a Moscow cemetery.

The American historian Herbert R. Southworth wrote: 'An event took place, later on in 1940, according to friends of [Burnett] Bolloten in whom he confided, that completely changed his interpretation of the Spanish Civil War. This event touched in some way on the murder of Leon Trotsky. One version is that Communist friends sought to coerce him into helping the assassin Mercader to escape – for instance, by offering him a safe house. It seems probable that Bolloten may have left papers concerning this matter, but to my knowledge, nothing has been published.' The editor of the book, Professor Preston, added a significant detail: 'Some years before his death, Bolloten told me that the beginnings of his break with Communism came in Mexico when he was asked to take part in some way – perhaps in helping the

---

[6] RGASPI, f. 17, op. 163, d. 1316, ll. 45–7. The decree awarded Ramón Merceder (in absentia); Caridad Ramonovna Mercader and Naum Isaakovich Eitingon – the Order of Lenin; Lev Petrovich Vasilevsky and Pavel Anatolievich Sudoplatov – the Order of the Red Banner; Iosif Romualdovich Grigulevich and Pavel Panteleimonovich Pastelnyak – the Order of the Red Star.

assassin get away – in the assassination of Trotsky. He said that he refused point blank.'[7]

In 1938, Bolloten left Spain for Mexico and went on to spend the greater part of the next decade living in Mexico City and working to reconstruct 'from limited materials and a limited knowledge of the subject, some of the principal political events of the Spanish Civil War and Revolution'.[8] With this in mind, he interviewed Communists like Constancia de la Mora and her husband, General Ignacio Hidalgo de Cisneros, as well as 'Carlos Contreras' (Vittorio Vidali). Whether he also met Eitingon or Grigulevich is not known. It is unlikely. But it is possible that he could have come across Caridad Mercader, which could be a reason for her urgent departure to New York.

In January 1941, Vasilevsky and Eitingon moved to Turkey where they tried – unsuccessfully – to organise the assassination of the German ambassador Franz von Papen in Ankara.

In 1942, a Soviet illegal named Alexander Kuper (aka 'Alejandro Kúper Kuperstein'), then aged 31, was sent on a clandestine mission to Mexico to prepare an operation to get Ramón Mercader out of prison. Alexander, the son of Siméon Kúper, a professor of the First Moscow Medical Institute, came from a Russian Jewish émigré family who left Russia long before the revolution. Like all his other family members, Alexander studied medicine (at the University of Santiago de Compostela, where he was active in the revolutionary student movement), joining the PCE at the beginning of the civil war. He first worked as an interpreter with Soviet military advisers and later as the cultural secretary of the PCE at the Soviet Embassy in Barcelona, leaving Spain for the USSR with the embassy staff. Nothing is known of what Alexander did in Mexico. His name does not figure in the VENONA decrypts and his cryptonym has never been identified. Maybe his was a small-scale auxiliary operation and he controlled Carmen Brufau Civit and a couple of other deep-cover agents who could be activated when necessary. But no information has been available so far. Kuper operated in Mexico until 1948 and then returned to Moscow, later leaving for Bucharest and Prague, arriving back in Spain in 1988. He died there a year later.

From December 1943, two senior Soviet 'diplomats' in Mexico City, Vasilevsky, alias 'Tarasov', and Pastelnyak, alias 'Klarin', had been very busy preparing a 'surgical operation', as it was reported to Moscow Centre,

---

[7] Herbert R. Southworth, '"The Grand Camouflage": Julián Gorkin, Burnett Bolloten and the Spanish Civil War' in Paul Preston and Ann L. Mackenzie (eds.) *The Republic Besieged: Civil War in Spain 1936–1939* (Edinburgh: Edinburgh University Press, 1996), 273; Paul Preston to author, 23 July 2009.

[8] Bolloten, *The Grand Camouflage*, ix.

to release Trotsky's assassin, Mercader, from prison. This large-scale secret operation, codenamed GNOME, had lasted for several years and ultimately failed. It involved Soviet intelligence operatives little known even to the experts like, for example, Soviet illegals Nicholas and Maria Fisher (codenamed CHETA or COUPLE) or Anna Kamayeva, as well as many other agents and collaborators, mostly foreign nationals. Among them were: Jacob Epstein (HARRY) and Ruth Wilson (NONA), a husband and wife couple; Juan Gaytan Godoy (JUAN); José Garcia Reyes (ANTON); Antonio Gomez Deans (OLIVER) and José Sancha Padros (REMBRANDT). All took part in the Spanish Civil War.

Directly or indirectly involved in Operation GNOME were Dolores Ibárruri, Georgi Dimitrov, Pablo Neruda (whose 'cultivation' by the NKVD began in earnest in May 1944), Vincente Lombardo Toledano (codenamed SH), a Mexican labour leader close to President Cárdenas, and David Alfaro Siqueiros (KON') who returned to Mexico at the end of 1943.

Coded messages between Moscow and Mexico City also mention active participants. NKVD assets wuch as Kitty Harris, codenamed ADA, a former mistress of two NKVD agents – the American Communist Party leader Earl Browder and the British traitor Donald Maclean; Margarita Nelken, appropriately codenamed AMOR, and her daughter Magda Nelken, codenamed KUKI (identified here for the first time). Elena Vásquez Gómez, codenamed SEDA, the private secretary of General Lázaro Cárdenas; Spanish communist leaders Vicente Uribe (DON), Jesús Hernández (PEDRO), Francisco Antón and Antonio Mije. And, of course Ramón Mercader himself, codenamed first RITA and then GNOME, and his mother, Caridad Mercader, now codenamed KLAVA, as well as his fiancé Raquelia Mendoza (JUANITA), also identified here for the first time. In charge of the operation in Moscow was Nahum Eitingon (TOM), who by that time had returned from Turkey, was promoted to Commissar of State Security and appointed Sudoplatov's deputy. Whether Bolloten played any role remains unclear as many participants were only known by their cover names.

In August 1944, the newly appointed NKVD head of station in San Francisco sent a letter to Moscow denouncing his colleague in Mexico City, Tarasov (Lev Vasilevsky). Tarasov, the letter claimed, had bungled attempts to liberate Trotsky's assassin and had adopted a grand life style. As his private residence, Tarasov rented a house with grounds employing two servants in addition to the staff allocated to him. The reporter added that Tarasov was spending too much time breeding parrots, poultry and other birds, without doubt after having visited him there. For the time being the report was filed and no action taken. On the contrary, after Tarasov/Vasilevsky returned from Mexico in late 1945, he was promoted to deputy chief of the Illegals Directorate and later served as department head of scientific and technical intelligence directorate. Thanks to his experience in Spain during the civil war, in April 1953 Vasilevsky was promoted to Sudoplatov's deputy in the 9th department (subversion and sabotage abroad), serving alongside Eitingon, who was briefly released from prison and reinstated in his rank and position. Their intelligence careers ended with the fall of Beria.

During 1943–5, as Operation GNOME was in progress, the NKGB (successor to the NKVD) station in Mexico City sent about 570 messages to Moscow Centre, while the Lubyanka sent 400 messages, many of them concerning the GNOME affair. These messages indicate that the Russians, as always, had two plans to facilitate their agent's release: a combat operation by a group of illegals to spring him by force, and an influence operation where the station drew upon American, Mexican and Spanish Communists, and fellow travellers to accomplish their mission. As already mentioned, both attempts failed.

In the last analysis, it was not only Trotsky's defects of character that destroyed him. The old Russian revolutionary, who was only 60 when Stalin's henchmen reached him, outlived himself. The second most important and prominent Bolshevik leader, the comrade-in-arms of Lenin, became an outsider. After he was expelled from the country, he had absolutely no prospect of overthrowing Stalin as leader of the USSR, although he could make it much harder for the Kremlin dictator to get sympathy and support from Western governments. Ironically, *Time* magazine named Stalin their Man of the Year twice – in 1939, several months before the murder of Trotsky, and in 1942 – less than two years after. The brutal imposed famine of the 1930s, mass arrests, executions and deportations of the Great Terror, senseless victims of the first months of the war – tens of millions of destroyed lives did not matter – so the life and death of just one individual could not trigger any emotions. It seldom does. Mainly, Trotsky had crossed Stalin, so Trotsky had to go.

Beria was arrested in June 1953 and executed. In July, Vasilevsky was dismissed from his post and soon expelled from the Communist Party and deprived of his military rank.

Eitingon, considered a supporter of Beria, was apprehended again and held in jail without trial at the Butyrka prison in Moscow for four years. In November 1957, he was put on trial, in which he was again accused of conspiracy against the regime. The court sentenced him to 12 years in prison. His rank and all his medals were taken from him. After Nikita Khrushchev's ouster from power in 1964, Eitingon was released but not exonerated.

Sudoplatov was arrested in August. He simulated madness to avoid being executed with Beria, and therefore was only tried in 1958. He was accused, among other things, of involvement with Mairanovsky's laboratory of death. According to Vadim Birstein, with whom we met in June 2012 in the St Ermin's Hotel at London's Westminster where the Special Operations Executive (SOE) and the Security Service (MI5) were quartered during the war, Beria and his accomplices committed terrible crimes against humanity. A special laboratory, which was established for experiments on the action of poisons on living humans, worked under the supervision of Sudoplatov and his deputy Eitingon from 1942 to 1946. For their 'work' they demanded only poisons that had been previously tested on humans.

Sudoplatov was sentenced to 15 years in prison. After serving the full term, like Mercader, he was released in August 1968.

On Friday, 24 May 1940, the day of the first attack on the Trotsky residence in Mexico City, Joseph Brodsky, one of the greatest poets of the twentieth century, was born in what is now known as St Petersburg. In 1963, Brodsky's poetry was denounced as 'anti-Soviet', and his papers were confiscated, he was interrogated, put in a mental institution and then arrested and deported to a remote village in the north of Russia, near the White Sea. Seven years after his return from exile, on 4 June 1972, KGB agents broke into his apartment and put him on a plane for Vienna, Austria. In 1987, he won the Nobel Prize for Literature. Brodsky wrote, 'The Last Judgement is the Last Judgement, but a human being who spent his life in Russia, has to be, without any hesitation, placed into Paradise.' I failed to ask Brodsky what he had in mind. When I first arrived in America in November 1998 to meet Alexander Genis, the author of *Brodsky in New York*, Brodsky was already gone. Over a cup of strong black tea in the Russian Tea Room on West 57th Street in Manhattan, Genis reminded me of another of Brodsky's dictums: life is a game with many rules but no referee. One learns how to play more by watching it than by consulting any book. Small wonder, then, when so many play dirty, that so many lose.

The Trotsky story would be repeated in the first decade of the twenty-first century.

Chapter 5

Tinker Tailor Soldier Spy? No, Another Circus

'One of the most remarkable public appearances ever made by a Soviet illegal took place on 6 November 1951, when "Teodoro B. Castro" attended the opening in Paris of the Sixth Session of the United Nations General Assembly...' With these words, Cambridge professor Christopher Andrew opens a chapter of his book about the KGB in Europe and the West.[1] And he is perfectly right.

In the hundred-year history of Soviet intelligence, this was indeed an extraordinary case. To the best of my knowledge, nothing of the sort ever happened anywhere, maybe only in Germany where a Stasi spy, Günter Guillaume, managed to penetrate a close circle of friends of West German chancellor Willy Brandt, becoming his personal aide. When, in 1974, Guillaume's spying was uncovered, the scandal led to Brandt's resignation and Guillaume's arrest. As usual, Markus Wolf masterminded the plot. Naturally, Wolf, Guillaume and the whole Stasi had worked for the KGB and this example demonstrates that a KGB mole or an undercover agent may not only be involved in assassinations but can successfully penetrate any level of a Western government.

This is not even to mention that prominent politicians and high-ranking intelligence officers themselves can be recruited as spies. Or that a talented Oxbridge student can one day become a collaborator and climb to the top of a hierarchy. And we do not know how many such 'moles' remain unmasked.

Throughout the course of the twentieth century, many famous people have at some point in their lives served as spies. Josephine Baker, Laurence Olivier, Ernest Hemingway, as well as famous British authors John le Carré, Ian Fleming, Graham Greene and Frederick Forsyth – these are just a few well-known names that immediately come to mind. But on that November day of 1951 in Paris, no one paid particular attention to a spectacular performance starring a Soviet undercover operator who had never been identified as a secret agent. Don Teodoro Castro Bonnefil, a respectable diplomat who by then had been promoted to Minister Plenipotentiary, was attending the

---

[1] See Christopher Andrew and Vasili Mitrokhin, *The Mitrokhin Archive: The KGB in Europe and the West* (London: Allen Lane The Penguin Press, 1999), 212.

opening of the United Nations General Assembly as a trusted and valued member of the Costa Rican delegation. His real name, however, was Iosif Grigulevich, known to his friends as Grig, a Soviet illegal whose previous expertise had been in sabotage and murder. Grigulevich is only mentioned in passing in *The KGB's Poison Factory* in connection with a failed attempt to assassinate Trotsky in Mexico in 1940. He and his wife were now posted to Italy, launching into entirely new careers. Naturally, it was only a cover.

In Santiago de Chile, Grig recruited a Costa Rican Communist and journalist, Joaquín Gutiérrez Mangel, who had been working in Chile as vice-consul of Costa Rica. Don Joaquín was happy to help his Soviet friend. He invented a story of one Teodoro Castro, the illegitimate son of a dead (and childless) Costa Rican notable, and managed to persuade the consul general, Alejandro Oreamuno Beeche, to give Don Teodoro and his spouse Costa Rican passports. Appropriate documents were issued and soon Mr and Mrs Castro left Chile with new, genuine Costa Rican documents and a letter of recommendation signed by Don Alejandro. Several months later they turned up in Moscow.

Although there were several Russian, American and British spies who had served their country as fully accredited and respected ambassadors, the story of Grigulevich remains the most intriguing. While I described it in full in *Stalin's Agent*, it is worth briefly reproducing it again here.

At the beginning of 1949, Grig and his Mexican wife were sent to Rome, where they set up a small import-export business. In the autumn of 1950, 'Teodoro Castro' arranged a meeting with the members of a visiting delegation from Costa Rica. The delegation included the leading Costa Rican politician of his generation and the moderate socialist head of the founding junta of the Second Republic, Don José Figueres Ferrer, as well as Don Daniel Oduber and Don Francisco J. Orlich, who were instrumental in establishing coffee exports to Italy. This meeting was a turning point towards new opportunities.

Grigulevich's success in winning Figueres' confidence probably played a decisive role in his future diplomatic career. Hoodwinked by Castro's fraudulent account of his illegitimate birth, Figueres decided they were distant relatives, and nepotism used to be an important part of Costa Rican political culture, so Bob's your uncle. Thereafter, according to his KGB file copied by Vasili Mitrokhin, Grigulevich became a friend of the future president.

In July 1951, Teodoro Castro wrote a letter to the Costa Rican foreign minister informing him that the head of the legation of Costa Rica in Italy offered him a post of first secretary of the mission *ad honorem*. Soon, Grigulevich received his diplomatic passport No. 2026, together with the

Presidential Decree from San José. On 9 November, Castro was chosen as Counsellor to the Delegation of Costa Rica to the VI regular session of the United Nations General Assembly in Paris. During the plenary session in the new UN building on the riverside of the Palais de Chaillot, Castro was introduced to US Secretary of State, Dean Acheson, and British Foreign Secretary, Anthony Eden.

In April 1952, Grigulevich/Castro was promoted to Minister Plenipotentiary of Costa Rica in Italy and, according to his KGB file, was on good terms with the American ambassador, Ellsworth Bunker, and his successor, Claire Boothe Luce. At the same time, he established friendly relations with the Costa Rican nuncio to the Holy See, Prince Giulio Pacelli, a nephew of Pope Pius XII (Eugenio Pacelli). Later, the KGB wits created a legend that, acting as 'Don Teodoro', Grigulevich was awarded the Order of Malta for his outstanding diplomatic service. Some even claimed that they saw the cross of the Order with their own eyes. This, of course, is pure fantasy. But after a visit to the Magistral Library and Archives of the Order on Via dei Condotti in Rome, I found out there's no smoke without fire.

During the assembly on 21 November 1953, the Grand Master and the Sovereign Council of the Order of Malta accepted Teodoro Castro into the Order, thus making him a member and Knight of Magistral Grace with an appropriate decoration, at that time known as Croce di Cavaliere Magistrale with the inscription *in gremio*. The inscription meant that the member of the Order came from a country where there was no Association or Grand Priory. It was noted that the new Knight came from a chivalrous and noble Christian family and was not only an ambassador of his country to Italy but distinguished himself by providing considerable and gratuitous financial help to the Italian victims of a major flood in early December 1951. 'A good Catholic enlivened by altruistic nobleness of spirit and behaviour', Don Teodoro was an ideal candidate to be accepted to the Order. The only problem was that neither the Grand Master nor the Sovereign Council knew at the time that 'Teodoro Castro' was a Karaite who did not follow the Hebrew Scriptures, a Communist atheist who had no respect for God or people, and a spy whose prime mission was to steal the secrets of foreign governments and murder those who refused to comply. Now they know.

Amazingly, Grigulevich was not the only Soviet spy in the Costa Rican Embassy at 24 Piazza Sallustio in Rome. A young civil attaché, Julio Cesar Pascal Rocca (known to the NKVD in Montevideo under the codename PEGAS) worked with Grigulevich in Latin America before joining him in Italy in December 1951. While in Rome, Rocca was regularly writing letters to the Foreign Ministry praising the wisdom, devotion and high-level contacts of Don Teodoro.

In several published sources it is claimed that Laura, the wife of Grig, who was known to the diplomatic corps in Rome under the name Inelia Idalina de Castro, helped her husband a great deal. However, discussing the details of his and Castro's meetings in Rome, Minister Volio told me: 'Castro and I were together at some social functions such as receptions and dinners, but I never met his wife and don't know whether she was in Rome at that time.'[2] Maybe she was not.

In July 1952, Castro was appointed Minister Plenipotentiary to Yugoslavia. 'While fulfilling his diplomatic duties in the second half of 1952,' Sudoplatov recalled, '[Grigulevich] twice visited Yugoslavia, where he was well received. He had access to the social group close to the staff of [Josip Broz Tito, the Yugoslav leader], and was given the promise of a personal audience with Tito. The post held by MAKS [Grigulevich], at the present time makes it possible to use his capabilities for active measures against Tito.' Under 'active measures', Soviet spymasters meant murder.

When Sudoplatov was reading this memo, shown to him personally by Stalin in his Kremlin office, Grigulevich was no longer part of the Special Tasks group. In 1947, he was transferred to the Fourth (Illegals) Directorate of the Committee of Information, or KI, a new unified foreign intelligence service. Grig's boss there was General Alexander Korotkov, who later headed the KGB operations base in Karlshorst. Having made his reputation for several pre-war missions to assassinate 'traitors' abroad, Korotkov, together with General Pitovranov, Deputy Minister of State Security, who also used to head the Karlshorst base, designed a plan to murder the leader of Yugoslavia.

From the very beginning it was Stalin's idea. Before Sudoplatov was summoned to the Kremlin to discuss this plan, Vasili Sitnikov, head of station in Vienna, was instructed to organise a meeting between Grigulevich and his Moscow bosses. In a safe house outside the city, the Costa Rican diplomat was asked in what way he could be most useful in this operation, taking into account his high post. As it was reported to Stalin, Grigulevich, then codenamed MAKS, suggested several possible ways to eliminate Tito. Meanwhile, the Interior Ministry (MVD) assured Stalin there was no doubt that 'MAKS, because of his personal qualities and experience in intelligence work, is capable of accomplishing a mission of this kind', as Sudoplatov later recalled. The MVD leadership then asked for Stalin's personal approval.

Soon, Sudoplatov received a *liternoe delo* – a personal file with a detailed assassination plan – that contained reports on Tito from the Belgrade station and copies of Moscow's instructions to the officers there. After that, he was

---

summoned to face a mixed team of Stalin's and Khrushchev's men who insisted that the murder of the leader of the independent state was in the best interests of the Soviet Union.

The appointment of a senior Costa Rican diplomat as Tito's assassin was approved and Grigulevich composed a farewell letter addressed to his wife to be made public should he be captured or killed during the assassination attempt. Naturally, he signed the letter using his assumed name. In the same manner, a letter was composed and placed on 'Jacques Mornard', the alias of Ramón Mercader, when Sudoplatov sent him to Mexico to murder Trotsky, an operation where Grigulevich also played an important role.

On 1 March 1953, it was reported to Stalin that Tito was unfortunately still alive. On the next day, after an all-night dinner at his Kuntsevo dacha, Stalin suffered a fatal stroke. The Master of the House, as he was known, died on 5 March. Tito survived him by almost three decades.

There are various theories suggesting that Stalin was poisoned. I have not specifically studied the case, but most public supporters of this theory claim that Beria, who was very close to the dictator, slipped warfarin into Stalin's wine and some suspect Khrushchev of complicity in the deed. Specialists note that Stalin's condition was consistent with the overdose of warfarin, a colourless, tasteless, anticoagulant drug.

On 25 April, at the White Palace in Belgrade, His Excellency Teodoro Castro Bonnefil presented his credentials as Minister Plenipotentiary of Costa Rica to Yugoslavia to Marshal Tito. As appropriate to such occasions, they had a small talk, but it was not in private. Together with the Costa Rican diplomat, there were representatives of seven other countries, so any 'hit' against the Yugoslav president was out of the question.

Until recently, researchers drew a blank on when and how Grigulevich abandoned his diplomatic post and returned to Moscow. None of the suggestions was, in fact, true. A short visit to the Costa Rican foreign ministry archive and a helpful hand of my friend, Ambassador Jorge Sáenz Carbonell, solved the puzzle. In November 1953, five months after Beria's arrest, Grigulevich/Castro was still a member of the Costa Rican delegation to the VII General Assembly of the UN Food and Agriculture Organisation (FAO). Only on 16 January 1954 did the government of Costa Rica formally accept his resignation as Minister Plenipotentiary in Italy. As in the case of Rocca, there is no record, however, confirming that a letter of resignation from 'Don Teodoro' had ever been sent.

'Due to a serious illness of my wife I have to leave for Switzerland today,' was the text of the telegram that foreign ministry officials in San José received on 5 December 1953. Judging by letters written from Rome (now in the National Archives of Costa Rica), Grigulevich left Italy on 10 December. Soon, along with his wife and baby daughter, he was in Vienna, which was still occupied by Allied troops and divided into four sectors. Colonel Evgeny Kravtsov, former chief of the German-Austrian desk at Moscow Centre, had just arrived to head the growing MVD and then KGB Vienna station. Without doubt, he was instructed to deal with Grig and his family personally. Grigulevich, Laura and their daughter Romanella successfully landed in a safe house in the Soviet zone and, after receiving a new set of documents, boarded the Vienna–Moscow train at what was then the Austrian capital's largest railway station, Südbahnhof.

Back in Moscow, Grigulevich was placed in the Latin American department of the USSR State Committee for Cultural Relations with Foreign Countries. This was a KGB-fronted organisation and Grigulevich did not complain too much. Later, while discussing his situation with friends who visited his two-room Moscow apartment, Grig suggested that his recall to Moscow was due to Korotkov's personal antipathy. 'He [Korotkov] – at that time chief of the Illegals Directorate – envied me,' Grig used to say. 'He couldn't stand it that I lived in luxury abroad. Korotkov himself didn't even finish secondary school and besides, he was against me because I was a Jew. Stalin died but he was not alone in inventing the Doctors' Plot.' After the collapse of the Soviet Union, books about both Korotkov and Grigulevich continued to be published in Moscow, praising them as heroes of Russia. In reality, after the arrest of Beria, Korotkov did his best to avoid the fate of his State Security colleagues – many of whom were arrested, dismissed from the service and occasionally shot following Beria's fall – and tried to avoid purges by purging Beria's cadres.

Sacked from foreign intelligence and moved to the KGB special reserve, Grig embarked on a new career as a senior researcher at the Ethnographic Institute of the Soviet Academy of Sciences, and he made a new life for himself as a writer and academic, an expert on Latin America and an authority on ethnography and religion. In the early 1960s, he started travelling abroad again.

Grigulevich died on 2 June 1988, survived by his daughter who looks exactly like her father. She is a Russian academic working in the Sector of Ethnic Ecology of the Institute of Ethnology and Anthropology, Russian Academy of Sciences. The name Romanella has long been forgotten and she is now giving interviews and takes part in public events as Nadezhda Iosifovna Grigulevich, a proud daughter of the great Soviet illegal. When her father passed away, his body was cremated and the ashes buried at the cemetery of the Donskoy Monastery in Moscow, where many of his former friends and colleagues from the 'murder bureau' have found peace.

In all Russian and many Western publications about him (and one book was even published in Costa Rica), Grigulevich is pictured as a veteran master spy whose first intelligence school was Spain, and as a great illegal who managed to become an ambassador of a foreign country and a Knight of the Order of Malta. But the truth is that this obviously talented man was not a spy, nor even an intelligence officer. His task was not to extract secrets or exert influence.

Grigulevich, whose portraits and adventures fill the internet and bookshelves, wasted a large part of his life travelling the world ready to kill for Stalin. As a Costa Rican diplomat, he was unable to collect intelligence of any value, and when the orders came from Moscow to murder Tito, he didn't have the chance. When Stalin died, and Beria was dealt with, Grigulevich was recalled to Moscow, and the KGB ceased their relationship with him. One of his many lives was over and another begun. He was awarded a doctorate in history without having to defend a thesis and became a member of the Russian Academy without any academic achievement. He has authored and co-authored fifty-eight books, which lost any value they had after the collapse of the Soviet Union because they are nothing more than communist propaganda. As a result, all his efforts only reinforced, rather than challenged, the Soviet leaders' misunderstanding of the West that continues to this day.

Chapter 6

Assassin Turned Professor

Only days after Grigulevich arrived in Moscow another Soviet assassin, this time posing as an Austrian businessman, was waiting for an urgent telegram from the Centre. It came on 8 February 1954. The telegram instructed him to move to Frankfurt am Main and get ready for a hit. Almost half-a-century later the would-be assassin told me his version of this story.

There is a passage in the Mikhail Bulgakov novel *The Master and Margarita* where Pontius Pilate first meets Jesus Christ, whose name in the book is given in its Hebrew spelling, Yeshua: 'Early in the morning on the fourteenth of the spring months of Nisan …'

On the evening of the twenty-fifth of the autumn month of Elul, long after the shofar (an ancient musical horn, like the modern bugle) was blown in Westend Synagogue, a man rang at the door of an apartment on Inheidener Strasse in Frankfurt. The apartment was occupied by Georgy Sergeyevich Okolovich, one of the leaders of the anti-Soviet émigré organisation NTS, known in English as the People's Labour Union. The business at hand was murder. But things took a very different turn when Okolovich opened the door. The caller came straight out with it on the threshold.

'I'm a captain in the Ministry of State Security,' he said, 'and I have been sent from Moscow to organise your assassination. I don't want to carry the order out and I need your help.'

This is how Gordon Brook-Shepherd described the episode in *The Storm Birds* after reading the file summary prepared for him by the SIS and how Khokhlov himself presented it for the Russian documentary about his life, *The KGB Liquidator*.

Had the assassin involved in the Litvinenko operation decided to stay in the West, a similar scenario could have taken place in London in 2006. Alas, he decided to play the role written for him in Moscow to the end. And he did. So, Sasha Litvinenko was murdered. There were, however, cases when a 'terminator' sent to the West to liquidate 'enemies of the Russian people' appeared to be having second thoughts about committing a crime and getting away with it.

Until that telephone call to my Vienna apartment fifty years after the events in Frankfurt, all I knew about that encounter at the door was what anyone could read in the many books and articles that reported different variations of the plot. But on Monday, 22 September 2003 (the twenty-fifth day of Elul, according to the Hebrew calendar), my caller – the same who had turned up at Okolovich's apartment – identified himself as Nikolai Yevgenyevich Khokhlov, a retired professor of California State University in San Bernardino, and a former captain in Pavel Sudoplatov's Special Tasks unit, officially known as Bureau Number One. Khokhlov's voice sounded firm and there was no trace of age in spite of his venerable 81 years. He still remembered many details related to the events as far back as the war as if it was yesterday, and he spoke clearly and consistently about what happened to him after he was sent on a murder mission to Germany in February 1954. I have also learned about his life and adventures before he retired as a Professor of Psychology at the CSUSB. And during our many long conversations that followed, it became clear that Khokhlov had not changed much over those decades. Surprisingly, he had not even lost his good command of German, which I tested at the earliest opportunity.

Born on 7 June 1922 in the town of Nizhny Novgorod, Khokhlov began studies as a professional variety performer after moving to Moscow. In the summer of 1941, days before the Nazi troops attacked Russia, the duet of whistlers 'Khokhlov and Shur' became a laureate of the All-Union Contest of Artists. Then, like many other young people of his generation, Khokhlov was recruited by the 3rd Department of the Secret Political Directorate of the NKVD to inform on the Moscow intelligentsia. And whereas another recruit might have remained a grass who snitched on his friends and colleagues, Khokhlov was diligent enough to become a fully-fledged agent signing his reports by the pseudonym WHISTLER, while getting more and more complex assignments.

In September, his wartime handler Mikhail (actually, Isidor) Borisovich Maklyarsky, deputy chief of Section 2 of the 3rd NKVD Department and later one of Sudoplatov's men, laid before Nikolai his first operational assignment. From now on his whistling act was to be used as cover for an underground stay-behind role, which would begin for him when and if Nazi troops took Moscow.

A surprise came when Sudoplatov appeared in the safe house, where the sabotage group of two men and two women was quartered, to announce that he had personally selected Nikolai, with his undistinguished face, bum chin and blond hair, for special training as an illegal. (The group leader was not Khokhlov but Grigory Salnikov, alias 'Sergey Palnikov', and it also included, besides Khokhlov himself, Khokhlov's pre-war flame Taisiya Ignatieva, a singer with the alias 'Ignatova', and Valentina Nesterova, alias

'Nina Meshcheryakova', a juggler.) Soon, Khokhlov began studying German under the supervision of a professional instructor from the department and was sent to several PoW camps to mix with German prisoners and improve his pronunciation and grammar. His acting experience proved as useful as his musical talent and his good ear for foreign languages, so by April 1943, Nikolai could quite successfully communicate in German. For me, it remains a question whether at this stage he was able to pass for a German because, even after a long period of professional training, without living for quite a while in a certain geographical area you pretend to be a citizen of this is virtually impossible.

After completing his training, Khokhlov, according to his own account, was sent to the occupied Minsk where, playing a German officer and dressed in a German uniform, he allegedly took part in the operation to assassinate the Generalkommissar for Weissruthenien (Belarus) Wilhelm Kube, who was blown into pieces in September 1943, triggering brutal reprisals against the civilian population. Remarkably, several other people received high government decorations for this operation, but not Khokhlov. At the end of March 1945, he was sent to Bucharest, Romania, posing as a Polish businessman and using a forged passport in the name of 'Stanislaw Lewandowski'. Because he was issued with two Walther pistols before his departure, Khokhlov quickly realised that his trip to Romania could be related to future terminations.

Soon, his former case officer Maklyarsky also left Moscow and settled in East Germany, where he stayed from May to September heading Special Task groups in Brandenburg, Chemnitz, Leipzig and Mecklenburg, before stepping down for health reasons. Back in Moscow, he was promoted to head of department in the Sudoplatov's Bureau Number One. (In 1947, however, Maklyarsky retired and served first as head of Sovexportfilm, the government organisation responsible for the export of Soviet films abroad, and then as chairman of the newly founded Gosfilmofond, the film archive. He would later make an outstanding career as a scriptwriter.)

Maklyarsky's successor as Khokhlov's case officer was Captain of State Security Nikolai Ivanovich Kovalenko. After General Sudoplatov personally visited Khokhlov in Bucharest, Kovalenko informed him that his mission to Romania as a sleeper agent would be a long-term affair. However, after spending four years there playing the role of a white-goods trader, Khokhlov had his first breakdown, panicked, and wrote several letters to Moscow asking to recall him to the USSR as soon as possible.

Illegals abroad are commonly victims of nervous failures. Under the tension, they may commit irrational acts. So, when his case officer met him on the apron upon his landing in Moscow in October 1949, he greeted Nikolai with a friendly, understanding smile. Khokhlov was given back his internal Soviet passport, cash for initial expenses and time to readjust to Soviet life. Arrangements were also made for him to meet his intelligence chiefs.

In the safe house on the arched lane off Gorki Street were all three of them: Lieutenant General Sudoplatov, Major General Eitingon and Lieutenant Colonel Kovalenko. In May 1938, after having assassinated one of the Ukrainian nationalist leaders in Rotterdam, Sudoplatov, then a low-level penetration agent, came to Spain where Eitingon, his former superior, was heading a substation in Barcelona. One of Eitington's agents was Grigulevich, posing in Spain as Brazilian refugee 'José Ocampo', and another agent was Ramón Mercader. Later, all three would take part in the assassination in Mexico of Stalin's 'Enemy Number One', Trotsky. The operation was planned and controlled by Sudoplatov.

During that meeting, a new target country was outlined for Khokhlov: Austria. And Sudoplatov's service had its own mission for its illegals. They were either 'sleeping' or active saboteurs, assassins and demolition men.

By the time the Allies had settled into post-war Austria, drinking coffee in Vienna's cafés and giving American cigarettes to their local girlfriends, the Russian espionage agencies were busy filling the Austrian police and security service with their agents. Hundreds of them, recruited from the former Austrian Schutzbund militia and the International Brigades in Spain, arrived from Russia after the war and many took positions in the Staatspolizei (federal police) or Austria's premier civilian intelligence agency, the Generaldirektion für die Öffentliche Sicherheit (General Directorate for Public Safety). The Interior Ministry itself was placed under Franz Horner, a leading Communist official who had fought in Spain, lived in Moscow during the war and had been parachuted into Yugoslavia by the GRU to help to organise an 'Austrian Liberation Army'.

One Anton Dobritzhofer, the chief of police in Vienna's proletarian district of Floridsdorf, was instrumental in providing documentation for Soviet illegals. Dobritzhofer had been a Schutzbund commander in Floridsdorf and, after the defeat in 1934 of the Socialist revolt, immigrated to the Soviet Union. In 1936, he was sent to Spain and returned to Moscow in 1939. Like almost every other former officer of the International Brigades who was allowed to come to the Soviet Union, he was recruited by the NKVD. After the war, Dobritzhofer surfaced in Vienna and, following a brief spell as the district police chief, rose through the ranks, ending his career in the Vienna City Police Directorate.

Khokhlov recalled that there was another communist recommended by Dobritzhofer, who had also fought in Spain and who after the war became an official in St. Pölten, the capital of Lower Austria. He was one of the sources helping Sudoplatov's Bureau Number One to obtain original Austrian documentation for illegals. A check in the archives points to Alois Schmutz, who joined the KPÖ in 1936 and during the same year had to emigrate to Spain, where he first settled in Seville, Andalusia. But when the civil war broke out moved to Málaga. After briefly serving in the UGT militia, he fought with the XI International Brigade, was promoted to lieutenant but in 1939 was interned in the Saint Cyprien concentration camp in France, where Dobritzhofer also served a term before he was permitted to travel to the Soviet Union. Later arrested by the Nazis, Schmutz was thrown into Dachau concentration camp, where he spent five years. After the war, he returned to St. Pölten.

In September 1950, Khokhlov was commissioned as an active duty officer of the Ministry for State Security (MGB), the predecessor of the KGB. As he continued to be an illegal, he was allowed and even encouraged to live undercover as a student of Moscow State University. Sudoplatov claimed in his memoirs that he even helped Khokhlov to be admitted as a full-time student without bothering to take any entrance exams.

In February 1951, Nikolai was summoned to a safe house where he met the deputy chief of the Austrian desk, Captain Tamara Ivanova – the same female operative who had taught him German in 1942 – and was given a new assignment.

For what is known in professional jargon as a test-run, his first trip around Europe, Khokhlov was first flown to Austria on a military aircraft. They landed in Bad Vöslau near his department's operational base (internally known as OGA – Operational Group Austria), because such Soviet facilities were well-guarded, and no Austrian passport or customs officer was there to check. Instead of the Austrians, deputy chief of the OGA, Major Saul Okun, and his assistant met Khokhlov there.

Saul Lvovich Okun was a formidable figure. For the few who knew him, he was a legend. Recruited to the NKVD as a student, he operated in the Baltic States during the Spanish Civil War, was sent to Hungary under the diplomatic cover of a Soviet consul general in 1939, joined the Sudoplatov Service when Nazi Germany attacked Russia in 1941 and, after the war, was posted to Austria. In 1956 Okun, aged 41, was ordered to go to Hungary on a sabotage mission but refused and was sacked on the spot. Now his true adventure began as he was appointed director of the legendary Prague on Arbat Street, which is still ranked among the best Moscow restaurants. One day in 1976, I invited my future wife for lunch at the Prague, where an ordinary guest could never get a table as they were always reserved for foreign diplomats, KGB operatives, party functionaries and celebrities. We somehow managed to get in and were seated at a table on the first floor. The dish of the day was sturgeon Moscow-style, so we ordered it. But as soon as a waiter appeared with our order on a large tray, he heard a whisper 'Okun' (the name is translated from Russian as 'perch'), after which all service personnel froze, and an inconspicuous man in a grey suit 'swam' through the dining hall ... Quite incredibly, Okun served as director of the Prague until 1995 – almost 40 years.

Vöslau Airfield, located 4km east of the town in the Soviet occupation zone, was often used by the Red Army command, USIA (Soviet Property Administration in Austria) and SMERSH for smuggling people and assets, transportation of confiscated (looted) archives, artefacts and other valuables, as well as for various 'special missions'. Today, Bad Vöslau Airfield is of local importance and primarily serves general aviation. Khokhlov, accompanied by Okun, was chauffeured south to Wiener Neustadt and quartered in a safe house on Ungargasse, only steps away from the main square. In July, he was cleared to proceed further.

This 1951 test-run turned out to be an easy and pleasant adventure. From April until August, with an Austrian passport in the name of 'Josef Hofbauer', Khokhlov travelled around Switzerland, France, Denmark, Belgium and Holland, collecting visas and border stamps and opening bank accounts. Just another innocent, middle-class citizen of Europe, as his MGB 'legend' suggested.

Khokhlov's next assignment – to murder 'an enemy of the people' – was to be in Paris, but it was suddenly dropped. Instead of Paris, he was sent to Karlshorst in East Berlin, the largest operational base of the MGB in Europe, controlling stations throughout East Germany and operating into the West. In Karlshorst at that time, Sudoplatov had thirteen officers from a so-called special 'illegal reserve', one of the most secret of the Soviet secret services. Khokhlov arrived there in April 1952 and, in December, Markus 'Misha' Wolf, aged only 29, was made chief of the foreign intelligence service of the German Democratic Republic, of which Misha was one of the founding members, maintaining daily contacts with the Karlshorst base that I first visited in the autumn of 1988. By that time, Wolf had already retired and was writing his first book, *Die Troika*, a sentimental memoir of himself, his brother – the film director Konrad Wolf – and their friends from their shared childhood in Stalinist Moscow during the 1930s. Eventually, he became quite active and successful as an author. One of his books was called *Secrets of Russian Cuisine* showcasing his favourite Russian recipes.

When I first came to East Berlin, a place known as Haus Moskau, that is, a two-storeyed Soviet gastronomic establishment with a restaurant serving borscht, Stolichnaya, pirogi and moderately priced Malossol caviar, had just undergone a major refurbishment to become Restaurant and Café Moskau. Opened in January 1964, it was part of Moscow's plan to have seven international culinary attractions – Haus Budapest with Hungarian cuisine, Haus Sofia, Haus Warschau and so on – to be built on Karl-Marx-Allee, which until 1961, eight years after Stalin's death, was still called Stalinallee. Then, apart from the restaurant upstairs and the café on the ground floor it also had a dance hall and a late-night basement bar. The roof was decorated with a life-size imitation Sputnik, a gift of the Soviet ambassador to illustrate Soviet space achievements. Once established, it became a popular place for black-market dealers and spies. Forsyth, then the Reuters correspondent in East Berlin, claimed that at Christmas 1963, he helped his news agency reduce its surplus of East German marks feasting there on a mountain of Beluga and Stoli 'to ensure that all the bugs in my bedroom could record were the snores'. A slip of memory, as it seems. Remarkably, the Sputnik is still there.

In Karlshorst, Khokhlov reported to his former case officer Lieutenant Colonel Kovalenko, while his immediate superior there was Lieutenant Yevgeny Savintsev. Sudoplatov's officers were the elite of the Karlshorst contingent. They were among the very few who had unlimited access to the large carpool and had special ID cards permitting them to go outside the well-guarded fence of the compound, even at night. East German police and Soviet military patrols that ran throughout the city were obliged to let them go under any circumstances and, if necessary, provide assistance. Even six decades later their names remain secret and they do not figure in any declassified documents or archives.

The chief talent-spotter of the Kovalenko group was Gustav Röbelen – an Austrian who, in 1929, became a member of the KPD and, in 1933, immigrated to France and then Belgium, where he was engaged in organising illegal border crossings for the Party. When the civil war broke out in Spain, Röbelen was sent there. In his memoirs, Khokhlov recalled that Röbelen was a former general in the International Brigades and also worked with Eitingon, later becoming 'chief of personnel of the Central Committee of the East German Communist Party'.

This is not true. In Spain, Röbelen was part of the first battalion of the XI International Brigade named after Edgar André, a German communist executed by the Nazis in November 1936. After guerrilla training in one of the NKVD schools, which I mention in my book *Stalin's Agent*, Röbelen took part in action at Madrid and Teruel. From autumn 1937, promoted to captain, he headed the personal security detail of Alexander Orlov, the NKVD resident in Spain. After a wartime mission in Iran, he was parachuted to Byelorussia in 1944 to join a partisan group and in 1946 returned to Berlin. From 1948 Röbelen headed the Abteilung zum Schutz des Volkseigentums (Department for the Protection of National Property) of the Central Committee of the SED, Socialist Unity Party of East Germany, which in 1953 became the new Abteilung für Sicherheitsfragen, in other words, the department responsible for the intelligence and security issues in the police, Ministry for State Security and the army.

The group to which Khokhlov was seconded was in Karlshorst to recruit and train future demolition men who were supposed to be covertly operating in the West. Their tasks included deep penetration with a view to sabotage, assassination and general mayhem. In this work, they coordinated their efforts with Markus Wolf.

Among the group were two agents who had been placed in the special reserve. One, named Kurt Weber (codenamed FRANZ), was recruited in Paris before the war. Weber later moved to the south of France, married and lived well on Moscow subsidies. When Hitler's army occupied France, he joined the French resistance, and on one occasion, demonstrating great bravery and resourcefulness, managed to get a fellow maquisard out of a Nazi prison hours before the latter was doomed to die. The rescued man's name was Hans Kukowitsch. They became friends and after the war returned together to Germany and settled first in the American Zone and then in the Soviet Occupation Zone, locally known as SBZ. Weber found a job at the police in Berlin-Köpenick. There, he was located by Savintsev and reactivated. He immediately suggested finding his wartime friend Hans. Savintsev found him in Potsdam, living with a youngish widow and bored with his inactive life. Soon Kukowitsch became agent FELIX.

At the end of August 1953, Sudoplatov was arrested. His deputy, Lev Studnikov, became acting head of the Bureau Number One, by that time renamed 9th Department of the MGB. Despite those minor changes, on the whole, it remained business as usual because already in September the new chief told Khokhlov that he had been selected for an important mission in West Germany – to 'liquidate' one of the NTS leaders in Frankfurt. The acronym stood for Narodno-Trudovoi Soyuz, for whatever reason translated into English as the National Alliance of Russian Solidarists. The scope of activities that the Special Tasks officers and agents were to carry out was registered in the files as Operation RHEIN. It was supervised by the deputy head of the Second Chief Directorate (SCD) of the MGB, Oleg Gribanov, then only a colonel but soon to be promoted to major general. Remarkably, Khokhlov's defection would not affect Gribanov's career in any way but in

1964 one of his subordinates, Yuri Nosenko, decided to remain in the West and Gribanov, by then lieutenant general and head of the SCD, was fired.

During our long conversations, Khokhlov always insisted that he was not to do the dirty work himself, although I did not believe him. According to Khohklov, two German agents, FRANZ (Weber) and FELIX (Kukowitsch), were chosen as hitmen. They were brought to Moscow and given a five-week intensive course by the most experienced officers the KGB could come up with. There were driving and shooting lessons, and the agents were taught how to spot and elude surveillance and avoid an ambush, how to 'dry-clean' and pull off brush contacts – in short, the tradecraft needed for a successful 'bang and burn' operation. Finally, they deposited their East German passports identifying them as 'Kurt Wetter' and 'Hans Schulze' and, thanks to the help of agents in the Austrian police, were given new bona fide Austrian documents in the names of 'Josef Leitner' and 'Hans Rotter'. By 31 December, they had safely reached Vienna and settled in different hotels.

Dedicated to its neutrality, Austria has long had counterintelligence and national security forces – the General Directorate for Public Safely and the State Police – so simple to evade and much penetrated by foreign intelligence agencies. Their presence in the Austrian capital is so considerable that, according to several published accounts, Mossad operatives refer to them as 'fertsalach', the Hebrew term meaning a fart. This may or may not be justified.

One day at the Wheeler's, Marco Pierre White's Oyster Bar and Grill Room in St James's, I met a former member of the Firm who used to serve as head of the SIS station in Vienna. He made no bones about what he was (I knew it anyway) and we hit it off well, both agreeing that since the early 1920s to the present day, Russian Intelligence Services (RIS) had enough agents in the Austrian police to get what they wanted. Perhaps the most vivid examples are the first post-war chief of the Vienna state police (Staatspolizei or Stapo), Heinrich Dürmayer, who was a former IB fighter in Spain, and his successor Gustav Hochenbichler, who was unmasked in the 1990s as the KGB agent SOROKIN and the East German agent BAU. (Hochenbichler's Stasi case officer was Colonel Hans Ulrich Fritz under diplomatic cover as Second Secretary of the East German Embassy in Vienna.) In the Mitrokhin files, seven Austrian police officers were identified as KGB agents. In addition, among the Russian assets, there's a high-ranking civil servant codenamed YERSHOV, recruited in or about 1981, who is probably still in place.

It was, therefore, no surprise that Vienna was selected as the base for the Khokhlov murder mission. Khokhlov arrived there on 13 January 1954 on a regular Aeroflot flight. He waited for an order to move, although he had been told that before the Berlin Conference (25 January–18 February) was over, no operations were to take place in Austria or Germany. His two German agents had, by then, been placed in a safe house in Baden near Vienna. Later, a KGB arms expert delivered the specially designed weapons. The telegram came on 8 February, when it was clear that the 'Big Four' foreign ministers – John F. Dulles, Anthony Eden, Georges Bidault and Vyacheslav Molotov – would not reach an agreement on principle issues, which were the international status of Germany and Austria still under the Allied occupation, as well as the Korean War and the Indochina War.

Three years earlier, in 1951, the Soviets tried to abduct Okolovich. A group of German agents controlled by the Karlshorst base crossed the inter-sectional border and arrived in the small town of Runkel, less than four and a half miles away from Limburg an der Lahn, where the NTS had its headquarters at the time. The group was equipped with ampoules of morphine, syringes and 15,000 German marks in cash. Two of the agents immediately gave themselves up to the authorities. The leader managed to escape to the Soviet Zone. All the spyware ended up with the police. A special bulletin of the NTS Executive Bureau, which reported on this failed operation and demanded vigilance from all members, was carefully filed among other documents in Moscow that Khokhlov was encouraged to study.

That was not the first attempt. In 1948, another group of agents was sent to Limburg but failed to find Okolovich. Instead, they talked to his wife, who became very suspicious and told them her husband rarely visited the place, which was true.

After the NTS headquarters were moved to Frankfurt am Main in 1952, all the MGB knew about Okolovich was that he was often seen at the offices of the Russian Information Agency (RIA) and that his wife worked at the Possev publishing house. It was not until 1953 that Moscow finally got a reliable source able to provide all of the missing details. In July, the agent reported that Okolovich lived at 3 Inheidener Strasse in Frankfurt-Bornheim, was officially employed by RIA, and that he was driving a black Mercedes with a such-and-such licence plate. Also attached was a recent photo showing Okolovich and his wife in the company of that agent. His name was Nikita Khorunzhy.

If we draw parallels between the two operations – the attempt to assassinate Okolovich and the poisoning of Litvinenko – we shall see that in both cases Russian Intelligence Services (RIS) were acting according to the same pattern, in other words, played it by the book. Remarkably, even the names of the penetration agents were identical. Thus, in March 2002 one Nikita

(Chekulin) was successfully infiltrated into the close circle of friends and supporters of Boris Berezovsky reporting on both Berezovsky and Litvinenko. Later Chekulin claimed, quite incredibly, that the murder of Litvinenko was organised by Berezovsky with the help of Sasha's wife Marina.

Nikita Khorunzhy was a Ukrainian and captain of the Red Army stationed in East Germany. A schoolmaster in civilian life, he defected to the West in 1948 and was accepted as a fully fledged defector claiming his motives were not political but personal. With a wife and two children back in his home town of Kherson, he lived in Germany with a German woman of his choice, named Elizabeth Werner, with whom he claimed he had fallen in love and wanted to marry. As he had initially arrived at the US military police post in East Berlin, Khorunzhy was recruited as an agent of the G-2 military intelligence staff of the US Army located at Griesheim.

Pretty soon he joined several anti-communist organisations and became an instructor at the 7707th European Command Intelligence Centre at Oberursel. At the same time, Khorunzhy (alias 'Georg Müller') was asked to arrange special training courses for NTS recruits in Bad Homburg, and several other places, where agents had been instructed before they could be parachuted into the USSR. It is believed he betrayed a group of four agents who were dropped into Ukraine in April 1953. On 27 April, two of them were arrested and identified as 'Vasili V. Vasilchenko' and 'Leonid N. Matkovsky', whose real names were Alexander Vasiliyevich Lakhno (codenamed ALEC) and Alexander Nikolayevich Makov (PETE). They named two others, who were arrested later that day. Those were Sergey Izosimovich Gorbunov (JOHN) and Dmitry Nikolayevich Remiga (DICK). Interrogated by the MGB, all of them confessed that they had been trained in a special camp in Bad Wiessee in Bavaria and named their American instructors, among whom was a 'Captain Holliday'. All four saboteurs were sentenced to death and executed.

It was, as usual, bad tradecraft because Khorunzhy was controlled from the Berlin Karlshorst base by means of couriers. One of them betrayed him, so the mole was arrested and, in 1954, sentenced to a long term in prison. Five years later he was one of the first Soviet spies to be secretly exchanged and returned to the Soviet Union. His further fate is unknown.

The Khorunzhy story is similar to that of Dmitry Kovtun, the second suspect in the Litvinenko investigation. Kovtun is a former Red Army officer, who was stationed in the old East German town of Parchim and after the Berlin Wall fell and the Soviet troops started to withdraw decided he would have a better life in the West. Instead of returning home, Kovtun and his East German wife, Inna Hohne, fled to Hamburg. Here, the former lieutenant started to explore local curiosities, starting with the seamen's zone known as St. Pauli. This, of course, included the famous Reeperbahn, the main thoroughfare of its raucous red-light district. This marriage swiftly collapsed because Kovtun drank a lot and dreamt of becoming a porn star, his first wife stated, and the inquiry into Litvinenko's death duly recorded. Although he lived off benefits, occasionally working as a dish-washer, refuse collector and, once, a waiter, he managed to marry again. His second wife was Marina Wall, who is also German. They soon divorced, and he returned to Russia. There, Kovtun contacted Andrei Logovoy, his childhood friend. They both came from army families and attended the same military academy. It is obvious that Kovtun was used in the Litvinenko operation unwittingly, which means he was absolutely unaware of the supporting role he was supposed to play. And there is no doubt in my mind that both Kovtun and Lugovoy knew nothing about polonium.

One episode in the Litvinenko case seems to contradict this version. It is mentioned in the inquiry documents that the day before the poisoning, that is, on Tuesday 31 October 2006, Kovtun, visiting his ex-family in Hamburg, told an acquaintance who he once worked with at an Italian restaurant that he was looking for a friendly cook in London. When asked what for, he explained that he wanted this cook to put a 'very expensive poison' into Litvinenko's food or drink.

Naturally, this story does not stand up to any criticism. The Litvinenko operation had been planned long before, going on for over a year after Lugovoy first visited London on a reconnaissance trip in 2004. The next time he came to the British capital – in September 2005 – he contacted Litvinenko for the first time in ten years and invited him to a meal in Chinatown, already knowing that Sasha was a fan of Asian food. Litvinenko, of course, reported this rendezvous to Berezovsky, and on 23 January 2006, Lugovoy (Berezovsky's former bodyguard) was attending Berezovsky's lavish 60th birthday party at Blenheim Palace in Woodstock, Oxfordshire. Lugovoy was seated with Sasha, Marina, Alex Goldfarb, Ahmed Zakayev and Zakayev's aide Yaragi Abdullayev (better known as Yasha) – all of whom, except Lugovoy, I met several times. On that very day, the fate of both Litvinenko and Berezovsky was sealed. Boris, who had thought he could rely on his professional bodyguards and Goldfarb as some sort of intelligence and analytical department in one person, but who never had any counterintelligence service, was not able to foresee that.

Kovtun joined the Litvinenko operation at the very last stage in October 2006, when everything had already been meticulously planned and prepared. It is absurd to think that he was sent to Hamburg only a few hours before the actual poisoning to look for a cook to 'put a "very expensive poison" into Litvinenko's food or drink' somehow, somewhere. His waiter friend was clearly bluffing, because he had read the story about the Litvinenko poisoning in London and Kovtun's alleged involvement and decided it would be very beneficial for him to be in the media.[1] At the same time, it is established without any reasonable doubt that on 16 October, when Kovtun visited London for the first time, he became seriously contaminated by a rare poison, of which he only learnt after the death of Litvinenko at the end of November. He was then hospitalised in Moscow and treated for several weeks. Still, during an interview with the German television team, who sent me the footage, Kovtun was unable to pronounce the name of the radioactive element correctly, calling it 'poloniumum'.

By the beginning of 1954, thanks to Khorunzhy, the MGB had enough information to launch Operation RHEIN, a murder attempt on Okolovich's life.

In my book *WHISTLER* (2005) and later in *The KGB's Poison Factory*, I describe in detail Khokhlov's adventures after he poured out his soul to the NTS leader. I revealed for the first time the names of several CIA officers who worked with him and an unknown side of his career as a CIA agent before he became an academic. But that was only one part of the story.

What secured Khokhlov a prominent place in intelligence history was not what he pronounced during his famous press conference broadcast to the world by the Voice of America: love for the family, 'conscience' reasons for changing sides, homesickness – usual stuff Soviet defectors say when they turn on their own country. This was not important. More important was the fact of his physical existence.

Since its first days, the Cheka had been sending assassins abroad to murder enemies of the Kremlin. From General Wrangel in 1925 to Colonel Litvinenko eight decades later (both died after drinking poison-laced tea), honest people who had been forced to leave their beloved Russia have told the world about those crimes. But before Khokhlov, there was not a single person who ever came to his victim with the words, 'I have been sent to kill you, but I refuse to do it and I leave myself at your mercy.' Khokhlov's statement had an enormous impact on Western governments and people, as much as Litvinenko's statement from his deathbed.

---

[1] The official published Litvinenko Inquiry legal document states in paragraph 6.192: '... as to the reliability of this evidence, the German police thought that D3 was lying.'

After the press conference, Khokhlov was invited to London for a lecture tour and gave an interview to the BBC. His story received the full glare of publicity. On 6 May 1954, he was flown to Washington, DC, on board a plane of the US Air Force.

After his arrival in the United States, Khokhlov became a persistent critic of Communist Russia, lecturing widely and giving interviews to the media, just like Litvinenko did. In September 1957, he returned to Europe to take part in an important conference that had been planned long before and announced in advance.

As I am seeking to demonstrate, this is the most important part. The pattern was repeated in virtually every case when a professional assassination operation was arranged or abetted. Khokhlov knew exactly when and where he was going to be on which date and, quite certainly, not only Khokhlov was aware of that. The same applies to Yushchenko, Politkovskaya, Litvinenko, Berezovsky, Nemtsov, Perepilichny ... the operation can only be carried out if the operators know well in advance that the victim will be in a certain place at a certain time. That is why I am saying with full confidence that Sasha Litvinenko could NOT have been poisoned in the Millennium Bar.

In 1957, Khrushchev was named *Time* magazine's 'Man of the Year', and the Botanical Garden of Frankfurt was chosen for several hundred anti-Communist activists from various lands to come and share their views on what could be done in the aftermath of Stalin's death and Krushchev's rise to power in the Soviet Union. The West had been watching the new Soviet leader for four years now, and the signals were that he prompted more consumer industries, freedom of the arts, better pensions, and freed thousands of political prisoners from the GULAGs. In the meantime, West Germany was admitted into NATO and, as a result, the Moscow-controlled military alliance, the Warsaw Pact, was formed. Thus, the future direction of US-Soviet relations seemed cloudier than ever and a compromise had to be found. The place was the hall of the Palmengarten, set amidst palms and greenhouses, where conventions and concerts were held.

According to Khokhlov, with whom I discussed this episode in every detail, on Sunday, 15 September 1957, the closing day of the conference, he addressed the audience briefly and then stepped out on the terrace and ordered a cup of coffee, of which he drank less than a half. He went out to see off some delegates from London and then came back to attend the entertainment programme. From behind closed doors leading to the concert hall, he could hear the performers and the sound of laughter and applause from the audience.

1-509

𝕱𝖊𝖉𝖊𝖗𝖆𝖑 𝕭𝖚𝖗𝖊𝖆𝖚 𝖔𝖋 𝕴𝖓𝖛𝖊𝖘𝖙𝖎𝖌𝖆𝖙𝖎𝖔𝖓
𝕌𝖓𝖎𝖙𝖊𝖉 𝕾𝖙𝖆𝖙𝖊𝖘 𝕯𝖊𝖕𝖆𝖗𝖙𝖒𝖊𝖓𝖙 𝖔𝖋 𝕵𝖚𝖘𝖙𝖎𝖈𝖊
𝖂𝖆𝖘𝖍𝖎𝖓𝖌𝖙𝖔𝖓 25, 𝕯. 𝕮.

May 19, 1954   *PERSONAL AND CONFIDENTIAL*
VIA LIAISON

Mr. Allen W. Dulles
Director
Central Intelligence Agency
Administration Building
Room 123
2430 E Street, N. W.
Washington, D. C.

Dear Mr. Dulles:

    *Your attention is directed to the case involving
Nikolai Evgenyevich Khokhlov, a Soviet defector, who was
brought into the United States on May 8, 1954, and who
appeared before a Congressional committee on May 11, 1954.
Repeated requests through our Liaison Representative have
been made for interrogation reports and an opportunity
to examine the miniature weapons that Khokhlov and his
accomplices were to use in an assassination assignment.
On May 11, 1954, we learned through the press that
Khokhlov was to be made available to a Congressional
committee prior to any interview conducted by this
Bureau. In view of the fact that we did not have the
benefit of any direct information indicating that
Khokhlov had no information concerning current Soviet
intelligence operations in this country, immediate
arrangements were made whereby a brief interview was
conducted prior to Khokhlov's appearance before the
Congressional committee.*

    *To date we have not had the benefit of detailed
information available concerning Khokhlov, nor have the
weapons been made available to us for examination. In
view of this most irregular and shabby treatment afforded
us in this matter, we strongly protest. Under the
circumstances I feel that no good purpose would be served
by either further interview of the subject or an examination
of the mentioned weapons. It should be clearly understood
that Khokhlov must be considered as your responsibility and
assurances are requested that in the future defectors such*

A letter from the first FBI Director (May 1924–May 1972) J. Edgar Hoover to Allen W. Dulles
of the CIA about Soviet defector Nikolai Khokhlov.

Nikolai suddenly felt very fatigued and thought it was due to three days of nervous tension, speeches and discussions. He ordered a glass of juice but immediately realised that he could not drink it as he suddenly felt a severe, persistent abdominal pain. When he heard the voice of Irene Salena of the Frankfurt Opera, he decided that in spite of the wave of nausea engulfing him, he should go and listen. Tomorrow he would sleep late, he thought.

Khokhlov returned to the concert hall and found a seat, feeling no better. He decided he'd better go out, which he did, and the fresh, cool air slightly revived him. He climbed into the car and in a few minutes was at his bed-and-breakfast guesthouse. Then he fainted.

When Khokhlov came around he felt feverish, his heart was beating rapidly, and he was shivering. Picking up his keys, he dragged himself to the entrance, feeling worse every minute. Somebody called a doctor and he himself managed to call Okolovich. At that time, he was already suffering from vomiting and diarrhoea. The paramedics transferred him to hospital.

All the rest was exactly like in the Litvinenko case. After some time, Khokhlov's hair suddenly started to fall out and his skin yellowed. The doctors ran a series of tests and the head physician brought in consultants. A skin specialist suspected thallium. Indeed, alopecia (hair loss) is a hallmark of thallium poisoning that occurs seven to twelve days after other symptoms, such as severe stomach pain, nausea, vomiting and diarrhoea begin. But in this case, a skin specialist was probably wrong.

Subsequent developments proved that the biochemists in the secret laboratory in Moscow knew their profession. While the German specialists were pouring all kinds of antidotes into him, Khokhlov's system continued to disintegrate at a galloping rate.

As a former officer from the department that was the main customer of the Naumov lab product, Khokhlov knew better than anyone that everything had been figured out in advance: the inexperience of Western physicians, the inertia of authorities, the scepticism of the public, as well as symptoms of gastritis to disguise the action of a new type of poison not used before and therefore unknown and undetectable.

On the afternoon of Sunday, 22 September, nearly a week to the hour after his collapse, the doctors discovered that an incredibly rapid process of destruction was going on in Khokhlov's bloodstream. The number of the white corpuscles was falling dangerously, and at one time a count showed a drop from the normal 6,000–7,000 to 700. A puncture into his chest bone produced a sample of the marrow, and a microscopic examination of it established that the blood-building cells in the bone marrow were dying off. The blood in his veins was gradually turning into useless plasma. The saliva glands in the mouth, throat and alimentary canal were drying up. It became difficult to eat, drink, and even speak. Khokhlov sank into apathy and was growing feeble. That Sunday evening, his friends later told him, he looked very much like a dying man. Exactly like Sasha Litvinenko sixty years later.

The doctors told Khokhlov's friends that he was almost certainly going to leave this world pretty soon.

'But from what?' Okolovich broke in. 'What is the cause of this? Is it possible that medical science is unable to determine what is killing him, and attempt to fight it?'

'Ah, medical science!' the good doctor responded. 'All that we know is based on experience. How can one fight an unknown poison?'

But the specialists of the Barnet Hospital in London, not to mention the UCLH that claims to 'employ leading health care professionals in an extensive range of clinical services', *had* this experience. Unfortunately, practising physicians do not have time to read espionage thrillers.

On Monday morning, 23 September, NTS held a press conference. Vladimir Poretsky, the chairman, recited Khokhlov's history and stated that he was suffering from poisoning by a *combination of drugs*. Okolovich also spoke and explained the reason why the Soviet government wanted to get rid of the defector. In the meantime, the patient, unable to take food, was being fed intravenously.

But unlike Sasha Litvinenko, Khokhlov was extremely lucky. On 27 September, the twelfth day of his illness, the Americans intervened. A group of American healthcare professionals arrived at the hospital and went into conference with their German colleagues in Khokhlov's ward. On the same day, he was moved from the Frankfurt University Hospital to the US Army facility, where doctors started to administer specialised treatment.

By the middle of October, Nikolai Khokhlov was discharged from hospital fully recovered. That was quite a miracle.

I am repeating all those details here because the two cases, Khokhlov's and Litvinenko's, are very similar. The official memorandum written by Colonel F.Y. Leaver, MC, Commanding Officer of the United States Army Hospital, Frankfurt, APO 757, US Army, stated:

Mr Khokhlov was admitted to the United States Army Hospital, Frankfurt, on September 27, 1957, as a transfer from a local German hospital.

He had been hospitalised there on the 16th of September with what appeared to be an acute gastroenteritis, however, several days after admission he developed a severe hemorrhagic skin eruption, ulceration of the mouth, some mental confusion, loss of body hair, and severe depression of the bone marrow with a total white blood count of 750 and virtual disappearance of granulocytes. It was the impression of the staff of the German hospital that this probably was caused by poisoning, very likely thallium.

On admission to this hospital on 27 September (11 days following the onset of his illness) he was acutely and critically ill with marked bone-marrow depression, high fever, and he was unable to eat because of the hemorrhagic skin eruption which involved not only the body surface but also included the mouth, throat, and mucous membranes. There was marked epilation and loss of hair on all body surfaces including the scalp. He was emotionally disturbed and sometimes confused.

As his condition was critical, he was immediately placed on the seriously ill list. He received special nursing care in a private room. His treatment consisted of antibiotics, ACTH, steroids, as well as local treatment for his skin and mouth lesions. His condition gradually improved. He has been able to be up and about his room during the past few days. Temperature was normal, and skin lesions cleared. The blood picture returned to approximately normal. He lost most of his body hair. At the time of discharge from the hospital on Tuesday afternoon, October 8, 1957, he was weak, but was able to eat without difficulty and was gradually regaining his strength. He was considered essentially recovered.

Symptoms and clinical findings are believed to have been due to poisoning, probably by thallium and/or other chemical agents. Toxicological studies were performed on his hair, skin, and urine, which were negative; however, no specimens from the early period of his illness were available for study.

Khokhlov's poisoning coincided with the successful launch of the first Soviet Sputnik, and he reflected upon this in his book, writing 'I, too, was an exhibit of the achievements of Soviet science'. Ironically, a life-size copy of this Sputnik would later decorate the roof of Restaurant Moskau in East Berlin.

During the next five years, Nikolai worked for the CIA in Vietnam and South Korea, and in 1962, as he told me, he sent an application to Duke University in North Carolina for admission as a post-graduate student to the Faculty of Psychology, although he had not completed his university education in Russia. Nevertheless, he was accepted because the Agency always had good relations with what was once known as Trinity College – not at the University of Cambridge, England, but at Duke's.

In 1967, after five years at Duke University, Khokhlov wrote a thesis and a year later defended his PhD in psychology. Immediately after that he left North Carolina and settled in California, joining the Department of Psychology at California State University in San Bernardino (CSUSB).

That, of course, could not happen without the CIA's help. And here begins a new and little-known life of Nikolai Yevgenyevich Khokhlov: his career as an American professor and specialist in parapsychology.

According to the official record, since his arrival at CSUSB in 1968, Dr Khokhlov's speciality was the perception of mental processes, theories of the bio-field and computer applications to research on personality. Remarkably, Khokhlov never mentioned anything about some very special studies done by his academic supervisor at Duke University, Professor Rhine, whose name, by weird coincidence, was the same as the assassination plot that sparked Khokhlov's defection in Frankfurt – Operation RHINE (in German Rhein). In the 1930s, Dr Joseph Banks Rhine, who was a leading specialist in parapsychology, with his wife, Louise Rhine, and other members of the parapsychology laboratory conducted experiments into extrasensory perception (ESP), having in mind such human psychic abilities as intuition, telepathy, precognition, clairvoyance, mediumship and psychometry. Other topics included displacement analysis, spirit revival, telekinesis and other aspects of parapsychology. In the background was the idea that alongside other God's creatures, human beings can perform things beyond the scope of known and recognised bodily senses.

Already in 1938, Rhine's experiments were heavily criticised by the leading academics who challenged the concepts and evidence of ESP. In the 1960s, however, when Khokhlov was still at Duke University, parapsychologists were increasingly interested in the cognitive elements of ESP. In September 1966, Khokhlov was at the Institute of Parapsychology presenting a paper called 'The Relationship of Parapsychology to Communism'. It was later published in Rhine's book *Parapsychology Today* (1968). Professor Rhine asked Khokhlov to stay and work on his staff at the laboratory, which would later become the Rhine Research Centre, once Khokhlov had earned his doctorate, but Nikolai declined and moved to California. In June 1968, Sheila Ostrander, a Canadian, and Lynn Schroeder, an American, were for whatever unexplained reason invited to Moscow to attend an international conference on certain specific aspects of parapsychology. They later published a book called *Psychic Discoveries Behind the Iron Curtain* (Prentice-Hall, 1970) about the astounding breakthroughs in psychic research in the Communist Bloc countries. Then the topic again attracted great professional attention of, among others, the CIA and DIA.

From the book, specialists learned of an astonishing Soviet development – the ability to control behaviour and consciousness telepathically. The first experiments dated back to the early 1920s when Dr Bernard B. Karzynski (often transliterated from Russian as 'Kazhinsky') published his first book in Moscow entitled *Thought Transmission* (1923), introducing his idea of the 'brain radio', by which he meant telepathy.

In 1973, a former US astronaut Edgar Mitchell together with investor Paul N. Temple founded the Institute of Noetic Sciences (IONS) in California, officially a non-profit parapsychological research establishment. The institute focuses on such topics as spontaneous remission – an unexpected improvement or cure from a normally fatal disease such as cancer; meditation; psychokinesis, which is a synonym to telekinesis, and the survival of consciousness after bodily death. Interestingly, Khokhlov seems not to have been associated with this institute in any way, which is hard to believe but at the same time possible if he belonged to a different school, because noetic science has always had its champions, but also critics. The latter stress that there have been no independent, double-blind experiments that support the main thesis that mind can move matter. Some aspects of the institute's work were described in Dan Brown's bestseller *The Lost Symbol* (2009), where one of the protagonists, Katherine Solomon, notes that human thought, if properly focused, has the ability 'to affect and change physical mass', which is more or less consistent with experiments conducted in Czechoslovakia.

In September 1975, the US Army Medical Intelligence and Information Agency prepared a confidential paper for the Defense Intelligence Agency (DIA) called 'Soviet and Czechoslovakian Parapsychology Research', which described some aspects of psychotronic research and, specifically, psychotronic generators (also called Pavlita generators after the inventor, Robert Pavlita). It was based on a concept of a man as a source of unusual energy, known for a long time as 'vital energy' or 'prana'. In contemporary Soviet and Czechoslovakian parapsychology, the paper said, this energy is called bio-plasmic or psychotronic energy. A recent newspaper article, quoting Pavlita, reported that his generators could serve as weapons. No details were given. But when flies were placed in the gap of a circular generator, they died instantly. In another test, the paper continued, Pavlita, who was demonstrating his generators to visitors at home, aimed it at his daughter from a distance of several yards. Her electroencephalogram changed, she became dizzy, and her equilibrium was disrupted. The document further stated:

Both Czech and US researchers have described Robert Pavlita's work with psychotronic generators as possibly the most important contemporary development in the field of parapsychology and as a major contribution to the deeper understanding, mastery, and utilization of biological energy for human advantage. Just as in the example of direct transfer of biological energy for medical purposes, the use of such devices is not necessarily intended to be beneficial. If Pavlita's devices can kill insects at present, their potential in the future after refinement and enlargement may well be for killing men. If bioenergy can be reliably controlled and focused by such devices, death could be caused by disruption of fundamental brain rhythms, heart control, or biological clock mechanism.

A year later, in 1976, Dr Khokhlov was secretly hired by the CIA again, this time to uncover psychic research going on in his former homeland. By whatever means, he found evidence based, it is worth noting, on second-hand sources, of over twenty well-funded laboratories working on psychotronic devices for military use. In an exclusive interview in September 2015, former major general Boris Ratnikov from the KGB's Ninth Directorate (later FSO, Federal Guard Service), confirmed there were indeed such R&D centres in Kiev, St Petersburg, Moscow, Novosibirsk, Minsk, Rostov-on-the Don, Almaty/Alma-Ata, Nizhny Novgorod, Perm and Yekaterinburg.

Khokhlov described one such laboratory in Moscow, which, he reported, mass-produced psychotronic generators that were tested on prisoners. Telekinesis was also used on prisoners, he claimed, to paralyse sections of their spinal cord by damaging the nerve cells with a telekinetic blast. In 1990, this information was corroborated by Oleg Kalugin, another former KGB general, who claimed that the KGB chairman and future Soviet leader Yuri Andropov gave orders to move full speed ahead with psi warfare in the early 1970s and obtained funding of 500 million rubles. At the time, the official exchange rate was one to three, so that's roughly 1.5 billion dollars. Khohklov's intelligence was further corroborated three years later by Igor Vinokurov and Georgy Gurtovoy in their book, *Psychotronic Warfare* (1993), published in Moscow.

In 1978, the USA launched its own psi program, which, like VENONA, had many codenames but finally became known as the STARGATE project. The DIA and a private contractor in California established a secret US Army unit at Fort Meade, Maryland, to investigate the potential for psychic phenomena in military applications. The project primarily concentrated on remote viewing, or the purported ability to mentally 'see' sites from a great distance. It was terminated in 1995 after a CIA report concluded that it could not be useful or reliable and that nothing other than reasonable guessing and subjective validation were operating. A later report by the American Institutes for Research, a non-profit organisation based in Washington, DC, concluded that 'remote viewings have never provided an adequate basis for "actionable" intelligence operations'.

This, however, should be considered carefully. As one professional reviewer has put it, in all cases support for the programme is personality-dependent, which means that when high-level officials supported the use of psychics, programmes flourished. But under opponents, they died. John Alexander, who reviewed the book *ESP Wars East & West* (2014) written by a group of experts, notes that one of the important participants of the STARGATE program, Joe McMoneagle, once described to him the work environment saying that virtually every day was 'like being in a knife fight in a phone booth'.

'One key difference in psi research effort between the US and the Soviet Union,' Alexander writes, 'was their [Soviet] emphasis on the development of psychotronic weapons. These were hardware systems designed to influence or control minds and possibly adversely affect the target's health. It was hypothesized that the victim could be driven to suicide or accidental death.' General Ratnikov, allegedly referring to a secret KGB file that, of course, cannot be independently verified, reported: 'The principle of remote exposure of humans to a psychotronic generator is based on the resonance of frequency characteristics of human organs – the heart, kidneys, liver, and brain. Each human organ has its own frequency characteristic. And if the same frequency is beamed at it by means of electromagnetic radiation, the organ enters into resonance, and the result is either acute cardiac insufficiency, renal insufficiency, or a person starts to behave inadequately. As a rule, those microwaves hit the most weakened organs that, for whatever reason, do not function properly. In some cases, a fatal outcome may also occur.' Having read this, I started thinking about the Berezovsky and Perepilichny cases.

The most interesting publications on a great variety of subjects – including psychotronic weapons and other electromagnetic (EM) weapons that interact with the nervous system of the target, extrasensory perception (ESP) and mind-control techniques – can be found in the period between the collapse of the Soviet Union in 1991 and the next five years, before the new KGB came to power again in Russia. Thus, for example, in early 1993, the newspaper of the US Army, *Defense News*, and numerous other print media reported that one former KGB general George Kotov, at the time serving in a senior government ministry post, told American visitors about Russian research into 'acoustic psycho-correction'. The process allegedly involved transmitting commands into the subconscious through static or white-noise bands. The Russians proposed a bilateral centre to safeguard mind-control techniques where US and Russian authorities could monitor and restrict the emerging capabilities. In reality, that meant the Russians wanted to continue their research and development programme using American money.

Janet Morris, then project director at US Global Strategy Council, a Washington-based think tank established by former CIA deputy director Ray Cline, was a key liaison between Russian and US officials. She contended that the mind-control capability had been demonstrated in the laboratory in Russia and should be placed under international restrictions at the earliest possible opportunity. It seems the CIA and DIA showed no interest, being rather sceptical about its potential battlefield use, so nothing came out of it. However, an article that appeared in the *Daily Mail* on 1 April 2012 (by coincidence, All Fools' Day), mentioned 'zombie' guns that can affect brain cells, alter psychological states, make it possible to transmit suggestions and commands into someone's thought processes, damage the functioning of internal organs, control behaviour or even drive victims to suicide. In March 2013, Boris Berezovsky was found hanged in Sunninghill, England, at his ex-wife's Berkshire mansion. Cause of death: undetermined – maybe suicide, maybe murder…

Back in late November 2006, we were having a drink with Ben Macintyre of *The Times*, who would later become a bestselling writer, in the bar at the Connaught, and I told him the thallium story of Khokhlov's poisoning. Ben promptly found Nikolai and published a lengthy article in his newspaper about the man who KGB poisoned with a radioactive substance but who lived to tell the tale. He even dug up a rare old photo of Khokhlov, taken at a London airport in 1954, from his newspaper's archives.

Steve LeVine read the article and got his chance. In June 2007, after months of telephone and email exchanges, he went to San Bernardino to meet Khokhlov. A year later Steve published his book *Putin's Labyrinth*.

As expected, the KGB veteran turned professor of psychology told Steve a lot of tales that, alas, had nothing to do with what really happened. Old habits die hard. But Steve has a talent of understanding people, a rare gift. He quickly realised that the figure in front of him was extremely sensitive, complex, and difficult, who felt misunderstood by almost everyone. Besides, the journalist found Khokhlov a deeply emotional and sometimes self-pitying man who didn't always own up to his embellishments.

Steve, however, describes his new acquaintance as: 'most often being extremely polite and possessed of a self-effacing sense of humour. He had a coughing fit at one point and his wife asked if he needed anything. "Yes, a new throat," he replied.'

Discussing the Litvinenko case with his guest, Khokhlov was sure that the successor agencies to his former department had carried out the notorious murder in London. For Steve LeVine, Nikolai and Sasha thus shared an unusual distinction. They were the only known victims of radioactive poisoning in the entire history of assassinations worldwide. But Steve, with whom we had established quite friendly relations and regularly communicated during all those ten years, was wrong. I have rechecked it again and it is highly improbable that Khokhlov was poisoned by a radioactive or, as he had put it, radio-activated substance. Had that been the case, he would have never survived. Nikolai Khokhlov succumbed to a heart attack in September 2007, aged 85.

The very last time Khokhlov was mentioned in the media was in an article by Andy Wright in *Atlas Obscura*, published in January 2017 and entitled 'The Russian Spy Who Convinced America to Take ESP Seriously'. I am not sure he really did it, but he had certainly made his contribution.

Chapter 7

From Russia with a Poison Gun

Exactly one year to the day after Sasha Litvinenko was poisoned, Oleg Gordievsky, a former high-value British asset who was once acting KGB station head in London, told his dedicated AR (Agent Resettlement) officer Keith that he had also been poisoned by the Russians – exactly like Litvinenko. Gordievsky did not only repeat that to his MI6 handlers personally, who at the time were no less than Sir John Scarlett and his head of the Russian desk Christopher Steele, but also to Lord Butler (Robin Butler, Baron Butler of Brockwell, former Principal Private Secretary to Margaret Thatcher, who in 2004 chaired the Review of Intelligence on Iraq's weapons of mass destruction). As usual, British journalist Tom Mangold was probably the first to hear the news about Gordievsky's poisoning. And while Tom contacted Oleg to get from him every precious detail of the story, his colleague Jason Lewis, then security editor for *The Mail on Sunday*, dialled my mobile phone number asking for an urgent interview. He caught me shopping in Waitrose, minutes away from Gordievsky's house up the hill. For those who do not know – this excellent supermarket chain originated from the partnership of Wallace Waite and Arthur Rose (hence 'Waitrose'), formed in 1908.

I first came to England in January 1989 and settled in a private country club in Barnet that seems not to exist any more. It was a very warm January, about 15°C or more, and I loved London at first sight. My dream had always been to move here but I was only able to do it years later when the Litvinenko story was in every newspaper. I had rented a small semi-detached house in the wonderful market town of Godalming, Surrey, and plunged headlong into the Litvinenko case.

Two decades earlier, the message from General Hendrik van den Bergh – the legendary chief of the South African Bureau of State Security, the dreaded BOSS – transmitted through Mike Geldenhuys, one of his ablest officers, was rather laconic: 'Tell anyone who asks,' it read, 'that I can't remember about Loginov, and I don't want to remember. Tell them I do not suffer from verbal diarrhoea. We should stay out of this,' Mangold, an investigative journalist for BBC *Panorama* for 26 years, later recalled. Whether Tom had indeed received this message directly from the general or simply invented it, did not matter. What's important is that he recorded it in his book. Yuri Nikolayevich Loginov, alias 'Edmund Trinka', was a Soviet agent, an illegal, arrested in South Africa in 1967.

On 12 August 1961, several months after Loginov returned to Moscow following his first operational trip abroad, a telephone call reached an officer of the CIA Berlin Operations Base, better known as BOB. A German police duty officer informed the Americans that a man accompanied by a woman had turned himself in and was requesting contact with representatives of the US government. The officer acted strictly according to the appropriate paragraph of a secret document called the 'contractual agreement'. Signed in April 1955, the agreement defined the guidelines for the US intelligence agencies' activities on German soil. This call was the last twist in the crumbling intelligence career of a remorseless Soviet liquidator named Bogdan Nikolayevich Stashynsky, who was to become widely known as 'The Assassin' and recently, thanks to Serhii Plokhy, as 'The Man with the Poison Gun', a book that he published in 2017.

Stashynsky was a schoolteacher born on 4 November 1931 in Borshevitsy, a small place on the Polish border between Lviv, Western Ukraine, and Kraków, Poland. It is usually assumed, based on his later testimony, that one day, caught riding a train home from the school without a ticket, the police pitched him for service as an informant. From his recently declassified Ukrainian MGB-KGB files, however, it becomes clear that while he was still 19 years old, Stashynsky was arrested as a member of the OUN (Organisation of Ukrainian Nationalists, established in 1929), interrogated and 'turned'. Whether it was this way or another doesn't really matter, but soon Bogdan began snitching on his comrades as Agent OLEG of the Ukrainian Ministry for State Security, part of the short-lived KI (Committee of Information) that in November 1951 would be transformed into the MVD (Ministry for Internal Affairs, formerly known as the NKVD).

All those changes, however, did not affect his 'work' in any way and in the summer of 1951 Stashynsky was assigned to a secret police task force that employed strong-arm and sometimes bizarre tactics to round up the Ukrainian nationalist underground, with which Stashynsky family members were directly involved. During this time, the young agent successfully penetrated a local OUN cell and managed to identify an OUN militant Mykhailo Stakhur, who he knew as 'Stefan', as the murderer of the Ukrainian communist writer Yaroslav Galan, passing this young man's details to the Stalinist secret police. Other operational successes convinced his superiors that he might be ready for more important assignments.

In 1952, this good-looking and sufficiently smart 21-year-old Ukrainian was invited by the Ukrainian Ministry of State Security (MGB) – which, although only a republican organisation, was the second largest and most important Soviet intelligence and security organisation after Moscow – to start training for undercover work abroad. For the next two years Agent TARAS, Stashynsky's new operational pseudonym, went through the intensive course in tradecraft and foreign languages in Kiev. From the very beginning, it was planned that he would operate undercover in West Germany using various 'legends' and posing as 'Franz Müller' or 'Erich Johann'. It was also planned that he should be first sent to East Germany or Austria to study German.

On 15 January 1954, the acting chief of the 2nd department of the Ukrainian MVD, Lieutenant Colonel Tkachenko, sent a letter to Colonel Studnikov in Moscow explaining that TARAS had been successfully penetrated into the local OUN branch and reported about 30 of its members, some of whom were liquidated, some arrested and shot, others sentenced to various prison terms, and one recruited. Tkachenko also stated that because TARAS was living undercover in Kiev, posing as a student of the pedagogical institute, and was currently on holiday, it would make sense to summon him to Moscow to finally decide how he could be used in the future.

As usual, at that stage, his chiefs viewed Stashynsky as an agent-in-training, who during his schooling would serve as a courier or an occasional cut-out for some more important intelligence assets.

Regarding foreign languages, like all other Soviet illegals before and after him – take, for example, the Anschlag couple arrested in Germany in October 2011 – at the beginning, Stashynsky spoke German with an easily identifiable Slavic accent, explaining that he had come from Poland. (Andreas and Heidrun Anschlag had lived in Germany more than 20 years with Austrian passports but because of their accent, they pretended that they had come from Latin America.) At the end of 1954, documented as 'Josef Lehmann', Stashynsky was transferred to Berlin-Karlshorst, the official operations base of Soviet intelligence in Europe deliberately placed there as an opposite number to BOB (Berlin Operations Base of the CIA).

After the war, Berlin was at the heart of the intelligence battle between the United States and the Soviet bloc and actually between Western intelligence services and the KGB with its satellites. Lehmann then moved to Chemnitz, known as Karl-Marx-Stadt under Communist rule, where he got a job as a manual worker to adapt to life in the West and improve his German. At the beginning of 1956, Stashynsky/Lehmann returned to East Berlin, now employed as an interpreter by the East German Bureau of Internal and External Trade (Sowjetzonales Büro für Deutschen Innen- und

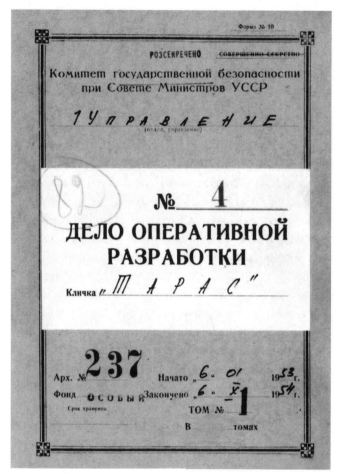

One of Stashinsky's KGB operational files on agent TARAS: Special Fund, vol. 1, file opened 6 January 1953, file closed 6 October 1954.

A Ukrainian KGB memo about paying a regular monthly fee to Stashinsky's father in Lviv, dated 6 September 1956.

Außenhandel). It was the job of the illegals section on the staff of the KGB representative at the East German State Security Ministry (MfS or Stasi) to place him there. The KGB compound known as military unit number 62504, at the time commanded by General Yevgeny Pitovranov, consisted of eleven buildings and was located in Karlshorst on Zwieseler Strasse. Until the fall of the now-infamous Berlin Wall, it housed several hundred Soviet intelligence personnel of the two main agencies, the KGB and GRU. Khokhlov was also stationed there for some time in 1952.

All this I did not know when I visited Karlshorst in 1989, but two years after Gorbachev's *perestroika*, the place was already half-empty, so rooms were easily available. By 1 September 1994, all personnel of the Soviet Army had been withdrawn to Russia. However, a few individuals stayed and among them was Lieutenant Dmitry Kovtun, then aged 28.

Back in the 1950s (as well as the 1960s and the 1970s), dating a foreigner was considered something extraordinary for a Soviet citizen. To do it secretly was out of the question because of a vast army of informers. That is if somebody was not a KGB agent or informer himself. In April, in the Tanz Casino located in the Friedrichstadtpalast in East Berlin Lehmann/Stashynsky met a 21-year-old hairdresser who introduced herself as Inge Pohl. She was German, lived in East Berlin, but worked in the American-dominated Western zone and was of common, sometimes sloppy appearance. As described by the media of the time, 'her hairdo was usually awry, intellectual interests limited, and her table manners wolf-like.'[1] He, in turn, was a charismatic young man backed by the Soviet government machine with a prestigious job in the foreign trade organisation. Nevertheless, for whatever reason, Stashynsky decided this simple girl was a good choice for him. As a safety measure, being aware of honey traps and other provocations from time to time set by both Soviet and Western secret services, he duly reported the contact but was assured the girl was 'clean'.

In January 1956, Stashynsky was summoned to a nondescript two-storey villa in Karlshorst, which was outside the compound, bound on the sides by Bodenmaiserweg, Zwieseler Strasse, Dewetallee and Arbertstrasse, where the main KGB residency was located. In a modestly furnished room on the first floor, he reported to Lieutenant Colonel Kovalenko from the 13th Department of the KGB's First Chief Directorate (Foreign Intelligence) – the successor of the 9th and 12th Departments – specialising in 'special tasks' or 'executive actions', such as sabotage, political murders and kidnappings.

---

[1] Steele, John L., 'Assassin Disarmed by Love: The Case of a Soviet Spy Who Defected to the West', *Life*, 7 September, 1962, 70–2, 77.

In Karlshorst, Kovalenko was Khokhlov's boss too. One of Kovalenko's men, Major Sergey Meshcheryakov, would become Stashynsky's case officer.

The first assignment given to Stashynsky in his new role was to travel to Munich and find a Ukrainian exile named Ivan Bisaga,[2] a Soviet agent and former aide-de-camp of the Ukrainian nationalist leader Roman Sushko. Sushko was the founder of the Ukrainian military organisation and later the Ukrainian Legion, who was assassinated in Lviv in January 1944. Bisaga managed to penetrate the Ukrainian émigré community in Bavaria and found a job on the staff of the anti-Soviet nationalist newspaper *Ukrainsky Samostiynik*, published in Germany and smuggled into Western Ukraine.

Bisaga (also known as Bysaga, Bissaga and Bysaha), who later returned to the Soviet Union and published his memoirs accusing former comrades-in-arms of internal squabbles and irreconcilable struggle of opposing factions of OUN leaders Melnyk and Bandera, was a small fish, but he regularly supplied his KGB controllers with valuable inside information. For several months Stashynsky's task was to secretly meet Bisaga, collect this information and pay for it. It was a typical cut-out job.

After at least five visits to Munich, during the next scheduled meeting with the agent in November 1956, Stashynsky asked Bisaga if he would be able to help in the planned abduction of Lev Rebet, an important political figure in the Bandera faction of the OUN, who was writing books and served as the editor of a number of anti-Soviet periodicals. Arrested by the Nazis in August 1941, Rebet had spent three years in the Sachsenhausen concentration camp. The idea of Stashynsky's KGB bosses was to bring Rebet to Kiev to face charges of extremism and anti-Soviet propaganda. Bisaga blankly refused because of the obvious risk for him. He also explained that in October he was questioned by the police on suspicion of anti-constitutional activities (*Verdacht nachrichtendienstlicher Tätigkeit*) – in other words, espionage. Shortly afterwards, Stashynsky brought him all the necessary documents securing Bisaga's free passage to the Soviet zone. Later, together with Vasil Galasa, Bisaga wrote his memoirs, filled with remorse and shame, *Za velinnyam sovisti*, which came out in Kiev in 1963.

---

[2] Ivan Bisaga, aka 'Nadiychin', 'Bard', 'Mikhail Babyak', was born in 1919 in Zakarpattia (Galicia), in south-western Ukraine. Joined the OUN and in 1939 immigrated to Slovakia and then Poland. Volunteered to the 14th SS-Division 'Galicia' when it was formed in 1943, serving in the secret section of its staff. After the war, Bisaga reportedly returned to Zakarpattia but in 1952 managed to flee to Austria and from there to West Germany. In some sources it is claimed that Bisaga was recruited by the CIA, but this information cannot be verified. From 1954, he was heading the local OUN organisation in Munich. Returned to the USSR in 1956. For his memoirs published in Soviet Ukraine, see the bibliography.

On a gloomy spring day in 1957, Stashynsky was summoned to a safe house in East Berlin where his case officer, Meshcheryakov, was waiting for him. The agent was informed that his new assignment would again be in Munich, but this time the plan to abduct Rebet had been abandoned. Instead, he was simply to 'liquidate' the nationalist leader or, plainly speaking, the Party entrusted him to 'trap the beast in his lair' and murder him.

At that time, Berlin Cathedral and the Reichstag were still in ruins and the whole Communist system did not look any better. In June 1953 the country had erupted in a series of riots and demonstrations that threatened the very existence of the regime. The uprising soon spread from Berlin to several hundred cities, towns and villages throughout East Germany and chants were heard calling for 'Death to Communism' and even 'Long Live Eisenhower'. In the words of Christian Ostermann, for the first time ever 'the "proletariat" had risen against the "dictatorship of the proletariat"'. Later, there were riots in Poland, and the then Soviet leader, Nikita Khrushchev, had to send in Soviet troops to help the pro-Moscow Polish government of Edward Ochab put them down. That, however, could not help the unpopular apparatchik, and Władysław Gomułka – the de facto leader of post-war Poland and a graduate of the International Lenin School in Moscow – became First Secretary (actually, head of state) of the governing United Workers' Party, also bringing several of his associates into the Politburo.

Following the example of the Polish workers, there were major riots in Hungary that started in October 1956 and were accumulating force until, on 4 November, Russian tanks rolled into Budapest killing several thousand people and restoring Soviet rule. Vladimir Kryuchkov, who masterminded the failed August 1991 coup d'état attempt against Michael Gorbachev, was stationed in Hungary at the time, assisting Ambassador Yuri Andropov in deceiving the Hungarian government about Soviet intentions until it was too late. Both Andropov and Kryuchkov were in some way involved in the suppression of the Hungarian Uprising in October–November 1956. Years after the collapse of the Soviet Union, with the benefit of hindsight, Christopher Andrew commented, 'Andropov remained haunted for the rest of his life by the speed with which an apparently all-powerful Communist one-party state had begun to topple.' A decade after the spontaneous uprising in Hungary was viciously crushed by Soviet tanks and troops, Andropov would not only become the KGB chairman, later ascending to the pinnacle of power in the Soviet Union as the General Secretary of the CPSU, but he would also make Kryuchkov head of Soviet foreign intelligence and later his own successor as the KGB chairman.

Khrushchev, the Soviet leader who had sent Soviet troops to Poland and, shortly after, to Hungary, was born in 1894 in a small village on the Russian side of what was then the symbolic border between Russia and Ukraine. In spite of his recorded Russian pedigree, for his whole life Khrushchev remained a Ukrainian to the tips of his shoes and most of all was troubled by the Ukrainian opposition in and outside the country, with its vigorous underground movement directed from West Germany by Western intelligence services, primarily the CIA and MI6. After the Khohklov operation rolled up, other candidates were sought for the 'special tasks' (meaning liquidations). One of those selected for the role of hitman was a German criminal, Wolfgang Wildprett, who was hired to assassinate Vladimir Poremsky, the chairman of the NTS and an ardent Soviet critic.

Poremsky was one of the founders and active members of the NTS, the People's Labour Union of Russian Solidarists, which he had headed for 18 years. From 1928, he lived and worked in Paris, from 1939 to 1941, as a researcher at the Institute of Applied Chemistry. After his election as the chairman of the NTS in January 1955, Poremsky had been very active in this movement. His last keynote address to the NTS activists took place in Moscow in December 1995.

When the war broke out, Poremsky and other leading members of the NTS executive council, including Georgi Okolovich and Alexander Trushnovich, all three with academic degrees, 'rallied to the Nazi course with a secret agenda to make themselves the new rulers of a puppet state inside the Nazi-occupied zone of the USSR', as Stephen Dorril wrote in his famous book about MI6 special operations. 'The NTS became an integral part of the Nazi propaganda, espionage and extermination apparatus in the East. Vladimir Poremsky was appointed director of education at an OMi school where he reported to the Gestapo on émigré "suspects". As head of a political department of the counterintelligence known as "Ingwar", Georgi Okolovich was responsible for combating the partisan movement in Byelorussia and in locating Jews who had escaped the mass shootings.'[3] After the war, several senior NTS leaders, who might have been tried as Nazi collaborators, avoided prosecution thanks to American protection. Only Dr Poremsky – 'a 200% Nazi' – was imprisoned as a war criminal but was released in 1946 following the intervention of MI6, because he managed to contact his former British intelligence sponsors before the final defeat of Germany. According to Stephen Dorril:

---

[3] Stephen Doril, *MI6: Inside the Covert World of Her Majesty's Secret Intelligence Service* (New York: Free Press, 2000), 409.

The Principal NTS Council members were the president and spiritual leader, Dr Poremsky; Georgi Okolovich, controller of secret operations, who worked for the Gehlen Org; Roman Redlich, Okolovich's deputy; Evgeny Romanov, liaison officer with MI6 and the CIA; Mikhail Olskej [*sic*, Olskiy], in charge of the internal security service and operations against other émigré groups such as the Ukrainian OUN-B[andera]; and an MI6 agent, Lev Rar, Director of the Foreign Organisations Branch (UZU). Working for the Nazis, Rar had been given a post at the Secretariat of the Vlasov Committee. After the surrender of Germany, he was held in the Fussen PoW camp and later moved to Britain, where he worked for the BBC.[4]

The Soviets certainly had some accounts to settle with them.

On 24 December 1955, Wildprett, a German criminal, flew to Frankfurt using a doctored document identifying him as 'Wolfgang Weber'. Exactly like Khokhlov before him, he had a pistol, a Walther PPK cal. 7.65 mm, a photo of Dr Poremsky, 500 West German marks in cash and an order to liquidate his victim. Like Khoklov, Wildprett had second thoughts and decided not to go ahead with the murder. However, he decided not to visit Poremsky at home but simply called him by phone, explaining what he had been ordered to do. On 29 December, Wildprett was apprehended by the Americans. It is a rather rare and unusual case in which the KGB, as it became known from March 1954, decided to use a common criminal to carry out a political murder for them. But they did.

Wolfgang Wildprett was born in Berlin in September 1929. He had already been arrested by the German police several times for burglary, fraud and embezzlement of funds when, shortly after the war, he met Herschel 'Henry' Liebermann in Paris. They soon met again in a Berlin prison, where Wildprett was serving a term for burglary and Lieberman for counterfeiting. In May 1954, Liebermann invited Wildprett to a café on Alexanderplatz in East Berlin and, knowing his circumstances, suggested he should start working for Soviet intelligence. For about a year Wildprett ran minor errands, receiving small cash payments. Then, in November 1955, Liebermann approached him again.

'What can you do for money, Wil?' Liebermann asked.

'For money, Henry, I can do anything.'

'Okay, then it is going to be 20k West German Marks and that's a bargain. You do away with somebody in Frankfurt, agreed?'

Then Wildprett was escorted to a cellar in Schlegelstrasse in East Berlin, not far from Nordbahnhof, where he was given a chance to test-shoot the

_____
[4] Ibid, 421.

Walther pistol. In a few days, with a forged document, he was already in Frankfurt am Main.

After several days and nights in Frankfurt's red-light district, Wildprett changed his mind and decided not to go ahead with the murder. 'So, he didn't kill me,' Poremsky later said, adding, 'I like Wildprett, and I still see him sometimes. In fact, I went to his wedding.'

While Stashynsky was sent to Munich to start a long surveillance routine establishing patterns of Rebet's movements and noting down his work schedule, a special KGB laboratory in Moscow was given orders to produce a new silenced weapon. As usual, the idea was that even after an autopsy the death of the victim should be attributed to natural causes. Though only 45, Rebet could not boast good health as, during the war, he had been interned by the Nazis in Sachsenhausen's infamous Zellenbau isolation cells (where four SOE agents were also held prisoner before being executed in 1945). This gloomy place in Oranienburg was primarily used for political prisoners.

In 1956, Rebet (who seven years before completed his doctoral dissertation) published his fundamental work *The Theory of Nations*. By the time Stashynsky started to shadow him in Munich, he was busy doing research in law, politics and sociology, also contributing articles to the Ukrainian émigré newspapers that were smuggled to the Soviet Union. The KGB considered Rebet an important theorist and ideologue of the OUN, a hated and feared opposition force. Rebet was also a one-time leader of the Ukrainian government in exile.

By the autumn of 1957, Stashynsky knew all that he needed to know about his man. At the same time, KGB scientists and engineers had developed a new weapon – the special technology laboratory modified their earlier model of a silenced tube gun into a poison gas gun while the chemical laboratory came up with the poison – hydrogen cyanide (HCN). When inhaled, it causes what is called 'chemical asphyxia', that is, immediate unconsciousness, convulsions and almost instantaneous death, ideally imitating myocardial infarction, commonly known as a heart attack.

The gas-firing gun was to be hidden in a rolled-up newspaper. When used against a target, the firing lever activated a firing pin, which detonated a percussion yap, rupturing an ampoule of acid. The acid evaporated into HCN and was propelled out of a small hole in the muzzle. The gun was just 7 inches (18 cm) long. The disadvantage was that it had to be fired directly into the victim's face.

In a short introduction to the *Life* article 'Assassin Disarmed by Love' by John L. Steele, reproduced in his book as a separate chapter, Allen Welsh Dulles, the first civilian director of central intelligence (February 1953– November 1961), wrote:

The Soviets had obviously tried to drill any human sensibilities out of Stashinsky for years, using a kind of Pavlovian deconditioning and hardening scheme in order to turn him into a perfectly functioning robot-murderer. To equip the human monstrosity, they hoped to create they also had invented new murder weapons whose use was clearly and solely for assassination purposes.[5]

Stashynsky's instruction was that after the hit he should clear the Munich area at once. He never told anybody about a support team and, when later giving evidence to the police, he presented the operation as an exclusively one-person show. In the KGB practise, however, there would have been a courier who secretly brought the gun for the killer or a diplomatic bag, somebody to watch the scene to be sure all was done properly and according to the plan, and another to evacuate the liquidator in case of an unexpected problem. This second role was assigned to the experienced officer of the Ukrainian KGB Alexander Svyatogorov.[6] It seems that Stashynsky decided not to betray his accomplices. The human element. Always the human element. And a little caution.

As part of the operation against Rebet, Stashynsky visited Munich three times – in April, May and July 1957. During those visits, he used a doctored German passport in the name of 'Siegfried Dräger' from Essen. Not to be caught unaware in case somebody asked him, he was sent to Essen to study his new 'legend' and familiarise himself with the place. Back in Munich, he booked a room in a hotel vis-à-vis the offices of *Ukrainsky Samostiynik* where Rebet was employed as editor-in-chief. From this room it was very convenient to watch all the movements of the target. Stashynsky noted that from time to time Rebet left the building and travelled to another address in the city centre where the editorial office of yet another Ukrainian émigré newspaper, *Suchasna Ukraina*, rented space. The assassin was quick enough to grasp the opportunity, as this second address seemed ideal for the hit

---

[5] Allen Dulles (ed.), *Great True Spy Stories* (London: Robson Books, 1984), 210.

[6] Lieutenant Colonel Alexander Panteleymonovich Svyatogorov (December 1913–June 2008) joined the NKVD in 1939. He took part in many executive actions, among others, the assassination of the German Colonel Georg Braun in Kharkiv (on 14 November 1941, Braun was blown up with several officers and NCOs of his unit); the assassination of the chief of the Lublin Gestapo Sturmbannführer SS Akkardt in 1944; and the kidnapping of the Abwehr officer Walter Feilenhauer – in both hits he acted with Anatoly Kovalenko, who later instructed Stashinsky in Karlshorst. After the war, Svyatogorov took part in several operations in West Germany, Austria and Czechoslovakia. He was sent to East Germany in 1956, remaining there until August 1961, when he was urgently dispatched to West Berlin to find and kill Stashynsky immediately after the latter's defection.

because Karlsplatz, where it was located, lies directly opposite the Main Railway Station of the Bavarian capital. Just in case, Stashynsky also followed Rebet to his home, not far from the Englisher Garten ('English Gardens'), a large public park stretching from the city centre far to its north-eastern quarters, where Radio Free Europe and later Radio Liberty (they merged in 1976) were headquartered from 1949 to 1995. His mission accomplished, Stashynsky returned to East Berlin and from there took an overnight train to Kiev to spend the holidays with his parents.

Several weeks later, on 12 October 1957, Stashynsky was waiting for his victim near the offices of the *Suchasna Ukraina* on Karlsplatz, a large square known as Stachus among the locals. The assassin entered the building just ahead of Rebet and started climbing the staircase. When he heard someone opening the door and getting into the small entrance hall, he turned and started to slowly descend, holding the gun rolled in a newspaper, as instructed, in his hand. He kept to the right of the staircase, allowing his victim – and he was sure it was Rebet, who he'd met before – to pass on his left. When they were on the same level, Stashynsky fired, ejecting the poison gas directly into the victim's face while continuing to go down, at the same time turning his head away. Before he left the building, he heard Rebet stumble but did not look back. At the door, he crushed the ampoule containing an antipoison that he had been given in Karlshorst and inhaled its contents. Seemingly unmoved, he left the crime scene, drowned the gun in a canal near the Hofgarten, a beautiful historical garden in the centre of Munich, and returned to the hotel. There, he burnt his Lehmann document and checked out, signing as 'Dräger'. Soon he was at the Hauptbahnhof and boarding the train for Frankfurt/Main. As it was too late for a return flight, he spent a night in a hotel and the following morning a Pan Am aeroplane with Stashynsky on board landed in Berlin-Tempelhof. Taking a taxi, he raced along the Kurfürstendamm and in twenty minutes was at the barrier leading through Checkpoint Charlie into East Berlin.

I crossed this border many times and was always surprised at the shocking difference between the two worlds. East Berlin, with its vast broad avenues, was always gloomy, with the sky full of dark, greyish clouds. It was often windy there and somewhat cool, while West Berlin just around the corner from the Friedrichstrasse border crossing and, especially in Ku'damm, was warm, sunny, full of life and wonderful scents.

I was there in the early morning of 9 November 1989, when the 28-mile (45 km) wall dividing Germany's capital came down – if not physically on that very day, but certainly symbolically. It so happened that I was standing alone in the middle of the Checkpoint Charlie crossing with large crowds waiting on the Western and Eastern sides. The feeling in the air was electric, as if some great force had been let loose. People were standing in anticipation of the miracle and, as Frederick Forsyth has put it, the problems of the future were still too far off to contemplate, had anyone wished, which they did not.

All that, however, happened three decades after Stashynsky was there, returning to his base in Karlshorst after the first 'hit'. At about that time, in the early 1960s, Forsyth was also in Germany, officially accredited as the Reuters correspondent in East Berlin. As he recalls in *The Outsider*, the book he considers his autobiography:

> The checkpoint was in the American sector of the four-power-divided city and in their glass booth the GIs were bowed over their radio [listening to the news]. You could have driven a herd of buffalo past them and they would not have noticed. The American barrier was up as always ... The East German border guards were the hardest of the hard and politically proof-tested before they got the posting. If needed, they would machine-gun anyone trying to climb the Wall to escape to the West.

According to Stashynsky's testimony, back in Karlshorst he reported to his case officer, who immediately informed the chief of the illegals section, Colonel Nikolai Gorshkov.[7] The latter reported to General Korotkov and after his approval sent a coded message to Moscow, informing Lubyanka that 'TARAS met in Munich a known individual, greeted him properly and everything turned out very well'. As already mentioned, TARAS was Stashynsky's codename.

After the post mortem was completed, the pathologist reported the cause of death as 'Eine hochgradige Atheromatose (Entzündung und Aufweichung) der Coronararterien mit weitestgehender Einengung der Lichtung des rechten umschlingenden Astes 5 cm nach der Abgangsstelle', in short, a well-progressed atheromatous disease resulting in atherosclerosis and causing the heart attack. Conclusion: no evidence of a violent death ('keine Anhalzspunkte für einen gewaltsamen Tod'), that is, Dr Rebet must have died from natural causes, according to the doctors. So far, so good.

This was, of course, not the first KGB murder of a Ukrainian opposition leader abroad. In May 1938, Pavel Sudoplatov, himself a Ukrainian,

---

[7] At the beginning of the war, Nikolai Mikhailovich Gorshkov was in charge of sending German and Austrian communists, selected and trained by the NKVD, behind German lines in collaboration with MI6. In 1943–4 he served as the NKGB resident in Algiers, Algeria, where he recruited a valuable source close to General Charles de Gaulle. In 1944–50, he was posted to Rome, and in 1954–5, to Bern. From 1957 to 1959, he headed the illegals section at the KGB base in Karlshorst. Colonel Gorshkov used the codename MARTYN.

assassinated Yevhen Konovalets, who a decade before took part in the first congress of Ukrainian nationalists in Vienna, where it was decided to form the Organisation of Ukrainian Nationalists (OUN). Konovalets was elected its chairman. Sudoplatov, at the time a little pawn in Stalin's terror machine, had been masquerading as a courier from the Ukrainian nationalist underground in the USSR for two years, establishing his bona fides with the émigrés. Konovalets met him alone in a restaurant in Rotterdam where Sudoplatov presented him with a box of chocolates and, after a short discussion, arranged to meet again later. Shortly after he left the premises, the bomb exploded killing Konovalets. As a result, Sudoplatov was promoted to head the Special Tasks group of the NKVD-MGB (predecessors of the KGB), which later became the 13th Department of the KGB, responsible for abductions and assassinations abroad. One day, Sudoplatov was summoned to the Kremlin and ordered to 'liquidate' Stepan Bandera, who became a symbol of the Ukrainian struggle for independence replacing Konovalets as the leader of the OUN.

From about that period, Stephen Dorril writes in his book, MI6 patronised Bandera's faction. Before the war, several individual members of OUN were recruited by the MI6 head of station in Finland, Harry Carr and his staff, and used as a network of informants inside the Soviet Union. Dorril, whose book was not well received at Vauxhall Cross, further notes that 'Carr, who was attracted by Bandera's brand of anti-communism, soon began to deliver funding and support for operations to infiltrate agents across the Finnish-Soviet border ... Andrei Melnyk, Richard Iarii and Colonel Roman Sushko, who was head of the OUN military organisation, continued to develop close ties with the Abwehr and opened an "excellent communications" channel to Admiral Canaris.'[8]

According to another source, MI6 first contacted Bandera through Gerhard von Mende, an ethnic German from Riga, in April 1948. However, nothing came of initial British approaches because, as the CIA learned later, 'the political, financial, and tech requirements of the [Ukrainians] were higher than the British cared to meet'. 'But by 1949,' Richard Breitman and Norman Goda note, basing their opinion on the NARA files, 'MI6 began helping Bandera send his own agents into western Ukraine via airdrop. In 1950 MI6 began training these agents on the expectation that they could provide intelligence from Western Ukraine.' And while the CIA flatly opposed to use Bandera and his people in their anti-Soviet operations and in April 1951 even tried to convince MI6 to pull support from him, MI6 refused, thinking that the CIA underestimated Bandera's importance. 'Bandera's

---

[8] Dorril, *MI6*, 224.

name,' they said, 'still carried considerable weight in Ukraine and … the UPA [Ukrainian Insurgent Army] would look to him first and foremost.' Moreover, MI6 considered Bandera's group to be 'the strongest Ukrainian organisation abroad'.[9]

Before the war, Bandera, who quickly became a popular nationalist leader, headed what was known as OUN-B, an aggressive militant 'revolutionary' faction of OUN as opposed to OUN-M under Andriy Melnyk, preaching a more conservative approach. In the spring of 1941, as claimed in the documents published by the Ukrainian Academy of Science, Bandera had a series of meetings with high-ranking representatives of German intelligence and his OUN faction received 2.5 million Reichsmarks for subversive activities inside the USSR. However, according to CIA records, the Gestapo invited Bandera for a conference, which apparently was a ruse to arrest him. He was detained in September 1941 and released, with his second-in-command, Yaroslav Stetsko, in late September or early October 1944, having spent this time first in the Prinz Albrechtstrasse Gestapo jail in Berlin and later in Sachsenhausen concentration camp. 'There is no information in the Directorate of Operations files,' a CIA document states, 'that he was ever involved in Nazi war crimes.' Regarding the absurd Soviet claim that Bandera had been 'Hitler's professional spy', the CIA categorically denies it, stressing that 'this claim was never substantiated'.[10] After the war, the Soviet authorities quickly learned that Bandera and Melnyk (who had found refuge in Switzerland while Yaroslav Stetsko escaped to Austria) had been actively collaborating with Western intelligence services and were once again organising an anti-Soviet underground movement in Ukraine.

First, in June 1946, what is known today as a Special Mission Unit (probably a small SMERSH group) secretly entered the US Zone to kidnap Bandera. Later, an attempt was made to obtain Bandera and Stetsko's extradition, but all Soviet efforts were to no avail. Bandera's daughter later recalled that the family was 'constantly obliged to flee from one place to another to avoid discovery'. They had moved from Berlin to Innsbruck and from there to the popular holiday resort of Seefeld in Tyrol before finally settling in Munich.

---

[9] Richard Breitman and Norman J.W. Goda, *Hitler's Shadow: Nazi War Criminals, US Intelligence, and the Cold War* (Washington, DC: The National Archives, 2012), 81–2.

[10] NARA, RG 263, Box 6, Folder 4, 'Stefan Bandera', 4, 292 and 293. According to the CIA files, a breakdown of Bandera's official titles would run something as follows: 1932-39 – chief of the homeland executive of OUN; 1939-43 – Providnik (leader) of OUN and chairman of the Provid; 1943–45 – unofficially Providnik; 1945–51 – Providnik of the foreign element of OUN (ZCh), ibid, 288. From 1951 and until his death in October 1959, Bandera served as OUN's Honourable Chairman.

The Soviet delegation at the United Nations Assembly charged that Bandera and Melnyk were running special schools to train undercover agents in sabotage and espionage work against the USSR. It must be added that the Russians never provided any details or documentary evidence to their claims.

While some in the CIA thought that the best solution would be the 'political neutralisation of Bandera as an individual',[11] British operations through Bandera expanded. An early 1954 MI6 summary noted: 'the operational aspect of this collaboration [with Bandera] was developing satisfactorily. Gradually more complete control was obtained over infiltration operations and although the intelligence dividend was low, it was considered worthwhile to proceed ...' Bandera was, according to his handlers' estimates, 'a professional underground worker with a terrorist background and ruthless notions about the rules of the game ... A bandit type if you like, with a burning patriotism, which provides an ethical background and a justification for his banditry. No better and no worse than others of his kind.' In the meantime, in Soviet Ukraine the words 'Bandera' and 'banditry' became synonyms.

Soon after Stalin's death in March 1953, General Sudoplatov and his friend and deputy General Eitingon were arrested and sentenced to long terms in prison, but Stalin's ambitions to destroy any actual or potential threat to the Soviet regime, even abroad, survived. In May, the executive action component of the MGB, Bureau No. 1, for carrying out sabotage, political murders and kidnappings became the 9th Department and, with the establishment of the KGB in March 1954, was redesignated as the 12th and then 13th Department. Now there were new people to carry out Kremlin's 'order to murder'. And because Stalin's successor, Nikita Khrushchev, represented the strong Ukrainian faction in the Politburo and the Central Committee, all Ukrainian affairs were given an absolute priority. The Karlshorst base was instructed to assist the Ukrainian KGB and, following his success in liquidating Rebet, Stashynsky was entrusted with a new murderous mission.

In May 1958, Sergey Meshcheryakov, Stashynsky's case officer in the illegals section in Karlshorst, summoned Stashynsky to inform him about a new assignment. This time it was to travel to Rotterdam to attend a memorial ceremony marking the 20th anniversary of the death of Colonel Konovalets. It is necessary, instructed Sergey, to photograph everybody who would be there as well as the grave itself. He did not explain why he needed all this and Stashynsky did not ask. Naturally, at the cemetery on 23 May he was not able to photograph anybody (our photo comes from another source),

---

[11] CIA/State Department – SIS/Foreign Office Talks on Operations Against the USSR, 23 April 1951, NARA, RG 263, E ZZ-19, B 9, Aerodynamic: Operations, v. 9, f. 2.

but he remembered the main speaker of the oration and managed to take a picture of his vehicle, an elegant dark-blue Opel Kapitän with the Munich registration plates M-DA 105. Without giving it a second thought, he relayed this information to Sergey and forgot about it. He was young, free, had some money to spend and would rather enjoy the company of his German girlfriend, Inge. Their regular dating continued until the autumn, when Sergey asked Stashynsky to go to West Berlin and buy a book or books written by one 'Stefan Popel', an obvious pseudonym meaning 'an outrageous guy'. The young man thought nothing of it and duly went to the Hugendubel bookshop in Tauentzienstrasse and checked their catalogue. The family business, founded in 1893, was as always happy to serve and quickly found the book, *Einführung in Schach*, which Stashynsky bought and brought to Sergey, who was genuinely surprised but did not show it.

As it sometimes, but not too often, happens in such cases, there was an amazing coincidence leading to confusion. Stefan Popel, the author of the book, was a real person who was born in 1907 in the former Austro-Hungarian empire and grew up in Lemberg, now Lviv, Western Ukraine. There, Popel studied foreign languages and, following in the footsteps of his uncle, chess master Ignatz von Popiel (the Polish spelling of the name), began to play chess, quickly rising to one of the most prolific and successful chess players of his time. In September 1939, Popel moved to Kraków and, in late August 1944, to the liberated Paris. During the next ten years, he took part in 18 international chess championships winning most of them. In 1956, Stefan Popel and his wife Valentina immigrated to the USA, and that was definitely not the person the KGB had been looking for.

The man the Ukrainian KGB was eager to find was born in Galicia, Austria-Hungary, in 1909 and also received his higher education in Lemberg. He later settled in Kraków, but in July 1941, shortly before Nazi troops attacked the Soviet Union, was detained in Berlin and only released under a written undertaking not to leave the city. His first name was Stepan although he often introduced himself as 'Stefan'. Both names derive from the Greek Stephanos meaning 'a crown' or 'a garland'. His German documents identified him as 'Stefan Popel', but his real name was Bandera, Stepan Andriyovych Bandera.

Bandera did not like the Soviets, Poles and Germans and they reciprocated. Bandera's father was arrested by the NKVD in May 1941 and shot. His sisters were also arrested and sent to the Gulag in Siberia. Bandera's brothers, both academics, were captured by the Germans and interned in the horror concentration camp Auschwitz, where they were killed by Polish inmates in 1942. As already mentioned, Bandera and other leading OUN members were arrested by the Gestapo on 15 September 1941. Released in October 1944, he established the OUN headquarters in Berlin, but when asked to help fight 'the enemies of the Reich', he refused to collaborate with the RSHA (ReichsSicherheitsHauptAmt), Nazi Germany's Main Security Directorate. By then, Bandera knew full well that Germany was going to lose the war. For a while he was in hiding, but after the war settled in Munich. There Bandera lived using the 'Stefan Popel' alias (according to his CIA file, Bandera's other aliases were 'Michael Kaspar', 'Stefan Donat' and 'Hubert Bula'), probably chosen because he knew about his famous countryman, the chess champion, whose name he borrowed.

Stashynsky's new mission was to travel to Munich and find the man who had been giving the oration for Colonel Konovalets in Amsterdam, the man with a dark-blue Opel-Kapitän. This time he was given a new set of documents identifying him as 'Hans Joachim Budeit', a real person who was living in Dortmund at the time – a rather risky practice for an undercover operation. Although Stashynsky was wrong about the book, the KGB already knew from their penetration agents that 'Stefan Popel' was indeed at least one of the pseudonyms that Bandera was using in Munich. Therefore, it was not difficult for the liquidator to find his target, who resided in Kreittmayrstraße, about half an hour walk from the historical city centre. His simple mission accomplished, Stashynsky flew back to Berlin to report to his case officer. In the meantime, he and Inge Pohl became engaged in April 1959.

At the end of April, Stashynsky was summoned to the Soviet capital where a room in the prestigious Moscow hotel Ukraina was reserved for him. Located inside one of 'Stalin's skyscrapers' in Kutuzovsky Prospekt, the hotel had often been used by the KGB. I remember living there for quite a while when my parents had been vetted before being allowed to travel to Arzamas-75, one of the 'closed' Soviet cities that officially did not exist. Later known as Arzamas-16 and Moscow-300, it is now called Sarov. In February 1943, Soviet scientists Igor Kurchatov and Yuri Khariton, under the supervision of Lavrenty Beria, the NKVD chief, began to work on the Soviet nuclear bomb and three years later Sarov disappeared from all documents and maps. The most secret Russian nuclear production facility is still located there. Polonium-210, one of the key components of the toxic poison that killed Alexander Litvinenko was, according to the experts, produced in Sarov.

In the wood-panelled and carpeted hotel room, Stashynsky was greeted by 'Georgij Aksentewitsch' [sic] – that was how this obviously wrong KGB officer's first name and surname were given to the German police and later reproduced by several authors. In reality, it was almost certainly Colonel Grigory Alekseyevich Korotya, who, in January 1953, returned from

Karlshorst where he had been posted for eight years. In Karlshorst, after serving as a SMERSH counterintelligence officer during the war, Korotya headed different operational departments of the MGB Berlin base, the last being Department A-3 – counterintelligence work against the Gehlen Organization. The visitor informed Stashynsky that the leadership was very satisfied with his performance and that his new target would be Bandera, aka 'Popel'. In early May, the KGB assassin returned to East Berlin. There, he was greeted by Korotya's former deputy, Vasili Ilyich Bulda, who until recently headed the 4th Department dealing with anti-Soviet emigration in Germany and was later promoted to deputy chief of the whole KGB 'Liaison Directorate' attached to the MfS.

On 10 May 1959, Stashynsky was on board a Pan Am DC-6Bs aircraft bound for Munich. Over a period of six months he made several trips to Bavaria, only to discover that there was no secure way to approach Bandera, who was experienced and careful, always carried a loaded gun in his shoulder strap and rarely went anywhere alone. Besides, the apartment building on Kreittmayrstrasse, a side street where he lived, was always locked.

It is generally assumed, based on Stashynsky's testimony in court, that he had many chances to murder Bandera during that May visit but something stopped him. At the time of his interrogation by the CIA at Camp King in Oberursel near Frankfurt, the US interrogation and intelligence command centre for Europe, Stashynsky explained that he changed his mind when Bandera caught a glimpse of him while he was still some distance away and felt that Bandera 'would be prepared to take evasive action'.[12] In his statement to the court, however, he said that some moral considerations stopped him, which is hard to believe. Regardless, one should always have in mind the flawed morality of an assassin's creed and the desire of any defendant to present himself in the best possible light.

In a KGB safe house in Berlin, Stashynsky told his case officer that he tried to open the door to Bandera's apartment house, but the five different keys that Moscow had provided didn't fit. Indeed, some broken key bits were later found in the lock housing. According to the investigation report, this was a standard lever-lock, which is usually harder to pick than pin tumbler locks. Moscow managed to sort out the problem and later the assassin was able to go in and out of the building whenever he wished. He used to practise at times when the premises were vacated so as not to attract

---

[12] CIA, 'Assassination of Stefan Bandera: Memorandum for the Record', 22 April 1976, 3: NARA, RG 263, E ZZ-19, B 14, declassified.

anybody's attention. In his testimony, Stashynsky described a problem with the key, but said that he had been asked to make a sketch from which an appropriate duplicate was produced. However, this is hard to believe because even an expert entry specialist can hardly create a duplicate key without working on the lock itself.

He was sent to Munich again, this time not only to test the new set of keys but also to check the address of another possible victim, Yaroslav Stetsko, who under the alias 'Dankiv' conveniently lived in the same Munich district as Bandera. Maxvostadt, the cultural heart of Munich, where both Bandera and Stetsko resided, is well-known in Germany not only for its many high educational establishments and art galleries but because such historical personalities as Bertholt Brecht, Vasili Kandinsky, Thomas Mann and even Hitler and Lenin lived here at some point.

In early October 1959, after Bandera had returned from an extended holiday in Italy, Meshcheryakov accompanied Stashynsky to the chief's office on the first floor of the main Rezidentura building. General Korotkov, himself a KGB assassin, once again explained to the young man that the Communist Party and the Soviet government entrusted him the mission of liquidating another enemy of the state, Bandera, which Stashynsky accepted without remorse. He was given a new improved weapon, the same German passport in the name of 'Budeit' that he had used before, and an air ticket to Munich via Frankfurt am Main. On 14 October, a year-and-a half after he first met Bandera in Rotterdam, Stashynsky arrived in Munich and checked into a small hotel. He later told investigators that he was alone and himself carried his new deadly weapon, a modified model of the tube gas gun, this time with a double barrel. This was unlikely, as it grossly violated the established KGB practise, but no one seemed to have noticed the discrepancy. Even today, in both London and Washington, there is a surprising lack of knowledge of many basic principles of the KGB operations.

On 15 October at about 12:45 p.m., the assassin was waiting for his victim near the house where Bandera rented an apartment on the third floor. At about one o'clock, Stashynsky spotted Bandera's Opel entering the driveway to the courtyard garage and let himself through the doors. As with Rebet, he went upstairs to the first floor to wait for his target to enter the house. Finally, he saw Bandera fiddling with his keys at the front door as he carried a basket full of green tomatoes in his right hand. (According to police files, Bandera was also carrying some cabbage wrapped in a piece of newspaper, as well as grapes and plums.) Stashynsky paused, bending down and pretending to tie his shoelace, on the one hand to keep his face hidden, as he had been taught in the spy school, and on the other giving him time before the door closed. It was still half open as he went down asking Bandera whether there was a problem with the door lock as Bandera was still trying to extricate the key from the door with his left hand. When the latter turned to him saying, 'Why, it works all right', the assassin fired both barrels point-blank into the victim's face.

He did not see the body fall. Stashynsky left the house, closing the door behind him and was off. On the way, he crushed the antidote vial in the gauze compress and inhaled the vapours, after which, on the way to his hotel, he discarded the keys and threw the murder weapon into a canal near Hofgarten at almost the same place where he had discarded the Rebet weapon. (Later German specialists analysed the pills that Stashynsky said he had been given to make him immune from poison. Their conclusion was that those pills were in reality not to immunise but, taken some short time before the hit, made the executioner lose all inhibitions and become so brave that nothing could stop him.) Neither of the guns were found.

The assassin left Munich at once taking a train to Frankfurt am Main. On the following day, he flew to Berlin, soon reporting to his handler in Karlshorst. Bandera – who was still alive – was found bleeding on the stairway. His wife called the ambulance and he died on the way to the hospital. A medical examination established that the cause of Bandera's death could have been potassium cyanide, which was found in his stomach. Several newspapers reported about a 'Mysterious Murder in Munich'.

After recuperating in Karlshorst for a month, the assassin was summoned to Moscow where, at a secret ceremony in early December, the chairman of the KGB pinned a highly valued combat medal of the Order of the Red Banner to his blazer. Stashynsky was not a commissioned officer but an agent, and accordingly did not wear a KGB officer's uniform. For official purposes, Stashynsky was supplied with a document stating that he had been a fellow at the Research Institute no. 946 and for his successes in solving an important scientific problem was awarded by the special Decree of the Presidium of the Supreme Council of the USSR dated 6 November 1959.

While in Moscow, the new 'intelligence hero', baptised in blood and granted the same honour that was bestowed on war veterans for their exploits, had a chance to meet all mandarins of the 13th Department. Among them were Colonels Hachik Oganesyan, the Armenian who recently joined the Special Tasks group, and Vasili Bulda, who he had met before, as well as General Ivan Fadeikin, the bespectacled chief who looked more like a schoolteacher than the ruthless commander of the KGB murder squad. (For two years, from 1952 to 1954, Fadeikin served in Karlshorst where he coordinated all Soviet intelligence operations against the West.) Stashynsky used this opportunity to ask Fadeikin for permission to go to East Berlin, where he intended to marry his girlfriend, Inge Pohl. The permission was finally granted by the KGB chairman.

On Christmas Eve, Stashynsky confessed to Inge what he had been allowed to say: that he was not 'Lehmann' and not German or Polish by nationality, but a Ukrainian working for the Soviet secret police. The young woman was obviously not overly surprised and agreed to go to Moscow with him. For this trip to the Soviet Union he was documented as 'Alexander Antonovich Krylov' and she as 'Inga Fedorovna Krylova', and they arrived in Moscow by train, together with several groups of East German tourists. On 9 March 1960, after two months in the socialist paradise, they returned to East Berlin. The KGB decided that after appropriate training, they would make an excellent 'illegals couple' for a long-term, deep-cover assignment in the West.

Stashynsky and Pohl were married in the registry office in Ost-Berlin-Mitte on 23 April 1960, with Stashynsky still posing as 'Josef Lehmann' and using his forged East German passport. Naturally, the bridegroom himself and his KGB bosses realised that this marriage, according to the Soviet or German laws, was not valid in the first place because 'Josef Lehmann' did not exist. However, from an operational point of view it was a marriage of convenience and thus perfectly all right as it could serve as a legal cover for the future couple of Soviet undercover operators.

By that time there had been some changes in the Karlshorst KGB base. General Korotkov was still there, now assisted by the new deputy chief, General Peter Grigoryev. Gorshkov had left to take a position at the headquarters in Moscow. His successor as head of the 7th illegals section was Colonel Nikolai Korznikov, a very experienced operator.[13] Stashynsky's case officer, Mescheryakov, was also recalled. Instead of Mescheryakov, Marius Yuzbashyan arrived in Berlin as deputy head of what by then became the 3rd illegals section.[14]

---

[13] Colonel Nikolai Alekseyevich Korznikov (1917–86) joined the NKVD foreign intelligence in 1939. During the war, he operated in the USA and France. He served in the 'A' special purpose unit (assassinations, terror and sabotage) until July 1944, when he was sent on a secret mission to the UK. Upon his return to Moscow in February 1946, he served as deputy head of various departments and then department head at the 13th Directorate of the MGB-KGB. From December 1959 to November 1962, he headed the illegals section in Karlshorst.

[14] Colonel (later Lieutenant General) Marius Aramovich Yuzbashyan (1924–93) worked in the MGB department in Lvov/Lviv and operated behind German lines from 1944 until the war end. After the war he returned to Ukraine but in 1954 was transferred to foreign intelligence. He served as the deputy head and then head of the 3rd illegals section of the KGB Karlshorst base from 1956 to 1970. He was promoted to the department head and

Colonel Svyatogorov took care of all the wedding chores. On 10 May, the couple returned to Moscow where Stashynsky enrolled as a first-year student on a German course at the Moscow Institute for Foreign Languages, the elite MGPIIYa-1, without taking the entrance exams. According to Stashynsky, when he and Inge lived in Moscow, his case officer was Sergey Sarkisov, who is also mentioned in the recent biography of Stashynsky written by the Harvard professor Serhii Plokhy, but I was unable to find this name in any KGB document of the period.

In September, Inge informed her husband – and he duly reported to his controller – that she was expecting a child. In January 1961 Inge was permitted to return to East Germany for the birth. She planned to travel back to Moscow with their infant son afterwards. Stashynsky had not seen him yet. But on 8 August 1961, Inge called Stashynsky in Moscow to deliver tragic news that their 4-month-old baby had suddenly died of pneumonia at the maternity hospital in Berlin. It must have felt to Stashynsky like God's retribution.

He was allowed to attend the funeral accompanied by Lieutenant Colonel Yuri Alexandrov from the Moscow KGB HQ. On 12 August, one day before the wall dividing East and West blocked any chance of escape, Bogdan and Inge boarded the elevated S-Bahn train to West Berlin. When they entered the shelter of a police station, darkness covered the city, as it prepared to be split into two worlds for twenty-eight years and one day.

That August was very hot and stuffy, and it was not easy for Herr Lehmann, who was properly documented and married to a real German girl, to prove to the formidable group of the CIA officers from the Berlin station that he was who he claimed he was.

The timing was not very fortunate for him, which Stashynsky could not know. In July 1959, William King 'Bill' Harvey, who had set about making Berlin the CIA's largest base (at its peak BOB had more than 200 employees), was preparing to return home. Harvey established sections for East German, satellite, Soviet and counterespionage operations, each with its head assisted by the deputy head. By 1955, he had in place four men who would later succeed him as chief of base. One of them liked to call it the Brandenburg School for Boys.

In August of 1959, one of the boys, David Murphy, who arrived in 1954 as Bill's deputy and head of Soviet operations, was not at all sure he would

---

then deputy head of the illegals directorate at the KGB Lubyanka headquarters (1972–88). From 1992, Yuzbashyan had lived in Yerevan, Armenia, working as security adviser to the major of the city. He was shot and killed in July 1993. The identity of the assassins remains undisclosed.

be appointed chief after Harvey's departure. Murphy thought he might be superseded by John Dimmer or William 'Bill' Hood, sometimes called 'the Vienna choirboys'. The ripples subsided, Bayard Stockton writes, when high authorities spiked the Austria desk's takeover of Berlin.[15] Murphy became chief of BOB in September 1959 and stayed until June 1961, with Dimmer as deputy.

Murphy was followed by William J. Graver, who had run the East German operations group under Harvey. Again, to Stashynsky's misfortune, on 19 August 1961, Lyndon Johnson was touring Berlin and paid a visit to the CIA station. The Berlin chief, Graver, did not mention Stashynsky but wowed the vice president with stories about how many East Germans, Czechs and Poles, military officers and civilians were snitching on the Soviet empire. 'However, if you *knew* what we had,' recalled Graver's subordinate Haviland Smith, 'you knew that the penetration of the Polish military mission was the guy who sold newspapers on the corner, not the roster of well-placed finks peddled to a starry-eyed LBJ. The only thing more routine than lying to Congress was ignoring it.'[16] In 1966 Graver, who later served in Vienna, yielded to Theodore 'Ted' Shackley, who had been chief of the Soviet satellite operations (SSO) carried out from the base. Ted Shackley arrived in Berlin in June 1954 after a tour of duty in Nuremberg, and Harvey, replacing Adam Horton, put Ted in charge of BOB's expanding Soviet satellite operations section.

Herbert 'Herb' Natzke, Shackley's deputy, was the last of the Harvey-trained BOB chiefs. He left Berlin in 1971, ending the Harvey era. That was the end of what became known to insiders as 'the Berlin Brotherhood'.

After his defection on 12 August, Stashynsky was briefly interviewed and flown to Oberursel near Frankfurt am Main. Murphy was not there anymore, and Graver, Shackley, Natzke and other chiefs were busy dealing with the news about the wall suddenly going up, which abruptly put an end to many of their efforts. According to CIA estimates, it severely inhibited Allied intelligence operations without incurring a similar disadvantage for the Eastern Bloc services.

'After the initial interrogation [in Camp King],' states a CIA memo of 22 April 1976, 'the conclusion was drawn that he would not be valuable

---

[15] Bayard Stockton, *Flawed Patriot: The Rise and Fall of CIA Legend Bill Harvey* (Washington, DC: Potomac Books, 2006), ch. 4. Stockton (1930–2006) was posted to Berlin in 1951 where he served under Bill Harvey for two years. He stayed in touch with Harvey during his next assignment in Pullach, Germany. Stockton resigned from the CIA in 1957 and became *Newsweek*'s bureau chief in Bonn and later London.

[16] Spencer Ackerman, 'The CIA's Failures', *The Nation*, 26 June 2008.

operationally as a double agent, that [Stashynsky] was not a bona fide defector and not the individual he purported to be. Because the assassinations had occurred on German soil, Stashinskiy [*sic*], on 1 September 1961, was turned over to German authorities.' However, the German police investigation preceding Stashynsky's public trial in Karlsruhe in October 1962 unearthed documents and witnesses to corroborate most of his story. The assassin was convicted and sentenced to eight years' hard labour. The judge declared that the main culprit was the Soviet government, which had institutionalised political murder.

This indeed was true. However, the information that reached Western intelligence circles in relation to Stashynsky's case was flawed. The KGB major Anatoly Golitsyn, himself a Ukrainian, defected to the CIA from his undercover post in Helsinki in December 1961, four months after Stashynsky. He reported that at least seventeen KGB officers had been sacked or demoted as a result of Stashynsky's 'treachery'. Fifty-five years later, Golitsyn's revelations cannot be corroborated by facts or documents.

Thus, nobody was actually punished except Yuri Alexandrov, Stashynsky's case officer, who accompanied him to Berlin but left him alone for some time. Alexandrov was allegedly expelled from the Party and sacked from the KGB. Stashynsky's controller, the legendary Ukrainian KGB 'liquidator' Alexander Svyatogorov, who this defector never mentioned to anybody, was recalled to Kiev. On 27 June 1961, General Korotkov died and was succeeded by General Aleksey Krokhin, the former chief of Directorate C/Illegals, and deputy head of the First Chief Directorate (FCD, Foreign Intelligence) of the KGB. After Stashynsky's defection, Krokhin remained in Berlin until 1964, returning to Moscow to his former position as deputy head of the FCD. In 1966, he was sent to Paris as the KGB head of station for the second time. His second tour of duty in France (he was first posted there from 1950–4) ended in 1971, and he retired from the Service three years later. Major General Grigoryev, deputy of both Korotkov and Krokhin, also stayed in Karlshorst until 1963, when Stashynsky was serving his first year in prison. Colonel Nikolai Korznikov, chief of the illegals section of the Karlshorst base from December 1959 to November 1962, was promoted. Upon his return to Moscow until September 1967, he headed a department in Directorate C and was later raised to deputy chief of the whole Illegals Directorate. Korznikov retired in 1982. His predecessor, Colonel Nikolai Gorshkov, also made a career at the Lubyanka HQ from 1959 to 1964, before heading the chair at KGB School No. 101. He was later sent as the KGB representative to Prague. Colonel Marius Yuzbashyan, who served as deputy of both Gorshkov and Korznikov from 1956 to 1965, returned to Karlshorst as chief of the illegals section in 1967. Like Korznikov, he had headed a department in Directorate C and was later appointed deputy chief of the whole Illegals Directorate (1972–8). Promoted to major general and then lieutenant general, Yuzbashyan headed the KGB of the Soviet Republic of Armenia for ten years until October 1988. An unknown assassin shot and killed him while he was jogging in the park in Yerevan.

Stashynsky's trial began on 8 October 1962 and lasted a week. The verdict was announced on 19 October and the self-confessed assassin was sentenced to eight years imprisonment. Unlike Sir Robert Owen in the Litvinenko case, the German high court judge unambiguously ruled that the Soviet government in Moscow was guilty of killing their opponents abroad and Stashynsky was their tool. At the time, no one thought of political correctness.

When he was finally released on New Year's Eve 1966, Stashynsky immediately became a problem for the German authorities. Nobody could figure out what to do with the former assassin. The Americans clearly didn't want him because of the Nosenko problem[17] and, accordingly, the BND also

---

[17] In his book, *The Man with the Poison Gun: A Cold War Spy Story* (London: Oneworld Publications, 2016), Serhii Plokhy writes: 'Had he been brought to the United States and placed under the authority of Angleton and his people at the CIA, Stashynsky most likely would have experienced the same kind of treatment that KGB defector Yuri Nosenko had been subjected to. Nosenko had spent three years in solitary confinement and was given drugs to make him tell the "truth".'

Yuri Ivanovich Nosenko offered his services to the CIA in Geneva in 1962, and suddenly defected during his next visit to Switzerland two years later. Because the CIA's Soviet Division believed him to be a KGB plant, Nosenko was unofficially arrested and kept in solitary confinement in Maryland from 1964 to 1967. There, the defector underwent psychological intimidation, sensory deprivation and it was one of the rare cases when ARTICHOKE (a top-secret CIA programme involving the use of drugs or chemicals in unconventional interrogation) had been used in an actual case. The declassified CIA file on the ARTICHOKE programme also mentions the Stashynsky case, referring to the *Newsweek* article 'A Killer's Confession' of 4 December 1961 briefly covering the Stashynsky case and mentioning his 'specially built squirt gun that fired a spray of vaporized cyanide at such high pressure that it penetrated the skin, killing instantly and leaving no mark on the corpse'. The author of the CIA document considered this 'very interesting as … in about 1950 we had in the ARTICHOKE a considerable interest in the hypospray'.

James Jesus Angleton's CIA's 31-year-long career ended on Christmas Eve 1974. He had successfully served under six CIA directors. Three of Angleton's senior aids in counterintelligence – Raymond Rocca, William Hood and Newton Miller – left with him. David Murphy was assigned to Paris as station chief in 1968, returning to Langley in 1973. He retired two years later and received the CIA's Distinguished Intelligence Medal. In 1967, Tennent Bagley became CIA station chief in Brussels, holding the post until his retirement in 1972. Both were senior officers, accordingly chief and deputy chief, of the CIA's Soviet Russia Division. There are still many intelligence veterans who remember them with admiration.

didn't take him on board as a consultant. It was finally decided he could be dispatched to a third country.

The Germans contacted South African Republican Intelligence (RI) because, as the retiring police commissioner Mike Geldenhuys told the *Cape Times* in March 1984, 'they were convinced [that South Africa] was the only country where he would be comparatively safe from KGB agents.' According to some reports, Stashynsky underwent intensive cosmetic surgery and was given a new family background legend and identity. It is not known how and where he had spent the three years after he was granted remission. Inge Pohl divorced her husband in June 1964.

In July 1969, after a dramatic spy swap on a border post between West and East Germany that had been delayed for three hours because Yuri Loginov, a Soviet illegal, did not want to return to the USSR – Geldenhuys prepared to fly from Germany to Cape Town in the company of a blond tanned man who looked nothing like a Ukrainian. Perhaps his eyes remained unchanged – the deep-set and expressionless eyes of an assassin that stared back with frank candour – but they were now covered by glasses.

During my research on this chapter, the image of Stashynsky resurfaced again. In August 2011, an obviously fake interview with him was published in one of Kiev's leading newspapers. The article was written by a freelance Ukrainian journalist with known ties to the Russian Intelligence Services and the SBU, the Security Service of Ukraine. It was the time when Ukraine celebrated its twentieth anniversary of independence while Victor Yanukovich was still sitting in the president's chair at the Mariyinsky Palace in Kiev, spending his free time at home in the luxury Mezhyhirya residence with its gold fixtures, monogrammed towels and crystal chandeliers in the toilets. This interview with 'Stashynsky' was retold in English by Professor Alexander Motyl of Rutgers University in his blog on the *World Affairs* website in November that same year. The idea was to present the former assassin as a double agent who had always been loyal to his KGB masters. This is nothing new, of course. The same trick was played in 1985, when Vitaly Yurchenko defected to the CIA in August and then came back some short time after, claiming he had been abducted. He was even given a government decoration and hailed as a hero.

Another indirect mention of Stashynsky was on 20 November 2006, when Litvinenko was dying in a London hospital. The newly appointed head of the SVR press bureau, Sergey Ivanov, on behalf of the Russian Foreign Intelligence Service, stated that 'Since 1959, when the Ukrainian nationalist Stepan Bandera was assassinated, Soviet intelligence and its successor, the

Hauptabteilung II/1   Berlin, 6. 12. 1986
                                       müh- ol

BStU
000315

Bestätigt

Abschlußbericht

zum Operativ-Vorgang ▓▓▓▓▓▓▓▓▓▓, Reg. Nr. 10727/61

Der OV ▓▓▓▓▓▓▓▓▓ wurde am 31.1º. 1961 durch die damalige
HA II/5 als Operativ-Vorlaufakte angelegt und 1966 zur
weiteren Bearbeitung an die ehemalige Abteilung XXI des MfS
übergeben.
Im September 1966 erfolgte die Umregistrierung zum Operativ-
vorgang.
Gegenwärtig sind im Index des Vorganges noch 2 Personen unter
ihrem Klarnamen und mit Pseudonym erfaßt.
Dabei handelt es sich um den ehemaligen inoffiziellen Mitarbeiter
des sowjetischen Bruderorgans

- Staschynskij, Bogdan-Nikolajewitsch
  geb. am   04. 11. 1931 in Bortschewice/Lwow

  alias

  Lehmann, Josef
  geb.am   04. 11. 1930 in Lukowek/VR Polen

  und seine ▓▓▓▓ Ehefrau

  ▓▓▓▓▓▓▓ geb. Pohl, Inge
  geb. am   ▓▓▓▓▓▓▓▓   in ▓▓▓▓▓▓▓▓▓

  alias

  Lehmann, geb. Pohl, Inge
  geb. am   ▓▓▓▓▓▓▓▓in ▓▓▓▓▓▓▓

Staschynskij, Bogdan hatte unter seinem damaligen operativen
Pseudonym - Lehmann, Josef- am ▓▓▓▓▓▓▓ in Berlin-Mitte
eine Ehe mit der damaligen DDR-Bürgerin Pohl, Inge geschlossen.

Am 12. 08. 1961 verließen beide ungesetzlich unter dem Namen
Lehmann die DDR und stellten sich in Westberlin imperialistischen
Geheimdiensten , wo Staschynskij, Bogdan umfangreichen Verrat
in bezug auf seine Zusammenarbeit mit dem sowjetischen Bruderorgan
beging.

Im Zuge seiner Verratshandlungen wurde Staschynskij, Bogdan in der
BRD inhaftiert und am 19. 10. 1962 vor dem 3. Strafsenat des
Bundesgerichtshofes Karlsruhe wegen Spionage und Beihilfe zum Mord
zu insgesamt 8 Jahren Freiheitsentzug verurteilt.
Davon soll er ca. 5 Jahre in einer bayrischen Haftanstalt verbüßt
haben und sei lt. westlichen Pressemeldungen auf Verlangen des
US-Geheimdienstes 1966 vorzeitig entlassen und nach den USA
ausgeflogen worden.

A secret Stasi document dated December 1986 showing that the investigation file 'Stashinsky/
Lehmann' is finally closed after almost three decades.

SVR, have not been involved in physical liquidations of individuals hostile to Russia'. This, of course, is a downright lie, as this book seeks to prove.

In April 2011, an English-language blog allegedly written by Stashynsky himself appeared on the internet, and soon after, a marginal group called the National Bolshevik Party of Ukraine called on the city authorities to name a local park after Stashynsky. Since 2014, after Russia annexed the Ukrainian territory of Crimea and started a hybrid war on its neighbour in Donbass, unidentified vandals have desecrated the grave of Bandera in the Munich cemetery Waldfriedhof at least three times.

I am sometimes asked what I think about Stepan Bandera and I always hesitate before giving an answer. In January 2010, the outgoing president of Ukraine, Victor Yushchenko, awarded Bandera the posthumous title of Hero of Ukraine, the highest decoration. The European Parliament condemned the award, recommending the new Ukrainian leadership to reconsider. But I believe they were not right because they did not have enough information, if any at all. Finally, who are they to give such a recommendation? All his life Bandera fought against Communist rule for a free, independent and prosperous Ukraine. He and his family suffered a lot and he was finally assassinated by the KGB in Germany, an act of terrorism on foreign soil. So much for the European politicians.

In the past ten years, I have spent a great amount of time and effort trying to locate Stashynsky, having contacted first the AFIO – American Association of Former Intelligence Officers – and then my acquaintances who used to serve in the CIA, DIA and FBI. All my enquiries were met with a wall of silence. I have even spoken to one American non-official-cover operative, who is my not-so-distant neighbour and who at the time was based in Johannesburg but maintained regular contact with the Agency people in Pretoria. He said no one ever mentioned Stashynsky, but this is probably because the Ukrainian lived in South Africa under an assumed name. I also asked Timothy Ashby, a prize-winning author whose career included a spell as a counter-terrorism consultant to the US State Department, to put out some feelers on Stashynsky to try and find out at least something, when Tim was travelling in South Africa, a country he knows very well. Without success.

It is possible that Stashynsky is still alive. If so, nobody knows where he now lives or what he does.

Why is this old case important for our investigation of the Litvinenko murder? Because it demonstrates that Russian Intelligent Services always employ new methods of killing people, invent new weapons and always use illegals, trained assassins to wipe out the enemy, that such operations are meticulously planned and take a considerably long time to execute that the place of execution is always fixed and that there is always enough time for the killer to escape. Except when he wants to surrender.

I've never been to South Africa, but working on this chapter I came across Forsyth's notes about his meeting with General van den Bergh in Cape Town. In his Africaans-inflected voice, the head of the Bureau of State Security insisted on telling the British writer (and at that time an SIS agent) a story 'to prove not only his legitimacy but his sanctity as well', as Forsyth recorded. After hearing the story, the writer concluded that the master of one of the most brutal secret police forces in the world (and Stashynsky's boss) was mad as a box of frogs. Quite barking mad.

Chapter 8

Road to Donbass

In 2005 the Orthodox New Year, or the Old New Year as it is called in Russia and Ukraine, fell on the night of 13 to 14 January. It was on this night that I arrived at the Rudolfinerhaus private hospital in Vienna's prestigious 19th district to interview Professor Nikolai Nikolayevich Korpan, then a little-known medical doctor and specialist in cryosurgery. Thirteen years later, also on the night of the Orthodox New Year, I once again visited Dr Korpan at his clinic, as if all those years had not passed since our last meeting.

Theodor Billroth, one of the most renowned and eminent physicians of the Austrian medical school, founded the Rudolfinerhaus in 1882 and it is now located on the street named after him. This private hospital is among the most modern medical establishments of the Alpine Republic, both in terms of its services and technical equipment. The Rudolfiner Society–Red Cross functions as the supervisory board for all facilities, including the campus and clinic itself. At the time of writing, the chairman of the board of directors as well as of the supervisory board was the Austrian businessman Georg Semler, also serving as the Grand Master of the Masonic Grand Lodge of Austria. He commanded a staff of about 200 of the Rudolfiner Society and more than 3,500 Austrian freemasons united in 74 lodges,[1] many of whom occupied and continue to hold leading positions in the country's medical establishments, media and judicial system. Professor Dr Korpan, the Honorary President of the International Society of Cryosurgery, has been employed by the Rudolfinerhaus since 1995.

On the morning of 13 January 2005, Nikolai was a happy and confident man who suddenly – thanks to a fortuitous combination of circumstances – became a trusted friend and personal doctor of Victor Yushchenko, the president-elect of Korpan's native Ukraine. It was only weeks before this that Dr Korpan felt he had personally saved the future president's life and helped in his own way to win the election. He immediately became famous and in high demand. Now, in January 2018, it was all in the past.

---

[1] Florian Horcicka and Ashwien Sankholkar, 'Die Freimaurer-Connection: Großmeiser der Skandale', *Trend*, 28.2.2012.

In *The KGB's Poison Factory*, I called the chapter about Yushchenko's poisoning 'The Ukrainian Patient'. Unlike all his predecessors, Yushchenko had a very difficult campaign running for the presidency. Victor Yanukovich, the former governor of the Donetsk province in Eastern Ukraine and later a prime minister, was an official candidate approved by Moscow. In November 2004, he initially won the second round, although his election was fraught with allegations of massive corruption, fraud and voter intimidation, documented by Western observers. This caused widespread protests and the Supreme Court ordered the revote. As a result, Yushchenko was elected 3rd President of Ukraine. Mass demonstrations and protests connected with this election campaign led to a political crisis and became known as the Orange Revolution. In the final re-run ballot, Yushchenko was a clear winner with 52 per cent. At the time no one could imagine that he would become President of Ukraine, although he always had great ambitions serving as Chairman of the National Bank and later as Prime Minister.

Yushchenko's wife is Catherine Claire Chumachenko, an American of the Ukrainian origin and a former State Department official. She worked in the White House during the administrations of Ronald Reagan and George H.W. Bush, later serving as the vice president of Ukraine-USA Foundation. Catherine met Victor Yushchenko working for the international auditors KPMG in Kiev.

On 26 July 2004, when speaking at a business forum in Yalta a short time before the presidential election in Ukraine, Putin accused secret services in Western countries of interfering with Russia's plans to integrate economically with Ukraine. '[Western] agents, in our countries and outside them,' he said, 'are trying to discredit the integration of Russia and Ukraine.' The former intelligence officer used the word *agentura*, the KGB term for networks of secret agents that penetrated foreign countries during the Cold War on behalf of the Kremlin. That was a Freudian slip: speaking about a Western threat, the President of Russia was contemplating his own covert action and clandestine activities. And it didn't take long for these activities to begin.

At the end of August, Vladimir Satsyuk, first deputy director of the Ukrainian Security Service (SBU), arranged a meeting with Yushchenko in his country house. Satsyuk, a graduate of the Frunze military school in Kiev, is a former Ukrainian businessman, banker and an MP. As a member of parliament, he headed the Committee on National Defence and Security and from there was transferred to the SBU. Yushchenko was accompanied to that meeting by his old friend David Zhvania, a wealthy businessman from Georgia. It is said that David is a distant relative of Zurab Zhvania, a Georgian politician and a former prime minister who died under suspicious circumstances in

February 2005. Zhvania's friend and compatriot, Thomas Tsyntsabadze, another Georgian businessman and the owner of a car dealership, himself a well-known figure in Kiev, volunteered to serve as their driver. Only a couple of days before, the SBU deputy was spotted in Moscow meeting his Russian colleagues from the FSB.

All tactical elements of the operation to poison Yushchenko were repeated in London according to the very same pattern. In fact, in the best by-the-book stickler tradition, this time against Sasha Litvinenko. I tried to explain this to my Scotland Yard contacts, and they listened very attentively, saying, 'Why don't you write about it? We have nothing like that in our library.' So I did. It transpired, however, that the Litvinenko investigation and public inquiry did not take my explanations into consideration.

It was Zhvania, a member of and, according to his own words, heavy donator to Yushchenko's new political party, who had been approached to organise this secret meeting between the SBU deputy director and the opposition candidate. Zhvania was a trusted person but also one of the two important contacts in Kiev for Boris Berezovsky, who was supporting and funding democratic institutions in Ukraine from his London exile. Another man who, for whatever reason, Berezovsky trusted was Alexander Tretyakov, a Ukrainian businessman and politician, who was very close to the future president. Tretyakov used to be Dr Korpan's patient in Vienna and it was he who recommended Nikolai to Yushchenko. It must be added that Zhvania knew another Georgian, Badri Patarkatsyshvili, from early childhood and Badri was the closest friend and business partner of Berezovsky. This is how Zhvania, by that time an MP, became a go-between for Berezovsky and Yushchenko – a typical miscalculation on behalf of Berezovsky.

Without seeing the files, it is impossible, of course, to accuse Zhvania of having any ties to Russian Intelligence Services. I haven't got any evidence except perhaps that he had served with the KGB border troops in Tbilisi. His involvement was revealed much later, in September 2007, after the poisoning of Yushchenko, when Boris Berezovsky sued Tretyakov and Zhvania, who had in the meantime become Emergency Minister of Ukraine, for misusing nearly $23 million of about $45 million that the tycoon had allocated for Yushchenko's campaign. More importantly, Zhvania took a firm pro-Kremlin position and joined an FSB-orchestrated propaganda operation designed to prove that there had never been any attempt on the candidate's life and all that happened in September 2004 was nothing but Yushchenko's subterfuge aimed at bringing himself to power.

By the end of August, a team of assassins had already infiltrated Ukraine and established themselves near Satsyuk's dacha and possibly even inside it. Video cameras and audio recording equipment were concealed on the veranda. The house was also bugged. Before the 'hit', the assassination team's task was to establish the target's profile: the pattern of his movements, his reaction to persuasion, his protection system and its weaknesses. Much of this information had already been available to Moscow controllers, including photographs of the target, plans of the dacha, maps of the surrounding area and the escape routes. The means by which the target would be assassinated had also been determined and a specialist delivered a sophisticated poison produced by a laboratory in Moscow. A support team consisting of the 'cleaners' should also have been available, this time not to dispose of the body, but to professionally clean up the place so that the future investigation would not find traces. Certainly also, a back-up team was ready for action should something go wrong during the planned operation. This is how it is usually done.

As all professional intelligence officers learn during their training, assassination is all about getting the target into a position where he cannot escape but remains unsuspecting. Those are special operations where the activities of executioners are both covert and clandestine. Contrary to what many people think, the terms 'clandestine' and 'covert' are not synonymous.

Here is a timeline of the events on the tragic day when Yushchenko was poisoned. On 5 September 2004, the Our Ukraine presidential nominee accompanied by his personal security detail plus two government bodyguards arrived in Chernigov, about 150 km away from Kiev, where Yushchenko would speak to a rally of his supporters. When they left, Zhvania called his friend, Thomas-the-car-dealer, and asked him to urgently bring a car, a Mercedes G-class SUV, a model known in Kiev as a 'Cube'. They left it in front of Zhvania's home, took Zhvania's black Mercedes-Benz sedan and rushed to Chernigov with Thomas behind the steering wheel.

At the end of the meeting, a local antique trader invited Yushchenko and his escort to his home to perform a wake for his wife, who had passed away days before. Yushchenko agreed and the host toasted his guests with some strong homemade alcohol distilled from bark.

All that time, Zhvania's Georgian friend Thomas was not only performing the role of a driver, but served as a liaison between Satsyuk, who was waiting in his dacha, and Zhvania, who did his best to control all movements of the opposition candidate. It was decided in advance that all communications would go only through him.

Both Zhvania and Thomas thought they were now driving to Satsyuk's country house, but Yushchenko's plans suddenly changed. He had already started drinking and agreed to visit a party organised by his friends. Like every Ukrainian, Yushchenko loved good company and long feasts around a groaning board. They stayed until evening eating fish and sushi and drinking red wine and brandy – an impossible combination – when Zhvania firmly said to Yushchenko: 'They are waiting for us at the dacha.'

Again, precisely according to his established psychological pattern, the future president let himself be persuaded – especially because by that time he was already quite intoxicated. Yushchenko and one of his government bodyguards went in the Audi. Zhvania was behind them in his own black sedan driven by his Georgian friend, while the rest of the security detail followed in a caravan.

When they reached Podol, an old district of Kiev, the motorcade stopped. A single car was waiting for them on the embankment. It was the same Mercedes 'Cube' – with the Kiev number plate 555-93 – that the car dealer brought to Zhvania that morning. (In *Poison Factory* I gave a different number: 555-55, as it was mentioned in earlier reports. Later Tsyntsabadze corrected it.) Following their boss's instructions, Zhvania's personal driver and one of his bodyguards brought the 'Cube' to Podol.

Here, Yushchenko's team changed cars again. Thomas Tsyntsabadze took the driver's seat of the 'Cube', as he had done during their previous visit to the same dacha. The future president settled down beside him, while Zhvania sat comfortably on the back seat. They quickly moved in the direction of the holiday village Osokorki, where Satsyuk and his boss, the director of the SBU General Igor Smeshko, were waiting for them drinking beer. Two government bodyguards were driving behind them in Yushchenko's Audi and Zhvania's sedan was brought back home by his personal driver.

There is no suggestion that the director of the SBU was involved in the operation. It seems likely that the only person there who was informed of the unfolding plot was Satsyuk, the host, and even he only in very general terms, and perhaps to a certain extent Zhvania. So, four of them retired to the veranda where a table was laid for what could easily become 'the Last Supper' for Yushchenko. There were, however, two or three other persons who inconspicuously attended the party and at least three or four waiting outside and in the house.

The substantial meal that night included a bucket of crawfish washed down by plenty of beer, then various salads followed by cold meats with vodka, and Uzbek pilaf as the main course. The pilaf, prepared by two Uzbek brothers, was served on separate plates by Taras Zalessky, a man close to Satsyuk with a very colourful biography. A professional sportsman, he had served in the regular police force before joining the department for combating organised crime. He then retired only to head the security service of a bank. For some time, when Satsyuk was an MP, Taras served as his personal assistant. At the time of an exclusive interview in Turkey where, in September 2007, journalists from the Russian language Ukrainian tabloid *Segodnya* found him living in a modest hideout, he was writing a book and editing the internet site 'Criminal Ukraine'.

As soon as I heard about the Uzbek cooks in Satsyuk's house, I remembered another Uzbek cook working in the Tajbeg Palace in Afghanistan, and President Hafizullah Amin entertaining his inner circle with his beloved Uzbek pilaf. The 'cook' was a Soviet illegal Mitalin Talybov, and although everyone at the table was eating the same meal, only Amin appeared to be poisoned.

When Satsyuk and his guests finished the pilaf, they had already emptied two bottles of vodka. Then Satsyuk and Zhvania retired to the house leaving Yushchenko and Smeshko alone on the veranda.

They settled in the house around a small table and Zhvania found a bottle of brandy, which they quickly emptied. It was followed by a large bottle of Scotch and at one moment a car dealer-come-driver, who knew both well enough to serve as a cut-out during that operation, also joined them.

After a while, Zhvania and the SBU deputy returned to the veranda and all enjoyed a dessert of watermelons, plums, grapes and other fruit, and coffee. Before the guests left at about 3:00 a.m., Zhvania took a photo of the two SBU chiefs in the company of the presidential candidate, with Satsyuk's friendly hand on his right shoulder. Then after half an hour, they arrived at Yushchenko's home where one of the government bodyguards took a photo of Zhvania, Yushchenko and Tsyntsabadze in front of their car. At least two in this company were markedly drunk.

When Yushchenko turned in he slept like a log, but in just a few hours started feeling a strong headache coming on.

The next morning, a UDO bodyguard arrived to accompany Yushchenko to his office but found him feeling very unwell. (The UDO – The Department of State Protection of Ukraine – a rough equivalent of the US Secret Service and successor of the 9th Department of the Ukrainian KGB, is the agency responsible for protecting all presidential candidates.) Catherine Yushchenko was really worried about her husband's condition. Yushchenko's terrible headache was followed by nausea and vomiting made worse by severe abdominal pain. He also felt his back was not in order and went to a sauna for relief. There was no relief.

On Wednesday, a council of doctors gathered to decide what could or should be done about Yushchenko's problem. They were nonplussed by the variety of symptoms but finally decided it was gastroenteritis, an inflammation of the gastrointestinal tract involving both the stomach and the small intestine. As this is a dangerous and potentially lethal disease, they wanted their patient to check in to the government hospital for closer examination.

On the same day, Catherine Yushchenko started to discuss a possible evacuation to a foreign medical facility. Zhvania, who was also there, advised against it. 'Are you going to make a mess of the election campaign by flying him to a foreign hospital with this diarrhoea?' he asked.

While Zhvania was musing about the subject, Yushchenko continued discussing with his wife what to do as the pain in his back was becoming unbearable.

On Thursday, 9 September, a doctor looking after him at home continued to insist on Yushchenko's hospitalisation as the tests showed that his lipase level was three times the upper limit of normal. That pointed to possible acute pancreatitis (for which alcohol is the second most common cause).

Catherine and Yushchenko's top aide Tretyakov realised it was time to fly away as quickly and as secretly as possible. They were lucky to get a private jet ready to be airborne at once and, after putting his finger in the air, Tretyakov came up with an obvious solution and called Dr Korpan, who appeared to be in Vienna and ready.

It was actually a not-so-random decision. In March, Catherine gave birth to their youngest child, Tarasik, in one of the best Vienna maternity hospitals. Both Yushchenko and Zhvania then flew to Austria to pick her and the child up. Zhvania also had a lot of business interests in the country. He even lived here for some time when he left Georgia.

Before their plane was cleared for take-off, a doctor who accompanied them to the airport gave Yushchenko an anaesthetic injection to reduce his pain. In the aircraft were Yushchenko, his wife Catherine and their five-month-old son, a government bodyguard, and Tretyakov and Yevgeny Chervonenko, Yushchenko's private guard. The jet landed in Vienna after midnight.

It took the Russians about twenty days to launch an international propaganda campaign against Yushchenko and the Rudolfinerhaus hospital. The incumbent president's son-in-law, Ukrainian oligarch and billionaire Victor Pinchuk (the founder and owner of EastOne Group, an investment and advisery firm registered in the UK) travelled to Vienna to make all necessary arrangements. There, according to Professor Dr Michael Zimpfer, at the time President and Chairman of the Board of the Rudolfiner Association-Red Cross (in charge of the Rudolfinerhaus Hospital), Pinchuk was introduced to Dr Lothar Wicke, who was serving as Medical Director and CEO of the Rudolfinerhaus. The Ukrainian oligarch persuaded him to hire a professional agency that, he explained, could handle all public relations work for the hospital. Soon, a PR team from the Paris office of Euro RSCG, part of Havas Group, headed by Yffic Nouvellon, arrived in Vienna. This particular agency had already worked for Pinchuk and his wife in Kiev and demonstrated that they were ready to exhibit a fair degree of professionalism and cunning in the execution of their job. Nouvellon was accompanied by one Ramzi Khiroun, who organised a press conference in the Rudolfinerhaus in late September.[2]

On 28 September, the Nouvellon team distributed a forged press release written by Nouvellon and Khiroun that was sent to the news agencies and international media offering evidence that Mr Yushchenko had not been poisoned.[3] Reuters, then still an independent international news agency headquartered in London, for whom Frederick Forsyth worked half a century ago, disseminated this fake news, stating that doctors of the Vienna hospital had ruled out the possibility of the Ukrainian patient's deliberate poisoning. Later, Yushchenko's staff traced the distribution of this falsified press release to TriMedia, a public relations firm with an office in Moscow.[4]

Apart from the international disinformation campaign, Nouvellon's team also arranged a press conference on Wednesday, 29 September, in which Dr Wicke contradicted Yushchenko's allegations of poisoning. From that day on, Wicke became a cause célèbre in the anti-Yushchenko propaganda war.

After that press conference, Dr Wicke was given a written notice signed by the Rudolfinerhaus president to retract his remarks. He told me he refused to do it. It was after that, Wicke claimed, that he received a telephone call. According to him, the caller introduced himself as 'a friend from Ukraine' and allegedly warned the old radiologist, who had nothing whatsoever to do with the treatment of Yushchenko, to 'take care as your life is in danger'. Wicke was immediately put under 24-hour police protection. (Later, the Rudolfinerhaus president Dr Michael Zimpfer issued an official statement making it clear that 'Dr Wicke had [only] once met with Yushchenko on administrative issues', adding that 'Mr. Wicke is a radiologist, and as a specialist, he can neither approve nor disprove Yushchenko's diagnosis'.)

Wicke's extraordinary statements started a battle. Speaking to the press on 4 October, Dr Korpan revealed that in the previous week his Kiev apartment had been searched and his neighbours questioned by Ukrainian investigators. On Thursday, 7 October, an Austrian criminal police squad arrived at Rudolfinerhaus with all their gear, including cars with flashing blue lights and sirens. The aim of the operation was the seizure of Yushchenko's medical

---

[2] See Marcel H. Van Herpen, *Putin's Propaganda Machine: Soft Power and Russian Foreign Policy* (Lanham, MD: Rowman & Littlefield, 2016), 56.

[3] Ibid.

[4] 'A poisoning … and an egging', *The Ukrainian Weekly*, 73/3 (16 January 2005), 7.

records, although it is hard to imagine what Austrian authorities intended to do with them.

On the following day, the second international press conference was held at the Rudolfiner conference hall with a crowd of journalists from many countries waiting in a long queue to get admission. Dr Wicke repeated his allegations that a 'medically forged diagnosis' had been circulated by someone 'not permanently employed in this clinic', referring to Dr Korpan. Wicke appeared especially irritated by one of Korpan's phrases in his draft of the medical conclusion stating (correctly, as it was established later) that 'the patient's condition may be caused by the administration of toxic agents that are not usually included in food products'.

Lothar Wicke was born in Vienna in 1941 and received his medical education at Vienna University. That year, 2004, was probably the most successful period of his career. In April his book *Atlas of Radiologic Anatomy*, 7th edition, was published by Saunders/Elsevier, one of the world's premier names in healthcare publishing. In July, he received the Austrian Cross of Honour for Science and Art 1st Class from the Austrian president Thomas Klestil. And in September, his name was in every international media because of his multiple press conferences, radio and television interviews claiming that Yushchenko had not been poisoned.

When quite by chance I observed Wicke in early spring 2005 going to a meeting with his contact in the Hotel Bristol, a police guard was still accompanying the old man. Wicke later said to the Austrian *Profil* magazine: 'I was not ready to be used as an instrument in the Ukrainian election manipulations.' In reality, that was exactly the role he continued to play long after several independent expert commissions concluded without any doubt that the Ukrainian patient had been deliberately poisoned.

The Bristol in Vienna is located right next to the State Opera and has been a meeting point not only for international political, cultural and business elite for more than 120 years, but has also hosted spies and venturesome men and women from all over the world. Sigmund Reilly, 'the ace of spies', used to stay in the Bristol. It was here that the Prince of Wales and Wallis Simpson sojourned at the height of their affair in 1936. Nikolai Artamonov, a triple agent, and his wife occupied room 341 on the third floor before Nikolai was abducted and killed by the KGB in December 1975. In December 2017, Georg Semler, Chairman of the Board of Directors of the Rudolfinerhaus and the Grand Master of the Grand Lodge of Austria was spotted in the Bristol Bar... not to mention Theodore 'Teddy' Roosevelt Jr., the 26th President of the United States and a Master Mason, who stayed in the Bristol during his visit to Austria. No wonder Wicke also chose this hotel as his favourite meeting place.

Pretending to be a tourist, I followed Wicke into the lobby and noticed that he was meeting one Philipp Buchner, who I didn't know then. I would meet him eventually, years later, in a small Russian bookshop at the centre of Vienna. He turned out to be the nastiest piece of work I have ever come across. A fake 'doctor', fake businessman, a fake intellectual and a scoundrel whose hobby was to destroy other people's lives.

Philipp Buchner reminded me of the character described by Forsyth – Sir David Hunt, the British High Commissioner in Lagos, who probably belonged to the same psychological type. 'An intellectual who had missed out on every plum in the diplomatic service, the trashcan of diplomacy, and seethed with resentment; a crashing snob and a racist who hid his unpleasantness behind a veneer of affability, about as convincing as a four-pound note.' Both Philipp and Lothar were freemasons. Buchner would be kicked out from his Austrian lodge, later joining a small international lodge in a neighbouring country. Wicke, as he himself told me during a meeting in the Bristol café, was a Master Mason with many years in the craft. In 2017, Philipp, also a Master Mason in the Blue Lodge and a 33rd degree Scottish Rite member was expelled from Freemasonry, which is a very rare and severe punishment. He has always maintained excellent relations with Russia, visiting the country regularly, while both his former wives are Russian. He once boasted at a party that his father-in-law is a GRU general who served under the cover of a Soviet diplomat at the UN Vienna headquarters. Considering his collusion with Russia, Philipp could have played a role in helping Russian operatives find the right way in Vienna in what concerned the Yushchenko affair.

Interestingly, neither Philipp, who in the meantime was arrested and put into prison,[5] nor Wicke were mentioned in the criminal charge against two Russians, Vladimir Vozhzhov and Mikhail Vladimir, brought by the BVT, the Austrian police force responsible for matters of national security and counterintelligence. Vladimir, a veteran Russian diplomat, had served in Vienna from January 1994 to March 2005. Vozhzhov, a GRU officer, first came to Austria in November 1994, operating under the official cover. His tour of duty ended in March 1999. After that, Vozhzhov visited Austria many times, usually to meet his agent in the Austrian Armed Forces, Bundesheer, or his most important source, Werner Greipl, the technical programme manager at Eurocopter in Bavaria.

The Austrian agent's name was Harald Sodnikar and the BVT investigators found out that Vozhzhov summoned Sodnikar, who had

---

[5] In October 2019, the Austrian newspaper *Kurier* reported that after his release from jail, Buchner went to Sofia, where he died in circumstances that remain unexplained to this day. It was the result of a major showdown between the Bulgarian and Russian mafia.

introduced him to Wicke sometime before, and instructed him to ask Wicke whether he could find a reliable colleague among the doctors who were treating Yushchenko at the Rudolfinerhaus. This doctor, according to the case file 70231/9-II/BVT/2/2003, for a reward of $100,000 in cash would have to issue an official document on behalf of the Rudolfinerhaus stating that their Ukrainian patient had *not* been poisoned. This failed because already in October, the Rudolfinerhaus president had issued a statement emphasising that only he, Dr Zimpfer and Dr Korpan were authorised to talk about the state of Yushchenko's health, and only with the patient's permission. Nevertheless, for a time, Wicke continued to support the version promoted by the Russians.[6]

While Yushchenko was shuttling between rallies and his hospital bed, Victor Yanukovich, Putin's favourite, the prime minister and the only candidate favoured by the Kremlin, a man who had twice, in 1968 and 1970, been convicted and imprisoned for robbery and assault, conducted his own rather clumsy presidential campaign with the Russian support. Anders Åslund, a Swedish economist and expert on the economic transition from a centrally planned to a market economy, who served as an economic adviser to both the governments of Russia and Ukraine, estimated that Moscow spent $300 million on the Ukrainian election.

Those were lost funds. Later, *The Sunday Telegraph* described those days: 'Mr Yushchenko and his glamorous blonde ally, Yulia Tymoshenko, formed a kind of "Beauty and the Beast" alliance against the Moscow-favoured Viktor Yanukovych. When Mr Yanukovych triumphed in what was seen as a rigged presidential election, Kiev's Independence Square filled with half-a-million protestors, who camped out night after night in sub-zero temperatures. People power finally triumphed when Ukraine's supreme court ordered the vote to be re-run on Boxing Day, ushering in Mr Yushchenko as president and Ms Tymoshenko as prime minister.'

Despite a very stressful presidential race, in mid-December Yushchenko was in Austria again with his family. At the Christkindlmarkt in front of the Vienna's Rathaus (City Hall) he was approached by a journalist from the Austrian *News* magazine.

'On 26 December the elections will be repeated. What result do you expect?'

'After these elections, the world will see a different Ukraine,' Yushchenko said. 'An open, optimistic country, free from corruption and criminality.

---

[6] See, for example, *The Telegraph* of 27 March 2005, 'I received death threats, says doctor who denied that Ukrainian leader was poisoned', as well as other reports by Bojan Pancevski and other correspondents from Vienna.

You shall see a country that will quickly integrate itself into the European community. Ukraine is part of Europe, there can be no more doubt about it.'

A beautiful but totally unrealistic dream.

More than a decade later, Ukraine would still have a long way to go to become part of Europe and Russia would make it incredibly difficult for anybody to realise the programme Yushchenko described in Vienna in December 2004.

Moscow viewed the events of November–December 2004 as a Western-inspired coup d'état in its backyard and did her best to oppose it. But it could do nothing against the hundreds of thousands who gathered on the Maidan. 'It is said that God is always on the side of the big battalions,' Voltaire wrote, and he seems to be right. Yushchenko had millions of his countrymen and women supporting him. (Asked why Alexey Navalny is not quite successful in today's Russia, I always say because he doesn't have big battalions at his back.)

Victor Andreyevich Yushchenko was only one step from becoming the president of the country that had been the second most important part of the Soviet Union, after Russia herself, for almost a hundred years. Against Russia's will, Ukraine would finally turn its face towards Europe after his election. This put his country on the road to war.

The trouble with Ukraine is that, historically, it had never been one country, but three. Those who live there say it still is. From prehistoric times migration and settlement in the territories that we now call Ukraine varied along the lines of several geographical zones. The Black Sea coast had for centuries attracted the attention of Mediterranean maritime powers. The open steppe, from the east across southern Ukraine and towards the mouth of the River Danube, formed a natural gateway to Europe. And the north-central and western territories, saturated with vegetation, supported a sedentary agricultural population. As in modern times, the border areas of these zones were places of regular military conflicts but also of cultural and economic transmission.[7]

A process of great migration began about the second century AD. In the 5th and 6th centuries the East Slavs occupied the forest and forest-steppe regions of western and north-central Ukraine and southern Byelorussia. From there, they expanded farther north and to the territories of what would become Russia with Moscow as its centre. On those lands, the East Slavs

---

[7] Here and elsewhere, for the review of Ukrainian history, I used *The New Britannica*, *Britannica*, Macropædia, 15th Edition (1995), vol. 28, 980–94.

Trotsky and other communist leaders at the 2nd World Congress of the Comintern, Moscow, July 1920. Upon arriving, delegates were provided with an assortment of reports, resolutions and books, including a copy of the recently published *Terrorism and Communism* by Trotsky. (*Archival photo*)

Trotsky and American admirers, Mexico. Signed: To Comrades Bobby and James Bartlett with best wishes Leon Trotsky, 5 April 1940. Comment: Jimmy Bartlett, far right, turned out to be an FBI fink. Harry DeBoer, on the left, was a solid citizen to the end. (*Archival photo*)

Trotsky's house in Coyoacán, Mexico City. The leader of the Bolshevik Revolution had lived here in exile from April 1939 until his assassination in August 1940.

Trotsky's study in his house in Coyoacán, where he was deadly wounded by the Soviet agent Ramón Mercader on 20 August 1940. (*Leon Trotsky Museum, Mexico City*)

Soviet agent David Alfaro Siqueiros (codenamed KON') in Lecumberry prison, Mexico City. (*Archivo fotográfico Héctor y María García*)

Trotsky's grave in the courtyard of his house in Mexico City. (*Leon Trotsky Museum, Mexico City*)

Restaurant Moskau, East Berlin. (*Photo: Günter Weil, Bundesarchiv, Germany, Bild 183-C0211-0006-001*)

NKVD/KGB 'Poison Factory' at the corner of Bolshaya Lubyanka Street and Varsanofievsky Lane, Moscow. Numerous medical experiments were performed here on human test subjects.

Checkpoint Charlie, Berlin, 1960s. Leaving the American sector. (*dpa*)

KGB-trained assassin, Bogdan Stashinsky, alias 'Josef Lehmann', murdered two Ukrainian exiles in Munich, West Germany.

Markus 'Misha' Wolf, legendary KGB-trained chief of the Stasi foreign intelligence. (*Courtesy Markus Wolf*)

Stepan Bandera, alias 'Popel', one of the victims of Stashinsky, giving an oration at the grave of Yevhen Konovalets on 23 May 1958. (*Stepan Bandera Museum, Stary Uhryniv, Ukraine*)

(Above) Bandera's journalist credentials issued by the West German authorities in the name of 'Stefan Popel'. (*Stepan Bandera Museum, Stary Uhryniv, Ukraine*)

(Below) Back to the USSR – the only KGB left on the territory of the former Soviet Union is in Minsk, Belarus.

Sergei Skripal (centre, standing) as an officer of an airborne division, Asia, 1977.

Boris Volodarsky as a Soviet Spetsnaz officer during parachute training, Lithuania, 1983.

Boris Volodarsky (far right), as a Soviet army cadet, 1975. Three young men in the centre have reached high ranks in the KGB, one becoming chief of the Byelorussian foreign intelligence (later ambassador and deputy foreign minister).

East Berlin, early morning 9 November 1989. (*dpa*)

Author at the world-famous
Checkpoint Charlie separating
two worlds. The Berlin Wall
has just symbolically fallen
and both sides – East and West
Berlin – got a chance to visit
each other, which eventually led
to the unification of Germany.
In the picture the crowds from
both parts of the great city are
hesitating whether to move or
not because in the past 40 years
it always ended with a shooting.

The second picture, taken by
the author, shows the same
place when the West German
side finally decided to move.

Nikolai Glushkov, Boris Berezovsky and Badri Patarkatsyshvili, LogoVaz Reception House (The Club), Moscow, 1995. (*Courtesy of Badri Patarkatsyshvili*)

The limousine of Boris Berezovsky after an assassination attempt in front of the LogoVaz Club, 7 June 1994. (*Photo: Alexei Ilyin, author's archive*)

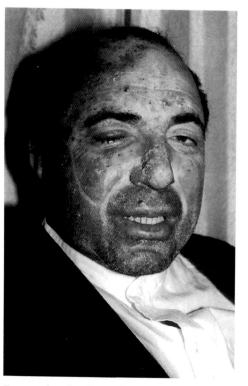

Berezovsky after the explosion, 7 June 1994.

Berezovsky's driver was instantly killed during the assassination attempt. (*Jean Philippe Girod/AFP*)

Registration ceremony of Badri Patarkatsyshvili and Olga Safonova (here with their son David), 16 May 1997, St Petersburg, Russia. (*Courtesy of Badri Patarkatsyshvili*)

Olga Safonova in Salzburg, March 1996, photographed by the author.

Arkady 'Badri' Patarkatsyshvili, Boris Berezovsky and Andrei Lugovoy, Georgia. (*Courtesy of Boris Berezovsky*)

Boris Berezovsky (right) and his bodyguard, Andrei Lugovoy, Moscow, 1998. (*Courtesy of Boris Berezovsky*)

Boris Berezovsky with his British bodyguard leaving Bow Street magistrates' court in London wearing Putin's mask, April 2003; in the background Vladimir Terlyuk. (*Getty image*)

Alexander Litvinenko, Boris Berezovsky, Ahmed Zakayev and Yuri Felshtinsky celebrating Berezovsky's 60th birthday, London, 23 January 2006. Lugovoy was sitting at the same table as Litvinenko and his wife, Marina.

On Wednesday, 8 May 2013, Luke Harding, a foreign correspondent for *The Guardian* in Russia (2007–2011) reported: 'The mercurial Russian oligarch Boris Berezovsky was buried in a deliberately low-key ceremony in Surrey, some six weeks after he was found dead on the bathroom floor of his ex-wife's mansion. Around 30 mourners including family, friends and his British lawyers attended the funeral, which was held amid tight security in Brookwood cemetery near Woking, Surrey. The service took place in a small brick chapel, overlooked by suitably Russian pines and silver birches, and under a dull, overcast sky.' The heavy oak casket, believed to contain the body of Berezovsky, was sealed throughout the burial ceremony. The grave was photographed in August 2018.

Lady Thatcher and Boris Volodarsky, Oxford & Cambridge Club, London, October 2007.

Boris Volodarsky and Michael Mann after the premiere of *Public Enemy*, London, 2010, when Mann was preparing to direct the making of a Litvinenko movie in Hollywood.

University Women's Club in a small enclave off South Audley Street, Mayfair. The KGB London station regularly left chalk marks on the Victorian lamppost outside the club to indicate the delivery of material to a DLB (dead letter box) usually located nearby. Intriguingly, while KGB spies were passing by 'reading'

the chalk mark, next door at No 3, Cubby Broccoli was busy casting unknown actor Sean Connery to play James Bond in a 1962 spy movie *Dr. No* with Ursula Andress. In December 2006, BBC's *Panorama* invited Volodarsky to interview Walter Litvinenko here.

MI6 agent Oleg Gordievsky and
his British companion Maureen on
the way from Buckingham Palace
where he was awarded the CMG
by the Queen, 18 October 2007.
(© *Boris Volodarsky*)

Boris Volodarsky and
Oleg Gordievsky CMG
at Buckingham Palace.
(© *Boris Volodarsky*)

Michael Shipster CMG OBE.
(*Public domain*)

Oleg Gordievsky in 2015, photographed in his house in
Surrey for *The Times* article celebrating his successful
exfiltration from Russia in July 1985.

Sergei Skripal (far left) in Valletta during his first undercover GRU posting as Cultural and Sports Attaché of the Russian Embassy in Malta. (*doi*)

General Anatoly Kuntsevich, the MoD overseer of the Novichok series R&D programme.

(Right and below) Boris Volodarsky in Salisbury as part of the ITN investigation team, 26 April 2018.

The first government of the Luhansk People's Republic, 2014. (*Courtesy of RFE/RL*)

HRH Prince Charles and Putin's personal bodyguard Victor Zolotov.

President Vladimir Putin and General Zolotov in Putin's Kremlin office. (© *Kremlin.ru*)

Russian President Vladimir Putin's working space at the Kremlin's Senate Palace. (© *Kremlin.ru*)

Denis Voronenkov, former Russian MP, assassinated on 23 March 2017 in the centre of Kiev, Ukraine, where he was living in exile. The public prosecutor general said Voronenkov was assassinated in a 'reprisal killing' following his testimonies against Kremlin officials and the deposed Ukrainian president Yanukovich. (*Valentin Ogirenko/Reuters*)

The gravestone of Alexander Litvinenko, poisoned in London on 1 November 2006 in a special operation carried out by the Russian Intelligence Services. Photographed in Highgate Cemetery shortly after the burial.

WHO WAS NEXT?

Anna Politkovskaya and Boris Nemtsov. With Boris Berezovsky – the most prominent Russian political figures assassinated by the Putin regime in the past decade. In her book *Putin's Russia* (2004) Anna wrote:

'I have wondered a great deal about why I have so got it in for Putin. What is it that makes me dislike him so much as to feel moved to write a book about him? I am not one of his political opponents or rivals, just a woman living in Russia.' Anna was born in New York City in August 1978 and assassinated in Moscow on 7 October 2007 – Putin's birthday...

'He was young, obviously very intelligent and had a strong, yet warm demeanour,' Edmond Pope, who met Boris Nemtsov in Russia, recalls. Nemtsov was assassinated on 27 February 2015 on a bridge near the Kremlin wall in Moscow.

The Russian 'Troll Factory' at 55 Savushkina Street, St Petersburg, said to be the headquarters of Russia's 'troll army'; it has now moved to Optikov Str., 4/3. (*Photo: Shaun Walker for the Guardian*)

began to build fortified settlements that would centuries later develop into important political and industrial centres. Among such settlements was Kiev, documented as going back at least 1,400 years. Built on the picturesque high right bank of the Dnieper River, it was gradually acquiring eminence as the centre of the East Slavic civilisation.

The formation of the Kievan state began in the mid-ninth century and it reached its Golden Age as the centre of Kievan Rus in the tenth–twelfth centuries. The name 'Rus', by which this vast area came to be known, remains a matter of controversy among historians. Kiev reached its apogee during the reign of Vladimir the Great who, in 988, adopted Christianity and had the inhabitants of Kiev baptised, thus entering the orbit of Byzantine Christianity and culture.

After a long period of decline, by the mid-fourteenth century, Ukrainian territories were under the rule of four foreign powers – the Golden Horde, the grand duchy of Lithuania, the kingdom of Poland and the grand duchy of Moscow, while the Crimea with its coastal towns and maritime trade was in the hands of the Venetians and Genoese. Competition between Lithuania and Poland over the former Galician-Volhynian principality ended with partition into Volhynia under Lithuanian rule and Galicia in possession of Poland. Thus, the grand duchy's control extended over virtually all Ruthenian (Ukrainian and Byelorussian) lands. Over three centuries of Lithuanian and Polish rule, Ukraine, by the middle of the seventeenth century, had undergone substantial social development.

Polish influence was still sufficiently strong in Ukraine, and Polish nobility continued to play an important role when it was partitioned along the Dnieper River, its western Right Bank still under Poland while Moscow got the eastern Left Bank plus the right-bank city of Kiev. In the following two decades the eternal peace treaty acknowledged the status quo and put Kiev under Russian control for many years, in fact, centuries to come. Polish rule in Ukraine came to an end towards the end of the eighteenth century after three partitions of the Polish-Lithuanian Commonwealth with each annexed territory becoming part of Imperial Russia, Habsburg Austria and the Kingdom of Prussia.

In the meantime, the Tatar Golden Horde, the westernmost successor of Genghis Khan's Mongol Empire, began to disintegrate, and one of its successor states was the Crimean khanate, which accepted the supremacy of the Ottoman sultans. Both the Crimean Peninsula and the large adjoining areas of land remained under the khanate's rule until its annexation by the Russian Empire in 1783.

During the same year, the gradual process of enserfment of the peasantry in the Left Bank culminated under Catherine II, better known as Catherine the Great. Nevertheless, the reforms stimulated the development of industry, especially in eastern Ukraine, notably the Donbass, attracting the labour force to the area from the whole Russian Empire and first of all from the marchlands. As a result, the emerging working class and the urban population became highly Russified.

In the nineteenth century, the development of Ukrainian intellectual life was closely connected with the emerging role of academia. Though primarily Russian institutions, modern universities were established first in Kharkiv, the second largest city in Ukraine, situated not far from the Russian border, then thirty years later in Kiev, and after another thirty years, in Odessa, contributing to the study of local history and ethnography. This is not to mention the University of Lviv, founded in January 1661 when John II Casimir Vasa, the king of Poland and grand duke of Lithuania, issued a diploma granting the city's Jesuit Collegium 'the honour of the academy and the title of the university'.

Although universities had a stimulating effect on the Ukrainian national movement, Tsarist repression and the largely rural character of Ukrainian society hindered the growth of a political movement. At the same time, masonic lodges had already been formed and chartered under the auspices of the Grand Orient of Poland long before the first two partitions of the Polish-Lithuanian Commonwealth. The oldest lodge on record, named Three Brothers, was formed in Volhynia, and then another one, Three Goddesses, in Lviv. One lodge, The Dying Sphinx, was created in Kharkiv, also under the Grand Orient of Poland as well as the first masonic lodge in Kiev, Immortality, established by the Russian officers. While they developed international relations focused on continental Europe, masonic lodges became more secularised and more politicised, similar to the Grand Orients of Belgium, France and Spain, and the Grand Lodge of Russia. In the north-eastern part of Ukraine, the Malorussian Secret Brotherhood was established and sought the independence of Ukraine in collaboration with the masonic movement that continued to spread rapidly all over the country. A secret society, Cyril and Methodius Brotherhood, advocated social equality and a federation of Slavic states under the leadership of Ukraine. In the second half of the nineteenth century, secret societies called *hromadas* ('communities') were formed in various cities. Several years later, primarily student-led *hromadas* were engaged in overtly political activities in ways that benefited the national liberation movement. One such group in Kharkiv published a pamphlet in 1900 that called for the first time for 'one single, indivisible, free and independent Ukraine'.

Following the Bolshevik uprising in Petrograd on 25 October 1917 (New Style – 7 November), Ukrainian-Russian relations, never quite amicable, deteriorated sharply. The Central Council of Ukraine (or Central Rada, the short-lived governing institution of the Ukrainian People's Republic) refused to accept the new regime's authority over Ukraine and proclaimed the creation of the Ukrainian National Republic (UNR). The Leninists, in turn, at the first All-Ukrainian Congress of Soviets held in Kharkiv declared Ukraine to be a Soviet republic and decided that Kharkiv should be its first capital. In January 1918, the Red Army launched an offensive and advanced on Kiev but in April they retreated from Ukraine. By the end of the year, in Kiev, the Executive Council, known as Directory and formed by the Ukrainian National Union, took power and officially restored the Ukrainian National Republic, reviving the legislation of the Central Rada. The Executive Council was headed by Symon Petlyura who was also a freemason, the Grand Master of the Grand Lodge of Ukraine and the commander-in-chief of the army.

During the same month, December 1918, the French occupied Odessa. This began the intervention that involved French, Polish and Greek troops. After four months, however, they were withdrawn, the Red Army defeated the White Army forces and General Wrangel, the last commander-in-chief, reorganised the remnants of his army and what was left of the Russian Imperial Fleet, and with the military situation deteriorating, he and all his men fled to Turkey aboard Allied ships.

Following the chaos of the war and revolution, Ukraine appeared to be divided among four states. Bukovina was annexed to Romania, Transcarpathia became part of the new Czechoslovak Republic, Poland took over Galicia and western Volhynia, and what remained was soon to be formally organized as the Ukrainian Soviet Socialist Republic. Moscow decided that Ukraine had to be Soviet and it had to be Soviet quickly.

Stalin's rise to power marked the onset of the breakneck industrialization and collectivisation that in Ukraine led to rapid economic and social transformation. The industrial output had increased fourfold, the number of workers tripled, and the urban population grew considerably. The result of this inhuman, barbaric collectivisation was a famine that took as many as ten million lives. The groundwork for the famine – the greatest demographic catastrophe to hit one single country in Europe since the Middle Ages – was laid by Stalin. According to Professor Donald Rayfield's research in the Russian archives, Stalin ordered to force the tempo of grain exports to 'establish our position on the international market', but also to get American help with producing tractors. In fact, the hidden goal was to produce tanks because tractors were of no use when there was precious little grain. Nevertheless, by 1931, Rayfield notes, 'from a starving countryside, over five million tonnes of grain were being exported to pay for turbines, assembly lines, mining machinery and the funding of communist parties all over Europe, Asia and America'. At the same time, for want of men and horses, not to mention tractors, women were pulling ploughs without any hope of sowing anything. The silence of the West, emerging partly from its economic depression paid for by the blood of millions of people, Russians and Ukrainians, is a blot on our civilisation.[8] That, however, did not stop the late British historian Christopher Hill from saying seventy years later of Ukraine in 1933: ' I saw no famine', and write after Stalin's death: 'He was a very great and penetrating thinker. Humanity not only in Russia but in all countries will always be deeply in his debt.'[9] When Stalin was still very much alive, settlers from Russia were forced to move to Ukraine to repopulate the devastated countryside.

In parallel with the industrialisation and collectivisation, the Kremlin, with the help of the Communist party of Ukraine, launched a campaign against 'nationalist deviations' – in all, some four-fifths of the Ukrainian intellectual and cultural elite was repressed or perished in the course of the 1930s.

In April 1939, Stalin proposed an alliance between Britain, France and the Soviet Union. His idea was that the three powers should jointly guarantee all the countries between the Baltic and the Black Sea against aggression. Neville Chamberlain, the British prime minister, did not like the plan. Several weeks before, on 26 March, he wrote in a private letter: 'I must confess to the most profound distrust of Russia … And I distrust her motives, which seem to me to have little connection with our ideas of liberty, and to be concerned only with getting everyone else by the ears.'[10] He was right because already in May Stalin's representatives started secret negotiations with Germany, by August Russia had swapped sides and at the end of the month signed the Nazi-Soviet Pact, having agreed not to go to war with each other and to split Poland between them. By mid-September, in accordance with the secret protocols of the pact, western Volhynia and most of Galicia were occupied by Soviet troops. In June 1940, northern Bukovina was annexed, all of them becoming part of Soviet Ukraine.

Ukraine's human and material losses in the aftermath of the Second World War were enormous. Up to seven million people perished. The material losses comprised almost half of Ukraine's national wealth. Nevertheless, as much as in the interwar period, the post-war reconstruction, totalitarian control and terror together with the Sovietisation of Western Ukraine remained the hallmarks of Stalin's rule.

---

[8] Donald Rayfield, *Stalin and His Hangmen: An Authoritative Portrait of a Tyrant and Those Who Served Him* (London: Viking, 2004), 183–4.

[9] Boris Volodarsky, *Stalin's Agent: The Life and Death of Alexander Orlov* (Oxford: Oxford University Press, 2015), 117.

[10] Keith Feiling, *The Life of Neville Chamberlain* (London: Macmillan, 1946), 603.

Most of the 'bourgeois nationalists' came from Galicia, Transcarpathia, Volhynia and northern Bukovina, as well as western Podolia, which had been forcibly brought under Moscow's rule. And the Soviet secret police used its murder weapons to eliminate their leaders. On orders from Moscow, Symon Petlyura, a leader of Ukraine's fight for independence and briefly head of state, was shot and murdered in Paris in May 1926. In October 1947, the young and popular bishop Theodore Romzha, who had called his parishioners to resist the Russian occupiers and was hated by Khrushchev, the Ukrainian leader at the time, became Moscow's assassination target.

Initially, the Ukrainian NKVD under Sergey Savchenko mounted the operation, using their favoured technique of a road 'accident', but the bishop survived and was hospitalised. In panic, Khrushchev called Stalin for help. A special group from the Sudoplatov's Bureau No. 1 flew from Moscow and on the night of 31 October, a new relief nurse was assigned to care for Bishop Romzha. Soon after midnight, she used the syringe provided by Mairanovsky to poison the priest with curare. In the morning he was found dead. The nurse disappeared. The 'terminations' of Ukrainian nationalist leaders in the Soviet Union and abroad, opponents of the Soviet regime, continued after Krushchev's ascendancy to the top echelons of power in Moscow.

This, and the countrywide celebration in 1954 of the tercentenary of the Russian–Ukrainian 'unification', was another sign of Ukraine's rising status within the Soviet Union. On that occasion, Soviet Premier and the leader of the monolith CPSU Khrushchev transferred control of the Crimea to Kiev.

Having emerged victorious after the sharp political struggle between powerful candidates, at the 1956 party congress he delivered a report that became known as the 'Secret Speech', which denounced Stalin's purges and ushered in a less repressive regime. Khrushchev was also the first to start a succession of Soviet leaders of Ukrainian-Russian pedigree in the Moscow Kremlin: Leonid Brezhnev, Yuri Andropov, Konstantin Chernenko and Mikhail Gorbachev all had Ukrainian blood flowing in their veins.

The 1991 Soviet coup d'état attempt, also known as the August putsch, organised in Moscow by hard-line members of Premier Valentin Pavlov's government including himself, the Vice President and the Chairman of the KGB, collapsed within two days. Gorbachev, General Secretary of the CPSU and (the first and last) President of the Soviet Union returned from his dacha in the Crimea, where he had spent three days under house arrest, to find the country in disorder. In the wake of the events in the Soviet capital, the Ukrainian Parliament, in emergency session, declared the full independence of Ukraine. The USSR finally imploded at the end of the year.

The official inauguration ceremony of Victor Yushchenko, the third democratically elected president of independent Ukraine, took place on Sunday, 23 January 2005 at about noon. Both Dr Zimpfer and Dr Korpan were present and also invited to the party that followed, parallel to euphoric celebrations in the Maidan, the capital's Independence Square. In March, doctors received a report from a research centre in Münster, Germany, confirming the dioxin poisoning. Korpan said to *Ukrayinska Pravda* that 'there is no doubt that Mr Yushchenko has been poisoned deliberately', and added that the amount of dioxin in his patient's body exceeded the norm by 5,000 times. This does not mean that the Ukrainian presidential candidate had eaten five buckets of dioxin. The dosage would have been measured in milligrams, but the concentration and toxicity were so very high because it was a tailor-made poison specifically designed for Victor Yushchenko, taking into account his age, weight, nationality and, most important, his medical record.

Five years after his impressive victory over the Moscow candidate, the man once hailed as democracy's battle-scarred poster boy who was putting his country on the European path, agreed to meet a London *Telegraph* correspondent who was eager to know and tell his readers what went wrong in Ukraine under Yushchenko's presidency.

A total of 18 candidates were nominated to run for the presidential election and among them: Yulia Timoshenko, incumbent prime minister; Victor Yushchenko, incumbent president; and Victor Yanukovich, former prime minister and leader of the Party of Regions. By December 2009, Yushchenko had been trailing far behind in the contest, scraping just single figures in some polls. In the first-round ballot in January, internationally recognised as meeting democratic standards, he came in fifth place with less than five-and-a-half percent support. As the *Telegraph* correspondent who interviewed him noted, after personifying the hopes of the Orange Revolution five years earlier, by the time of the new election, Yushchenko symbolised the way its glow had faded, having failed to secure either European Union or NATO membership. He wasn't even able to negotiate a 'bezvíz' – a new word popularised by the Ukrainian media and meaning that the citizens of Ukraine could visit the EU member states without visas.

Independent observers also pin some blame on Yushchenko for failing to use his momentum to give the Ukrainian Parliament and the bureaucracy the proper household cleaning they so much needed. The highest country's legislature remained full of corrupt, criminal MPs who only used their mandates as a means of personal protection against prosecution. Besides, due to constitutional wrangling and a problem with the so-called party-switching that occurs quite commonly in Ukraine, when a partisan public figure holding elected office changes his or her political party affiliation, not because of their political convictions but in exchange for favours, it was and is difficult to carry out any reforms.

Many Ukrainians also question whether the Yushchenko-Timoshenko leadership duo really merited their orange halos in the first place, the same *Telegraph* article claims. They certainly did when there were the right advisers and consultants on their side during the days of the Orange Revolution. But after they left, having done their job, it would appear that despite her attractive face and a masterly created image, Timoshenko might often act as a quarrelsome opportunist who could be manipulated and put in a gridlock. Like, for example, in January 2009, when she signed a natural gas supply contract with Putin, then the Russian prime minister, at prices that were ruinous for the Ukrainian economy.

After having interviewed Yushchenko in Kiev, Colin Freeman of *The Sunday Telegraph* wrote that, 'although viewed as competent and honest, [the Ukrainian president] comes across as slightly plodding. Certainly, interviewing him is not like meeting some Eastern European Tony Blair – he is prone to monologues rather than soundbites, and reluctant to concede fault'.[11] Well, we know senators, MPs and even presidents who produced remarkable soundbites but were impeached, fired, disgraced or committed suicide not because of what they said, but because of what they did. President Yushchenko served his term with dignity.

Yushchenko was also criticised for naming Stepan Bandera a 'Hero of Ukraine', one of the country's highest honours, during the last days of his presidency and for his campaign to demolish communist monuments. Ironically, the statue of Lenin in Kiev survived until 2013, three years after Yushchenko's defeat, when it was toppled by activists. At the same time, monuments to Bandera had begun to spring up across western Ukraine, while to the east of the Dnieper River, particularly in Kharkiv, Luhansk and Donetsk, people under the influence of post-war Soviet propaganda continued to call him a Nazi puppet. Naturally, no one in Brussels cared to carry out any research and the MEPs, with their permanent chip on the shoulder, easily swallowed Moscow's ideological fodder, describing Bandera as the 'OUN fascist'. In reality, Bandera never set foot in today's Ukraine after 1934, spent much of the late 1930s in a Polish prison and almost the entire war in a Nazi concentration camp.

---

[11] Colin Freeman, 'Ukraine's Orange Revolution sours', *The Sunday Telegraph*, 27 December 2009.

Finally, President Yushchenko came under fire for calling on the international community to recognise the famine of the 1930s as genocide. Stalin's policies provoked the tragedy, he declared, which left millions of people dead from starvation and related diseases. 'There is now a wealth of historical material detailing the specific features of Stalin's forced collectivisation and terror famine policies against Ukraine,' Yushchenko wrote in the article 'The Holodomor', published by the *Wall Street Journal* in November 2007. (My own article, 'Terror's KGB Roots', came out in the previous edition.) Many countries, including the USA, recognised Holodomor as an act of genocide and 'deliberate act of mass-murder' committed by Stalin and his hangmen. One of the leading Russian historians, Oleg Khlevniuk, sent me his new biography of the dictator with a sub-chapter 'Famine', in which he very neatly summed up the situation, concluding that the Stalinist leadership was only able to retain power by using the most savage repression.

> The famine, which reached its peak over the winter of 1932–1933, took the lives of between 5 million and 7 million people. Millions more were permanently disabled. In a time of peace and relatively normal weather, agriculturally rich regions were ruined and desolated. Although the famine was a complex phenomenon, posterity has every right to call it the Stalin Famine. The Stalinist policy of the Great Leap was its primary cause; moreover, it was Stalin's decisions in 1932 and 1933 that, instead of easing the tragedy, made it worse.[12]

This concerns not only Ukraine but also other areas of what was once known as the Soviet Union. At its peak, the famine afflicted the territory populated by more than 70 million people. Secret OGPU and Communist Party reports are filled with accounts of widespread cannibalism, paint horrific pictures of mothers murdering their children, and describe deranged activists robbing and tormenting the population.

Long before the January 2010 Ukrainian election, Christina 'Chrystia' Freeland, a journalist who was appointed Canada's Minister of Foreign Affairs in January 2017, argued that for the Kremlin, a Yanukovich victory was important for philosophical, political and geopolitical reasons. 'Philosophically,' she wrote, 'a triumph for "managed democracy" and state capitalism in Ukraine would have been a validation of Russia's own renunciation of open democracy in favour of President Vladimir Putin's increasingly overt neo-authoritarianism. Politically, installing the Kremlin's

---

[12] Oleg V. Khlevniuk, *Stalin: New Biography of a Dictator* (New Haven and London: Yale University Press, 2015), 117.

man in Kiev would have been a victory for the neo-imperialist vision that Putin and his supporters have been propagating to shore up domestic support. Geopolitically, the Kremlin made its traditional calculation that vassals make better neighbours than independent states.'[13]

In the lobby bar of the refurbished Dnipro Hotel, where I first stayed in 1977, just minutes away from Kiev's main square, one of Ukraine's leading investigative journalists told me: 'I have no trust in these candidates, but the Orange Revolution did at least two things – there is a free media now, and it made our political leaders more disposable. That is, people can change them whenever they think it is necessary.'

Like Poland, Romania, Russia, Slovakia, Timor-Leste, Zimbabwe and several other countries, Ukraine is using the two-round electoral system. The second round of voting between Viktor Yanukovich and Yulia Timoshenko took place in February 2010. The exit polls indicated that Yanukovich had been elected, which was later officially confirmed. His inauguration was attended by a number of EU and American functionaries, such as: Catherine Ashton, former EU High Representative; James Jones, former US National Security Advisor; Boris Gryzlov, former Russian Interior Minister and a close ally of Putin; and the Patriarch of Moscow and All Russia, who conducted a public prayer service. The Primate of the Russian Orthodox Church, Vladimir Gundyaev (Patriarch Kirill), was elected to this post, the Russian media claim, because of his close collaboration with the Russian Intelligence Services and open support for the communist regime. Even after Gundyaev was elected as Patriarch of Moscow, he would continue to praise Stalin and the Soviet regime. For obvious reasons, Yushchenko and Timoshenko did not attend the ceremony.

That winter, the conflict that plagued the previous campaign became even sharper as far as various ethnic groups were concerned. Eastern Ukraine regarded Russian as their first language and continued looking to Moscow to help improve their living, while Western Ukraine felt their kinship with Europe. Irrespective of these differences, many Ukrainians wished to stand strong for genuine Ukrainian independence.

Victor Yanukovich had been in office for exactly four years, from February 2010 to February 2014, when he was ousted as a result of the Euromaidan Revolution. Euromaidan is the second act of the Ukrainian revolution for independence, which also became known as the Revolution of Dignity. This time it was because apart from being a grafter and a corruptionist[14] who

---

[13] Chrystia Freeland, 'Up from under', *Financial Times*, 8–9 January 2005.

[14] Unsurprisingly, the international media was unanimous in this case. See, for example: Jeremy Kline, 'Cowards in the Ukraine', *The Statesman*, 27 February 2014; Maxim Tucker,

would still be tolerated in modern Ukraine, Yanukovich rejected a pending EU Association Agreement choosing instead, under Moscow's pressure, a Russian loan bailout and closer ties with Putin's regime. Shortly after his ouster, the former president fled to Russia.

This led to mass protests, and the young Ukrainians eager to see their country as an integral part of Europe rather than an industrial appendage of Russia once again occupied Kiev's Independence Square to demonstrate their disagreement. Four months later, Ukraine appeared to be on the brink of a civil war as violent clashes between protesters and special police forces led to nearly 130 deaths and many injuries. On 21 February, Yanukovich fled Kiev in panic with the help of the Russian special forces, leaving behind his sumptuous private residence with golden lavatories, a private zoo with ostriches and peacocks, a helipad and a baroque marble construction that on closer inspection turned out to be a backyard barbecue. In short, as one report has put it, a disgraced and ousted Russian puppet has left behind a palace monument to greed, corruption and bad taste.

By a secret decree signed by President Putin, Yanukovich was granted Russian citizenship and settled with his mistress in a guarded inner ministry guesthouse near Moscow. Vladimir Satsyuk, former deputy director of the Ukrainian security service SBU, accused of taking part in the operation to poison Yushchenko, was also granted Russian citizenship. When Ukraine asked for their extradition, in an echo of the Litvinenko case in Britain, Moscow announced that it does not extradite its citizens.

Mykola Azarov, who succeeded Yanukovich as the prime minister of Ukraine, also fled to Moscow. At the end of January 2014, immediately after his resignation, he briefly visited his family in Vienna and then hurriedly left Austria because of a pending international wanted list for abuse of power. In January 2015, the Interpol placed Yanukovich, Azarov, their former finance minister and nine other suspects on its wanted list on charges of 'misappropriation, embezzlement or conversion of property by malversation' – most of them with a 'red notice', indicating an extradition request. However, they were soon removed following a legal complaint. Interpol says the appropriate information is still available in its restricted-access database, which makes no sense.

'Ukraine's fallen leader Viktor Yanukovych "paid bribes of $2 billion" – or $1.4 million for every day he was president', *The Telegraph*, 31 May 2016; Samuel Rubenfeld, 'Corruption Currents: Ruling Reveals Yanukovich Corruption', *The Wall Street Journal*, 10 January 2018; and finally, 'Ukraine Sentences Ex-President Yanukovych in Absentia to 13 Years in Prison', *RFE/RL*, 24 January 2019.

Less than two days after Yanukovich absconded with millions of dollars, gold, diamonds and other valuables, Russia occupied the peninsula of Crimea and the Crimean city of Sevastopol in a well-prepared military operation. Both were announced sovereign Russian territory in March. Exactly as with the case of the Abyssinia crisis in 1935 and the Czechoslovakia crisis in 1938–9, which began with the German annexation of the Sudetenland, the great powers and the League of Nations (today the UN) did not react in any decisive way, in spite of all international agreements, assurances and guarantees that they had signed. For the most part, the UN as well as the EU, British and American pronouncements were empty gestures that were not enforced and completely ignored by Moscow.

In April 2014, Austrian authorities began an investigation of Oleksiy Azarov, the son of Mykola Azarov, among several other Ukrainians close to the former government, on suspicion of money laundering, and already in March, the influential Ukrainian oligarch Dmytro Firtash was arrested in Vienna on an FBI warrant just weeks after Yanukovich fled to Russia.

Firtash was released on a record 125-million-euro bail but ordered to stay in the country. His defence lawyer was Dieter Böhmdorfer, former Austrian Minister of Justice, and he managed to persuade the judge not to extradite his client. However, in February 2017, the Austrian appeals court approved the extradition on corruption charges, violating the Foreign Corrupt Practices Act (FCPA). It was also established that Paul Manafort, who managed Donald Trump's presidential campaign, was involved in a secret deal with Firtash to buy high-end real estate in New York. Right after the decision to extradite him, Firtash was detained again by the Austrian police, serving a Spanish warrant separate from the extradition ruling. Spanish authorities were seeking his arrest for charges of money laundering and reported ties to organised crime.

Firtash is a Moscow asset. How the Moscow–Madrid criminal chain worked was initially established by Litvinenko when the British SIS seconded him to the Spanish investigators' team more than a decade ago.

At the end of 2013, a deal between Cargill, an American privately held global corporation, and Ukrainian Land Farming (ULF) was settled with Cargill acquiring 5% of the company owned by Oleh Bakhmatyuk, a Ukrainian oligarch and former banker. Several years earlier, Bakhmatyuk suddenly moved from the oil and gas sector to agricultural business, selling off his assets in a string of lucrative regional gas distribution companies to Firtash. Apart from ULF, he also owns Avangardco, which is listed on the London Stock Exchange. In April, during a press conference in Kiev, an Austrian MP accused Bakhmatyuk of involvement in one of Europe's largest banking scandals. Austria's Hypo Alpe Adria bank was the subject of a criminal investigation and it was announced, based on the investigation documents, that its Ukrainian subsidiary lent 57 million euro to Bakhmatyuk's companies, subsequently losing most of these funds. At least 2.5 million of the borrowed money was spent on the luxury property in Fontana, Lower Austria, where Bakhmatyuk's family resides. The latest news about Oleh Bakhmatyuk mentioned that the Austrian Finanzpolizei was investigating alleged money laundering of 35 million euro.

From the beginning of March, protests by pro-Russian and anti-government groups took place in the Donetsk and Luhansk provinces, together commonly called the Donbass. The word 'Donbass' is a portmanteau formed from two words – 'Donetsk' and 'Basin' that together refer to the Donetsk coal basin, which has been an important coal mining area since the late nineteenth century when Donetsk was the centre of coal mining and Luhansk of machine building and the chemical industry. After the Russian annexation of Crimea, protests and demonstrations in the Donbass area escalated into an armed conflict between the separatist forces and the Ukrainian government. With Russian help and support, which included political pressure, propaganda, supplies of arms, ammunition, anti-aircraft weapon systems, tanks, military personnel, advisers, armed mercenaries and volunteers, Russian paramilitaries were reported to make up between 15 to 80 percent of combatants. Thus, what seemed to many like a local conflict between insurgents fighting the central government in Kiev for 'independence', or a civil war between eastern and western parts of Ukraine, evolved into a dangerous war in Europe where Ukraine is trying to defend itself against an international aggressor – the Russian Federation.

In May 2014, Petro Poroshenko, a former secretary of the National Security and Defence Council of Ukraine in the administration of Victor Yushchenko and a former Minister of Foreign Affairs in the government of Yulia Timoshenko, was elected president, winning more than 54% of the vote in the first round. It was Poroshenko, then an MP, who served as interpreter, helping Dr Zimpfer, the Austrian anaesthesiologist, to keep Yushchenko alive and kicking during the latter's election campaign in spite of the candidate's poor condition after poisoning.

At the time of Poroshenko's inauguration, armed separatists headed by pro-Russian henchmen declared the separatist zones independent peoples' republics of Donetsk and Luhansk, abbreviated as DPR and LPR. Igor Girkin/Strelkov, a Russian Spetsnaz officer who was in charge of the 'rebel' movement in eastern Ukraine from the very beginning, was recently quoted as saying, 'You make yourself look like a total moron if you say that [the Donetsk and Luhansk Peoples' Republics] were formed by themselves.'

During his visit to Berlin, the newly elected Ukrainian president stated that separatists 'do not represent anybody'.

The New Year 2015 started badly for both Russia and Ukraine. On the night of 27 February, on a bridge not far from the Kremlin walls, a Russian opposition leader was cruelly gunned down ahead of a march against a war in Ukraine. The murder of Boris Nemtsov made headlines around the world and, hardly noticed by anyone, signalled to the Russian Intelligence Services to have a free hand in Ukraine. It was a very tricky operation that is still not fully recognised as such.

Fast-forward only two weeks and in March, Oleksandr Peklyushenko, a former regional governor, was found dead with a gunshot wound to his neck. An active member of the Party of Regions, he had been accused of using excessive force, together with pro-government thugs, to disperse demonstrators at the height of the protests against President Yanukovich's rule.

A few days later, Victor Yanukovich Jr, the younger son of the former president, drowned in Lake Baikal after driving in a VW minibus onto the ice. All five people who were with him survived. The young man was a fan of extreme driving and it is hard to say whether it was a mere accident or something more sinister.

On 15 April, Oleg Kalashnikov, a former MP and likewise a member of the Yanukovich's Party of Regions, was shot and murdered in his Kiev home. For the record, Kalashnikov was one of the activists hired to organise a series of anti-government protests known as anti–Maidan. It didn't work so he was expendable.

The day after Kalashnikov's death, another political murder took place in Kiev. This time a Ukrainian journalist was gunned down outside his home. Oleg Buzyna, who had never concealed his pro-Russian views, was, like Kalashnikov, active in anti-government circles.

'A journalist should never join the Establishment,' Frederick Forsyth notes, 'no matter how tempting the blandishments. It is our job to hold power to account, not join it. In a world that increasingly obsesses over the gods of power, money and fame, a journalist and a writer must remain detached, like a bird on a rail, watching, noting, probing, commenting but never joining.' Oleg Buzyna decided to ignore this golden rule, so he perished.

Between January and April 2015, more than ten people who were active political and business players during the Yanukovich regime were found shot, hanged, drowned in a bathtub or had jumped from a window.

Remarkably, Elena Bondarenko, an MP representing the Party of Regions, as if referring to this chain of mysterious deaths made a statement at the end of April accusing the authorities of threatening opposition politicians with assault. The Junta, she said (meaning the legitimate government), in their struggle for power in Ukraine is using methods that have nothing to do with democracy. The free world is losing another outpost – Ukraine, she speculated, as if her party and the Yanukovich regime in general had any ambitions of joining the free world instead of becoming Russian marionettes.

Bondarenko's statement echoed an article published on 21 April 2015 in *The Nation* entitled 'At Least 10 Opposition Figures Have Died in Ukraine Just this Year'. In the article, James Carden, the executive editor working for the American Committee for East-West Accord, warned that overthrowing democratically elected governments 'is not a promising recipe for building the kinds of "civil societies" that we are told are in America's interest'. Mr Carden further suggested that 'American journalists and US policymakers might do well to focus more closely on the full dimensions of what is unfolding in Kiev rather than to continue to simply parrot the post-Maidan party line'. Instead of a comment, I shall add that Mr Carden is a graduate of MGIMO, the Moscow State Institute for Foreign Relations.

A year later, mysterious murders continued and in October 2016, *Foreign Policy* published a report entitled 'Is Russia Killing off Eastern Ukraine's Warlords?' with the subtitle 'After a string of brutal murders, Donbass leaders are worried that someone very powerful wants them dead'. The article tells how a separatist commander – a 33-year-old mercenary – was assassinated in Donetsk by a remote-controlled bomb planted on his apartment building's elevator. It further describes how a former prime minister of the LNR purportedly 'committed suicide' – exactly like other former officials in Kiev – by hanging himself in a prison cell in Luhansk, where he had been placed after being accused of plotting a coup. Just days earlier, a separatist field commander was gunned down in a Moscow restaurant. Earlier that year, another warlord, the founder of the so-called Ghost Brigade of the pro-Russian LHR combatants, was killed in an ambush. Finally, shortly before Christmas, a Cossack ataman was assassinated by a car bomb, just hours after his own wedding. And these are only the most notable figures.

My latest information is dated August 2018. Several telephone calls from Kiev – all from the British and American journalists accredited there asking me to comment on the assassination of the leader of the Kremlin-backed self-proclaimed Donetsk People's Republic (DNR) – made me activate some sources in Kiev, including a good-looking blonde named Olena, Press Secretary of the SBU. The 'head of state' and 'prime minister' of DNR Alexander Zakharchenko, 42, was blown to pieces when an explosive device, planted in a vehicle parked near a café in the centre of Donetsk, went off killing him and seriously injuring one of his acolytes. Olena's office sent me a short note in Ukrainian without any comment suggesting I contact the chief. The SBU, a very weak security service because it has been fully penetrated by Russian agents since the day of its foundation, later issued a statement saying Zakharchenko's death could have been the result of infighting between rival separatist factions or an operation by Russian special forces.

I found the situation weird enough to contact Taras Kuzio, a British academic who is a research associate at the Canadian Institute of Ukrainian Studies and an international expert on Ukrainian affairs. Taras responded promptly. 'Concerning the killings in Kiev,' he said, 'I have always suspected they were undertaken by people within the Donetsk clan with ties to organised crime because they felt they needed to clean up house. Witnesses are bad for business.' I disagreed, arguing that those murders were sophisticated, efficient, and required close access – signs of tradecraft that suggest Russian involvement. Regarding Donbass, my interlocutor was of the same opinion as the *Foreign Policy* analysts, namely that the Russians were murdering their own who would not play by Moscow's rules, that these deaths often involve corrupt warlords falling out in turf wars over power and money, and, this was new, that some of the assassinations were the result of operations conducted by Ukrainian special forces. I thought it could hardly be the case, simply because the SBU and Interior Ministry did not have enough capacities and experience for such covert operations.

Indeed, two main theories were circulating among experts. Some believed the killings were likely the result of infighting among rebel chieftains. As they sought to consolidate their rule and reap the rewards of the region's lucrative black-market deals and smuggling routes, they were turning on one another.

Others were of the opinion that Russia could be behind the assassination campaign. The argument was that after labouring to build the region's governments and pumping arms and money into defending them, the Kremlin was interested in extricating itself from the quagmire of eastern Ukraine, hoping to do so by making the breakaway 'republics' seem respectable. That required eliminating thugs and former field commanders who had trouble following Moscow's orders. One well-placed source speculated: 'Some … are saying that handlers higher up the chain are cleaning up first-generation rebels to destroy any incriminating evidence and remove witnesses to war crimes. The Kremlin needs its proxies to have a more acceptable public face.'[15] At any rate, whoever is killing the Ukrainian separatists, the fate of the separatists is predetermined.

---

[15] Jack Losh, 'Is Russia Killing Off Eastern Ukraine's Warlords?', *Foreign Policy*, 25 October 2016. See also Pavel Kanygin, 'Why was the separatist leader of Donetsk assassinated?', *Meduza* (Riga), 4 September 2018.

Perhaps the most blatant political assassination to date took place in March 2017, when a former Russian lawmaker was shot dead on a busy street in central Kiev. Denis Voronenkov, who had spoken out against Vladimir Putin was gunned down outside the upmarket Premier Palace Hotel. He died on the scene. A firefight broke out between Voronenkov's bodyguard and the assassin. Both were wounded and taken to hospital, where the assassin died a few hours later. It was obviously a contract killing but the killer was not a trained professional, so he was also expendable.

The assassination coincided with a fire and explosion at a huge Ukrainian Army ammunition depot in the country's east that prompted the evacuation of more than 20,000 people. This time the authorities firmly blamed it on Russia, suggesting an escalation of Russian special operations inside Ukraine.

Another less known and less 'public' assassination happened in Kiev in June – Colonel Maxim Shapoval, the commanding officer of the Ukrainian Spetsnaz, was killed by a car bomb, which was without doubt the work of the Russian GRU. It looks like this secret operation in Kiev was an absolute copy of another operation when a Chechen politician was killed in the same manner – by a bomb that blew his car apart in Qatar in February 2004. Three undercover GRU officers were then arrested in Doha.

By the time this book was sent to press, the Russian aggression has not ended, and the situation not improved. It has got worse. The DNR and LNR governments have increased the size of their 'armies'. These continued to be quietly equipped with torrents of Russian weaponry shipped out covertly by the Moscow government, which hypocritically tried to assure one and all that it remained neutral. The war was going on and there seemed to be few routes for winding down the conflict. Ukraine was not going to give up territory that it justly considered her own, while Putin risked losing face – both within his constituency, the Russian ruling elite, and on the world stage – if Russia withdrew too readily from the morass.[16] Any agreements or international conferences aimed at reviving the stalled peace process in Donbass would be doomed to failure.

In January 2018 in Vienna, I met Dr Michael Zimpfer and Dr Nikolai Korpan – two doctors who saved Yushchenko's life. Michael was as open and friendly as usual. He had studied at the Harvard Medical School and received his MBA diploma at the University of Chicago, so his English was perfect. In 2001, he had been elected president of the Rudolfinerhaus, but after seven years of successful presidentship was not re-elected. A year earlier he had stepped down as the anaesthetist-in-chief in the Department

---

[16] Jack Losh, Foreign Policy, 25 October 2016.

of Anaesthesia at the Vienna General Hospital (AKH). At the time we met, Professor Zimpfer had been a leading specialist at the Vienna Medical Centre (Zentrum für Medizin und Gezundheit).

Nikolai – who I had not seen for more than ten years – was very circumspect in his statements, carefully weighing every word.

'Any problems because of the Yushchenko case?' I asked.

'No, no problems at all, everything's fine.'

In reality, this was not quite true, especially after two Austrian Social-Democratic ('Red') MPs questioned the credibility of Dr Korpan during several parliamentary sessions, which could lead to his losing his medical practice and certainly his reputation. But unlike his colleagues Zimpfer and Wicke, Korpan retained his position at the Rudolfinerhaus, travelling widely and perfecting his cryosurgical methods. He said he was still in touch with his former Ukrainian patient, whose portraits were hanging on the wall of Dr Korpan's office. After I gave him a signed copy of my *Poison Factory* book, which he had not read, Nikolai suddenly said: 'You know what? Yushchenko's case is as complex as that of President Kennedy, whose assassination more than five decades ago remains a mystery. I reckon there will pass many years before all true details of this affair come to light.'

I believe I know Ukraine rather well. My grandfather came from Vasilkov, a small town near Kiev where, like many, he was employed at the local leather factory. I visited Ukraine many times before and after it became independent and while in the 1970s and 1980s it looked like a prosperous Soviet republic that enjoyed a special status within the Soviet Union, after the declaration of independence in August 1991, Kiev turned into a typical post-communist provincial capital like Minsk, East Berlin, Warsaw or Bratislava. By now, of course, they have all changed and Ukraine is getting better but, as one witty observer remarked, taking two steps back in Kiev is still much easier than taking one step forward. It seems the newly elected Ukrainian president Vladimir Zelensky has already had time to realise this.

Chapter 9

Of Mice and Moles

I arrived in Godalming in November 2006 – the day Sasha Litvinenko died. Oleg Gordievsky invited me to stay with him for a while because he needed help with the avalanche of media requests related to this extraordinary case. He first placed me in a very comfortable hotel named The Inn on the Lake on Ockford Road, just opposite the local masonic hall, then I moved to his spacious house on the hill before relocating to the Rose and Crown, which had several rooms upstairs for guests. It is one of the oldest and smallest pubs in the town and I love it until this day, visiting whenever there is an opportunity. Valentina arrived late on Christmas Eve and we happily celebrated the end-of-the-year holidays together until it was time for her to leave and for me to return to our temporary office in Shepherd's Bush.

Exactly one week before Sasha's funeral, on 1 December 2006, *Panorama*'s editor Sandy Smith signed a letter on behalf of the BBC confirming that Blakeway/3BM was officially commissioned to produce a documentary on the poisoning of Alexander Litvinenko. The programme would be broadcast as *Panorama*'s 'How to Poison a Spy' on BBC One at the end of January 2007, at peak time. After that, John Sweeney, a reporter then working full-time for the BBC, became a regular and perhaps the most important visitor to our Shepherd's Bush premises. He was not dependent on us. The success of our project was dependent on him. And paraphrasing Mahatma Gandhi, he was not an outsider of our business; he was part of it. At the end of the day, it turned out that we were probably part of John Sweeney's business, but that is another story.

One day, John O'Mahony, a self-shooting producer and director employed by Blakeway TV for this project, asked me to invite Ahmed Zakayev, Litvinenko's Chechen friend, Walter Litvinenko, Sasha's father, and Sasha's half brother Maxim, so that we could interview them all in one place. John carefully chose the venue, which turned out to be University Women's Club at 2 South Audley Street in Mayfair. In the evening, I reported to Gordievsky about the events that had occurred during the day and he immediately remembered the address.

As it happens, in April 1985, although a political intelligence officer, Lieutenant Colonel Gordievsky received a highly classified instruction from the PGU headquarters, internally referred to as Moscow Centre, to use the Audley Street address as part of a dead letter box (DLB) operation. Such tricks of the trade were used by intelligence services during the Cold War. Without the tremendous advantage of today's technical means, the only way to communicate with an agent or illegal was by 'brush contact' or 'dead letter box'. An example of a real-life brush contract or pass could be seen in the surveillance videos of the Russian illegals released after their arrests in the United States in the summer of 2010 as part of a Freedom of Information Act request. This FBI investigation operation became known under its codename GHOST STORIES. Two video clips in the public domain show Russian spy 'Christopher Metsos' swapping information in a brush contact with his case officer who was working undercover as an official from the Russian mission in New York in May 2004.

A brush contact is a fleeting meeting between two intelligence operators when one passes information or instruction to another. The brush contact should be planned in 'dead ground', for example, a narrow spiral staircase of a cathedral or a dog-leg in a passage where prospective observers cannot get too close. In reality, brush contacts are difficult to pull off reliably because, apart from the watchers, a video camera may be secretly mounted in a place of a possible contact, like in the above-mentioned FBI operation.

DLB exchanges or dead drops are more reliable but they require greater organisation and more complex preparation. In the Gordievsky case, he was instructed to go down South Audley Street just a few blocks below Grosvenor Square, not far from the southern part of the American Embassy, and find a small enclave called Audley Square, where there is a prominent Victorian lamppost. A white figure '8', his coded telegram read, is painted at the base of the lamppost on the roadside, about a metre above the pavement. This lamppost is easily seen from a car passing slowly by (and one can only drive rather slowly there). A light blue chalk mark below the figure '8' was to signify that the DLB would be loaded at a fixed time in a previously agreed place, on that occasion Brompton Oratory. If Gordievsky was the one loading the DLB, a short time beforehand he was to make sure that the signal was read. If he was supposed to clear it, that is, to secretly empty the contents of the container, whatever it was – a fake hollow stone, a film canister, a cut-out book or any other concealment device – he would first have to make sure that the DLB was loaded and then leave a signal that he had successfully emptied it.

The advantage of the dead drop is that this method does not require intelligence operators to meet directly and thereby the security of the operation is higher. The principal disadvantage of DLBs is that they are occasionally discovered by the public – often by small children, or as a result of surveillance. Thus, in many known cases, clearing a DLB presented a considerable risk and often an immediate arrest of an agent 'red-handed' because the adversary knew the place and was lying in wait. A more sinister consequence of discovering a DLB would be if the opposition decided to booby trap it. Although it never happened in Moscow, there are examples from other countries.

What Gordievsky told me about this KGB 'tradecraft in action' was not so interesting or exciting because we had studied it all, and much more, during our Spetsnaz training, first as part of Operation RYAN and then again on my own special course as a GRU illegal. Although I never had a chance to use my skills in a real-life operation, we practised all forms of secret communication assiduously.

Operation RYAN – a Russian acronym for a nuclear missile attack, usually understood as a surprise nuclear missile attack on the USSR by the United States – was a Cold War intelligence programme initiated in May 1981 by Yuri Andropov, then chairman of the KGB and member of the Politburo. Because Gordievsky played a pivotal role in revealing details of the operation to the British and was the primary, and for a long time the only, source on RYAN, all that he said was taken for granted. For the British and American governments, Gordievsky's reports offered penetrating insight into the mindset of the Soviet leadership and it was a feeling of deep contentment to realise they were so well informed about its plans and fears. And fears were there all right because members of the Politburo were among a few people in the country who, at least since the Cuban missile crisis, knew very well that the nuclear strike was something the Soviet Union could not withstand.

Besides Gordievsky, other KGB and GRU sources provided corroborating information so what Gordievsky, codenamed FELIKS by the British, said and Christopher Andrew wrote in the book *KGB: The Inside Story of its Foreign Operations from Lenin to Gorbachev* (1990) is generally considered to be true and correct. As Professor Andrew later put it, 'RYAN's purpose was to collect intelligence on the presumed, but non-existent, plans of the Reagan administration to launch a nuclear first strike against the Soviet Union – a delusion which reflected both the KGB's continuing failure to penetrate the policy-making of the Main Adversary and its recurrent tendency towards conspiracy theory'.[1]

---

[1] Christopher Andrew and Vasili Mitrokhin, *The Mitrokhin Archive: The KGB in Europe and the West* (London: Allen Lane/Penguin Books, 2000), 278; and Christopher Andrew and Oleg Gordievsky (eds.), *Instructions from the Centre: Top Secret Files on KGB Foreign Operations, 1975–1985* (London: Hodder & Stoughton, 1991), ch. 4.

However, it is often forgotten that in a secret speech to a KGB conference in May 1981, Andropov announced that, by decision of the Politburo, the KGB and GRU were for the first time to collaborate 'in a global intelligence operation, codenamed RYAN'. Remarkably, the role of the GRU in it is widely ignored although at the time the CIA had at least three long-established and reliable sources: General Dmitry Polyakov, codenamed GT BOURBON and ROAM; Colonel Vyacheslav Baranov (GT TONY), recruited while based in Dhaka, Bangladesh, sometime in the 1980s and arrested in Moscow in August 1992; and Colonel Sergei Bokhan, codenamed GT BLIZZARD, the GRU station deputy head in Athens. In May 1985, Bokhan, who had worked for the CIA for ten years, was suddenly recalled to Moscow. With a sense of foreboding, he contacted his CIA case officer, Dick Reiser. Five days later, after stops in Madrid and Frankfurt, he landed at Andrews Air Force Base in Maryland, leaving behind his wife and daughter. Bokhan was extensively debriefed by the CIA, FBI and DIA, but anything that he said about RYAN remains secret.

What he probably could not say, because he did not know, was that after the announcement of the American SDI ('Star Wars') programme in March 1983, on the express orders of the GRU director Pyotr Ivashutin, several groups of officers with a good command of English, each group about a battalion or 300-strong, were gathered from various parts of the country at secret Spetsnaz bases. Disguised as paratroopers, they were to be trained in advanced insertion techniques and learn how to effectively use C-4 plastic explosives and methods of sabotage to conduct special operations behind enemy lines in case of war. Divided into 30 ten-men squads or teams, they were modelled after the Israeli Sayeret Matkal commandos to be able to perform tasks that included deep penetration with a view to reconnaissance, tampering and general mayhem. Operation RYAN began to wind down in 1984, although in August there were still high-level meetings with the East German Stasi to discuss its particulars.

In the summer of 1984, I was informed that our preparations for the planned military operation behind the lines (the name RYAN had never been mentioned) would be suspended and that as a former group commander I was now promoted to the rank of captain and would start special training on an individual programme. In May 1985, I was very busy learning German and studying details of several European cities, only hearing about Gordievsky's adventures at that time about twenty years later.

In August 2003, we were sitting in a comfortable Brussels apartment that belonged to Tennent H. Bagley, better known to his friends as Pete, and Oleg was telling us about the events of May 1985 when he was suddenly recalled to Moscow and appointed head of the KGB station in London. Pete, a CIA veteran, had served for 22 years in the Agency's clandestine service where he handled Soviet spies and defectors, before becoming chief of Soviet Bloc counterintelligence. At the time of his summons to the headquarters, Gordievsky had been a fully-fledged agent of the British SIS for ten years.

Gordievsky was the son of a KGB officer and the brother of a KGB illegal, and like many children from such families attended the Moscow State Institute of International Relations, known as the MGIMO, the MFA establishment producing diplomats and spies. He graduated in July 1962, already aware that in August he would join the KGB but, in the meantime, decided to spend his holidays in the recreation summer camp in the Crimea on the Black Sea. Here he met his good friend Stanislav 'Stas' Kaplan, who he calls 'Lazlo Barany' in his memoirs.[2] Like Gordievsky, Kaplan was a former MGIMO student, a good athlete and womaniser, and they had a great time together. After two months, Stas left for Prague and Oleg returned to Moscow to be driven with other recruits to the Higher Intelligence School (later School no. 101, then the Andropov Institute and now the SVR Academy). For the MGIMO graduates, there was a one-year course after which Lieutenant Gordievsky was sent to serve at the First Chief Directorate of the KGB, in its Directorate N (Illegals), where his older brother Vasilko had served. In 1966, newly married and a member of the Communist Party, he was posted under the diplomatic cover of Third Secretary to the KGB station in Denmark as a Line N (support of illegals) officer.

After his first unremarkable tour of duty abroad, Gordievsky returned to the Lubyanka headquarters in January 1970, where his immediate boss was Pavel Gromushkin, who since 1938 had worked at the section known as Documentary Support. From the very beginning this section was headed by the Austrian Georg Killich, alias 'Miller', and one of Gromushkin's colleagues there was William Fischer (who later became known as 'Colonel Abel'). Gromushkin, who specialised in forging documents for the illegals, lived a long life, passing away in Moscow at the age of 95.

Gordievsky and his first wife, Yelena, a KGB captain, were redeployed to Copenhagen again in October 1972. This time he was sent as a Line PR officer (political intelligence and 'active measures', that is, propaganda and disinformation) undercover as Second Secretary of the Soviet Embassy. He

---

[2] Oleg Gordievsky, *Next Stop Execution* (London: Macmillan, 1995), 198. Although there are names of serving and former officers, agents and operations of the British intelligence and security services mentioned in this chapter, I have not identified any person or clandestine operation that, to the best of my knowledge, had not yet been widely reported in the media or books.

knew, of course, that in Prague, after coming back from Moscow, his Czech friend Kaplan had started to work as a journalist but was soon invited to join the 1st Directorate of the Ministry of the Interior, where he was assigned to the Third Division (political intelligence: Western Europe). That was the Czechoslovak equivalent of Oleg's own new unit – 3rd Department of the First Chief Directorate. Headed by Dmitry Yakushkin, it was responsible for clandestine operations in Great Britain and Scandinavia.

While heads of the KGB station in Copenhagen, usually with a diplomatic rank of counsellor, came and went, Oleg, still a major, was promoted to Press Attaché of the embassy. One evening of 2 November 1973 there was a knock on the door of the apartment that he rented. When Oleg came out to see what was happening, to his great surprise he saw his old friend Kaplan.

Gordievsky could not know that after the one-year-long intelligence officer's course, in July 1969, Stanislav 'Daníček' Kaplan left for a holiday in Bulgaria where he managed to defect to one of the Western secret services. During his debriefing, Kaplan compiled a list of his friends who could be of interest to his new masters. Among others on the list was his Russian fellow student and Moscow Track & Field Club member Oleg. First, MI6 dispatched Kaplan to West Germany, where he tried to persuade a Czech citizen to change sides, and then on a 'fishing expedition' to Copenhagen. Upon his return, 'Daníček' reported that Gordievsky might be a candidate for recruitment and that the best way would be to set up a honey trap. On 19 November 1970, shortly after his trip to Denmark, the higher military court in Příbram sentenced Kaplan in absentia to 12 years imprisonment for defection abroad and attempted spying, although at the time the Czech authorities had no information about the defendant's involvement with the Russians.

'When the British made a move,' Gordievsky remembered later, 'it caught me off-guard. Having become enthusiastic about badminton, I had taken to hiring a court at the ungodly hour of 7 a.m. I would pick up a girl student called Anna, drive her to the court, and have an hour's match.' In his book, *KGB Against MI6* (2000), General Rem Krasilnikov, a KGB spy-hunter, writes that it was Ole Stig Andersen, head of the Danish Politiets Efterretningstjeneste (PET) who had sent 'student Anna' to Oleg. In reality, Mr Andersen headed the national security and intelligence service of Denmark later, and at the time that Gordievsky was pitched, during his second posting in Copenhagen, it was the PET chief Jørgen Skat-Rørdam who was helping the British to set up a trap. Gordievsky never provided further details but said that one morning in December 1973 he was in the middle of a game, when a man suddenly appeared beside the court, not in sports gear but dressed for the office. It was obvious, Oleg notes, that he wanted to speak to him. He identified the man as Dick Balfour, 'one of the best-known diplomats on the Copenhagen circuit: in his early forties, tall, with dark-brown hair and a good-looking typically English face.'[3] Describing the episode in *The Times* article in July 2015 devoted to the 30th anniversary of Gordievsky's escape from Russia, Ben Macintyre writes that the MI6 officer later admitted that he was uncertain whether he was recruiting Gordievsky or the other way round. 'Had this been an adulterous love affair,' Ben playfully comments, 'it was the moment when one side says to the other, "My husband doesn't know I am here".'[4]

Naturally, Ben could not have imagined that in April 2018, the Honourable Ivor T.M. Lucas, a British diplomat and husband of Christine Mallorie Coleman-Lucas (likewise a British diplomat), would die and that several newspapers, including *The Times*, would publish an obituary. Among other things, it would be remembered that one of Mr Lucas's coolest postings was to Copenhagen, where he had served as Counsellor from 1972 to 1975 and that MI6 used a British Embassy diplomat to recruit Gordievsky.

Lucas denied any involvement. 'Nothing to do with me,' he would later tell his eldest son. 'That was your mother's lot.'[5] While the role of Mrs Lucas remains unknown, the man who successfully recruited Gordievsky was the SIS head of station Robert 'Rob' Browning. Assisted by Skat-Rørdam's men, secret meetings with the would-be star agent were arranged in a safe house in Skovlunde, a small Danish town about 10 miles west of Copenhagen.

Once it had become clear that Gordievsky was the genuine article and not interested in an instant defection, a VCO (Visiting Case Officer) was sent from Century House to finalise his enlisting. Colin Figures, who later became Chief, flew out from London and met FELIKS, a codename given to Gordievsky by MI6, in a safe house in the older Gammel Skovlunde suburb of the Danish capital. After his recruitment, Gordievsky was handled by John Davies and then Philip Astley.

---

[3] Gordievsky, *Next Stop Execution*, 200.

[4] Ben Macintyre, 'The greatest spy story of the Cold War', *The Times*, 4 July 2015. In his September 2018 article in *The Times* also devoted to Gordievsky, Macintyre names the British officer 'Richard Bromhead, the MI6 head of station in Denmark', another alias.

[5] *Telegraph Obituaries*, 'Ivor Lucas, diplomat', 28 May 2018. Interestingly, Michael John Smith, serving a 20-year sentence for passing secrets to a KGB contact, in his letter from HMP Full Sutton, York, to James Fallows of US News & World Report dated 22 November 1997, writes about Gordievsky: 'His credibility was further questioned by my lawyers, because they were informed that Gordievsky did not volunteer to become a British agent in the 1970s as he claimed, but was blackmailed into it by a sexual affair (or trap) while working at the KGB station in Copenhagen.'

Oleg's agreement to collaborate with British intelligence in late September 1974 included a set of conditions. He would bring all secret documents that might come his way, but should not be involved in 'technical' operations like secret photography or eavesdropping. His meetings with SIS handlers would be limited to his postings abroad, never taking place in Moscow or other areas within the territory of the USSR, because KGB's counterintelligence, its Second Chief Directorate, was so skilful that no one ever managed to beat them. Finally, he was also prudent enough not to ask for any remuneration for his services – if he survived, and Agent TICKLE was very strongly determined to survive, this would come. He appeared to be right on every point. Over the next three years, Gordievsky delivered a treasure trove of high-grade political intelligence but, Macintyre notes, much of his information was simply too sensitive to be used.

In 1976, Mikhail Lyubimov, using the usual diplomatic cover of a Counsellor, arrived in Copenhagen as the head of the KGB station and Gordievsky's superior. Before Denmark, Lyubimov had been posted to London for four years and became infatuated with the English way of life, fashions and customs for the rest of his days, only to be expelled in 1965. After a short tour of duty in Denmark, he returned to the headquarters serving as deputy chief of 3rd Department, responsible for covert operations in the UK, Australia, New Zealand and Scandinavia. Lyubimov and Gordievsky quickly became friends, but in March 1978, Oleg's posting to Copenhagen was coming to an end as well as his marriage to Yelena, and he soon returned to Moscow.

There, he divorced his wife and married a woman 11 years his junior, who had been his mistress in Copenhagen and who gave birth to their two daughters – Maria, born in April 1980, and Anna in September 1981. Gordievsky was posted to London and the family arrived at Heathrow on 28 June 1982. Naturally, his new wife knew nothing about his involvement with SIS.

On his second evening in London Oleg, a middle-ranking officer reporting to Colonel Igor Titov, the head of Line PR and deputy resident, called a secret number that was given to him during his last meeting with Phil Astley in Copenhagen. A meeting was arranged for early July. Titov, a TASS correspondent in London from 1974 to 1979, was posted here again in February 1982, succeeding Ravil Pozdnyakov who, upon his return to Moscow, was promoted to head of 3rd Department. During his second tour of duty in London, Titov was representing the Soviet magazine *New Times*. In March 1983, after MI6 discussed it with Gordievsky, he was declared *persona non grata* and expelled. Back at headquarters, Titov would eventually be placed in charge of the British sector while Gordievsky, as expected, succeeded him in London as head of Line PR.

About a week after his initial call, Gordievsky made his way to the Holiday Inn on Sloane Street, where he was met at the lobby by his old case officer Philip, who had been flown from East Berlin especially for the occasion, and a slightly older woman, who would be introduced as Joan. She would become his London debriefer along with a new man, who Gordievsky describes as 'Jack' in his memoirs. It was John Scarlett (later Sir), a future Chief of MI6. With John as his handler, Oleg was extremely lucky.

After Titov was PNG'd on 31 March with two GRU officers, Sergei V. Ivanov and Gennady A. Primakov, Gordievsky took his place, rising one rank higher. To bolster his reputation, MI6 provided him with some useful contacts, like Neville Beale, member of the Greater London Council (GLC) representing Finchley from 1981 to 1986. Mr Beale was educated at my alma mater – the London School of Economics – as well as the Sorbonne and Hague Academy of International Law. His importance to the KGB, as he jokingly explained to me during a brief meeting in Gordievsky's house in the spring of 2007, was his apparent closeness to the prime minister, as Margaret Thatcher was not only the leader of his party but also represented the same constituency in the House of Commons. During the three years Oleg spent in London, his 'agent' recalled, he lunched with Beale every few months in some of the best restaurants, all expenses paid by the KGB.

Though Gordievsky, contrary to what he later claimed, was run by SIS rather than the Security Service's K3 section (the section that recruited and ran Soviet agents), his was a combined operation. 'In collaboration with SIS,' Christopher Andrew writes in his *Authorized History of MI5*, 'the small group in the Security Service who were indoctrinated into the case set out to strengthen Gordievsky's position within the London residency in two ways. The first was by giving him apparently impressive (though unclassified) information designed to enhance his reputation within the KGB as a political intelligence officer – work for which his role as a British agent left him too little time.'

The second was to justify the expulsion of more senior officers in the London residency. As part of Gordievsky's promotion programme, the head of station, Arkady Guk, was expelled in May 1984 and Leonid Nikitenko, his deputy responsible for Line KR (counterintelligence), was appointed acting head with Gordievsky in tow. However, until his official tour of duty in London was over, MI6 didn't dare touch Nikitenko so as not to raise suspicions to their prime source. Plans of John Deverell, director of K3, to declare Nikitenko, the acting resident, *persona non grata* in order to clear the way for Gordievsky, according to Andrew, were abandoned as counter-productive.

In January 1985, Gordievsky was summoned to Moscow for a high-level briefing to be informed that he had been chosen as a possible candidate to replace Guk and that Nikitenko was scheduled to leave London at the end of April. Indeed, Boris Korchagin duly arrived, and Nikitenko left for Moscow on 2 May. Korchagin, formally First Secretary in charge of cultural affairs, followed him shortly after when 25 embassy officials were ousted in September as a result of Gordievsky's defection.

During his department's annual party conference in Moscow, Gordievsky was officially introduced as the 'resident designate in London' and, as such, paid a visit to all department chiefs concerned including General Yuri Drozdov, the longest-serving chief of Directorate S, Soviet illegal intelligence, who succeeded at this post Gordievsky's former boss General Anatoly Lazarev and General Vadim Kirpichenko. Kirpichenko was in charge of Operation STORM-333 when Soviet special forces stormed the Tajbeg Palace in Kabul and assassinated Afghan president Hafizullah Amin and his 11-year-old son. It happened on 27 December 1979. By that date, Captain Skripal was already there and I was in bed recovering after a severe bout of influenza, so my trip to Afghanistan was cancelled, to the great annoyance and displeasure of the military commissariat.

By the beginning of February 1985, Gordievsky was already back in London. After Nikitenko left, Gordievsky took temporary command of the London KGB station, although still a lieutenant colonel. However, this had lasted for only two weeks.

With a staff then of approximately 2,300, SIS was by far the smallest service compared to America's CIA and Russia's KGB. Its officers were divided into an intelligence branch, or 'IB', of about 350 men and women, and about 800 who were general service or 'GS' officers. Those serving in the SOV/OPS department of the IB regarded themselves as the elite because although the Service was expanding its operations throughout the world, the Soviet Union was still the focal point of its activities. Sir Percy Cradock, a trusted advisor to the then prime minister, Margaret Thatcher, appointed Chairman of the Joint Intelligence Committee (JIC) in early 1985, believed the Cold War would go on forever and – not without reason – subscribed to the view that Moscow's far-reaching goal was world domination.

Cradock relied on the assessment reports from the JIC offshoots, known as Current Intelligence Groups (CIG), where the most influential was the CIG on the Soviet Bloc chaired by Harry Burke, a senior GCHQ officer. His group, apart from a notetaker, would include the Head of J Division from

GCHQ (this Division dealt with the Warsaw Pact states) and the Head of the Soviet Bloc controllerate from SIS.

At least two authors who researched the subject, Mark Urban and Stephen Dorril, concluded that the assessment system at the top British intelligence echelons relied to a great extent on the US efforts. 'More than anything else,' Urban writes, 'British intelligence is a system for repackaging information gathered by the USA. Most intelligence relates to foreign or defence policy, most of that intelligence is sigint [signal intelligence], and the vast majority of sigint processed at Cheltenham had been obtained from the USA.' Urban estimates that at the time when Mikhail Gorbachev came to power as General Secretary of the CPSU, between 80 and 90 per cent of intelligence flowing to the JIC was derived from the NSA-GCHQ sources.

A similar situation applied to much of MI6's own CX output, which relied to a great extent on sigint rather than on humint (human intelligence) having, as usual, little or no information on the inner workings of the Kremlin. 'What we were less successful at,' John Scarlett admitted, 'is getting into the mindset of the [Soviet] leadership.'[6] The situation remains largely the same with the only difference that elint (electronic intelligence), which began in England just before the Second World War, is now playing a leading role. This explains why so much effort was devoted to trying to impress the American counterparts though, as Urban notes, they were increasingly uninterested. One would say for obvious reasons because, during the eighties, the CIA and FBI maintained a vast network of agents, having penetrated the Soviet system high and low. On the contrary, in the UK, those members of the British establishment who had access to the weekly survey of intelligence known as the Red Book were not impressed. David Mellor, Mrs Thatcher's youngest minister, who was appointed to the Home Office in 1983, described them as 'humdrum'.[7]

When Gordievsky was serving as a Line PR officer in London from June 1982 to May 1985, except for his information about his fellow KGB and GRU men and their agents, he was only able to deliver political intelligence. As one author puts it, his achievement was mainly in delivering understanding, not secrets. Stephen Dorril, a British academic, author and journalist, notes in this connection:

---

[6] Gordon Corera, *The Art of Betrayal: Life and Death in the British Secret Service* (London: Weidenfeld & Nicolson, 2011), 267.

[7] See Stephen Dorril, *MI6: Inside the Covert World of Her Majesty's Secret Intelligence Service* (New York, London, Toronto, Sydney, Singapore: The Free Press, 2000), 747–9; and Mark Urban, *UK Eyes Alpha: The Inside Story of British Intelligence* (London: Faber & Faber, 1996), 4–7, 24, 31, 41, 73 and 288.

Gordievsky's information was not always well received, as it did not fit in with the well-ingrained prejudices of the Service. He was 'often puzzled by SIS's preoccupation with the KGB's modest operational successes' and was concerned that so much time was wasted by his MI6 handlers 'asking questions about agents and penetrations and so on. They didn't ask me elementary questions about politics. I assumed that it was because they knew about these issues, but they didn't'. MI6 had always exaggerated the role of the KGB, and Gordievsky's briefings that 'the Party was the boss. The KGB was the servant, particularly in foreign affairs,' were often rejected. His reports, however, were welcomed by Foreign Office officials and the assessment staff, who had long believed that MI6 was 'obsessed with fighting the opposing intelligence service rather than putting more effort into finding out more about the wider world'. The problem was that so much was invested in 'Sovbloc' operations, which were regarded by the elite Intelligence Branch officers as 'the route to the top'.[8]

For almost 11 years, Gordievsky had been their star prize, although his position within the embassy was by far less valuable than that of an agent-in-place in Moscow, like Oleg Penkovsky, for example. Even so, 'with Gordievsky it meant that MI6,' according to Derek Boorman, Chief of the Defence Intelligence Staff, 'was able to exploit everything that he meant in terms of exerting sensible leverage with the CIA.'[9]

Because he was considered a very high-value asset, Gordievsky was run with such secrecy that only a handful of MI6 and MI5 officers knew of his existence, as conventional wisdom has it. Oleg told me, for example, that Eliza Manningham-Buller, a future Director-General of the Security Service, was indoctrinated into the secret of his existence as a double agent while Michael Bettaney, a British intelligence officer working in the counter-espionage branch of MI5, who allegedly shared a room with her, was not. That is why, according to Gordievsky, when Bettaney decided to turn some of the secret MI5 files to Arkady Guk, head of the KGB station in London, he knew nothing about Gordievsky's role and thanks to the latter's efforts got caught.

This is obviously one of the legends invented by Gordievsky, especially after Mrs Manningham-Buller was appointed head of MI5 in October 2002. Having joined in 1974, she progressed from typing up transcripts of tapped telephone conversations between Warsaw Pact diplomats to becoming an expert on counter-terrorism. According to her BBC profile, she was heavily

[8] Dorril, *MI6*, 742–3.
[9] Ibid, 749.

involved in the Lockerbie investigation, served as MI5's liaison officer in Washington and became director of the agency's Irish counter-terrorism branch T2, spearheading the fight against the Provisional IRA. If it is true, as claimed by the media, that during the early 1980s only five people knew that Gordievsky was a British agent, this was quite certainly not Manningham-Buller.

Regarding those 'five people', apart from Margaret Thatcher, who was indoctrinated into the Gordievsky case in December 1982, Sir Geoffrey Howe was also informed on becoming Foreign Secretary six months later, as were several other FCO officials like, for example, Sir Julian Bullard, deputy PUS and political director. Sir William Whitelaw, Home Secretary, was taken into the Service's confidence on 24 January 1983 and so was his successor Leon Brittan (later Lord Brittan of Spennithorne). From September 1975, SIS had been passing all intelligence received from Gordievsky to MI5 and specifically its K Branch (counterespionage). That meant among those indoctrinated were four DGs: Sirs Michael Hanley, Howard Smith, John Jones and Tony Duff; Cecil Shipp, who became DDG in 1982; Director K (John Deverell); plus several members of K3, K6 and K7 sections. And this is only in MI5. The secret of Agent FELIKS was nevertheless preserved in spite of the fact that Michael Bettaney had been trying to sell his Service's secrets to the Russians while Gordievsky was in London, and Miranda Ingram, a former colleague of Bettaney in K Branch, left MI5, became a whistleblower and later worked in Russia as the *Daily Mail* Moscow correspondent. Because SIS was the principal agency running Gordievsky, among those who knew about him were: Robert Browning who, disenchanted with intelligence work, resigned from SIS in 1975; Sir Maurice Oldfield, the Chief when Gordievsky was recruited in Copenhagen; Sir Arthur (Dickie) Franks; and, at the crucial time of Gordievsky's posting in London, Sir Colin Figures. Finally, there were Sir Christopher Curwen, who oversaw one of the Service's greatest coups – getting agent FELIKS out of Russia; the head of the Soviet Bloc controllerate (C/CEE), head of Soviet Operations (H/SOV/OPS) and head of the Moscow station (H/MOS); officers John Davies and Philip Astley in Copenhagen; Gordievsky's London debriefers John Scarlett, Stuart Brooks and Joan; plus a couple of GS and TOS staff.

Across the pond, Burton Gerber, the chief of the CIA's Soviet/East European (SE) Division, also knew that his British colleagues had a source in the KGB and was determined to identify this source. Although Gerber did not respond to my email request, it is generally considered that he assigned Aldrich Ames, whose job was to oversee operations in the USSR, to find out who that mysterious person known in the division's records as GT TICKLE could be. Gerber was not jealous, although while this agent had actively or passively been working for the British, six successive CIA station chiefs, including Gerber himself, managed to serve in Moscow. The new boss of SE Division was curious.

Rick Ames was chosen for his new CIA headquarters role as counter intelligence branch chief in SE Division in September 1983, that is, over a year after Gordievsky arrived in London. He could speak and read Russian, was considered a KGB specialist and had some previous experience in handling Soviet cases. The division's Personnel Management Committee, comprising the SE Division chief, his deputy, the chief of SE operations and a couple of other chiefs voted on the choice. Ames's official job description was Chief, Soviet operational review branch in the Operational Review and Production Group of the Soviet/East European Division of the Directorate of Operations (DO). As such, he had access to all the Agency's Soviet cases, including all its human assets as well as clandestine operations inside the USSR.

According to Pete Earley, who had interviewed Ames in jail for almost two weeks, Ames quickly realised that he possessed an extraordinary treasure. When he joined the SE Division, the CIA had more spies working in Moscow than at any previous time in its history. From the files, he could trace at least twenty-five agents and a hundred covert operations. The enormity of the Agency's access to Soviet secrets was breathtaking, he thought, explaining to Earley, 'We had penetrated every aspect of the Soviet system; we had spies in the KGB, GRU, Kremlin, scientific institutes – everywhere.' As a result of Ames's treachery, they had all been betrayed to the KGB and only a few survived.

According to the legend supported by all who write about it, SIS decided to hide Gordievsky's identity from the American 'cousins', but it didn't stop the CIA from trying to figure out where London was getting its information. 'Burton Gerber', his former deputy and then successor, explains, 'was determined to identify the British source and assigned the SE Division's chief of counterintelligence, Aldrich Ames, to puzzle it out. By March 1985 Ames thought he had the answer – Gordievsky. Ames sent a cable to the CIA's London Station asking whether Gordievsky fit the profile. The answer was yes, and the CIA concluded – without being officially told – that Gordievsky was a British mole.'[10] To me, this seems pretty far-fetched.

Oleg also disagrees. 'There was also the problem that some of the CIA officers are not all that brilliant,' he wrote in an article in *The Spectator* about Ames

---

[10] Milt Bearden and James Risen, *The Main Enemy: The Inside Story of the CIA's Final Showdown with the KGB* (New York, NY: Random House, 2003), 46.

soon after the American traitor's arrest. 'The level is not as scintillatingly high as one might expect. They make up for it by working hard and being thorough, but there are some things you can't make up for that way.' About Ames, who he had met twice during his CIA debriefing, Gordievsky recalls: 'He wouldn't have known my name at that time, but he would have heard about the kind of information that was coming from me.' And then he says, 'I remember that when I first started working for the British in London, I was very eager that they should pass over my information to the Americans. The MI6 officer who was working with me — a very thorough and protective woman [Joan] — was adamant: No! Absolutely not! The CIA leaks like a sieve!'[11]

In his autobiography, published a year after that *Spectator* article, Gordievsky stressed that he [Ames] 'never knew my name, he told the Russians that the British had a source with access to the highest level of KGB intelligence'. That was it.

Alan Edwin Petty – a former MI6 officer and personal assistant to the Chief, Sir Colin McColl, – writing under the nom de plume 'Alan Judd', is of the same opinion as Gordievsky, dismissing Ames as socially inadequate. 'He was an incompetent and slipshod spy and would have been caught long before had the CIA not been equally slipshod in its approach to personal security,' Mr Judd writes in his review of Pete Earley's book *Confessions of a Spy*. '[The CIA] had all the right rules and procedures but did not apply them, which meant that Ames walked unheeded from his office with carrier bags of documents, avoided serious questioning of his new-found wealth and was never properly called to account for his drunkenness.'[12]

At the end of his book, even Bearden has to reconsider:

> Oleg Gordievsky was another unresolved case. He was recalled to Moscow in May 1985 ... before Ames's fateful meeting at Chadwicks. The fact that the KGB questioned but did not immediately arrest Gordievsky suggests that they lacked the hard evidence they had against the other compromised agents. Ames has been held responsible for betraying Gordievsky, and there is no doubt that he identified him to the KGB. But he did so on June 13, by which time Gordievsky was already back in Moscow and under hostile interrogation. Since his arrest, Ames has consistently told the CIA and FBI that he betrayed Gordievsky at Chadwicks in June, when he first gave the KGB his long list of Soviet agents. Both agencies are convinced he is telling the truth.[13]

---

[11] Oleg Gordievsky, 'Aldrich Ames, my would-be killer', *The Spectator*, 5 March 1994, 15.

[12] 'The sorry story of slipshod espionage', *The Telegraph*, 15 February 1997.

[13] Bearden and Risen, *The Main Enemy*, 516.

As correctly noted by Stephen Dorril, the Ames affair has left a deep impression on the Anglo–American intelligence community. In London, the Intelligence and Security Committee of Parliament found it unacceptable that two years after a major betrayal, the Americans had still not provided responsible British agencies with a detailed read-out of the damage Ames did to UK assets and agents. The report went on to express concern that MI6 had not started considering the matter until November 1995.

And here we come to the first of Gordievsky's riddles: was he really identified to the KGB as a British agent and if yes, who did it?

The timeline of events is extremely self-evident. On Friday, 17 May 1985 – the date must be remembered because wittingly or unwittingly it is given incorrectly in almost all published accounts, including Gordievsky's autobiography and the *Authorized History of MI5* – Oleg was sitting at his desk in the Soviet Embassy in Kensington. A cypher clerk brought in a telegram from headquarters summoning him to Moscow as soon as possible. There was nothing sinister in the text: he, 'Comrade Gornov', was to appear before 'Comrade Mikhailov' (Chairman of the KGB, Victor Chebrikov) and 'Comrade Alyoshin' (Vladimir Kryuchkov, head of the First Chief Directorate, or PGU) to discuss his possible appointment as head of the London station. Gordievsky was also to report on the situation in Britain after Gorbachev's successful visit there in December followed by his election as General Secretary in March. 'Gordievsky's briefs,' the Official Historian of the British Security Service, notes, 'doubtless impressed the Centre as well as Gorbachev, almost certainly influencing the decision of the FCD Third Department in January 1985 to recommend his appointment as London resident in succession to Guk.'[14] It was clear Britain was steadily moving to become the most important Western partner for the new Soviet leader. During their final meeting at the safe house, Joan and Stuart Brooks, Oleg's MI6 debriefers, were very laid-back and rather positive about his upcoming trip to Moscow and were anxious to know Chebrikov's plans for Britain. He duly arrived in the Soviet capital on 19 May. No one expected there could be a problem.

All the rest we know exclusively from Gordievsky. A week after he appeared in Yasenevo spending several idle days at the KGB foreign intelligence headquarters, he was invited for lunch by General Victor Grushko, First Deputy Head of the PGU. The car took them to a comfortable bungalow near a compound of cottages for important foreign guests. Apart from Grushko, Gordievsky claims, two other KGB officers were present: General Sergei

---

[14] Andrew and Mitrokhin, *The Mitrokhin Archive*, 725.

Golubev and Colonel (later General) Victor Budanov. The first was deputy chief of Directorate K (counterintelligence) and headed the 5th Department in charge of internal security at headquarters and stations abroad. The second, Budanov, his deputy, who Gordievsky did not know, was expelled from London in 1971, later also serving as head of the 5th department, then deputy head of the KGB in Karlshorst, East Germany, and from 1991 head of Directorate K. Both were the right persons to interview a candidate to be appointed resident in London. It was a typical job interview with sandwiches and brandy and without too much stress, according to Grushko, who later published a book about his work in the KGB with a special chapter on Gordievsky. However, Gordievsky insists that he had been interrogated, even drugged, but did not confess. Then for whatever reason, he was not detained but sent to the KGB sanatorium, while his family left for a long summer holiday in Azerbaijan, where Leila took the girls off as planned to have a proper rest at her father's dacha on the shore of the Caspian Sea.

It is established that during his meeting on 13 June at the Chadwicks restaurant with Sergei Chuvalkin of the Russian Embassy in Washington – almost a month *after* Gordievsky was summoned to Moscow – Ames handed over documents identifying twenty Soviet assets in the CIA register including TICKLE (Gordievsky). Among those were Adolf Tolkachev (SPHERE and VANQUISH) – a scientist captured four days earlier and shot after a quick trial; Sergei Bokhan (WORTH and BLIZZARD), a GRU colonel and deputy head of station who had been spying for the CIA for ten years (he was successfully exfiltrated from Athens at the end of May); Leonid Poleshchuk (WEIGH), lieutenant colonel, KGB Line KR in Lagos, Nigeria, arrested while unloading a dead drop in Moscow in August, shot. Gennady Smetanin (MILLION), a GRU lieutenant colonel in Lisbon, who offered his services to the CIA two years before, was recalled to Moscow and arrested in August, and shot. Gennady Varenik (FITNESS), KGB lieutenant colonel, Line N working under a TASS cover in Bonn, Germany, who approached an Agency officer in Vienna, where he had been posted (Varenik was lured to Karlshorst in November, arrested in February 1987, shot). Sergei Vorontsov (COWL), KGB major, Second Chief Directorate, Department for Moscow and Moscow region, arrested in January 1986, and shot; Valery Martynov (GENTILE), KGB lieutenant colonel, Line X, Washington, arrested in a sting operation upon his arrival in Moscow in November 1985, shot in May 1987. Sergei Motorin (GAUZE), KGB lieutenant colonel, Line PR, Washington, operated as a correspondent for the Novosti New Agency (APN), recalled to Moscow and transferred to Department 'A' specialising in black propaganda and disinformation. Arrested in November 1985, shot.

Among those who survived, Dr Vladimir Potashov (MEDIAN), a postdoctoral research fellow at the Institute for the USA and Canada Studies, worked as an interpreter to Harold Brown, an American scientist who served as US Secretary of Defense during a visit to Moscow. In 1981 Potashov, on a business trip to Washington, met Brown and asked him to introduce him to a CIA officer because, as he explained, he had some important information to offer. Brown agreed to help and that was perhaps the first time in history a high-ranking US official played a role in the recruitment of an agent. Betrayed by Ames, Potashov was convicted in July 1986 of espionage after passing sensitive documents to the CIA. He was released after six years, slipped out of Russia during a shopping trip to Poland and sought asylum in the US Embassy.

Another example is Boris Yuzhin (encrypted KAHLUA by the FBI and GT TWINE by the CIA), KGB lieutenant colonel, Line PR San Francisco. In 1975, the KGB sent Yuzhin to the University of California, Berkeley, posing as a student, where he was recruited by the FBI in a honey trap. Three years later, Yuzhin returned to the USA, this time using the cover of a TASS correspondent in San Francisco. Back in Moscow four years later, he was transferred to Directorate K (foreign counterintelligence) and arrested after his name had been passed over by Ames. He was convicted in 1986, paroled in 1992 and left with the family for the USA in 1994. At the time of writing, he was living with his wife and daughter in Santa Rosa, California.

In 1985, Lieutenant Colonel Vladimir Piguzov – codenamed GT JOGGER by the Central Intelligence Agency, a KGB officer recruited in Jakarta, Indonesia, seven years earlier after his tour of duty assigned to the KGB's Andropov Institute – dropped from sight. This was an especially mysterious and sinister loss, for Piguzov had not been in contact with the CIA since 1979, when he had returned to Moscow. Having been given up by Ames in June 1985, Piguzov was arrested in February 1987, tried and executed.

In 1982, Vladimir Vasilyev (ACCORD), a GRU colonel under cover of the Soviet military attaché, volunteered to a US military representative in Budapest. He was turned over to the CIA to handle and his case officer was at the same time a woman and a civilian, which did not please him very much. Two years later, Valisyev returned to Moscow. Taken into the KGB's custody in 1986, he was executed the following year.

Perhaps the most extraordinary and tragic story is that of the GRU general Dmitry Polyakov, a man the FBI and CIA called TOP HAT, ROAM, BOURBON and BEEP. Polyakov volunteered to supply the FBI with information in the early 1960s. 'By the time he dropped from sight in 1980,' Bearden writes, 'Dmitri Polyakov had provided American intelligence with the most voluminous and detailed reporting on the Red Army of the entire Cold War.'[15]

There were six others whose names and codenames Ames handed over to Chuvalkin on 13 June 1985 in one of Chadwicks' long and darkly wooded booths. In his book, Pete Earley claims they are still living in Russia, so these agents are not identified. Their codenames are VILLAGE, GLAZING, TAME, BACKBEND, VEST and EASTBOUND. The latter was a radar scientist from the Akademgorodok, a university centre for science, education and research in the town of Novosibirsk in Russia.

As soon as the agents were fingered by Ames or Robert Hanssen, a KGB mole in the FBI, they were immediately arrested by General Krasilnikov's men. But not Gordievsky. The double agent himself and the officials who profited from the sheer fact of his existence explain this discrepancy by saying that, for whatever reason, his case was handled not by the Second Chief Directorate, responsible for such investigations, but by the PGU – First Chief Directorate (foreign intelligence). However, the truth is that from May to September 1985 the Gordievsky case was not handled by anybody in the KGB because no one suspected him of treachery before they learned about it directly from the British side. Not even his wife.

It is true that psychoactive drugs were used by the KGB, especially its Directorate S, which controls the illegals, to check the reliability of its agents. The trustworthiness of those who operate overseas for a long time was and remains a constant concern of the security officers from Directorate K (foreign counterintelligence). Having spent several years in Directorate S (illegals), where his older brother also served, Gordievsky certainly knew the procedures and described them correctly. I also heard about the 'truth serum', as it is known, like scopolamine, pentothal, amobarbital (amytal sodium) or others mentioned in Chapter 3, but had no chance to try it on myself and never observed its action on humans.

Gordievsky's description of his 'hostile interrogation' in Yasenevo generally corresponds to what could really happen when an illegal returned to Moscow for a visit or obligatory holidays. One day he or she would be invited to have lunch or dinner in a safe house with a lot of booze. At a suitable moment, a drug like SP-117 would be administered and a specialist would start asking questions. Usually it works, and the substance can loosen the tongue of even the toughest intelligence operators while the next morning a person cannot remember anything.

---

[15] Bearden and Risen, *The Main Enemy*, 189.

The problem is not whether any special pharmaceutical preparation (SP) was or was not used during his late May lunch with KGB bosses. The problem is that at that time Gordievsky was quite certainly *not* under any suspicion as an agent of a foreign power. There was no sense or reason to bug his apartment, install hidden cameras or arrange surveillance, as he described in his autobiography, because it had initially been presumed that he must be 'clean'. Otherwise, it would make no sense – only three months before – to get him acquainted with special resident's codes and means of secret communication with Moscow as well as show him highly classified documents, as had been done. And if Ames indeed figured out TICKLE's real name, which is very unlikely because Gordievsky was not an American asset and the real name of a source had never been disclosed by SIS, the Russians would not know it until mid-June. Even if they somehow learnt that the London station was leaking, Gordievsky would probably be the last person to suspect due to his exemplary biography and service record. There were plenty of other candidates in the London station, including Leonid Nikitenko, long-time head of Line KR, and Valery Prokopchik, head of Line X (scientific and technical intelligence).

'At the time I was the party secretary of 3rd Department,' Yuri Solonitsyn, who later served as personal assistant (Head of Secretariat) to Vladimir Kryuchkov, the Chief, says in an interview, 'and Gordievsky was my deputy. He had always been an excellent party comrade and, having spent so much time together, also sharing a drink or two, I would never think he might be a traitor. But he already was.'[16]

What happened next is well-known from the books *Next Stop Execution* (considered to be Gordievsky's autobiography) and *Sokea peili* (with Inna Rogatchi) that came out ten years after the events, in addition to multiple published accounts and several documentaries.

To warn the British that he was in danger, FELIKS had to appear on a certain street corner at 7:00 p.m. on a Tuesday, 'and stand by a lamp-post on the edge of the pavement holding a plastic Safeway shopping bag.' Next, he writes, 'at 11 a.m. on the third Sunday after that, I would pass a written message by brush-contact in St Basil's Cathedral, on Red Square.' The first attempt, we learn, was on Tuesday 11 June, meaning that the next contact was planned three weeks later on 30 June 1985.

This plot, of course, is an important element of drama to introduce tension into the narration. First, there were no grounds to worry because it was also

---

[16] Leonid Mlechin, *Istoriya vneshnei razvedki: Kariery i sud'by* (Moscow: Tsentropoligraph, 2011), 24.

his planned vacation time. Secondly, to give a danger sign and then wait for three weeks until the next meeting sounds unreasonable, to say the least. And indeed, as shall be seen, in reality the escape plan was quite different.

By mid-July, a month after the meeting at Chadwicks, Gordievsky must have heard of something big happening in Washington. At the time, the First Directorate was leaking like a sieve and frank, informal corridor conversations were a norm. And although he was on holiday at a KGB sanatorium, Gordievsky was keeping his finger on the pulse.

Like every man living a double life, he had a well-developed instinct of self-preservation. 'The biggest threats to each side's spies are agents coming over from the other side and snitching on them.' Gordievsky understood that better than anybody else but this adage, coined by none other than Aldrich Ames, only became known to him many years later. First of all, he called his 'agent' Neville Beale, cancelling their next lunch because, Oleg explained, he had been recalled to Moscow where he was now in a sanatorium. Neville immediately alerted his MI6 contacts who, in turn, informed the Moscow station. On Tuesday, 16 July, Gordievsky arranged a late dinner with his father-in-law in the village of Davydkovo on the Moscow M3 route, where Mr Aliyev had a country house, which perfectly suited Oleg's meeting appointment with SIS at Kutuzovsky Prospekt. He could not imagine that it was the same lamppost that had already been used in the Penkovsky operation.

At 4:00 p.m., Gordievsky headed out of his house at 109/2 Leninsky Prospekt[17], inhabited by the KGB employees. The house was built in 1976 and Oleg acquired a new co-operative apartment there while still in Copenhagen. After spending almost three hours 'dry-cleaning' (professionally correct but in reality, a profoundly meaningless exercise if and when you are under surveillance in Moscow) arrived on station perfectly in time. After some minutes he saw Andrew Gibbs, First Secretary of the British Embassy, munching a Mars chocolate bar and carrying a green Harrods bag. As he passed within four or five yards, he stared straight at Oleg and continued walking, so the agent realised that his signal had been read and understood. On the same day, a YZ (highly classified) telegram was sent to London. This set in motion the rescue plan codenamed Operation PIMLICO.

Whether or not PIMLICO succeeded, the attempt would spark a diplomatic firestorm that was very clear to number 10 Downing Street, the

---

[17] In Gordievsky's own memoirs and all subsequent publications, the house number is given incorrectly. Gordievsky gives it as '103 Leninsky Prospekt' (*Next Stop Execution*, page 1); in Chris Andrew's book, it is '109 Leninsky Prospekt' (*KGB: The Inside Story*, page 10); and Ben Macintyre simply says 'Leninsky Prospekt' not bothering to mention any number (*The Spy and the Traitor*, pages 275 and 279).

Foreign Office, and to Sir Bryan Cartledge, the new British ambassador who had only taken up his post a few weeks before and was preparing to fly to Moscow that Thursday. The prime minister knew about the plan, but she was at Balmoral Castle visiting the Queen. So Charles Powell, Mrs Thatcher's private secretary, flew to Scotland and drove to the castle. 'Telling a miffed equerry that he needed the prime minister at once, and alone,' Ben Macintyre writes, 'Powell told Mrs Thatcher that the Pimlico signal had been flown, and requested approval to proceed.' There were only four days before the danger signal was displayed, and the exfiltration operation must have been accomplished.

The escape plan was drafted by Joan but revised and approved by Patrick, at the time H/SOV/OPS. It required FELIKS to be at the rendezvous point at 2:30 p.m. on Saturday 20 July. Near kilometre-post 836 in the vicinity of Vyborg only 24 miles south of Russia's border with Finland was a loop road in a wide D-shape marked by a large rock. It was hidden from the main road by trees and bushes.

On Wednesday, Oleg bought a second-class ticket on the overnight train to Leningrad for the following Friday. On Friday afternoon, he hastily repeated his usual anti-surveillance drill known to all intelligence branch officers as 'Moscow rules', and by 5:00 p.m. reached Leningradsky station, the oldest of Moscow's nine railway terminals. On the same day the newly arrived British ambassador, Sir Bryan, was hosting a cocktail party where all diplomats, including members of the SIS station, were in attendance. At almost the same time that Oleg boarded the train, two senior MI6 officers and their wives left the embassy reception and set off in the direction of the Finnish border. The ruse was for the wife of Andrew to fake a minor medical emergency requiring treatment in Helsinki while her friend Clare, Viscountess Asquith, would go in order to keep her company. Their husbands, both First Secretaries, would be dragged along feigning reluctance. On the way Raymond Asquith, the head of MI6's Moscow station, took the lead in his white Saab especially selected by TOS for this operation. His deputy, Andrew Gibbs, drove the second car, a silver Ford Sierra. As additional cover, Raymond and Clare would take with them their baby daughter, Frances Sophia. At the pre-arranged place in the woods, the pick-up had taken less than 80 seconds.

In his memoirs *Conflict of Loyalty*, published in 1994, Geoffrey Howe (later Baron Howe of Aberavon), then Secretary of State for Foreign and Commonwealth Affairs, describes how at the last minute, on Saturday 20 July, 'two senior officials (one from the FCO, the other from SIS)' visited him at Chevening House, a country residence in the parish of Chevening in Kent, and how he 'gave authority for the plan to go ahead', a decision endorsed by the prime minister.

One day in January 2007, some time before the *Panorama* investigation of the poisoning of Litvinenko, where I acted as a chief consultant, was due to be aired by the BBC, Oleg told me with a meaningful and somewhat mysterious expression on his face that he and Maureen were leaving for Portsmouth and would not be back until the next day. I was left behind to look after the house, which is indeed a substantial two-storey home on the hill but hardly a 'stockbroker-belt' estate, as described in the media. It is, however, considerably better than that of any other KGB or GRU defector in Britain like, for example, Vladimir Rezun, Vladimir Kuzichkin, Mikhail Butkov, Victor Oshchenko or Sergei Skripal, not to mention Victor Makarov.

Upon his return I quickly learnt the big secret – Gordievsky was invited to deliver a lecture to the next IONEC – Intelligence Officer's New Entry Course – part of which was traditionally taking place in Fort Monckton, an atmospheric and well-hidden base for MI6, officially known as 'No. 1 Military Training Establishment'. The 'Fort' is a historic military installation on the eastern end of Stokes Bay, Gosport.

In September 1780, five years after the American War of Independence began, the Governor of Portsmouth Lieutenant General Sir Robert Monckton ordered to start construction works to defend Stokes Bay. It was completed just before the French revolution and was renamed Fort Monckton, after the governor. It is only about an hour by train from Godalming to Portsmouth Harbour where Oleg and Maureen were met at the station and driven along a winding road through the guarded gatehouse to the main wing. Here, they were lodged in a luxury suite reserved for the Chief, at the time Oleg's former case officer Sir John Scarlett. Only a few weeks before, John and his wife Gwenda privately visited Oleg for a 'family' dinner at home. Although the local Waitrose offers a decent selection of wines, Oleg and I travelled to Fortnum & Mason on Piccadilly to buy a special bottle for his guests along with a large circular wooden box of Époisses from Fromagerie Berthaut.

Gordievsky's lecture to IONEC is traditionally a story of his remarkable escape from Russia. For years he used to tell it to almost every IONEC, providing a dramatic account of tradecraft in action, as one of the former students who attended the course in 1991–2 has described it.

According to the story related by that student, after Gordievsky was suspended from work and his passport confiscated while the KGB conducted further inquiries, he managed to get word of his plight to the station in Moscow where a mid-career officer, the Honourable Raymond Horner, was the number two, designated MOS/1 by the headquarters. (As no 'Raymond

Horner' was in the Moscow Embassy list at the time, one may presume that Oleg had in mind Raymond Asquith, who would eventually become 3rd Earl of Oxford and Asquith or Lord Oxford as he is now known, and Katherine Sarah-Julia Horner, an MI6 officer who was indeed posted to Moscow in 1985. Thus, from two real characters, he created one fictional.)

Every station has on its standing orders at least one plan for exfiltration of defectors in such emergencies, Oleg told his listeners. The exfiltration plan in Moscow was to smuggle the agent over the Finnish border. A support team had already reconnoitred a route from Moscow, and Horner had a Saab 900 as his official car, which in 1985 was the only car with a large enough boot to comfortably hold a grown man. This luxury foreign automobile, assembled in Finland, was a front-engined, front-wheel-drive vehicle that originally contained a number of unusual design features that distinguished it from most other cars, making it a preferred model for the operation. However, Oleg added, it caused some resentment amongst Horner's FCO colleagues because they were obliged to drive uninspiring British models in inconspicuous colours.

As his daily routine, Gordievsky narrated, he took a stroll in Gorky Park, followed closely by his round-the-clock surveillance team. Horner identified a patch of 'dead ground' where the agent would be momentarily out of sight of his followers, and spent the day driving around Moscow practising his anti-surveillance skills. On a designated evening he arrived at the spot at exactly the same time as Gordievsky, who leapt into the Saab's capacious boot. Horner immediately drove out of Moscow and started a long and nerve-wracking ride to the Finnish border not daring to communicate with his hidden passenger because his car could have been bugged. Even after they crossed the border, it was too risky to speak so, to let Oleg know that he was now out, safe and free he played his hidden passenger's favourite piece of music over the car stereo. It was *Finlandia*, Op. 26 by the Finnish composer Jean Sibelius, written at the end of the nineteenth century as a covert protest against censorship from the Russian Empire. In order to circumvent the restrictions, *Finlandia* had to be performed under alternative names at various musical concerts, one of such names being *Happy Feelings*. After that, agent FELIKS, Gordievsky, has been referred to in MI6 by the codename OVATION, a reference to this piece and that episode.

Yet another story of Gordievsky's escape from Russia was told by the British writer Nigel West, the pen name of the former Conservative Party politician and MP Rupert Allason in his book *The Friends*, published in 1988, three years after the exfiltration operation. In West's account, the circumstances of Gordievsky's passage back to England were 'quite extraordinary'. 'It took place,' West reveals, 'while Moscow's local security apparatus was at full stretch coping with some 30,000 students attending the 12th World Festival of Youth. Coincidentally, a cocktail party was held at the British Embassy by the ambassador, Sir Bryan Cartledge, and Gordievsky was smuggled past the Soviet militiamen guarding the Embassy gates in the back of a guest's diplomatic car.'

The operation, according to West, further developed in the following way. 'After spending the night in the Embassy,' he writes, 'Gordievsky climbed into one of the two specially adapted Commer vans that periodically carry non-urgent diplomatic freight north by road to Helsinki via Leningrad. Once across the frontier at Vybourg-Vaalimaa where, by convention, diplomatic vehicles and their passengers are exempted from checks, Gordievsky's arrival in the Finnish capital was concealed by the unusually large retinue accompanying the British Foreign Secretary to attend a European Security Conference. Once his journey to England had been completed, the lengthy debriefing session began.'[18]

If I did not know personally almost all participants of Operation PIMLICO (Oleg told one of his co-authors it was codenamed MAGICIAN TRICK), I would call it the second Gordievsky's riddle, asking: which of the three stories of his miraculous escape from Russia is true?

On the morning of 16 June 2007, I woke up very early to get a copy of *The London Gazette* before a telephone call from Natalie Golitsyn, the London correspondent of Radio Free Europe/Radio Liberty. Both Natalie and I knew there would be an important announcement and were ready. A day before, Oleg and Maureen left for Ireland, and I was to answer all incoming calls. Natalie's was the first at 8:00 a.m. and I was happy to share the news – Gordievsky was appointed Companion of the Most Distinguished Order of St Michael and St George (CMG) for 'services to the security of the United Kingdom' in the Queen's Birthday Honours for that year.

After the traditional October ceremony at Buckingham Palace, where Oleg received his award in person from the Queen, we gathered for a luncheon at the spacious and well-appointed Oxford and Cambridge Club on Pall Mall. The party was organised by Michael Shipster, CMG OBE, a former British diplomat serving, among other places, in Moscow and Washington, who was educated at Oxford, and Sergei Cristo, a Russian-born activist of the Tory Party. Among the guests were participants of Operation PIMLICO including Raymond Asquith who, after Moscow, served as a counsellor at HM Embassy in Kiev. Another British diplomat, Michael Davenport, a keen tennis player

---

[18] Nigel West, *The Friends: Britain's Post-War Secret Intelligence Operations* (London: Weidenfeld and Nicolson, 1988), 163.

who was posted as First Secretary to Moscow in 1996 and at the time served as FCO Director for Russia, South Caucasus and Central Asia was also there as well as Glenmore S. Trenear-Harvey, a former RAF pilot, writer and broadcaster specialising in geopolitical, security and intelligence matters. Seva Novgorodsev MBE, a radio presenter from the BBC Russian Service, was, as usual, the life and soul of the party. Seva was quite famous in the former Soviet Union for his witty talk shows like BBSeva and others. His real name turned out to be Vsevolod Borisovich Levinstein. Not that it mattered in any way. New Forest East Conservative MP and Shadow Minister of State for the Armed Forces Julian Lewis, also an Oxford alumnus, and Liam Fox, another Conservative MP, then Shadow Defence Secretary, were also present. My wife and I were lucky to be seated together with the Cambridge professor Christopher Andrew and were deeply engaged in an interesting conversation when a steward announced the arrival of Lady Thatcher.

It was the most extraordinary meeting and we happily spent a few hours with the former prime minister, who was indeed an outstanding personality. At one moment Lady Thatcher asked whether it was now known for sure who betrayed Oleg and after a short and rather-awkward pause I had to say: 'No, madam, it has not been established so far,' after which no one dared to comment. At the end, Michael Shipster stood up, took out a card from his pocket and read what he said was an extract from Gordievsky's personal file. 'Back in 1974,' he began, 'setting out on the path that would eventually bring him to Britain, Gordievsky wrote a letter to the head of MI6, laying out his motivations.'

> My decision is not the result of irresponsibility or instability of character on my part. It is a decision that has been preceded by a long spiritual struggle and my agonising emotion. But even deeper disappointment of developments in my country and my own experiences have brought me to the belief that democracy and the tolerance and humanity which follow it, represent the only road for my country … If a man realises this, he must show the courage of his convictions and do something himself to prevent slavery from encroaching further upon the realms of freedom.

I have asked Michael to let me have this card or its copy for my future book, but he refused, saying with a smile: 'A good try, Boris, but sorry, this is strictly confidential.' Actually, it was not. With a slightly different wording, this passage appeared in print in both Oleg's book published in Finland and in the already mentioned article by Ben Macintyre in *The Times*.

The rest of the party went on extremely well, the food was superb as well as the wine and I introduced Valentina to Raymond Asquith, great-grandson of the former British prime minister, who together with his wife played a prominent role in the rescue operation.

Rewind to July 1985. When the cars approached the rendezvous point, they swerved onto a loop road behind the curtain of trees and bushes, where Gordievsky was hiding, and screeched to a stop. A small, dishevelled figure emerged from the undergrowth and climbed into the boot of the Ford. The thermal blanket was quickly laid on top of him to foil heat-detecting sensors at the border and, in violation of the cover story that called for the two couples to pretend to have stopped for a picnic, they slammed shut the boot and rushed towards border control. Two checkpoints after the last petrol station they passed without delay and only stopped in the official border area. While the guards scrutinised their diplomatic passports, Clare Asquith, daughter of an architect, suddenly did something creative and spontaneous. She took the baby from the back seat of Saab and began changing her nappy on top of the boot of the Ford above where Gordievsky lay. Then she dropped the nappy on the ground in front of the sniffer dogs that were quickly led away to inspect other cars. In a few minutes, the Ford started up and began to pick up speed. I wonder if Lady Frances Sophia Asquith, now in her thirties, ever learnt that many years ago her dirty nappy probably changed the course of the Cold War.

The rest is known. On the other side of the border, in the forest right after the Vaalimaa crossing point, they were met by an impatient but happy group led by Michael Shipster, then a rising star of the FCO. Naturally, happy and smiling, Stuart and Joan were also there as well as Margaret Mildred 'Meta' Ramsay, the future Baroness Ramsay of Cartvale and member of the House of Lords. A fluent Russian speaker, at the time she had served as Helsinki head of station. After a short telephone report to the SOV/OPS chief who had masterminded the whole operation, the rescue team went on their way to Helsinki while others piled into two Volvos for a marathon drive to Tromsø in northern Norway, a small town on the island with a nice mild climate thanks to the Gulf Stream. They spent the night in the care of Andrew Fulton, head of Oslo station, who would one day be elected chairman of the Scottish Conservative Party, and on the next day took an SAS flight to Oslo and, from there, a BA flight to London. Oleg was then accommodated at a Security Service safe house in the Midlands where the Chief, Sir Christopher, was flown by helicopter to visit him, accompanied by Gerald 'Gerry' Warner (later Sir). Gerry would become a lifelong friend. He later rose to MI6's Director of Counterintelligence and Security, was then promoted to Deputy Chief, before leaving the Service to be appointed Co-ordinator for Intelligence and Security at the Cabinet Office.

OXFORD AND CAMBRIDGE CLUB

LUNCHEON
THURSDAY 18ᵀᴴ OCTOBER 2007

Cream of Celeriac and Apple Soup with Crispy Parma Ham

***

Poached Fillets of Lemon Sole with Trout mousse and Chive Butter Sauce
Parsley New Potatoes
Fresh Peas

***

Cappuccino Parfait with Coffee Crème Anglaise

***

Coffee

Club White Burgundy
Club Claret

The luncheon menu of the Oxford and Cambridge Club celebrating Gordievsky's CMG award,
18 October 2007.

After five days of rest, familiarisation and friendly questioning by Deverell and Brooks about his last two months in Russia, Gordievsky was set up at Fort Monckton for a lengthy debriefing. This lasted over two months and was conducted by the principal Kremlinologist of MI6, Gordon Barrass, who is now a visiting professor at the LSE IDEAS but previously served as Chief of the Assessment Staff in the Cabinet Office and member of the Joint Intelligence Committee long before John Scarlett headed the JIC.

On 17 May 1988, three years to the day since Gordievsky's sudden recall to Moscow, Stella Rimington, Director of Counterespionage (a position known in those days as 'K'), reported to the management board that the debrief of Gordievsky had been completed: 'It has been the longest and most comprehensive debrief ever undertaken by the Service; over 1,300 specific briefs from sections has been answered and 2,500 reports issued within the Service.'[19] In the book *The Great Cold War* (2009), based on his experience, Professor Barrass comes to the conclusion that 'one lesson stands out above all others – neither side was infallible in the judgements they made about their adversary'. This idea was formulated by Brent Scowcroft, national security adviser under US presidents Gerald Ford and George H.W. Bush.

Other less-experienced and less-knowledgeable observers note that 'those who dealt with Britain's most famous spy against the Russians, Oleg Gordievsky, recount his greatest value was in helping Margaret Thatcher understand the last Soviet leader Mikhail Gorbachev's peaceful intentions'. To which Charles Powell, who, as Mrs Thatcher's private secretary, was influential on foreign affairs, remarked: 'I don't think intelligence as such played a big role in our view of Gorbachev.'[20] That is probably why Mrs Thatcher's memoirs briefly put on record her 'highest regard' for the former British agent inside the KGB, but say nothing about the impact on her of the intelligence he had supplied before his defection.

Before leaving the Oxford and Cambridge Club, we arranged a quick photo session with Lady Thatcher, realising it was a truly historic moment. I never saw 'The Iron Lady' again, but three years later the 85th birthday party of, in the words of David Cameron, 'the greatest peace-time prime minister of the twentieth century', was still celebrated at No. 10.

After the collapse of the Soviet Union, the KGB was de-facto and de jure dissolved at the end of 1991. From its last chairman, Vadim Bakatin,

---

[19] Christopher Andrew, *The Defence of the Realm: The Authorized History of MI5* (London: Allen Lane/Penguin Books, 2009), 730.

[20] Stephen Dorril, *MI6: Inside the Covert World of Her Majesty's Secret Intelligence Service*, 751. See also, Stephen Grey, *The New Spymasters: Inside Espionage from the Cold War to Global Terror* (London: Viking/Penguin Random House, 2015), 294. The author adds: 'But his [Gordievsky's] actions ultimately assisted his country's leader.'

SIS learned that for several weeks after Gordievsky's disappearance from Moscow, his former colleagues had no idea what had happened to him. After he came back from the sanatorium but failed to call or come to the office or to his friend's dacha as expected, his wife Leila, who by that time had returned from Azerbaijan, telephoned the emergency number she had been given. She was assured that there was no need to worry because, officially, Oleg was on vacation and could have been anywhere merely having a good time and a proper rest. His department officers were not lying or pretending – they simply knew nothing about him.

On 15 August 1985, the Kremlin was officially informed of Gordievsky's defection. Recently declassified secret files show the frustration of Sir Bryan Cartledge, the ambassador to Moscow, at the ensuing round of tit-for-tat diplomatic expulsions after news of Gordievsky's defection reached the Soviet capital. For a long time, UK government officials wrestled over the timing of the defection's public announcement, finally choosing 12 September. This became known within departments as Operation EMBASE. On the same day, twenty-five Soviet intelligence officers were expelled. 'We are making it clear to the Russians, on my personal authority, that while we cannot tolerate the sort of intelligence actions which Gordievsky has revealed, we continue to desire a constructive relationship with them,' Mrs Thatcher wrote to US president Ronald Reagan on the day the defection was revealed to the Russian side. After the British ambassador broke the news of Gordievsky's defection to an MFA official in his usual diplomatic manner, the latter was furious and attacked the 'blatant activities' of SIS, adding that the Soviet authorities knew of the role 'assigned in this to first secretaries Gibbs and Asquith'.

When the Russians retaliated, expelling twenty-five British Embassy personnel, most of whom were not intelligence officers,[21] Mrs Thatcher ordered six more expulsions. Sir Bryan, who used to serve as private secretary (Overseas Affairs) to two British prime ministers, fully appreciated the brilliant operation carried out by the officers from his embassy: 'We have achieved an extraordinary victory,' he wrote later in summing up the affair. However, he was aghast when he heard about the mass expulsion of the Soviet officials from London. In an irate cable to London, he offered two adages, the first being 'always quit while you are ahead', and the second – 'never engage in a pissing match with a skunk: he possesses important natural advantages'.

---

[21] The 25 Britons ordered out of the Soviet Union included 18 embassy staff, five journalists and two businessmen. The most senior diplomat on the list was Viscount Asquith. Two other First Secretaries, two Second Secretaries, two Vice Consuls and five attachés were also ordered to leave. Six other embassy staffers on the list were administrative and technical personnel.

From the very beginning, intelligence experts realised that SIS used Gordievsky to reinforce its reputation at home and abroad after the spy scandals of the 1950s and 1960s. Gordievsky was welcome as a living proof that British intelligence was not penetrated any more and could run a long-term agent safely and securely.

In September 2007, Oleg invited me to attend the memorial service for Nicholas Bethell, the 4th Lord Bethell, of whom *The Telegraph* wrote that he was 'an unsung hero of the Cold War ... tall, stooping and with a quick, nervous smile, and furtive, sidelong glances, he seemed almost to embody the cloak-and-dagger world in which he moved'. From the church, we all moved to Lord Bethell's home, not far from the Russian Embassy, where James Bethell, his eldest son who inherited the title, gave me a copy of his father's book *Spies and Other Secrets* (1994). 'A successful operation would do wonders for MI6's credibility in the intelligence world,' Nicholas Bethell writes, 'and would leave Britain with a valuable "property", a storehouse of priceless information which even the CIA would find useful. It would impress the Americans, and this is something that British intelligence always likes to do.'

Twenty years after Oleg's glorious defection, the excitement was over. Some time before, trips to the Fort and Cambridge, where he delivered lectures to the young intelligence officers on the IONEC training course as well as young scholars at Professor Andrew's study group of intelligence seminars at Corpus Christi, gave him satisfaction and reassurance that he was still needed and were important to his morale. Now it all seemed meaningless. He was still suffering from post-usefulness syndrome remembering the heady days of VIP treatment, champagne, caviar and oyster receptions, first-class commuting to the London headquarters with a fat consultant's fee when he didn't know how to spend the money that he received. All-expenses-paid trips to visit friendly intelligence services in Washington, Paris, Vienna, Berlin and Sydney, and international conferences where he had been praised as a true Western intelligence hero. It was all over, every tiny detail of his training, all his KGB colleagues, superiors and subordinates, illegals he ever dealt with or heard about, every important moment of his entire KGB career had been sucked from him. Like that of other defectors before and after him, his value to the West and the sense of importance that this had brought was long gone and he was bored and demoralised.[22] The only satisfaction he got

---

[22] Cf. Richard Tomlinson, *The Big Breach: From Top Secret to Maximum Security* (London: Cutting Edge, 2001), 102.

came from regular visits by John Scarlett, who considered him a friend. One day it all changed.

Gordievsky did not like Sasha Litvinenko. He refused to receive him when Litvinenko defected and when Sasha met and befriended the legendary Soviet dissident Vladimir Bukovsky, who had lived in Cambridge since he was exchanged for the Chilean communist politician Luis Corvalán in December 1976, it was Vladimir who begged Gordievsky to accept Sasha. Gordievsky agreed but when Sasha, Marina and their young son Tolik arrived, asked Maureen to drive them to his friend, Martin Dewhirst, while he himself went to the pub. Martin would eventually become Sasha's translator at various functions.

Gradually, their relations warmed, although Gordievsky hated when Sasha came with two mobile phones using both of them for his long discussions with whoever was on the other side of the line. At the end of 2001, Litvinenko asked to put him in touch with 'Mishki' – either MI5 or MI6 or both – explaining that his experience of fighting Russian organised crime could be of great value. Gordievsky hesitated but after a while called his contact at Vauxhall Cross to arrange a meeting. Sasha obviously created a good impression because already, after a few months together with a fresh alias, Edwin Redwald Carter, he received a matching British passport and driving licence – a product of MI6's Central Facilities (CF) department – from his case officer. Berezovsky also came to visit and after Oleg learned that Sasha had started working for MI6, which the latter was happy to share with his mentor, Gordievsky boldly proposed to recruit Berezovsky as well. As soon as Sir John learnt about it, he dismissed this idea on the spot. So Boris had never been a British agent, contrary to what the Russian media alleged.

Litvinenko's being in touch with MI6 did not stop him from working full time for Berezovsky, who quickly learned about Sasha's newly acquired contacts at the London Ziggurat, the SIS headquarters on the Thames which, like other defectors, Sasha was not even allowed to enter.

One of the public actions with potentially far-reaching consequences was masterminded by Berezovsky. It was due to take place in Brussels on 17–18 October 2006. Both Litvinenko and Gordievsky were to take part. The plan was to arrange a press conference at the European Parliament where the keynote speakers would be Gordievsky, Litvinenko and Yuri Shvets – all three former KGB officers now living in the West.

Berezovsky knew that some British, American and European politicians had been closely collaborating with the Kremlin and were actually paid by the so-called Russian oligarchs, in fact, several nouveaux riches from the

IN THE HIGH COURT OF JUSTICE   1997-9-A-No 173
QUEEN'S BENCH DIVISION   1997-B-No 240

B E T W E E N:

                    NIKOLAI GLOUCHKOV
                                           Plaintiff
              BORIS BEREZOVSKY   Plaintiff

                          and

              (1) JAMES W MICHAELS
              (2) FORBES INC
                                           Defendants

                    _____

                          AFFIDAVIT

                    _____

I, OLEG GORDIEVSKY, care of 1 Gresham Street, London EC2V

7BU, MAKE OATH and say as follows:-

1.   Background

I am a former senior officer of the Soviet intelligence

and security organisation (the KGB). I spent altogether

23 years in that agency, specialising in Germany,

Scandanavia and Britain. In 1985, when I had to ask for

political asylum in this country, I was acting head of

the KGB station in London, and my military rank was

colonel. For the 11 years prior to 1985, I was the prime

In 1996–7, Boris Berezovsky and Nikolai Glushkov sued *Forbes* for defamation over an article written by Paul Klebnikov. Oleg Gordievsky acted as an expert witness at the trial.

former Soviet republics of Russia, Ukraine and Kazakhstan. Putin has long been watching his Western partners with a level of contempt. And how else, a Russia expert asks, can you treat them if the chancellors and premieres of the great European states are lining up to serve as flunkeys at his gas stations for a miserable reward of 2 million euros a year?[23] This is no big news today and it is enough to name Gerhard Schröder, who served as Chancellor of Germany until November 2005; Alfred Gusenbauer, Chancellor of Austria from January 2007 to December 2008; Paul Manafort, President Trump's campaign chairman from March to August 2016, and many others, but it was something quite extraordinary a decade ago. Litvinenko's accusations that Romano Prodi – an Italian politician who had served as the President of the European Commission and twice as the prime minister of Italy (Prodi's second term was between May 2006 and May 2008) – was a KGB 'confidential contact' were part of this plan. Naturally, the whole story of the former KGB General Trofimov telling Litvinenko about Prodi's involvement with the KGB was an invention.

Gordievsky, as a senior officer, was to deliver a lecture on the Soviet penetration of the European political parties mentioning the Comintern, Cominform and the Cold War with the names of British politicians acting as Soviet penetration agents, agents of influence and confidential contacts, and reviewing the first six years of Putin's presidency. Litvinenko and Shvets were to prepare their parts. Since March, as Oleg has told me, 'they had pulled the wool over the faces [*sic*, eyes] of the very distinguished MEPs [Members of the European Parliament], very solid former military officers' drawing a red herring across their path. Because Litvinenko did not speak English, he could not communicate with the MEPs himself, so he was using the services of Bukovsky's assistant, Pavel Stroilov.

In February, Litvinenko was interviewed in Italy, on camera, by Mario Scaramella (one of the advisers to the Mitrokhin Commission). During the interview, Sasha made the same allegations against Prodi. The Mitrokhin Commission was an Italian parliamentary commission set up in 2002 to investigate the KGB penetration of Italian politics. It was presided by Senator Paolo Guzzanti (Forza Italia) and in its investigation actively used secret files from the so-called Mitrokhin Archive shared by SIS with the Italian security services as well as other security services of Europe and America.

Unusually, in 1995 the Italian government banned its secret services from dealing with documents provided by the British. These were copies of secret KGB files identifying more than 250 Soviet agents and collaborators

---

[23] See Andrei Piontkovsky, 'The cult of death: About Putin's "Da"', *RFE/RL*, 24 May 2018.

among the Italian political, business and financial elite, including the press, magistrates and courts. The papers had been meticulously copied and later brought to London by the KGB archivist Vasili Mitrokhin. Only part of this treasure-trove was published by Christopher Andrew in the form of two thick volumes covering Soviet intelligence operations in Europe and the West and the battle for the Third World. The classified part of the archive was given to the appropriate governments for consideration. In Italy, under the premiership of Romano Prodi, nothing was done about those potentially scandalous papers. When Prodi became the president of the European Commission in May 1999, he was asked how this material could be kept from prosecutors and the press for so long. The former Italian prime minister responded that he had never heard about such documents. And indeed, no investigation was ever carried out.

Among others, Stroilov, on Litvinenko's request, contacted Gerard Batten, a British politician I first met at the Litvinenko funeral and who, until August 2019, served as the leader of the UK Independence Party. Batten is one of the founding members of UKIP and was first elected as an MEP in the 2004 European parliamentary election for the London constituency ironically on the basis of seeking the withdrawal of the United Kingdom from the European Union. During his first term of office, Batten served as a member of the European Parliament's Subcommittee on Security and Defence and was appointed UKIP's official spokesman on Security and Defence.

In April 2006, Batten stated that a former FSB agent, Lieutenant Colonel Alexander Litvinenko, had been told that Romano Prodi used to be the KGB's 'man in Italy', demanding an inquiry into the allegations. He told the European Parliament that Litvinenko 'had been warned by FSB deputy chief General Anatoly Trofimov that there were numerous KGB agents among Italian politicians'. As reported by the Brussels-based *EU Reporter*, 'another high-level source, a former KGB operative in London, has confirmed the story.' This unidentified 'high-level source' was Gordievsky, but the whole story involving Trofimov was made up by Litvinenko and Berezovsky.

Colonel General Anatoly Trofimov (ret.) was assassinated near his house in Moscow on 10 April 2005. He joined the KGB in 1962 and served as a special investigator specialising in political cases like those of academician Andrey Sakharov, human rights activist Sergei Kovalev, orthodox priest Father Gleb Yakunin, dissident Nathan Shcharansky, journalist Alexander Podrabinek and KGB captain Victor Orekhov, known as 'the KGB dissenter'. Orekhov (who now lives in the US) was arrested by Trofimov twice, in 1978 and 1995, serving different terms in the inhuman conditions of the Russian penal camps. Trofimov also investigated the famous Yeliseyev grocery store affair. The general manager of this exclusive Moscow food hall was arrested and shot in the 1980s on fabricated corruption charges. In October 1993, following the orders of President Boris Yeltsin, Trofimov's men detained the opposition leaders of the Supreme Soviet, and two years later he was promoted to deputy head of the Federal Counterintelligence Service (FSK) and head of the Moscow FSK directorate. General Trofimov was dismissed in February 1997 after two of his subordinates were arrested on heroin trafficking charges. At the time of his assassination, he was acting as security chief of the Russian private company Finvest. During his long career in the KGB and its successors, General Trofimov had nothing to do with foreign intelligence and could not have had any information about anything related to Italy or any other country, not to mention foreign politicians.

On 26 April 2006, Batten repeated his call for a parliamentary inquiry, stating: 'former senior members of the KGB are willing to testify in such an investigation, under the right conditions … It is not acceptable that this situation is unresolved, given the importance of Russia's relations with the European Union.' At about the same time, I received an email from Gordievsky asking me to compile 'a list of the prominent communist leaders connected with the Comintern, Cominform, the International Department [of the Central Party Committee], KGB and GRU'. 'The countries of special interest are Italy, France, Spain, Britain, Germany and Austria,' he wrote. However, on 6 October, Oleg informed me that for various reasons 'the whole action collapsed'. During a lunch near London's Waterloo station, Gerard Batten confirmed to me that a big media event was indeed planned in Brussels with Gordievsky and Litvinenko. He complained that MEPs usually had very little time to make their position known to other members and the event was not easy to organise.

The poisoning of Sasha made Gordievsky's life more exciting again. For days and weeks, there were queues of British and foreign journalists and television crews from all over the world in front of his house willing to interview the famous defector. Part of the job of answering questions was given to me in spite of the fact that I was quite busy working on the BBC *Panorama* investigation with John Sweeney and John O'Mahony at the spacious Shepherd's Bush studio. It did not stop even after the programme was aired by BBC One on 22 January 2007 at prime time with three of us – Oleg, Maureen and me – watching in Gordievsky's house. I soon left for Oslo where a contract with Egil Ødegård, CEO and producer of Filmhuset AS, a Norwegian film production company, was signed to produce a similar documentary, this time without Peskov.

At the end of February 2007, I was in Rome discussing the developments with Guzzanti and visiting Scaramella in his historical prison, Carcere di Regina Coeli. Built in 1654, it is the best-known correctional facility in Italy, also serving as a police academy. The senator was received politely by the director himself, a pleasant Italian of medium height, and a group of senior officers accompanied us as we crossed the guarded space with everything looking more like a Catholic convent, as it initially was, than a gaol. From there through an inner yard, we went into another, more modern building and climbed to the third floor. While Paolo discussed the convicts and their problems with the prison governors, I was accompanied into a solitary cell where Mario was waiting. We had about forty-five minutes one-to-one with no one interfering.

Mario, who I saw hours before he and his family left London on Christmas Eve to fly home to Naples, told me about his arrest at the airport by the local police and security chiefs and the search of his properties. The police broke down the doors of all Scaramella's family houses and confiscated his computers and documents. After the arrest, Mario was kept in solitary confinement, though the police failed to produce any formal accusation.

He told me about the prosecutors' demand that he sign a statement accusing Senator Guzzanti of manipulating evidence to compromise Berlusconi's political rival, Prodi. He also described the arrest of six Ukrainians, who were charged with smuggling arms when two VOG 25P grenades were found in their cargo. These were no toys and VOG, known as the 'Frog', is especially vicious. After being fired from a grenade-launcher and before exploding, it springs about a metre into the air and then detonates, killing a lot of people. Amazingly, after they had been several months in custody, the case against the Ukrainians collapsed 'for lack of evidence'.

Leaving the complex, Paolo and I met Amedeo, Mario's father.

'It is purely political,' he said, 'my son is a political prisoner.'

'*Mi dispiace*,' I tried to calm the man. '*Posso solo dire che faremo del nostro meglio*. We shall do our best.'

Mario Scaramella was finally released after Prodi lost a vote of confidence in the Senate in January 2008 and had to step back from Italian politics.

In January, I was back in Godalming after Christmas and New Year holidays in Vienna and immediately noticed Oleg's sudden change of mood.

'What happened?' I asked.

'You shall soon know,' he said, 'the Office found out it was a KGB attack.'

'Oh, really?' I could not believe my ears because I knew exactly what happened the previous November before I left for Austria. 'And who attacked you?'

He did not answer, and we went to the Star, a no-frills Victorian boozer on Church Street, where we had spent many a happy hour with Maureen, Jill, Martin Dewhirst, and others, including my wife and son. On the same day, two senior officers of the Surrey police Special Branch visited me at home.

The interview was long but friendly and continued for several days. I have learnt that on 22 January, Oleg sent a letter to Robin Butler, Baron Butler of Brockwell. Sir Robin, who is the same age as Gordievsky, has had a high-profile career in the Civil Service for 37 years, serving as Private Secretary to five British prime ministers, including Margaret Thatcher. Along with Mrs Thatcher, he narrowly escaped the assassination attempt by the IRA against the top tier of British government in October 1984 at the Grand Hotel in Brighton. Twenty years later, Lord Butler chaired the Review of Intelligence on Weapons of Mass Destruction, which assessed the use of intelligence in the lead up to the 2003 Iraq War. After retiring from the Civil Service, he had been Master of University College, Oxford, for ten years and in this capacity sent an invitation to Oleg, who he knew well personally, to visit the college and give a lecture to students.

Gordievsky responded with the following story. The previous November, he said, exactly one year after the poisoning of Litvinenko, there was a KGB attempt to poison him as well. After having spent seven days in a coma (which is not true) and another seven days recovering, he suffered several damages to the body as well as paralysed fingers. However, what distressed him, Oleg complained, was that MI6 and Special Branch, particularly the Guildford Special Branch, were trying to suppress knowledge and other details of that KGB operation because, for some reason, it better suited their sense of political correctness. Oleg reminded them that the same happened in the cases of Georgi Markov and Alexander Litvinenko and concluded that it stemmed from the MI6 Chief's obsession with co-operating with the KGB, which he, Oleg, did not like. He stressed that in MI5 they understood the situation much better, not being restricted by silly foreign policy considerations. That was why they were taking an honest and proper position on the investigation, he declared. Lord Butler's correspondent concluded the letter by saying that he did not regard this information as confidential because he was irritated by the position taken by some above-mentioned bodies. Jill Telfer, Oleg's secretary, put a signed copy in the envelope and sent it by regular mail to Oxford.

Initially, this did not help much. In the course of the meticulous investigation and multiple forensic analyses, it was established without any doubt that in the evening, Oleg took several pills, including Xanax, and washed this mixture down with wine and then brandy, which is extremely dangerous and may even be fatal. As should have been expected, it caused severe drowsiness, weakness and clumsiness. He lost consciousness and the next morning fell from the staircase leading to the first-floor bedroom, hurt himself and could not open the front door to Jill. She immediately telephoned me. I did not see Oleg for a week and was not there but advised to call an ambulance and the police, which Jill did. They arrived together, and the paramedics had to wait until officers broke the door and found Oleg in a terrible condition. However, after about a week he was out feeling well enough to invite Maureen and me for a drink in several nice pubs around Godalming and preside over a London launch of the book *Allegations* (2007) by Litvinenko, Sasha's 'selected works', edited and translated into English by Pavel Stroilov. Pavel was there, of course, busy with the book presentation while Gordievsky, Bukovsky and Zakayev were sitting on the dais along with the other guests of honour, including Litvinenko's father Walter. I recorded the date – it was 22 November 2007.

During the next few years Stroilov, officially a law student, published three more books – *Behind the Desert Storm* (2011), *The Inglorious Revolution* (2013), and *Road to Freedom: How Britain Can Escape the EU* (2014), the last two titles with Gerard Batten. About the first book and its author, publishers say: 'Pavel Stroilov is a Russian historian living in London after being granted asylum by British Judges in 2006. He fled Russia in 2003 after successfully stealing 50,000 unpublished top-secret Kremlin documents from the archive of the Gorbachev Foundation. Stroilov and other researchers were given access to the archive in 1999 but were brusquely refused permission by Mikhail Gorbachev himself to copy significant parts of the collection. Over the next few years, after secretly watching the archive's network administrator enter the password into the foundation's computer system, Stroilov was able to copy the archive and send it to secure locations around the world. Most of the originals remain classified to this day.'

In December, Godalming was beautifully decorated for Christmas, and I was leaving for Paris and then Vienna to see my family, secretly dreaming of returning to my second home as soon as possible. As mentioned, as soon as I returned, visitors from the Surrey police were at my door.

Until March, however, nothing changed except Oleg, who cut all communications with me and I couldn't figure out why until the chief of Special Branch visited me with another senior officer one day. From them, I learned that Oleg was accusing me of poisoning him. In a letter to his friend Ken Warren, Oleg wrote: 'The person whom I call the culprit is Boris Volodarsky who to my annoyance lives in Godalming.' Oleg was asking his old friend to help put me behind the bars.

In an email to another friend, dated 31 March 2008, Gordievsky reported that he had sent an angry letter 'to the Office', meaning MI6. 'There I was quite direct,' he explained. 'I said the enclosed text shows once again that the Office had entered into a criminal collusion with the corrupt Guildford Police.'

Kenneth Robin Warren, an alumnus of King's College London and, like myself, of the London School of Economics, had been an MP for Hastings and then Hastings and Rye for 22 years until his retirement in 1992. Without doubt, a kind and very well-connected man, he immediately decided to do what he could for Oleg. Ken thought it best to use the services of his trusted confidante by the name of Jeremy H. Taylor, who used to live in Farnham near Godalming and who he considered totally reliable, with connections of high value that Jeremy would be able to use at once in Oleg's interest.[24]

Indeed, Mr Taylor managed to pull a few strings and Oleg soon learnt that the right people at the top had been informed and a review of everything had been instigated.

After a while, two new police investigators appeared. Those were a young and good-looking female officer Jamie, Detective Constable, Serious Crime Investigation Team, and Mark Chapman, Detective Sergeant, Crime Operations, both from the Surrey police headquarters at Mount Browne. They turned out to be nice people and did everything properly and correctly.

On Friday afternoon, 4 April, I was at Waitrose buying something for dinner when a telephone call from Jason Lewis of *The Mail on Sunday* stopped me. Jason had learned that Surrey police officers had been ordered to reopen the inquiry after pressure by senior intelligence figures, including former MI5 DG Dame Elizabeth Lydia Manningham-Buller. He had also discovered that Lord Butler, the head of the inquiry into intelligence failures in the run-up to the war in Iraq, was understood to have queried why the case had not been taken more seriously. We discussed the matter with Jason while Tom Mangold called Gordievsky to listen to his version of events. Their article appeared in *The Mail on Sunday* on 6 April: 'Special Branch is investigating an alleged attempt to murder Oleg Gordievsky, the KGB double-agent who spied on Russia for British intelligence at the height of the Cold War. The former Soviet colonel, who escaped to Britain in 1985, says he was poisoned by a Russian assassin who visited him at his secret safe-house in Surrey.' Scroll down for more, suggested my computer when I was reading the article online, so I did.

---

[24] Correspondence between Oleg Gordievsky and Sir Kenneth Warren, March–April 2008.

'He lay unconscious and "close to death" for 34 hours,' the story went on. 'He spent a further two weeks recuperating in a private clinic paid for by his former bosses in MI6. But he claimed that his former MI6 paymasters had attempted to cover it up. He said MI6 forced Special Branch to drop its initial investigation into the case. He told *The Mail on Sunday* that he was certain he was the victim of a Kremlin-inspired assassination attempt. "It was obvious to me I had been poisoned," [Gordievsky stated].'

Oleg was furious and did not want to hide it. Talking to Tom, he accused MI6 of abandoning him. He also said his would-be assassin used a 'variant or derivative of thallium'. This no doubt came from my small book published a year before, to which Gordievsky wrote a foreword. In the book, I discuss the case of Nikolai Khokhlov, who was allegedly poisoned by radioactive thallium in Frankfurt in 1957. Oleg picked the story up.

Both journalists noted that the fact forensic tests had failed to identify the poison or any other suspicious substance in Gordievsky's body did not surprise him. He told them: 'KGB poisoning is based on the poison being undetectable.' I wonder how Porton Down experts then managed so quickly to identify the nerve agent that knocked out Skripal and his daughter in Salisbury in March 2018.

Oleg said: 'On the third day that I was in hospital, the deputy head of Special Branch in Guildford visited me and said there was no crime, no poison. I realized that they wanted to hush up the crime. If they are saying I am not affected by the poison, why did I spend two weeks in hospital? The fact that no evidence of poison was initially found means absolutely nothing.' Fortunately, or unfortunately, no evidence of any poisonous substance has ever been found in Gordievsky's body. Asked whether he thought there could be any other explanation for his illness – perhaps too much stress after Litvinenko's murder and a very demanding media campaign that followed, he said, 'The stress is made only by MI6'. 'Refusing to investigate a crime is not nice,' he added. 'Special Branch were ordered by MI6 not to investigate.'

Playing by the book, Jason Lewis accurately noted that *The Mail on Sunday* 'understands that Gordievsky suspects one of his long-term friends, a former Russian military intelligence officer, of administering the poison'. 'When this man was at my house, he had ample opportunity to insert the poison into food and drink, to which he had access,' Gordievsky said. Four days later, in his letter to *The Sunday Times*, Oleg called the *Mail on Sunday* article the worst production of the gutter press. In his next public interview, this time with Natalie Golitsyn of the Radio Free Europe/Radio Liberty, he accused my wife of poisoning him on orders from the KGB. Valentina was then summoned to the Godalming police station and questioned for several hours, with her statements duly recorded and filed. Fortunately, they never disturbed her again.

When this book went to press, Gordievsky continued to receive a Ministry of Defence pension, equivalent to that of a British Army colonel. His welfare and security for all his time in Britain have been overseen by the Re-Settlement Group for Defectors within MI6, and his own dedicated AR (Agent Resettlement) officer visits him at least once a month providing all possible help. An intelligence source described to WorldNetDaily how suddenly all hell broke loose 'over why Manningham-Buller had taken time out from feeding her animals to get involved in current decisions within the intelligence services and why Lord Butler had intervened'.

After spending the best part of his long life in the UK, Gordievsky should have known about Anglo-Saxons. Thirty-three years in Limeyland should have taught him to be wary of that Anglo-Saxon habit of giving you a very hard punch on the jaw without warning. I am paraphrasing Forsyth, but again I admire the Forsyth style. In his recent autobiography, *The Outsider*, the best British spy writer argues: 'The biggest fear of all is not that you have run out of tradecraft or luck, but that far away back home some bastard has betrayed you ... That is why Dante put the traitor in the final circle of Hell.'

Chapter 10

The Oligarch

Boris Berezovsky is an extraordinary figure, hugely underestimated by the West. 'I am a businessman who turned to politics, an entrepreneur, and a communications executive,' he writes in his book *The Art of Impossible* (2006) published both in Russia and in the USA. 'But in Russia and in the West, I have been called an oligarch, someone who wielded unknown power in the Yeltsin years and who does not believe in democracy. This was an unfair portrayal, but I never felt seriously compelled to refute it until recently.'

The book, which covers three volumes and was co-authored by the Russian-American historian Yuri Felshtinsky is, unfortunately, little known. Boris further explains:

> The current situation in Russia has made it necessary for me to tell the world of concerns I have for the future of democracy there ...
>
> I had hoped that Mr Putin would preserve the fundamental accomplishment of the Yeltsin era – the national commitment to democracy – while correcting some of the mistakes from that time. But his performance in the year he has been in power – he was elected in March but has been running the country since August 1999, when Boris Yeltsin named him as his successor – has been a disheartening disappointment. Not only did Mr Putin not start solving these pressing problems, but he initiated the dismantling of some revolutionary achievements of the Yeltsin era.
>
> He has formally (so far only formally) destroyed the basis of the democratic federation by replacing elected representatives in the upper chamber of the Russian Parliament with appointees. Moreover, he abrogated for himself the power to dismiss regional governors elected by the people. In doing so, the new president concentrated all the country's political power in his hands.
>
> Most recently, he has taken steps to subordinate the mass media and has begun using law enforcement agencies to put pressure on both independent businesses and political opponents ...
>
> Mr Putin continues to insist on a military solution to the ethnic conflict in Chechnya, a path leading nowhere. The fear of the authorities' unchecked power has begun to find its way back into the everyday lives of ordinary Russians.

By and large, Mr Putin is gradually heading toward authoritarian rule. For ages the supreme leader of Russia – be it a Tsar, general secretary or president – wielded practically unlimited power …[1]

Boris Berezovsky and I were not friends, but we knew each other and met several times. There was a period when I needed his financial support and he immediately agreed to help, providing a grant through his International Foundation for Civil Liberties (IFCL) headed by Alex Goldfarb. For various reasons, unrelated to Boris, it never materialised and now I am quite happy that it did not happen. At least I can in all conscience say that I never received money from Berezovsky. But many, very many people did: British lords, Russian, European, American and other politicians and MPs, ministers and PR specialists, bureaucrats of all ranks, army, intelligence and police officers, journalists, actors, husbands, wives, children, and young women. Even heads of states and terrorists. You want names?

There are many books written about Berezovsky starting from *The Godfather of the Kremlin* (2000) by Paul Klebnikov to the latest *The Time of Berezovsky* (2018) by Petr Aven presented by the author in Waterstone's Piccadilly in April 2018. I believe the most authoritative among them is *Death of a Dissident* (2007) written by Alex Goldfarb with Marina Litvinenko. It is certainly a treatise about Berezovsky and the title fits perfectly with the content. The title says it all. Whatever the authors planned or wanted, it is Berezovsky who was a dissident, another 'prophet unarmed' and then 'prophet outcast' after Trotsky, not Sasha Litvinenko. About six years before a coroner recorded an open verdict on the death of probably the most interesting, controversial and mysterious figure of post-communist Russia, when the Goldfarb's book was published, nobody could know that Berezovsky, who directly or indirectly financed it and was one of its very first readers, was already as good as dead.

In the close circle of Berezovsky's associates, Litvinenko was the first victim. Then came Badri, aged only 53. Berezovsky's body was found on Saturday afternoon, 23 March 2013, in a mansion belonging to his former wife Galina Besharova. Three former wives and six children survived him. With the benefit of hindsight, one may say that it was easily predictable that the former oligarch would die a violent death. Some, including Boris himself, feared it, and quite a few were plotting it. Nikolai Glushkov, another man close to Berezovsky, feared it too. He was found dead at his London home in March 2018.

---

[1] Boris Berezovsky, 'Putin Reins in Russia, at a Price', *The New York Times*, 22 September 2000.

It is interesting to talk about Boris Berezovsky, his former good old friend Petr Aven writes. '[Boris was] bright, fearless and never petty-minded. And he paid the full price.'

Berezovsky was a mathematician, which he sometimes called himself before he became a businessman and then plunged into politics. In mathematics, twenty-three is a prime number. Because of their nature, many prime numbers but especially 23 have occult powers and are seen by many to have a mystical significance. Boris was born on 23 January and gone on 23 March (William Shakespeare was born and died on 23 April). The most famous and most quoted of the Psalms is number 23 (KJV): 'The Lord is my shepherd; I shall not want. He maketh me to lie down in green pastures; he leadeth me beside the still waters.' Each parent contributes 23 chromosomes to the start of human life and the average human physical biorhythm is 23 days. The Knights Templar, a Catholic military order, which was among the wealthiest and most powerful, had 23 Grand Masters. On the night of 23 March, Russian emperor Paul I was murdered in his bedroom in the newly built St Michael's castle in Saint Petersburg by a group of his dismissed officers. He was succeeded by his son, the 23-year-old Alexander I ...

I suddenly remembered Boris's omnipresence at the Highgate cemetery during the Litvinenko burial and later at the memorial ceremony but Aven recalled that Berezovsky hated to attend funerals and did not like visiting sick friends in hospital.

The first assassination attempt on his life was on 7 June 1994. Berezovsky's first official company was a Soviet-Italian joint venture known as LogoVAZ, a combination of the Italian firm Logo Systems, an old partner of the AvtoVAZ, or Volga Automobile Plant, a Russian car manufacturer producing dismal vehicles of the Trabant class known in the West as Lada, and the Russian automaker. The joint venture was not a car dealership at the beginning; it was to adopt new automated processes to bring the production a little bit closer to the modern automotive industry standards. Contracts for the Fiat, Mercedes and Volvo brands came later. True to himself, Boris decided he needed an exclusive company venue in central Moscow and set up The Club (officially, the LogoVAZ Reception House), spending £1.5m to restore a rather modest turn-of-the-century merchant's house where he would entertain politicians, ministers, businessmen and guests from all over the world. On that sunny June afternoon, at 5:20 p.m., Berezovsky's grey Mercedes 500 pulled out of the gates of The Club as a radio-controlled improvised explosive device placed in a blue Opel parked nearby exploded. The blast blew out windows in the eight-storey house across the street and wounded people passing by. The driver was killed instantly but Berezovsky and his bodyguard suffered only minor injuries. Neither Boris's deputy for security matters nor the head of his personal protection detail could figure out how it could have happened. Both, as it turned out, were not security professionals.

Later, Litvinenko suggested it was someone at the Lada automaker who had put a contract on Boris – law enforcement agencies had no means to investigate at those times, so there were only wild guesses and rumours. Sasha thought it was because Berezovsky sent one of his lieutenants, Nikolai Glushkov, to act as a financial director at the car factory and someone feared that his or her shadow deals with intermediary firms would become known. Litvinenko, then a senior officer at the FSB's Division of Operations against Criminal Organisations (URPO), suggested it was most likely the Kurgan Gang, who specialised in contract killings. They had their own people in the Moscow police, he said, and even in the FSB. According to the Russian businessman Yuri Scheffler (Shefler), the owner of SPI Group who lives in London, Vladimir Rushailo often visited his Moscow restaurant with leaders of the Kurgan Gang. Rushailo was then head of the Serious and Organised Crime Command of the Moscow police and at the same time head of the Serious Organised Crime Directorate of the Interior Ministry (similar, but not identical to the British National Crime Agency).[2]

Litvinenko's URPO was nothing but a Special Tasks unit similar to that headed before and some time after the war by Pavel Sudoplatov. Sudoplatov was a KGB general so secret that no one knew about him until he published his book *Special Tasks: The Memoirs of an Unwanted Witness* (1994), which instantly became an international bestseller and brought him world fame in spite of the book's multiple factual errors. But it was the first and remains the only serious publication about Soviet special secret operations in the West written by their principal organiser. Among other 'wet jobs', Sudoplatov was in charge of the operation to assassinate Trotsky in Mexico. He and his service became a role model for many secret KGB departments, including URPO. When Litvinenko was there, the division was commanded by General Yevgeny Khokholkov, whose claim to fame was his role in the assassination of the independent Chechen president Dzhokhar Dudayev.

In late December 1997, General Khokholkov's deputy informed Sasha and several of his colleagues that their next assignment would be the assassination of Boris Berezovsky, who, until November, was Deputy Secretary of the Security Council of Russia, a very important government post. Putin was

---

[2] Petr Aven, *The Time of Berezovsky* (Moscow: AST/Corpus, 2018), interview with Yuri Shefler (in Russian).

its secretary in 1999, and for the previous decade, the Security Council had been headed by Nikolai Patrushev, former FSB director.

Naturally, the URPO officers didn't want to carry out this assignment and informed Berezovsky who, in turn, informed the Kremlin. On the next day, the deputy chief of the presidential administration summoned them to report, listened to all of them carefully until they had finished, and promised to do something about it. By mid-April nothing had happened, and they finally gathered at the Berezovsky dacha and recorded a video testimony. This video has never been shown to the public, but after a discussion with the Service director and a visit to the prosecutors, the whistle-blowers and their boss, General Khokholkov, were suspended pending the outcome of the internal investigation.

In the middle of June, Valentin Yumashev – a journalist who married Yeltsin's daughter Tatiana and at the time headed the powerful Presidential Executive Office – summoned Boris to the Kremlin. They knew each other quite well, and for a while, Berezovsky served as Yumashev's counsellor advising him on major government appointments. Valentin, with whom I was acquainted when he was working for the popular *Ogoniok* magazine, asked the tycoon for his opinion about one of Yumashev's aides by the name of Vladimir Putin.

'Why?' Boris enquired.

'We are considering him for the FSB directorship. Kovalyov is being dismissed because the president does not trust him.'

'Sure,' Boris said. 'I support Putin 100 per cent.'

At the end of July, Putin was appointed FSB Director. On that occasion, Berezovsky's life was saved. 'A process,' Goldfarb notes, 'instituted by Sasha's URPO whistle-blowers and steered behind the scenes by Boris, plucked their future nemesis from obscurity and placed him in charge of one of the world's most powerful spy services.' This, of course, is not right because the FSB is only a domestic security service and not a 'spy' organisation. But it was an important first step to real power and, with Berezovsky's help and encouragement, Putin successfully made all other steps to become the President of Russia. Which, without doubt, placed him in charge of one of the most powerful, cunning and ruthless secret services in the world.

On 13 November 2000, Boris was having his usual breakfast at the Château de la Garoupe with a magnificent view of the Bay of Nice. According to several sources, in 1907, British MP Charles McLaren, Baron Aberconway, bought 4 acres at the point of the Cap d'Antibes. He hired an English architect to build the property. It features a long façade with half-moon windows and a long stairway leading to the sea. The garden, which was maintained by McLaren's wife, has a wonderful pergola with 12-metre-high rose bushes, irises and begonias. At times the house was rented or visited by various celebrities, including Pablo Picasso. The property passed to the owner's daughter Florence and her husband, Sir Henry Norman. Norman expanded it and added an extra storey to the house. In 1999, this elegant French château, one of the few chateaux *privés les plus chers au monde*, was purchased by Berezovsky for €22 million euro.

Also present at breakfast were his life partner Elena Gorbunova, and Alex Goldfarb. At one moment Boris announced that he was going to Moscow 'for a few hours' to answer the summons 'as a witness' in the Aeroflot fraud case. It took some serious efforts to persuade him to stay and in the end, Boris agreed and dictated his famous statement: 'They force me to choose between becoming a political prisoner or political émigré, and I am choosing the latter.' That was certainly a wise decision, but it did not solve his problems in Russia.

One of those problems was his television channel ORT. According to its bylaws, major decisions in the company required the approval of 75 per cent of the board of directors. At the time, Boris's loyalists such as Konstantin Ernst, general director and executive producer, Tatiana Koshkareva, director of information programmes, Sergei Dorenko, deputy general director and the main anchor, and Badri Patarkatsishvili, Boris's partner and ORT's Chief Operating Officer, controlled the board and with it the network. To gain full editorial control, one had to turn any or all of them.

Dorenko was summoned to the Kremlin but refused to take an offer. After some time, Ernst called Badri: 'I know that I am a piece of shit,' he said, 'but I will go with the winning side. It's pointless to resist. Sorry.' Remarkably, Ernst had previously been quoted as saying that Trotsky was and remains 'an international star of the past 100 years, a popular hero and the de facto producer of the October Revolution'. In 2017 he would act as one of the producers of the (very mediocre) feature film about the founder of the Fourth International.

In mid-December, the Kremlin sent a messenger. Roman Abramovich flew from Moscow for a weekend. His villa was a ten-minute drive from Boris's château. 'You understand, of course,' he told Boris and Badri during a meeting, 'that if they wanted, they could take your share in ORT and you'd get nothing. But to make it easier, we agreed that I would buy your 49 per cent out.'

By mid-January 2001, the transaction was complete. Ernst remained CEO, and on his initiative, the ORT was renamed The First Channel (they call it 'Channel One Russia'). Koshkareva was appointed editor-in-chief of *Nezavisimaya Gazeta* ('The Independent Gazette'). She later left journalism to become an administrator. Dorenko's television career was abruptly finished. In modern Russia, any individual who does not willingly become a conformist is forced to fall in line until he is 'all right'. Recently, Dorenko has been working for a Moscow radio station. In the summer of 2001 Badri fled to Georgia, making use of his Georgian citizenship. The controlling stake in the channel as of 2018 belonged to the state (51%). Of the rest, 25% belonged to National Media Group, chaired by Alina Kabayeva, former MP and rumoured to be Putin's 'girlfriend', and 24% to Abramovich. Both Director-General Konstantin Ernst and Executive Producer Alexander Feifmann report to Kabayeva.

Berezovsky's new role as a symbol of the Russian opposition to the current Kremlin regime, albeit, like Trotsky, from exile, and a sponsor of all that was considered to be democratic in a non-democratic Russia, was announced by Elena Bonner at a press conference in Moscow. The press conference was organised two weeks after that memorable breakfast at the Château de la Garoupe, on 30 November. Bonner, the 77-year-old widow of the Nobel Laureate who defied the Soviet system, said that she had accepted a $3 million grant from the New York-based Berezovsky foundation (the future IFCL) as an endowment for the Sakharov Museum and Civic Centre in Moscow. Her husband, nuclear physicist Andrei Sakharov, who died two years earlier, was a well-known Russian dissident and activist for disarmament, peace and human rights.

'For Boris and me,' Goldfarb, the director of the IFCL, writes, 'awarding the first grant to Sakharov was a gesture ripe with symbolism. Elena Bonner had been the first among Russia's human rights activists to say that Putin represented "modernised Stalinism" at the time when Boris was still Putin's "brother". Three decades earlier Sakharov had become an emblematic figure, symbolising modern resistance to tyranny. The grant to the Sakharov Center was meant to underscore the continuity of Soviet oppression under Putin and the permanence of dissidents' resistance. From the outset it defined the colors of the new foundation.'[3] By May 2001, the IFCL had awarded 160 more grants to various organisations across Russia that represented protest movements. Soon, a signal came from a group of democratic politicians who wanted to set up a new political party. The objective was to run in the 2003 election to the State Duma, the lower house of the Russian Parliament, on the anti-Putin platform.

---

[3] Alex Goldfarb with Marina Litvinenko, *Death of a Dissident: The Poisoning of Alexander Litvinenko and the Return of the KGB* (London: Simon & Schuster, 2007), 238–9.

When Sergei Yushenkov, a veteran of Russia's democratic politics, and Vladimir Golovlev, another dissident MP, returned after visiting Berezovsky in France, Yushenkov announced the formation of a new political party, Liberal Russia, with Boris and himself as its leaders.

Golovlev was assassinated on 21 August 2002. His killers were never found. Yushenkov was shot dead in front of his house in Moscow on 17 April 2003, just hours after the Liberal Russia registration had been completed. Berezovsky applied for political asylum in Britain and was living in London while being kept informed of the Russian prosecutors' demands for his extradition.

Spring 2003 was quite stressful for the tycoon. Several months before, the Office of the Prosecutor General of Russia sent another request to London demanding the extradition of him and Yuli Dubov, Berezovsky's old and close friend and business associate. Boris was almost certain that the British were not going to extradite him but on 23 March, he and Dubov were arrested and transported to the police station. It was, of course, a formal act and they were soon released, but the episode left an unpleasant feeling for quite a while.

On 2 April, the newspapers reported: 'Russian oligarch Boris Berezovsky, fighting extradition to Russia on fraud charges, is released on £100,000 ($160,000) bail by Judge Timothy Workman, pending hearings scheduled for October. Speaking to reporters outside Bow Street Magistrates' Court in London, Berezovsky dons a satirical mask of President Putin to underscore his claim that the case was a farce.'

Later that day Berezovsky and Dubov were giving a press conference in Le Méridien Hotel in Piccadilly after preliminary hearings at Bow Street Magistrates' Court, when a tall man approached Nikita Chekulin, who had recently joined Berezovsky's London team, and started a conversation. The choice of target was correct as Chekulin had already been working for Russian intelligence. The stranger's name was Vladimir Terlyuk (I have misspelt it in *Poison Factory* because in all Russian media he was named as 'Teplyuk'), who would later figure in the British court documents as 'Terluk'.

Terlyuk was strange. According to some sources, he was born in Karaganda, Kazakhstan, in 1951, but even ubiquitous Russian journalists in the country where virtually any information could be bought for a dime were unable to dig up anything on him or his life. That is until May 2000, when he applied for foreign travel permission, received a Kazakh passport and a year later left for Germany. This total lack of information on Terlyuk's fifty years spent in the former Soviet Union, this inability of researchers to get more than his official passport data, presents reasonable grounds for suspicion and speculation. He was also noticed stalking Berezovsky at the 6th Russian Economic Forum, which opened in London on the next day, 3 April 2003, where his presence could not be explained.

I met Terlyuk only once at a seminar in the London University of Westminster in Regent Street on 2 February 2007, where it was seemingly not his business to attend and he uttered no sound as he towered in a front row as a silent and indifferent observer. I remember him as being tall, rather skinny, with a wrinkled face, standing out in the crowd, letting himself be photographed, wearing a grey suit and speaking poor English.

At the seminar, the floor was given exclusively to Julia Svetlichnaya and James Heartfield, who were introduced as researchers at the Centre for the Study of Democracy, University of Westminster. Both made headlines in Europe and the USA with their stories about Litvinenko. As already mentioned, just in front of the speakers' table I noticed Terlyuk. During the whole conference he never said a word, hardly understood much of the discussion as it was in English, but was busy hurriedly making notes. Shortly before the event, he invited Martin Dewhirst, Sasha's interpreter, who was sitting with me in the conference room, to meet privately in a café at Victoria Station. There, Terlyuk repeated his old story that Berezovsky offered him millions of pounds for giving false evidence to the Metropolitan Police. Strangely, it seemed he wanted to stir up anew some old allegations that had been discredited four years earlier and generally had no relevance any more. The reason was unclear until two months later.

When Terlyuk was spotted again talking to Chekulin, on 13 May at Boris's next court hearing, a call was immediately placed to find out who he was. Terlyuk introduced himself to Litvinenko as 'Vladimir Ivanovich' (later the Kazakh immigration authorities would state that his patronymic should be 'Afanasyevich') and said that he had been living in England for four years, applied for asylum, which was still pending, and started a small trading company. He claimed his only reason for seeking Berezovsky's company was to do business with the tycoon. Litvinenko immediately suspected Terlyuk of being a Russian agent – dressing, speaking and behaving like one.

This did not sound too far-fetched. There is something in the tradecraft called a 'passive probe' when someone, not necessarily an agent, is sent on an intelligence mission just to observe passively and record details about the target location or organisation. I heard that Terlyuk had been recruited in the late 1970s when he worked in the special garage belonging to the 9th Directorate of the KGB. Credit should be given to Berezovsky's security for spotting him.

Some time later, Litvinenko brought Terlyuk to meet Goldfarb in a coffee shop on Leicester Square. There, Terlyuk confessed that he was moonlighting for the Russian Embassy. According to Terlyuk, in 2002 two Russian diplomats approached him in a London park. They knew his old KGB pseudonym, the one he used to sign his reports years before.

'They said I should work for them, otherwise they would report my past to the immigration authorities, and I would be deported,' Goldfarb recalled Terlyuk telling him. 'Of course, I had not mentioned the KGB in my asylum application,' he added, 'so I had no choice.'

'What kind of work have you been doing?'

'Going places, writing reports. Russian events, for example. Or, say, details of parking, service elevators and emergency exits in a department store. With Berezovsky, I was supposed to get friendly with one of you and report whatever I heard, that sort of thing.'[4]

Amazingly, even after he had been uncovered and confessed, Terlyuk continued to consort with Berezovsky's people including Goldfarb, Litvinenko, Litvinenko's English friend and interpreter Martin Dewhirst, and even Julia Svetlichnaya, then a post-graduate student of the University of Westminster who met Sasha for a series of interviews in May 2006. Terlyuk attended all magistrates' court hearings in 2003 until Boris was granted political asylum. He was omnipresent. No wonder in May the security officials in the courtroom asked Terlyuk to identify himself and made notes of his passport data.

He reappeared a few weeks later and Litvinenko brought him to a sushi restaurant in Soho. This time he had a new assignment, Terlyuk reported. His Russian Embassy contact told him to buy a fountain pen of a special make, and then see whether he could walk with it through a metal detector to get into the Bow Street courthouse.

This information sounded important enough for Goldfarb to arrange a meeting with Berezovsky's lawyer, George Menzies, who agreed to meet Terlyuk and draft his statement for the police. Terlyuk, however, never showed up. In the meantime, Litvinenko had submitted his own statement about their Leicester Square conversation to Special Branch and wrote reports to MI5 and MI6. In turn, Goldfarb also alerted the police and contacted David Leppard of *The Sunday Times*.

'In early September,' Goldfarb writes in *Death of a Dissident*, 'Judge Workman told Boris's lawyers that the extradition hearings would be moved from Bow Street to the Belmarsh Court, where high-security cases are usually heard, thanks to a request by the Metropolitan Police. They believed that there was a credible threat to Boris's life. Then suddenly, on September 11, the Home Office granted Boris asylum without any explanation. The next

---

[4] Goldfarb and Marina Litvinenko, *Death of a Dissident*, 301.

day, Judge Workman threw out the extradition request, noting that it was now "quite pointless".[5]

On 21 September, David Leppard commented in his slightly belated article in *The Sunday Times*: 'An agent for the SVR, the former KGB, is said to have been sent to Britain to stab Boris Berezovsky, the Russian billionaire, with a pen filled with poison as he attended a London court hearing to contest his extradition on fraud charges.' David further claimed, 'The Russian spy is said to have confessed that he had orders to smuggle a cigarette lighter filled with a lethal poison into London's Bow Street magistrates' court where Berezovsky was due to attend the extradition hearings.' In his article Leppard quoted an unnamed Whitehall official who allegedly confirmed that: 'MI5 had been approached by a man claiming he had been sent to Britain to murder the tycoon and they had referred the matter to the police. The plot is understood to be under investigation by Scotland Yard.'

Upon his return to Russia, in his writings and public statements Chekulin maintained that Berezovsky had offered Terlyuk millions in cash for a false testimony and that Litvinenko had drugged the poor Kazakh and then video-recorded him 'confessing that he was dispatched by the FSB to kill Berezovsky' – a video that influenced the Home Office decision on Berezovsky, he claimed.

These statements, produced not only for Russia but also for export, had their effect:

London, House of Commons

Boris Berezovsky

Dr Julian Lewis [Conservative MP for New Forest East]: To ask the Secretary of State for the Home Department if he will make a statement on the outcome of police investigations into the claims made during the hearing of the extradition case against Boris Berezovsky that an assassin had been sent from Russia to attack him.

Ms Hazel Anne Blears, MP [then a Home Office minister]: The Commissioner of Police of the Metropolis informs me that the Metropolitan Police Service was made aware of an alleged threat to Boris Berezovsky. Inquiries made were unable to either substantiate this information or find evidence of any criminal offences having been committed. Investigations into this matter have been concluded.[6]

---

[5] Ibid, 302.
[6] UK Parliament, Publications and Records, Hansard written answers for 13 January 2004: Column 654W.

Speaking about journalism, Walter Cronkite, often cited as 'the most trusted man in America', noted that objective journalism and an opinion column are about as similar as the Bible and *Playboy* magazine. Whatever the *Sunday Times* reported and, ironically, David Leppard, who I also met, published almost the same text ten years later describing another case, Boris Berezovsky was not granted political asylum in Britain because of Terlyuk's supposed 'confessions', Litvinenko's statements to the police and MI5, or Leppard's opinion column. As the above-quoted document shows, they could not be substantiated. As usual, the Russians underestimated and failed to understand the dominance of justice in the country they still refer to as Foggy Albion.

Litvinenko's assumptions and Leppard's writings made Boris feel completely baffled. 'Can you believe it,' he exclaimed discussing the story with Goldfarb, 'that they would attack me with a chemical weapon? Volodya [Putin] must be really insane!' Then, no one could imagine this was indeed going to happen in Salisbury in March 2018. The victim's name was not Berezovsky, who had long been out of reach by that time, but someone would be quite insane to attack a person in this country by using a chemical weapon.

From his new home in King's Road, Chelsea, known as Stanley House, a fine seventeenth-century mansion with a large garden purchased by Boris in 2005, Berezovsky and his associates, who were labelled by the media The London Circle of Russian Exiles, launched a fierce propaganda campaign. Berezovsky publicly stated that he saw his political mission as bringing down Putin's regime either by force or by organising a 'bloodless revolution'.

On 22 November, one day before Sasha Litvinenko died, I wrote in *The Wall Street Journal* that whatever the truth, this poisoning also looks to be directed against Boris Berezovsky. How? Lord Timothy 'Tim' Bell,[7] a friend of Berezovsky who handled the Litvinenko poisoning affair with the media, explained.

'Boris,' he said, 'you have cast yourself as the archenemy of Putin: politically, personally, and ideologically. Reasonable people believe that you are on the good side in this crusade, even though they may question your motives. For the people at large, this is all pretty irrelevant because it's all about politics in a faraway land. But this time the situation is very different. A crime has been committed on British soil ... '

---

[7] Lord Bell is best known for his advisory role in Margaret Thatcher's three successful general election campaigns and his co-founding and running of Bell Pottinger, a British PR firm. Bell has recently resigned as his company's chairman to set up an advisory firm (Sans Frontières Associates, the original name of the public relations firm he registered before it was renamed Bell Pottinger).

Interestingly, Lord Bell was not able to correctly predict the reaction of the British public. 'The [Litvinenko] story,' he speculated, 'will reach many people, who will react intuitively. The problem is that most people will not *want* to believe it was Putin. People are instinctively averse to the idea of governments or presidents ordering murders. The more it seems obvious, the deeper they will go into denial. You will be going against the tide [he said to Boris], and you are the anti-Putin. If people don't want to think it was Putin, then they'll think it must be you. The louder you say it was him, the more this will happen.'[8] What Lord Bell said was very true about Russia, where most of the people still think that it was Berezovsky who poisoned Litvinenko, and until this day the government propaganda supports this version. However, in the West, it was totally different. Speaking about the possible role of Berezovsky in the Litvinenko affair, Judge Sir Robert Owen had the following to say: 'In summary, I am quite satisfied that Mr Berezovsky bore no responsibility for Mr Litvinenko's death.'

In April 2007, Terlyuk suddenly reappeared, and again he was assigned the same role. The Russian television programme *Vesti Nedeli*, broadcast by the TV channel RTR Planeta, the equivalent of BBC Two's *Newsnight*, showed him 'in obscurity' and using the alias 'Petr' repeating word for word the story he told Martin Dewhirst of how Berezovsky offered him millions of pounds for pretending to be an assassin sent by Moscow to kill the oligarch. At the same time, he claimed, Litvinenko had witnessed an attempt by Berezovsky to avoid extradition and get political asylum by obtaining false evidence from a Vladimir Terlyuk. He also suggested that Berezovsky was party to threats to Mr Terlyuk's life. That was the reason, 'Petr' claimed, for Berezovsky receiving political asylum in Britain. After Berezovsky filed a lawsuit against Terlyuk and the television channel, Terlyuk denied in court that he himself was the person called 'Petr' and featured in silhouette in the TV programme, but the judge said he had 'no doubt'.

All these tales have already been rejected by the British authorities long before. This time Berezovsky sued the broadcasting company VGTRK, but their defence lawyers asked the judge to refuse jurisdiction over the claim on the basis that the interviewee – Terlyuk alias 'Petr' – was a Russian state-protected witness, part of the bigger case against Berezovsky. Nevertheless, Mr Justice Eady ruled that both RTR and Terlyuk were liable for damages. The High Court awarded Berezovsky £150,000 ($224,000), the BBC reported.

On 18 July, I met Alex Goldfarb for a late breakfast at the Hilton Hotel on Park Lane. On that day, British media reported yet another story about

---

[8] Goldfarb with Marina Litvinenko, *Death of a Dissident*, 321–2.

the plot to assassinate Boris. The suspected assassin was only named as Mr 'A'. Alex explained that the man's name was Movladi Atlangeriev who had 'a long association with the FSB' and that the Metropolitan Police possessed intelligence that he had come to the UK to assassinate Berezovsky. He was detained on 21 June in the same Hilton, located conveniently around the corner from Boris's office, where we were sitting, on suspicion of conspiracy to murder, but was released without charge to immigration officials two days later. No incriminating evidence was found and Atlangeriev was quietly expelled to Moscow.

Several days later, Ahmed Zakayev invited Gordievsky and me for a long *shashlik* lunch at his home in Muswell Hill. Oleg arrived with Maureen and because Valentina was in London, she was also happy to join me. *Shashlik* or *shashlyk* is a popular dish of skewered and grilled cubes of meat, best of all marinated lamb, with pieces of onion and vegetables. Ahmed was a great master of making *shashlik* with his son Shamil helping him. He told us that Movladi Atlangeriev, known among his associates as Ruslan, born in 1954, was a childhood friend of a future Chechen president Ahmad Kadyrov, father of Ramzan Kadyrov. Ruslan began his criminal career in the 1970s with burglaries of rich foreign students' flats together with another Chechen by the name of Khozh-Ahmed Noukhaev, a future prominent Chechen politician. Russian media reported that eventually both were recruited by the KGB. In the 1990s, Atlangeriev and Noukhaev had dealings with Berezovsky, it was claimed, and in the 2000s collaborated with the FSB in their operations in the North Caucasus. Nikolai Patrushev, the head of the Security Service, reportedly valued Atlangeriev's services in Chechnya so much that he awarded him with an engraved pistol.

Paul Klebnikov, an American journalist who wrote a book about Berezovsky called *The Godfather of the Kremlin* (2000), also published a book about Noukhaev with the self-evident title *Conversation with a Barbarian* (2003). Soon after it came out, Klebnikov was shot dead in Moscow. The FSB first accused Berezovsky and then Noukhaev of the murder. Noukhaev disappeared without a trace in February 2004.

After he returned from London, Atlangeriev, nicknamed 'Lord' and 'Lenin', was kidnapped in Moscow and is widely believed to have been murdered in Chechnya. Mentioning him in the Litvinenko inquiry report, Sir Robert stressed that if the intelligence that the police are said to have received about Atlangeriev was true, this event was evidence that even at the time of Litvinenko's death, Russian secret services were prepared 'to arrange the assassination of leading opponents of the Putin regime in London', meaning Berezovsky.

In 2009, Yumashev and his family suddenly became Austrian citizens.

On Monday, 25 March 2013, the Press Bureau of the Thames Valley Police officially reported that a post-mortem examination was carried out on 67-year-old Russian national, Boris Berezovsky, who was found dead at a residential property in Mill Lane, Ascot, on Saturday. The results of the post-mortem examination carried out by a Home Office pathologist showed that the cause of death was consistent with hanging. It was not reported, however, that the body of the dead man was unequivocally identified as that of Boris Berezovsky. Police and forensic scientists concluded the man had committed suicide.

However, Professor Bern Brinkmann, an internationally renowned medico-legal expert and forensic scientist who was employed by members of Berezovsky's family, said that his examination of autopsy photographs had led him to conclude that the person in question had not killed himself. Professor Brinkmann submitted a report to the inquest that included the suggestion that the 67-year-old had been murdered by a number of assailants and then suspended by his scarf from the shower rail. 'The strangulation mark is completely different from the strangulation mark in hanging,' the expert wrote. Killers could have throttled their victim in a bedroom, he asserted.[9]

The Berkshire coroner Peter Bedford said that after hearing evidence from such an eminent witness, he was not able to conclude that Berezovsky had taken his own life.

The police statement said: 'Thames Valley Police and the South East Counter Terrorism Unit carried out a thorough investigation into the unexplained death of Platon Elenin formerly known as Boris Berezovsky. This included the deployment of an experienced Home Office pathologist to examine the body in situ and conduct the subsequent post mortem. His findings were considered alongside examination of the ligature, detailed toxicology, physical evidence recovered from the scene and the deceased's medical history. The investigation could find nothing to support the hypothesis of third-party involvement.'

Nevertheless, after the two-day inquest at Windsor Guildhall in March 2014, the coroner recorded an open verdict.

Six weeks after being found dead on the bathroom floor of a house that belonged to Berezovsky's ex-wife, Berezovsky's body was laid to rest in a deliberately low-key ceremony in Brookwood Cemetery near Woking, Surrey. I was not there. The *Telegraph* reported the service took place in a small brick

---

[9] Correspondence between Professor Brinkmann and the author, 9 August 2018.

chapel, overlooked by suitably Russian pines and silver birches, and under a dull, overcast sky.

Boris Nemtsov, Russia's deputy prime minister during Yeltsin's second Presidency, warned Berezovsky that Putin would not accept a kingmaker by his side: 'He [Putin] will never forgive you for supporting him.'[10] Nemtsov would be shot in Moscow in February 2015.

I know Alex Goldfarb believes in what the British police say. And he believes in the Old Testament: When Ahithophel [Absalom] saw that his advice had not been followed he saddled his donkey and set out for his house in his hometown. He put his affairs in order and hanged himself.[11]

'He was a friend. I miss him. I'm very grateful to Boris. Through him, I felt the touch of history,' Goldfarb told the reporter at the funeral.

I talked to Alex in July 2018. He was suing two Russian propaganda TV outlets, Channel One and RT, which have publicly accused him of Sasha Litvinenko's murder.

Remarkably, Yuli Dubov, another friend, noted: The games that Boris used to play had to be interesting to him. The interest that he got when playing a game with an impossible result always complicating the conditions of this game – that was his main motive.

For me, the life of Boris Berezovsky, the oligarch who single-handedly started the New Cold War, could end in only one of two ways – either he must be killed by Putin or simply disappear. But if he was destined to die a violent death, as some feared and quite a few were plotting, we shall know that the violence will be in the thought and the action of the assassins, not in his dying. You may succeed in silencing one man, but that silence comes at a price …

---

[10] See Masha Lipman, 'Boris Berezovsky: An Oligarch Dies', *The New Yorker*, 26 March, 2013.

[11] This is The King James Version (KJV), 2 Samuel 17:23. It ends with 'So he died and was buried in his father's tomb'. The New Revised Standard Version (NRSV) is different: 17:23 *Hanged himself.* No doubt the premonition that Absalom had embarked on a disastrous course prompted the rejected counsellor to take his own life lest he die the death of a traitor at the hands of David.

Chapter 11

A Venomous Agent

In early July 2010, I discussed a potential prisoner exchange with Steve LeVine, who was writing an article for *Foreign Policy* magazine. It was published one day before Reuter's Moscow correspondent Guy Faulconbridge broke the news of the spy swap. On 9 July, on the upper floor of Vienna International Airport, a large group of observers and journalists, including myself, gathered to watch the YaK-42 passenger jet of the Russian Ministry of Emergency Situations landing with four passengers. They were brought directly from their respective penal colonies to Domodedovo Airport south of Moscow and thence to Austria.

At the same time, Vision Airline's American Boeing 767 was taxiing on the tarmac. It contained nine Russians and one Vicky Peláez, a Peruvian national and US citizen, all mistakenly known in the West as 'sleepers'. Just to explain, in reality, they were not 'sleepers' but active intelligence operatives, some of them commissioned officers including one general – a Hero of the Soviet Union – and some civil employees of the Russian foreign intelligence service, the SVR. The Hero, Mikhail Anatolyevich Vasenkov, the oldest in this group, was deployed in or about March 1976 with a Uruguayan passport in the name of Juan José Lázaro Fuentes. Officially, he was the husband of Vicky Peláez. All ten were professionally known as illegals. Not only have the Soviet Union or Russia been using them widely, but also countries such as Britain and the USA. In Langley, they are known as Non-Official Cover agents or operatives, usually abbreviated as NOCs, and at Vauxhall Cross as natural cover officers. An SIS veteran explained that 'illegals are officers so carefully trained in natural cover that they can live in the target country for extended periods without arousing suspicion'. In the group of Russian illegals arriving from Washington on that day, there should have also been an eleventh person – a man posing as 'Christopher Robert Metsos', who had assumed the identity of a deceased Canadian boy. But after being briefly detained at Larnaca Airport in Cyprus, he managed to skip out after posting bail. Metsos was subsequently exfiltrated to Russia by the local SVR station. His real name was Pavel Kapustin and he was a colonel of the SVR Directorate S (Illegals) and controller of the group.

This spy swap, quite unprecedented in history, became possible because a senior officer of the same Directorate S, Colonel Alexander Poteyev, defected to the United States, the country for which he had secretly worked for about ten years as an agent-in-place, that is, as a CIA 'mole' within his own intelligence organisation. Poteyev, who is being very well guarded by his American hosts, betrayed all the Russian agents and operatives that he knew. Apart from this group of ten, there were also Russian illegals in Canada, Germany and Spain and quite possibly in other countries, including the UK.

Among those who were sitting on board the Russian plane were the former SVR colonel Alexander Zaporozhsky, the former KGB major Gennady Vasilenko, the former GRU (Soviet and then Russian military intelligence) colonel Sergei Skripal, and Igor Sutyagin, the former arms control researcher at the Moscow Institute for USA and Canada Studies, which usually employs former KGB and GRU officers and collaborators. Whatever Sutyagin's previous affiliations were, if any, he was arrested in 1999 and sentenced in April 2004 to 15 years hard labour on charges of high treason. The British government insisted that Skripal and Sutyagin were handed over to London although there were other candidates in Russian prisons and labour camps suitable for this pure 'American' exchange. Among those who stayed was the GRU colonel Alexander Sypachev, who had been convicted on charges of attempted espionage and sentenced to an eight-year prison term in 2002 after he had contacted the US Embassy in Moscow offering his services.

Following a short stopover in the UK, the Boeing continued its flight with only two passengers, among whom, as already mentioned, was Vasilenko who had been fingered by a Russian mole in the FBI, Hanssen (RAMON). The other was Zaporozhsky, thanks to whose efforts Hanssen was identified as a Russian spy, arrested, sentenced and put behind bars. He is currently serving 15 consecutive life sentences in a US prison. In his turn, Zaporozhsky was lured out of his home in Cockeysville, USA, back to Russia, detained by the FSB agents once his plane touched down and escorted to Lubyanka for interrogation.

After landing at RAF Brize Norton in Oxfordshire, Skripal and Sutyagin were transported to Latimer House for debriefing. When this was over, Sutyagun was given a well-paid job at the prestigious Royal United Services Institute (RUSI) on Whitehall and Skripal received a British government pension equal to that of a colonel in the British Army. SIS also bought him a house in Salisbury, Wiltshire, which, rather unusually, was registered in his real name. His family – wife, son and daughter – received long-term British visas and he got a British passport.

Sergei Viktorovich Skripal was born in Kiev, Ukraine, on 23 June 1951. After school he chose a military career and at the age of 17, instead of going into the army, joined the military engineering school (college) named after Andrei Zhdanov, who after the Second World War was thought to be the successor-in-waiting to Stalin but died soon after the war. After graduating in 1972, like many other junior officers, Lieutenant Skripal went to study at the Kuibyshev Military Engineering Academy in Moscow, where he enrolled in the sapper course. He was then lucky to be sent to one of the airborne divisions, the VDV or *desant* (after the French 'descente'), which means to drop or parachute.

On Christmas Day 1979, large numbers of Soviet airborne forces began to land in Kabul as part of the operation STORM-333 and Captain Skripal was among them. After his tour of duty was over, he was invited to join the GRU, the military intelligence arm of the Soviet Army. Like in other countries, it focuses on gathering and analysing military information to assist commanders and the country's leadership in their decisions. It was a very prestigious transfer to the elite club of General Staff officers.

His first intelligence assignment after the compulsory post-graduate course at the Military Diplomatic Academy was to Malta, posing as Cultural and Sports Attaché of the Soviet Embassy in Valletta. He returned to Moscow in 1990 after a five-year posting in this charming island country in the Mediterranean Sea, where SIS has always maintained only a one-man station. Malta was a paradise for intelligence officers of all trades, but as a junior staffer, Sergei hardly attracted anybody's attention.

It is usually a mistake to call intelligence officers posing as diplomats or journalists 'spies'. They are not spying in the full sense of this word but controlling assets and sources – that is, those who collect secret information and those, usually illegals, who help to do it – by serving as a cut-out, a mutually trusted intermediary. Sometimes, illegals themselves run a productive agent or source whose position is so sensitive that it would be too risky for a station officer to approach them. Members of the local station under the roof of an embassy may empty or fill dead-letterboxes, act as talent spotters and recruiters, run agents and write reports. They can also sometimes obtain documents and equipment that could be of use to their organisation, various scientific institutions or other consumers. Spies are those who wittingly or unwittingly provide an intelligence service of the adversary with secret information.

After some time at the headquarters in Moscow, popularly known as 'Aquarium' after the book written by the GRU defector Captain Vladimir Rezun, penname 'Victor Suvorov', Skripal was posted to Madrid and accredited at the office of the Russian Military Attaché. (Like in many other instances in his book *The Skripal Files*, Mark Urban is wrong by claiming, on page 62, that Skripal's position was that of Scientific and Technical Secretary. In reality, Skripal served in Madrid as Assistant Military Attaché.)

At the time, Russia was suffering in the aftermath of *perestroika*, which had resulted in the total collapse of the system. The Soviet ruble had no value and there were no goods in the shops or food in the grocery stores. Seizing the chance to leave the country, albeit temporarily, all Soviet representatives abroad had a 'nose for business'. This, of course, had quickly become known to the intelligence and counterintelligence services of Europe and America, which began hunting for Soviet intelligence officers accredited at the embassies or as foreign correspondents.

There are at least four classic ways of acquiring spies and informants, but the most common method of recruiting an agent is to send out a 'talent spotter' to look for a senior functionary of 'the other side' who, as former MI6 agent Frederick Forsyth puts it, 'may appear disenchanted, resentful, dissatisfied, bitter or in any way susceptible to recruitment'.

Skripal's potential was first spotted by the Spanish intelligence service, the Centro Nacional de Inteligencia (CNI). Among the candidates, the talent spotter had tabbed a 'possible' and an access agent moved in starting, as usual, with a casual friendship growing deeper and warmer every week. In October 1994, a man Russian counterintelligence call 'Luis' suggested to Skripal a business venture selling Spanish wine to Russia. Eventually, the 'friend' asked his new pal to do him a small favour by providing a minor and inconsequential piece of information about the Russian market they were both planning to explore. By February 1995, the 'wine merchant' had allegedly managed to sell a batch of wine barrels to Russia and Skripal was paid $6,000 in cash.

Usually, the motives for being recruited to serve another country vary. In this case it was money, encouraged by sweet talk and flattery. As Forsyth admitted in his autobiography written after many years of spying for the British government, most spies who turn on their own country do so because they share a monstrous vanity, a conviction that they are truly important. Skripal did it because he simply wanted his family 'to live a normal life' at a time when senior diplomats were stealing electric bulbs and rolls of toilet paper from the embassy for their homes because salaries were often delayed or not paid at all.

Eventually, it was decided that such a potentially high-value asset would be better run by SIS with whom the CNI, like its predecessor, had a close working relationship. In July 1995, the Russian was handed over to a British agent calling himself 'Paul', who had just come back from a tour of duty in Africa and was himself a former military intelligence officer, albeit junior. Skripal was given the codename FORTHWITH, as we are told, and began to produce volumes of high-grade intelligence, which was sent to London and sometimes even to Washington. In February 1996, he met with Paul for the last time and a monthly retainer of $3,000 was agreed. It was also agreed – very wisely – that the agent would not have any contact with his British handlers in Moscow. In April 1996, Skripal returned to the Russian capital.

A type-1 diabetic, he suffered increasing health problems and in 1997 resigned his commission as an operational officer and was moved to the personnel department, where he was promoted to its acting head position. From there, travelling to Malta and sometimes Malaga for holidays, he provided his new case officer (who he knew as 'Steven') with valuable intelligence including GRU operations, agents, and other GRU officers stationed in various parts of Europe. From August 1997, his recruiter, Paul, had been based in Estonia accredited as First Secretary of the British Embassy in Tallinn. Once, Skripal was able to deliver the whole GRU telephone book with hundreds of names in it. The agent was paid in cash between $5,000 and $6,000 a meeting, keeping his money in a good Spanish bank with a solid international reputation. Two years later Sergei retired from the GRU having secured a job at the Foreign Ministry's Administration Department.

In October 1999, he called the secret phone number given to him by Paul, which he had memorised, asking for an emergency meeting. His SIS case officer immediately flew to Spain only to discover that Sergei needed $10,000 immediately. After a short explanation, he received the money the next day.

In 2001, Skripal had to leave the Foreign Ministry because of ill health, having secured a job at the Ministry of Municipalities in the Moscow provincial government. He was invited there by an old GRU friend and was not surprised to see several former colleagues occupying various ministerial posts. The reason was that general Boris Gromov, a hero of the Afghan war who had retired from the army, had been elected governor of the Moscow region in January 2000. (In November 2007, Gromov was re-elected for the third term, always sharing a close bond with Afghan veterans and especially the VDV.) He was then elected to the State Duma, the lower house of the Federal Assembly of Russia.

Unlike what has been claimed in the Russian media, Skripal and his family lived very modestly, sharing a two-room apartment between Sergei, his wife Lyudmila and their children Alexander and Yulia. Skripal was advised not to spend his money ostentatiously and to his office in an old Russian Niva, an off-road vehicle produced specifically for the rural market. No one ever suspected him of being in touch with a foreign intelligence organisation. Until one day.

In October 2004, the SVR foreign counterintelligence department contacted their colleagues in the FSB and GRU with breaking news. A top Russian agent inside the Spanish CNI reported that SIS had a senior GRU officer working for them. A copy of his operational file was secretly handed over to a cut-out, an illegal who had operated in Spain for two decades under the name Henry Frith and who was known at the SVR Yasenevo headquarters as Sergei Yurievich Cherepanov, born in Russia in 1955. Cherepanov/Frith urgently called his case officer, Petr Yakovlevich Melnikov, accredited as Counsellor at the Russian Embassy in Madrid, and arranged a meeting. Soon the file was in Moscow. A telephone call was immediately made to Skripal's home only to find out that he was on holiday in Turkey.

Indeed, Skripal's next meeting with his case officer was in Izmir, a metropolitan city on the Turkish Aegean coast. The meeting with Steven was arranged at one of the two local Hilton hotels, with good air conditioning and a perfect view of the hilltop Velvet Castle, built during the reign of Alexander the Great, which overlooked the city. The meeting went well and Skripal was able to deliver a few valuable snippets of intelligence, which he managed to collect during his social functions with former GRU colleagues. It seems he also produced some fairly important intelligence because, according to the Russian media, in the course of that meeting at the Hilton he was paid $20,000. He returned to Moscow where both the FSB and GRU watchers were already waiting for him, secretly recording his every movement. Skripal was not detained upon arrival, only watched and filmed carrying a Louis Vuitton bag (quite certainly a fake). Three years later the former last leader of the USSR Mikhail Gorbachev was pictured driving by the Berlin Wall with a similar but genuine Louis Vuitton Keepall 45 Monogram bag in the advertisement shot by Anne Leibovitz.

Colonel Skripal was detained on 15 December 2004 near his house in Moscow. Ben Macintyre wrote in his article in *The Times* that Skripal's shoulder was said to have been deliberately wrenched from its socket during the arrest. This is certainly an exaggeration – after a few cases when in such circumstances people committed suicide by swallowing a cyanide pill, officers who make the arrest are very careful not to allow it, but they never use excessive force. In August 2006, Skripal was convicted of high treason and sentenced to 13 years in a penal colony. He was stripped of his military rank, but his sentence was reduced because he agreed to cooperate with investigators. In July 2010, he was unexpectedly released, pardoned by the Russian president (at the time Dmitry Medvedev) and flown to London. His troubles seemed to be over forever.

WANTED BY THE FBI

CHRISTOPHER ROBERT METSOS

Conspiracy to Act as an Unregistered Agent of a Foreign Government; Conspiracy to Commit Money Laundering

Photograph taken in July 2010

DESCRIPTION

Aliases: Christopher R. Metsos, Pavel Kapustin, Gerard Martin Kelleher, Diego Cadenilla Jose Antonio, Luis Miguel Alarcon-Correas, Patrick Allen Woolcocks, Peter Michael Franklin, Graham Douglas Cox, Pavel Gukov, Sean Proinnsias O'Donaill

Date(s) of Birth Used: June 16, 1956, April 7, 1954, November 17, 1959, October 20, 1955, June 21, 1956, March 17, 1956, October 9, 1953, April 27, 1958, June 1, 1954, December 30, 1954	Place of Birth: Canada
Hair: Light Brown (Balding)	Eyes: Brown
Height: 5'11" to 6'0"	Weight: 180 to 195 pounds
Sex: Male	Race: White
Nationality: Canadian	Scars and Marks: Metsos has a scar on his chest and burn/pock marks on his arms.
NCIC: W560713749	

REWARD

The FBI is offering a reward of up to $50,000 for information leading to the arrest of Christopher Robert Metsos.

REMARKS

Metsos may have fled to Russia. He has travelled the world extensively. He may wear a moustache and eyeglasses. Metsos is trained in martial arts and holds a black belt.

CAUTION

Christopher Robert Metsos is wanted for failing to register as an agent of a foreign government as required by United States law. This occurred from 1993 to 2005. During that time, Metsos allegedly took part in a money laundering scheme, causing money to be illegally transferred to other United States-based co-conspirators who were also unregistered agents of a foreign government. A federal arrest warrant was issued for Metsos in the United States District Court, Southern District of New York, on June 25, 2010, after he was charged with conspiracy to act as an unregistered agent of a foreign government and conspiracy to commit money laundering. Metsos was arrested in Cyprus on June 29, 2010, but posted bail and fled.

SHOULD BE CONSIDERED AN ESCAPE RISK

If you have any information concerning this person, please contact your local FBI office or the nearest American Embassy or Consulate.

Field Office: New York

One of the most successful Russian 'illegals', Colonel Pavel Kapustin, alias 'Christopher R. Metsos', acted as group leader and controller for a number of Russian undercover agents who brazenly operated in the US before they were all caught red-handed and arrested in June 2010. Kapustin managed to escape and is now on the FBI 'Wanted List'.

Several days earlier, on 28 June, a British intelligence agent approached 'Frith' near his home in Madrid. He obviously knew everything about the Russian illegal and made him a blatant offer to change sides. Frith/Cherepanov, who spoke English as if he was born in New Zealand, which he was not, politely declined. In the morning, he was already on board a plane taking him to an Eastern European capital. Shortly before Skripal's arrest, Cherepanov was in Moscow. Recently re-elected President Putin personally presented government awards to 'Christopher Metsos' (Kapustin), 'Henry Frith' (Cherepanov), Anna Chapman (Kushchenko) and other Russian illegals during a ceremony at the SVR Yasenevo headquarters. A couple from Germany, 'Herr und Frau Anschlag' (Alexander and Olga Rost), joined them later. The couple have worked undercover for more than 20 years. In late December 2006, 'Paul William Hampel', another SVR illegal, was deported to Russia from Canada. His real identity is known but not publicly disclosed.

In July 2007, Roberto Flórez García, a 41-year old former employee of Spain's National Intelligence Centre (CNI) was arrested on Tenerife. The head of the CNI, Alberto Saiz, said the mole had been selling information to an unnamed country from 2001 to 2004 although he had been working for the intelligence service since 1991. He added that Mr Flórez was richly rewarded for handing over the identities of agents and CNI activities to a foreign power. It was established without doubt that the country was Russia, although the Russian Embassy in Madrid denied having anything to do with the spy.

In February 2010, Roberto Flórez was convicted of treason and sentenced to 12 years in prison by a Madrid court. But then something strange happened. In December 2010, five months after Sergei Skripal arrived in the UK, the Supreme Tribunal reduced Flórez's term to nine years. And this is not all. From time to time, Mr Flórez mysteriously disappeared from the prison of Estremera, a modern facility about 70 km from the capital where he was being incarcerated, and then came back as if nothing had happened. His wife even moved from Tenerife to Madrid to make full use of those favourable penitentiary conditions. It seems that somebody was very keen to establish how Flórez thought he had been uncovered, what exactly he knew and betrayed, and what information his Russian handlers were seeking to get, apart from what he had already delivered.

Colonel Skripal was not the only GRU officer residing in the West, but he was the most recent 'acquisition'. Therefore, after settling in Salisbury he remained in regular contact with MI6, from time to time lecturing at the Sandhurst and Fort Monckton in Gosport but also helping where his experience and expert knowledge were most needed. And this concerned a wide area of problems including the most important hotspot of recent times – Syria.

A Syrian government organisation, the Scientific Studies and Research Centre (*Centre d'Etudes et de Recherches Scientifiques*), better known by its French abbreviation CERS, was established in 1971. Two years later, President Hafez Al-Assad transformed the centre into the main agency for the development of modern weapons for the Syrian army. Ten years later, the director-general of the CERS was raised to ministerial rank and the production of chemical weapons became one of its main projects. According to the US Special National Intelligence Estimate (SNIE) of 15 September 1983, the USSR and its satellites started to deliver chemical warfare agents (CWA) to the centre with delivery systems for military CWAs like vesicants, pulmonary toxicants, incapacitating agents and neurotoxic agents.

In the early 1990s it was reported that CERS had started to produce sarin, VX and mustard gas, receiving the expertise, technology and materials from Russia. Later, North Korea delivered to Syria Hwasong-6 tactical ballistic missiles, a derivative of the Soviet R-17M (Scud-C). All contacts and works had been supervised by the Soviet GRU, an intelligence arm of the Army General Staff. In 1991, a rather shadowy figure by the name of Anatoly Kuntsevich – who from 1964 to 1981 had served at the military-chemical R&D centre (Institute 33) in Shikany and from 1972 supervised the development of neurotoxic agents/organophosphorus compounds – was suddenly awarded the Lenin Prize, a kind of a Soviet domestic equivalent of the international Nobel Prize.

Little known in the Soviet Union and Russia, the general and academician Kuntsevich, Hero of the Socialist Labour, was then promoted to deputy commander of the Soviet Joint Chemical, Biological, Radiological and Nuclear Defence (CBRN) troops and in 1992 became President Yeltsin's adviser on the chemical weapons ban treaty. Ironically, as reported by Vil Mirzayanov,[1] early that year Russia and Syria signed an agreement whereby Russia undertook to deliver new types of chemical weapons to Damascus. Among them was the infamous Novichok series synthesised at the Russian State Research Institute of Organic Chemistry and Technology and tested at the Shikhany chemical testing ground near Saratov under the supervision of Kuntsevich. Mirzayanov used to head the department there and was in charge of the facility's protection from Western intelligence, surveillance

---

[1] See Vil Mirzayanov and Lev Fedorov, 'Otravlennaya politika', *Moskovskie novosti*, (20 September 1992); and Vil S. Mirzayanov, *State Secrets: An Insider's Chronicle of the Russian Chemical Weapons Program* (Parker, CO: Outskirts Press, 2008). See also David Wise, 'Novichok on Trial', *The New York Times*, 12 March 1994.

and reconnaissance capabilities. According to Mirzayanov (who left Russia and settled in the United States), in conformity with the agreement, all necessary components were delivered to CERS in May. In 1993, Kuntsevich was appointed chief Russian representative at the military research centre of the Syrian CERS facility in Jamraya, the highly secretive base established in the 1980s.

The Chemical Weapons Convention Bulletin of March 1996 quotes President Clinton's letter that he wrote to Senate Foreign Relations Committee chairman Jesse Helms in response to the latter's concerns about General Kuntsevich, the erstwhile chairman of the Russian Presidential Committee on CBW Convention Problems. The US president's letter, released in January 1996, states: 'Any activities aimed at smuggling materials for weapons of mass destruction — whether nuclear, chemical or biological — are of vital concern to the United States. That is why we recently imposed chemical weapons-related sanctions against General Kuntsevich. That is also why we are so determined to bring the Chemical Weapons Convention into force and to do so as soon as possible.'[2] Before this letter was made public, Kuntsevich was nominated as a parliamentary candidate for the Liberal Democratic Party of Russia (LDPR), but later dropped out of the race. The same party also nominated Andrei Lugovoy, who was elected following the scandal that broke out after the barbaric poisoning of Alexander Litvinenko in London.

The letter ends: 'I share your concern about General Kuntsevich's smuggling activities. I am convinced, however, that once the CWC is in force in Russia and other countries, proliferators like General Kuntsevich will find it both more difficult and more costly to carry out their deadly activities. The CWC is in our national security interests. I urge your Committee to complete its consideration of this vital treaty this fall.' However, in February 1996, unidentified intelligence sources were quoted by the New York *Daily News* as holding Kuntsevich largely responsible for the purchase by Iran and Syria of Russian designs for the production of the nerve agents VX and 'Novichok-5', also known as A-232.

A couple of years later, experts in the UK, US and Israel started to express concern about these new agents designed to be undetectable by standard NATO chemical detection equipment and able to defeat existing chemical protective gear. In 1999, Michael Ross of the Mossad was instructed to find out as much as possible about Russian deliveries of modern chemical

---

[2] See *Chemical Weapons Convention Bulletin* (CWCB), 31 (March 1996), 16, Ref. 28 November [1995], last paragraph.

weapons to Syria. In his book *The Volunteer* (2007), Mr Ross recalls making a telephone call to the Presidential Administration of Russia after Vladimir Putin had become the country's leader. He was assured that no efforts would be spared 'to stop this private smuggling business'. At the end of March 2002, General Kuntsevich suddenly died on board a plane departing from Syria where, the former Mossad operative notes, 'He'd just delivered stolen precursors for Novichok, a Russian-made [nerve] agent several times more deadly than conventional nerve gases.'

Several recent publications add an interesting note to this old story.[3] A Soviet general behind the development of a deadly nerve agent used in a poisoning attack in the UK (in March 2018) raised concerns in Israel in the 1990s, *The Times of Israel* reports. The Jewish state was worried. It was furious that General Kuntsevich was trying to sell his knowledge to Syria. 'On 29 April 2002 [*sic*], in circumstances that remain unknown, Kuntsevich died during a flight from Aleppo to Moscow,' the newspaper quotes Ronen Bergman's book. 'The Syrians appear to be confident that the Israeli intelligence had succeeded in reaching and poisoning the general.'

In early September 2017, Reuters and several media outlets reported on the Israeli attack hitting a military site in Syria's Hama province. The air strike killed two soldiers and caused material damage to the facility near the town of Masyaf, the official statement said. The location of the facility is significant because it is 30 miles from a Russian airbase. A report from Jerusalem specified that the air-strike on the al-Talai Scientific Studies and Research Centre took place overnight and that Western intelligence reports had linked the target to Syria's chemical weapons programme. In a conference call with journalists, the former Israeli national security adviser Yaakov Amidror said: 'I know the organisation and facility. For many years it has been one of the Syrian centres for research and development for weapons systems including chemical weapons ... and weapons that have been transferred to Hezbollah.'

Hezbollah and Russia are strategic allies. At the same time, reports from Moscow mentioned that the CERS facility was guarded by Russian GRU Spetsnaz units, while the laboratories were staffed by Russian research scientists. Whether there were any casualties among the Russian personnel is not known.

Although Mossad is one of the best intelligence services in the world, it often uses information provided by friendly British and US agencies. The

---

[3] See, for example, Anonymous staff writer, 'Did the Mossad kill a Russian general for peddling deadly nerve agent to Syria?' *The Times of Israel*, 17 March 2018; and Ronen Bergman, *Rise and Kill First: The Secret History of Israel's Targeted Assassinations* (London: John Murray, 2018) – 'A masterpiece', Christopher Andrew is quoted on the cover.

aforementioned article in *The Times* noted that the inclusion of Skripal in the spy swap was an anomaly since he was not an American 'asset'. Britain, it said, pressed for Skripal to be swapped and the CIA agreed – a recognition perhaps of the high quality of material Britain had shared from the FORTHWITH files.

But the old files and achievements dating back to the late 1990s were certainly not the only reasons for the Russian 'hit'. Until his poisoning in March, Skripal was the only intelligence source in the West who could provide British and American services with reliable estimates of the Russian GRU activities in Syria and elsewhere. And although he didn't know people and specific operations any more, he knew the system from the inside, had practical knowledge and experience like no one else because this cannot be learned from the textbooks and manuals. With the loss of such a high-value asset it is more difficult to analyse intelligence coming from sources in the field.

There's also another possibility. An experienced intelligence officer who has something to offer to the West will rarely, if ever, contact a representative of a Western intelligence service even when stationed abroad, not to mention at home in Russia. Colonel Sypachev tried and was quickly caught. The reasons are obvious. In Moscow and St Petersburg, the FSB mobile surveillance teams are very skilled and work extremely well.

There is simply no chance for any informal contact without being detected even during a diplomatic reception or an official party. Abroad, a wrong move can cause suspicion from the ever-watching colleagues or there may be a Russian asset within the ranks of a Western service, like in the case of the CNI. We also remember Kim Philby and the Konstantin Volkov case as well as two notorious moles Ames and Hanssen, who betrayed many people, nearly all of whom were later shot. Therefore, the most reliable way is to call somebody who is known to maintain friendly relations with a trusted contact at Vauxhall Cross in London or the George Bush Center in Langley, Virginia. This can be done from any place provided this person's postal or email address or telephone number is known. If not, the daughter can always deliver an innocent letter from a former pal of her father.

Like almost every other Soviet and Russian defector before him (although he was not a defector in full sense), Skripal easily adapted to life in a small English town. He certainly liked a snort (local slang for a drink) or two and was often photographed with a pint of beer in a local pub or restaurant. People from the social club he frequented also mentioned that he liked vodka, and obviously whiskey and brandy, the usual stuff. I know several KGB and GRU defectors and it is always the same – a small market town, a newspaper in the morning, pub, lunch, and a visit from 'the Office' once a month. As a rule, this visit is not by someone who recruited the defector but by a dedicated AR officer from the resettlement section appointed to take care of the former asset or agent who has been exfiltrated, swapped, or managed to flee to the West.

According to his neighbours, Skripal was friendly and polite but not easy to understand because of his heavy Russian accent. There are some Polish waitresses and other service staff in Salisbury who comprehend Russian, as well as some Polish delicatessens selling groceries that Skripal enjoyed and where he could speak his native language. He also liked to talk to taxi drivers and often travelled abroad or, to be precise, asked to be driven to Heathrow Airport. In the meantime, Yulia was planning to get married to her boyfriend, had started some serious refurbishing of a small apartment where they lived and on 3 March, came to visit her father because she did not want to leave him alone on what would have been Alexander Skripal's 44th birthday. Alexander was her brother, and Sergei's only son, who died in St Petersburg in July a year before but was buried in Salisbury in the local cemetery, right near the gates. Yulia arrived at Heathrow at 2:40 p.m. and went straight to her father's house.

Facing the magnificent Salisbury Cathedral is an ecumenical Christian institution known as Sarum College. A wooden staircase and a short corridor on the first floor lead to the nineteenth-century chapel designed by the Victorian architect William Butterfield. It is available for hire and it is in this chapel that the congregation of the Greek Orthodox Church of Saint John the Forerunner gathers for worship. Here, a *panihida*, or memorial service, can be arranged with the priest for a Saturday.

Panihida for departed Orthodox souls is a short service, which is chanted in front of the crucifix and memorial table. Usually, those attending will hold a lighted candle throughout the ceremony, and a dish of *koliva* (a ritual food of boiled wheat) can be blessed and shared after the service. The service lasts for approximately 20 minutes. It is followed on Sunday morning by the liturgy. In the Slavic practice, *prosphora* are sent up by the faithful at the start of the liturgy together with 'scraps' of paper containing the names of Orthodox living and departed who they wish to have commemorated during the liturgy. A *prosphoron* (the single form of *prosphora*) is a loaf of leavened bread used in Orthodox Christian and Byzantine services. As a part of the Divine Liturgy, a cube is cut from the centre of the *prosphoron*, referred to as the Lamb (it is this Lamb which is consecrated to become the Body of Christ and from it both the clergy and the laity will receive Holy Communion). The remainder of the blessed bread is divided into pieces and distributed at the end of the

Liturgy. It is often served together with some red wine symbolising the body and blood of Jesus Christ. For those, who present their prosphora together with the name of the faithful living or departed, the priest will remove a triangular piece as well as several smaller particles while he prays for each of the persons listed.

In a simplified version, Sergei and Yulia could have taken their *prosphoron*, brought by Yulia from Russia, to the Orthodox church on Saturday evening to be blessed by an Orthodox priest. They would be obliged to share it on Sunday morning and eat while fasting before going to the cemetery or at the cemetery itself beside the graves of their loved ones, with a shot of vodka. It was established they had visited the graves of Lyudmila and Alexander Skripal that Sunday. From there they went to attend the Eucharist that began in Salisbury Cathedral at 10:30 a.m., spending the rest of the morning listening to the preacher's reading from *Exodus*, which was difficult for them to understand, and then *John*, whose words about 'the glory of the only Son', a glory received 'from the Father' seemed very fitting. They also enjoyed Bach's imposing *Fantasia* in C minor, a relatively short piece performed, as always, on the great 'Father' Willis Organ of 1877, before going to the town centre again shortly after 1:00 pm.

Remarkably, although this is how the last two members of the Skripal family could have been poisoned, it is only one of several possible scenarios and is not supported by any evidence. As a matter of fact, the government has not released *any* evidence so far. The official version – that the nerve agent was 'smeared' on the door handle of Skripal's house – seems unlikely to me. According to various scientific research papers, Novichok agents, also known as the 'N-series', have a higher density than air and will therefore tend to collect in low-lying areas. They also have a low viscosity so their use on the doorknob may be problematic. The stories about Russian agents rushing through Europe applying poisons to door handles may be good for the next Bond movie, but not for real life. Thus, we still do not know how Sergei Skripal and his daughter were poisoned and how Detective Sergeant Nick Bailey got involved. What is absolutely clear, however, is that if it was indeed the neurotoxic agent of the N-series (A-234, as the Russian Embassy in London was officially informed), it was not administered perorally (through the mouth) because the victims would have been dead within minutes.

Unsurprisingly, regarding the chemical and physical properties of A-234, the agent most likely used in Salisbury, its reactivity and toxicity, the usual answer is NDA – no data available. All requests for information under the Freedom of Information Act either to the Home Office or to the Ministry of Defence are being considered under the exemptions in sections 24(1), 31(1)

Sir Mark Sedwill KCMG
National Security Adviser
Cabinet Office
70 Whitehall
London
SW1A 2AS

H E Mr Jens Stoltenberg
Secretary General
North Atlantic Treaty Organization

13 April 2018

Dear Secretary-General,

Thank you again for your invitation to me to brief the North Atlantic Council on
15 March regarding the recent attack in Salisbury. I am pleased that we have
been able to remain in close contact with you and NATO Allies following this
attack, and particularly grateful for the measures taken by you and many Allies
in response.

As you are aware, yesterday the Organisation for the Prohibition of Chemical
Weapons published their report summarising the analysis of environmental and
biomedical samples relating to the investigation into the attempted assassination
of Mr Skripal and his daughter. Thank you for the public comments you have
already made regarding this. As signatories to the Chemical Weapons
Convention, all NATO Allies have received the full report, and several will take
part in next Wednesday's meeting of the OPCW Executive Council which the
UK has called.

The OPCW's analysis matches the Defence Science and Technology
Laboratory's own, confirming once again the findings of the United Kingdom
relating to the identity of the toxic chemical of high purity that was used in
Salisbury. OPCW have always been clear that it was their role to identify what
substance was used, not who was responsible.

I would like to share with you and Allies further information regarding our
assessment that it is highly likely that the Russian state was responsible for the
Salisbury attack. Only Russia has the technical means, operational experience
and the motive.

Letter from the British national security adviser Sir Mark Sedwill to the NATO Secretary
General Jens Stoltenberg, explaining the Skripal case.

and 40(2) of the Act, which relate to national security and law enforcement matters. So, the answer is 'No'.

However, information about overexposure effects is not so sparse. Usually, signs and symptoms are the same regardless of the route the neurotoxic agent enters the body – by inhalation, absorption, or ingestion.[4] These signs and symptoms are normally followed by cessation of breathing and death.

More than a year has passed since Sergei and Yulia Skripal were found unconscious on a park bench in The Maltings shopping centre in the middle of the ancient English cathedral town, and there are still questions. Was his poisoning in retaliation for the destruction of the Syrian chemical weapons centre where Russian scientists and the GRU Spetsnaz guards died? Where a lot of Russian money and technology have been invested for years and where highly toxic nerve agents, including Novichok compounds, have been secretly produced for the Syrian and Russian arsenals of murder weapons. Or was it simply to silence him as a valuable consultant to the British and US secret services and occasional middleman between them and his former GRU colleagues? Was Yulia poisoned by chance or was it a planned attack on the last two surviving members of the Skripal family?

Once again, I am re-reading Forsyth, this time *The Fist of God*, published more than twenty years ago.

'All wars must teach lessons,' he writes. 'If they do not do so, they were fought in vain and those who died in them did so for naught.' The last six decades of what was known as the Cold War gave two clear warnings if the powers that be have the wit to access them. The first is that it is madness for any civilised nation of the world possessing sophisticated modern weaponry and the means for its production, to sell these artefacts to the crazed, aggressive and dangerous dictators for short-term financial or political profit. The second lesson concerns the collection and evaluation of information. With the invention of the complex computer systems, many hoped this could forever be given to machines. The reality shows the opposite.

During the last decades, technical advances in the gathering of electronic and signals intelligence were so impressive that the free world, where Russia does not belong, was led to believe, as the scientists produced their expensive

---

[4] The above-mentioned signs and symptoms are: runny nose; tightness of chest; dimness of vision and miosis (pinpointing of the eye pupils); difficulty in breathing; drooling and excessive sweating; nausea; vomiting; cramps and involuntary defecation and urination; twitching, jerking and staggering; and headache, confusion, drowsiness, coma and convulsion. As already stated, these signs and symptoms are followed by cessation of breathing and death. For details, see Steven L. Hoenig, *Compendium of Chemical Warfare Agents* (New York: Springer, 2007), 85–7.

gadgets, that computers alone could do the job of maintaining peace in the world. While artificial intelligence demonstrated by machines was extolled to the skies, the role of human intelligence was downgraded. What becomes plain, however, is that the situation has changed. It also turned out that for certain tasks in certain places and under certain circumstances, there is still no substitute for the oldest intelligent machine on Earth: a human brain. I believe Sergei Skripal, who so clearly believed he was living unnoticed in semi-retirement, paid heavily for that simple fact.

On 26 February 2019, in an interview to the Interfax news agency, Sir Laurie Bristow KCMG, Her Majesty's Ambassador to the Russian Federation stated, 'I can confirm that they [Sergei and Yulia Skripal] are alive. I can confirm that the request or offer of the Russian Embassy [in London] to see them has been passed to them, they don't want to see members of the Russian Embassy … It's their choice.'

I immediately remembered Charles Maurice de Talleyrand-Périgord, French politician and Napoleon's chief diplomat, a great conversationalist, gourmet and wine connoisseur, who is also hailed as a statesman of great resourcefulness and craft. Better known simply as Talleyrand, he became famous for this quote: 'A diplomat who says "yes" means "maybe", a diplomat who says "maybe" means "no", and a diplomat who says "no" is no diplomat.'

In September 2019, Russian television channel NTV, controlled by Gazprom Media, broadcast a four-part documentary series entitled *Novichok from Salisbury*. In one of the episodes, they reproduced a recorded message allegedly left by Sergey Skripal on his mother's answering machine with 9 May Victory Day greetings. There was no mention of any voice authentication but that would not be of any real help anyway. Whether this call is the work of Russian or British secret services remains unclear.

For those who are interested – an aspect of artificial intelligence (AI) that is sometimes overlooked is just how good it is at creating fake audio and video.

Chapter 12

Epilogue

From the one-party terrorist state to the Putin presidency: "We'll wipe them out in the shithouse"

Probably the best intelligence historian of all times, Professor Christopher Andrew noted that the latest research on the period between 1917 and 1991, the rise and fall of the Soviet Union, undermines the common assumption of some non-specialists of a basic symmetry between the role of intelligence in East and West.[1]

In classic terms, secret intelligence offers insight into what the other side in any confrontation might be thinking (as opposed to what it is saying). It is especially important when open democratic regimes have to do with closed regimes and/or regimes supporting highly controversial activity. In such circumstances, as a former Chairman of the Joint Intelligence Committee (and the former Chief of SIS) Sir John Scarlett acknowledges, well-informed intelligence can make a big difference to policy.

In the early Soviet as well as in post-Soviet society, intelligence has played a different role. The first Soviet secret police was the Cheka. Its successors, the NKVD and KGB fulfilled the functions of both the security services and the overseas intelligence agencies right up to the collapse of the Soviet Union and disintegration of the country and were central to the functioning of the state system in ways that intelligence communities never were in Western governments. Alexander Herzen, a great Russian writer and thinker, known as the 'father of Russian socialism', has often been quoted as saying that what he feared for the twentieth century was the prospect of 'Genghis Khan with a telegraph' – a traditional despot with all the power of a modern state at his command. With Lenin, Stalin and Putin, Herzen's nightmare became a reality. His *aperçu* was wrong in only one aspect – all of them were not aliens but locals. And as well as the telegraph, they had machine guns, large and small nuclear devices, nerve agents and psychotronic weapons – in other words, after the Bolshevik seizure of power in 1917, Russia has been and

---

[1] Andrew and Mitrokhin, *The Mitrokhin Archive*, 707–35.

remains a closed regime conducting highly controversial activity and with very dangerous potential.

The foundations of the one-party terrorist state were laid by Lenin – the mastermind of the Cheka concept and its most ardent supporter within the Bolshevik leadership. Lenin dismissed any protests against its brutality as wimpish 'wailing'. 'With Lenin's personal encouragement,' Christopher Andrew writes, 'the Cheka gradually permeated every aspect of life under the Soviet regime.' Lenin's 'faithful pupil' and follower Stalin used the OGPU and NKVD, the Cheka's successor agencies, to carry through the greatest peacetime persecution in European history. Victims included the majority of the Party leadership and the high command, and even commissars of state security responsible for implementing the Great Terror. Andrew concludes, 'Among Western observers, unable to comprehend that such persecution was possible in an apparently civilised society, there were some textbook cases of cognitive dissonance.'[2]

In the field of psychology, cognitive dissonance is the mental discomfort experienced by a person who simultaneously holds two or more contradictory beliefs, ideas, or values or otherwise, as Professor Andrew puts it, the difficulty all of us have in grasping new concepts that disturb our current view of the world. This was also typical of a report compiled for the Litvinenko inquiry by a British authority instructed to provide expert evidence on Russian history and politics, which the coroner praised as 'most impressive and helpful'.

Assassinations have been an integral part of Soviet foreign policy from Lenin to Putin. Already in the 1920s there was a Special Tasks group operating from Paris that reported directly to the chief of the secret service. The group specialised in sabotage, assassination, burglaries, black propaganda and general mayhem. Its members were hunting early Soviet defectors Georges Agabekov and Boris Bazhanov and were responsible for the assassinations of Alexander Dutov, Ignacy Gintowt-Dziewałtowski, Symon Petlyura, Baron Peter Wrangel, Ignatz Reiss. They were also responsible for the abductions of the former tsarist generals Alexander Kutepov and Yevgeny Miller, the extermination of the leading Trotskyists in Spain and Western Europe and the plan to assassinate General Franco during the Spanish Civil War and Hitler after he attacked Russia.

As is well-known, Stalin was obsessed with 'liquidating' his arch-adversary Trotsky and his supporters in Russia and abroad. Trotsky was killed in August 1940, when the Second World War had already begun, after the first botched assassination attempt three months earlier. Before he died in March 1953,

---

[2] Ibid, 709.

Stalin's final political act was a plan to murder Josip Broz Tito, the Yugoslav leader.

After Stalin's death, Soviet illegal Nikolai Khokhlov was sent to West Germany to 'neutralise' an émigré leader in Frankfurt am Main, and another illegal, Bogdan Stashynsky, became known for liquidating two Ukrainian personalities in Munich using a specially constructed poisoned gun. In the 1970s, KGB general Oleg Kalugin personally took part in the abduction attempt in Vienna of the Soviet defector Nikolai Artamonov, who died on the way to the Czech border. Three years later, Kalugin supervised an operation to liquidate Bulgarian defector Vladimir Kostov in Paris, who survived, and Bulgarian dissident Georgi Markov in London, who died as a result of 'an umbrella murder' carried out by an illegal.

As well as underestimating the importance of the Soviet and now Russian secret services' role in the functioning of the state system, Western observers have often underestimated the power and influence of its security and intelligence chiefs, as well as that of personal bodyguards of the Russian leaders, starting from Stalin and culminating with Putin. A succession of the Cheka-OGPU-NKVD leaders following its founder, Felix Dzierżyński, nicknamed Iron Felix, responsible for the Red Terror, took an active part in mass executions. Yagoda, Yezhov and Beria, all three secret police chiefs under Stalin will be remembered for the millions of innocent victims before, during and after the war. Beria, who was placed at the helm of the secret police at the end of the Great Terror, emerged as the second most powerful man in the country. He was also put in charge of the GULAG, the Soviet forced labour system, and the construction of the first Soviet atomic bomb. After Stalin's death, Beria became the first secret service chief to make a bid for supreme power. However, other members of the Politburo, fearful of his ambitions, arranged his execution on 23 December 1953.

It was assumed thereafter that a chairman of the new Committee for State Security, better known as the KGB, would never be given an opportunity to become the leader of the USSR. That proved correct in only one case, when its dynamic and relatively youthful chief, Alexander Shelepin, who made little secret of his plans to become the leader of the party (and thus, automatically, the head of the state), was effectively sidelined after Khrushchev's overthrow by Brezhnev.

Brezhnev's successor in November 1982 was Yuri Andropov, a long-time chairman of the KGB. His former assistant and successor as the KGB chief, Vladimir Kryuchkov, suddenly emerged as a ringleader of the abortive coup in August 1991 that sought to topple Mikhail Gorbachev, the general secretary of the Communist Party, Chairman of the Supreme Soviet of the people's deputies, the first and the last Soviet president.

Yevgeny Primakov, during his long career, occupied a number of important posts, serving as foreign minister, Speaker of the Supreme Soviet (the highest legislative body of the country that also formed the Council of Ministers), the first head of Russia's new overseas intelligence agency, the SVR, and finally as Prime Minister of Russia. By the spring of 1999, though disclaiming any ambition to succeed the first Russian president Boris Yeltsin whose second term in office was coming to an end, Primakov topped opinion polls of potential candidates and was considered by many, including Boris Berezovsky, as a real threat to Yeltsin's future successor. After the fierce anti-Primakov campaign in the media, orchestrated by Berezovsky, and following the advice of his assistants and advisers, the president sacked Primakov in May 1999.

Yeltsin appointed Sergei Stepashin as Primakov's successor. Stepashin, a graduate of the police academy, military-political academy and the finance academy, had served for over a year as the head of the FSK, predecessor of the FSB, and then justice minister and interior minister, before he was appointed as prime minister in May 1999. In August, he was succeeded by Vladimir Putin, a former KGB officer who had served for five years in East Germany. 'For the third time in less than a year,' Professor Andrew notes, 'Yeltsin had confounded most Kremlin-watchers by choosing as his prime minister a present or former intelligence chief. Yeltsin caused further incredulity by declaring that Putin would be the next president.'[3] On New Year's Eve, before the end of his term, Yeltsin announced that he was stepping down and that Putin was succeeding him as Acting President. After Putin's victory in the March 2000 presidential election, he was hailed as Russia's 'absolute leader' who has no rivals. When ten years later, in August 2010, Riz Khan asked Masha Lipman, Russian political analyst and commentator, and me whether it was going to be 'a hot summer for Putin', then temporarily the prime minister, on the eve of the upcoming presidential elections, we both said 'No'.

In March 2012, Putin received 63.6 per cent of the vote securing a record third term in the Kremlin. A year later, Berezovsky was gone. In their primary role – to defend the Russian state against dissent in all its forms – the KGB and its successors were strikingly successful.

Professor Brinkmann, with whom I discussed the case in August 2018, is an authoritative specialist held in high repute by his colleagues worldwide. It was Brinkmann who managed to prove that the Italian banker Roberto Calvi,

---

[3] Ibid, 733.

dubbed *banchiere di Dio* ('God's banker') by the media because of his close association with the Holy Sea, who was found hanging from scaffolding beneath Blackfriars Bridge in London in June 1982, had been murdered. After two coroner's inquests (the first inquest decided he had committed suicide and the second returned an open verdict) and an independent investigation by Kroll Associates, it was ruled it was not a suicide but an assassination. More than 23 years after the banker's death – again twenty-three – five people were accused of killing him. Calvi was a member of the unrecognised pseudo-masonic lodge Propaganda Due (P2), who referred to themselves as *frati neri* (black friars) while the main shareholders of his bank were leaders of the Sicilian mafia, which suggested that either mobsters or 'brothers' were involved in Calvi's death. In the end, all five suspects were acquitted of the murder.

Like Berezovsky's family, Calvi's family never believed the official version. Brinkmann's 2002 report as well as that of his Italian colleagues, forensic experts in Rome who confirmed Kroll's initial conclusions, led prosecutors to reopen the case.

In March 2014, Brinkmann's evidence made the cause of the death of the 67-year-old man, believed to be Boris Berezovsky, impossible to determine in the verdict. Few people, including the coroner, believe there were reasons for Berezovsky to commit suicide, while his friends and family never thought this could ever be the case. Katya Berezovskaya, Boris's daughter, pointed the finger at the Russian government. She told the inquest there were people interested in having her famous father killed. The motive, she suggested, was obvious. For more than a decade Berezovsky had been warning the world that President Putin was not merely a danger to Russia and its people but was capable of menacing other countries, too.

'I don't think they liked what my father was saying,' Katya testified. 'He was saying that Putin was a danger to the whole world, and you can see that now'.

'I am plotting a new Russian revolution,' Boris Berezovsky told the *Guardian* in April 2007. 'We need to use force to change this regime,' he said.

Boris was firmly behind the media campaign after the poisoning of Sasha Litvinenko and without Berezovsky's efforts (and money) the world would never have known about this crime. Boris would quite definitely be better equipped to answer the inquiry's rather clumsy question, 'whether it is structurally or practically possible for "the Russian State" to commission the assassination of an individual whom such criminal groups of individuals perceive as a threat, at the behest of such groups or individuals, or to provide protection to Alexander Litvinenko's killers'.

After considering all aspects of the case to the best of his knowledge, the expert of the inquest made the following conclusion:

> The Putin administration has always been demonstrably secretive, manipulative, and authoritarian with a ruthless commitment to protecting its interests at home and abroad. The number of known unknowns is therefore disturbingly high. But about the FSB's involvement in some of the killings of people who mounted a struggle against the administration, whether by arms or with pens, there can be little reasonable doubt even though there is as yet no direct proof of such involvement in most of the particular cases. The Russian authorities have been reluctant to claim responsibility even when the killed individual was someone they had designated as a danger to state security ... Despite the absence of irrefutable evidence, however, I find it hard to believe that Patrushev as FSB Director was not also somehow involved in some of the other killings under consideration in my report. I recognise that my opinion rests on circumstantial evidence but have concluded that too much of the evidence points in this direction for it to be mere coincidence.
>
> It remains unclear that Putin gave anything beyond a general sanction to the broad line of action that Patrushev apparently followed; but it appears to me unlikely that Putin did not exercise – at the very least – some oversight of Patrushev's activities. Although there can be no unconditional confidence even about this particular feature of their close and long-term collaboration, the widespread suspicions that I have itemised about both Patrushev and Putin are reasonable and have yet to be dispelled.

Intelligence is not a precise science. It never provides the whole answer. But in any case, the requirement for intelligence and its assessment should be placed with professionals, not amateurs. It is the norm, not the exception, that those who are not fully informed of the realities of history are the most fervent believers of falsehoods.

In this book, I have shown how a harmless operation of exfiltrating an agent from Russia had been coordinated with the Foreign Office and sanctioned personally by British prime minister Margaret Thatcher. Can there be any doubt that the Russian president personally authorised the murder of the notorious traitor who claimed that the FSB had planned to kill Berezovsky? Who gave chapter and verse to convince everybody ready to listen that the series of explosions that hit four apartment blocks in the cities of Buinaksk, Moscow and Volgodonsk killing around 300 people and injuring more than 1,000, was the operation of the FSB agents? That the official explanations of the explosive devices found in the cellars in Ryazan were false? Who helped to uncover and arrest members and top leaders of Russia's largest criminal syndicates that operated out of Spain? Who could expose a Russian mole deep into the Spanish National Intelligence Centre? And finally, whose attacks on Vladimir Putin climaxed in 2006 with a personal accusation of paedophilia? The coroner concluded that the operation to kill Sasha Litvinenko 'was probably approved by Mr Patrushev [?!] and also by President Putin.' Also, in the coroner's view, 'the polonium 210 in question either must have come, or even probably came, from Russia'.

There are also doubts and even an open verdict in the Berezovsky case – many people, both in Russia and in the West, believe it was suicide and Putin had nothing to do with it. In addition, there is the as yet unexplained death of a young and healthy businessman in Weybridge on the River Wey and the strange poisoning of a former double agent and his daughter. In the case of the businessman Alexander Perepilichny, the Home Secretary had won a High Court order that sensitive material would not be disclosed at an inquest into his death, thus making it a farce. In the Skripals' case, some commentators seriously consider the possibility that 'rogue elements' within the Russian state or its Spetsnaz Special Forces might be involved. Those whose job it is to think about all this sometimes tend to forget that in the past decade the above mentioned strange deaths happened in England, not Siberia, 'though there is as yet no direct proof of such [Russian secret services] involvement in most of the particular cases', the Litvinenko inquiry heard.

I shall again point out that even a simple case of exfiltrating a British mole from Russia had to be discussed with and approved at the highest level in the UK. It is impossible for me to consider that the use of the radioactive poison, the death of the Kremlin's Enemy No. 1, and the chemical warfare nerve agent attack in Salisbury were not approved by the highest level in Russia.

When I learnt over sake-steamed abalone at the Japanese restaurant Umu that all this is being done by the FSB or Spetsnaz, I realised that what the British newspaper-reading public has been told for years is complete bunkum. Because FSB is the abbreviation for the Federal Security Service, the principal security agency of Russia and it is not involved in the operations overseas. And Spetsnaz are special forces of the Russian Army controlled by the military intelligence directorate that may be involved in covert but not in clandestine operations abroad. Unlike in Britain or in the USA, for such operations there are specially trained illegals in both the SVR and the GRU.

It is my strong conviction that the conclusions of the Litvinenko public inquiry and the Berezovsky inquest must be reconsidered and the ongoing Perepilichny investigation should be given more public and media attention. I also believe there's still a lot to be done in the Skripal case. Many things remain unclear. For example, I do believe Gary Aitkenhead, the chief executive of the government's Defence Science and Technology Laboratory (DSTL), who said that Porton Down experts were unable to verify the precise source of the nerve agent. He also said there was no known antidote to Novichok. So, if they want me to believe that Sergei Skripal is alive, I want to see him, along with his daughter.

Certain guiding principles should also be revised. The early security services were based on complete secrecy and limited accountability and the British establishment have always taken up extreme positions on them. It was assumed that the activities of the secret services should remain as secret as possible for as long as possible. 'It is the essence of a Secret Service that it must be secret,' Austen Chamberlain remarked speaking to the House of Commons as Foreign Secretary in November 1924, 'and if you once begin disclosure it is perfectly obvious to me, as to hon. Gentlemen opposite, that there is no longer any Secret Service and that you must do without it.'[4]

Secrecy is basic, says John Scarlett. Also, sometimes you know things that are difficult to share with other governments and certainly with the public. But then, without sharing information including intelligence, it can be difficult to mobilise international understanding and support. In the Skripals' case, these were granted on credit.

I also do not like defectors. Even the word itself sounds bad to me. Dante divides circle nine, the circle of treachery and the final circle of Hell, into four regions. The second region, Antenora, he reserves for those who betrayed their political party or their homeland. Putting defectors aside for now, one of Moscow's chief priorities has been to seek to prevent all dissidents and dissenters achieving international recognition. 'We'll waste them in the outhouse' is not only about terrorists, as is usually assumed, but it is also about all Kremlin opponents.

I walk out of my house with its excellent evergreen garden hedge and in a few seconds am already on High Street. Turn left at Whitley's Jewellers, my neighbours, and passing by Boots, WHSmith and the Santander I reach the Pepperpot, so-called because of its shape. It is the iconic symbol of our small market town built in 1814 at the junction of High Street and Church Street. As in every other English town, Church Street is so-called because of the church. For more than a thousand years, the Church of St Peter & St Paul has been a centre of Christian worship. It is the oldest building in town looking great in both winter and summer. The dramatic spire, says the tourist leaflet, is a symbol of God's eternal presence and the beautiful

---

[4] Parliamentary Debates (Commons), 15 December 1924, col. 674.

architecture and craftsmanship seen in the windows, carvings and masonry all inspire reflection and a sense of belonging. Indeed. The Star, one of the snug local places that advertises itself as 'a fab pub run by fab people' is also conveniently on the way to the station. I sometimes drop by for a shot of brandy. Our nineteenth-century railway station often wins Best Small Station Pride Awards. It is only 37 miles down the line from London Waterloo, which means 40 comfortable minutes to the centre of the best city in the world. I absolutely love it. You must belong here to understand ...

Appendix I

Alexander Perepilichny:
An Unexplained Death

It all began as the Soviet Union splintered in the early 1990s. At that time, Mitt Romney was the CEO of Bain & Co., a Boston-based consulting firm. When he became the Republican Party nominee for President of the United States in the 2012 election, Romney's role at Bain had received almost no public scrutiny even though an investigation into Bain's business activities found that the consulting firm helped two corporate titans as they vied to move forcefully into the Russian market.

Bain's Russian business wasn't about charity or eco-friendly goods and services. It was about smoking and puffing, and the deals were about cigarettes. 'And that work,' *The Huffington Post* investigation report claims, 'sent Bain into the shadows of the post-Soviet economy – including helping to orchestrate anonymous, convoluted cash transactions to keep major deals hidden from regulators and competitors.' The report goes on to assert that 'it was part of a free-for-all that involved wholesale looting of major industries, as Western technocrats helped facilitate the transfer of Russia's wealth into the hands of a few oligarchs. This set in motion a populist backlash that helped sweep Vladimir Putin into power, giving the Kremlin dominance over a country Romney has recently called the "number one geopolitical enemy"'.[1]

Bain was in the middle of all this using taxpayer money to help it gain footholds in Russia. In the early 1990s Bain's co-founder Ralph Willard formed Bain Link, a subsidiary aimed at generating business in once-forbidden markets of the Soviet Union. Bain's employee Sushovan Ghosh became the vice president at this venture. To Mitt Romney and his colleagues at Bain & Co. in Boston, and later in its London and Moscow offices, it was a chance to rake in money. Ghosh reported directly to Romney, who was excited about the Russian market. 'He was my boss,' Ghosh said. Romney's number one in Bain Link, Willard, later explained in an interview: 'We had this idea – wouldn't it be cool to be the first ones in this mysterious place?'[2]

Their partner in Moscow was Abel Aganbegyan, a leading Soviet and Russian economist of Armenian descent. He was one of Mikhail Gorbachev's chief economic advisers and among the first Soviet economists to voice the need for a radical change – *perestroika* in Russian – of the economic and business infrastructure of the Soviet Union. 'Aganbegyan,' according to *The Huffington Post* reporters, 'would help supply Bain with Moscow-based researchers and networking contacts, which eventually

---

[1] See Jason Cherkis and Zach Carter, 'Mitt Romney's Bain Made Millions on Big Tobacco in US, Russia', *The Huffington Post*, 9 October 2012.
[2] Ibid.

brought Willard to the Kremlin.' One of the first candidates whom Aganbegyan recommended to the Americans was a fellow Armenian named Igor Sagiryan who would eventually become the managing partner at Bain-Link.

Igor Sagiryan was born on 8 February 1952 in Tbilisi, Georgia. In 1974, he graduated from the Moscow State Institute of International Relations – the main recruiting pool for Soviet and Russian diplomats and spies. Three years later, in 1977, he completed his post-graduate studies with a candidate of science degree (MPhil) at the semi-secret USA and Canada Institute (now Institute for US and Canadian Studies) of the Russian Academy of Sciences where many of the former Soviet spymasters found their post-retirement employment. From there Sagiryan was sent to work in the Committee of Youth Organizations (KMO) of the USSR, the successor of the Communist International of Youth, a Comintern youth wing staffed by the agents of various Soviet secret services. From 1984 to 1987 he headed a department there. After the KMO, Sagiryan was promoted to the International Department of the Presidium of the Supreme Soviet of the USSR, where he remained until 1989, that is, until the time when Gorbachev's new economic 'restructuring' encouraged the formation of private companies.

Working at the International Department did mean regular contact with the KGB. In 1989, Sagiryan was invited by Aganbegyan to head Link Consulting, a Soviet-Swiss joint venture, and a year later was recommended to Ralph Willard. Bain acquired the Swiss part of the joint venture and promptly sent Igor to Harvard Business School. In Boston, he was introduced to Romney and upon return to Moscow became a managing partner in Bain Russia, where he would stay for ten years.

Willard, Bain Link's president, decided that the firm should deal with Western companies seeking to invest in the Soviet Union. In March 1993, two years after the Soviet Union collapsed, the US government gave Bain & Co. a $3.9 million contract to advise the then-president Boris Yeltsin's administration on the privatization of the Russian economy. 'Romney's consultants,' states the report, 'helped foreign firms and aspiring oligarchs decide how to corral Russia's riches – including writing an official manual that outlined how best to navigate the process. At the same time, Bain leveraged its contracts with senior Russian officials to arrange sweetheart deals for its tobacco clients. The Soviet Union's downfall meant rich rewards for any company able to move quickly, and the timing was right for the US and British tobacco companies eager to control the cigarette market. In 1992, a year before it won the US government contract, Bain approached British American Tobacco (BAT) – the international conglomerate behind Kool, Lucky Strike, Pall Mall and Benson & Hedges – offering a lucrative partnership in Russia. It worked.'[3]

Romney's personal involvement with Bain's tobacco business is unclear, but as the consultancy's CEO, he was responsible for its work. Ghosh and another former colleague who was interviewed said they reported to Romney. 'Bain and Romney would not discuss their respective involvement in the Russian tobacco market,' says the report. And Romney could not even remember one of his former Russian partners who would play a key role in the affair that in December 2012 would result in the signing of what became known as the Magnitsky Act by the US president.

---

[3] Ibid.

Besides working privately for BAT, Bain, as mentioned, was a top adviser to Yeltsyn's administration with a multimillion contract from the USAID (United States Agency for International Development), an agency of the US government that answers to the foreign policy directives of the State Department and is primarily responsible for administering civilian foreign aid and development assistance. AID, as it was abbreviated in Russia, had been using personnel contracted by one of the many American accounting companies now administering State Department contracts with employees working in the economic section of the US Embassy in Moscow. One such contract employee, Michael Dasaro, was the first American citizen with direct ties to the embassy to be murdered. He was killed in his apartment in Central Moscow in 1993. Although a Russia expert, he was convinced, like many of his colleagues, that the so-called Russian mafia or organised crime had made inroads into all aspects of Russian life including AID's multimillion-dollar effort to change state-run enterprises into private businesses, known as the privatization program. 'He had contacts and he knew that the criminal element had taken over privatization,' Dasaro's friend said.[4] They could not imagine that it was the Russian secret service taking over both privatization and the criminal element.

USAID told the investigators 'it could not determine whether Bain violated any American conflict-of-interest rules by working simultaneously with a private corporation and the Russian government.'[5] But in February 1993, weeks before they were awarded the government contract, Bain arranged a meeting between BAT executives and Aganbegyan. The meeting was chaired by Aganbegyan's protégé, Igor Sagiryan, who boasted to BAT that the 'Russian government has named Bain Link its principal adviser in its privatization efforts'.[6] In a September 1993 memo, cited by *The Huffington Post*, BAT's Edouard 'Elias' Ettedgui (later Group Chief Executive of Mandarin Oriental International Limited) noted that Bain was 'somewhat different from our other advisers' because 'approximately half' of the Bain staff 'works for the Russian government'.

In 1994, Bain was instrumental in the acquisition of the former Imperial Tobacco Factory in Saratov (STF) by BAT using a complicated shell transaction. 'It does appear Bain engaged in illegal, or at least highly unethical, actions,' noted David Katz, an economics professor at the University of Massachusetts at Amherst, when shown the relevant documents. He said the Bain-BAT transaction fitted a pattern of illegal activity in Russia at that time: 'Sending a payment for Bain's work to an individual employee was a typical technique,' for Western companies engaging in 'tax evasion, money laundering, and/or to hide its involvement in a shady deal and its connections with very unsavoury characters.'[7] By the second half of 2018, BAT-STF's production had reached 45 billion cigarettes a year in Russia.

For Igor Sagiryan, his eight-year involvement with Bain was a very good business school. In 1999, he was transferred to Renaissance Capital, then the largest

[4] See Seymour M. Hersh, 'The Wild East', *The Atlantic*, June 1994.
[5] Cherkis and Carter, 'Mitt Romney's Bain Made Millions on Big Tobacco in US, Russia', *The Huffington Post*, 9 October 2012.
[6] Ibid.
[7] Ibid.

investment company in Russia, founded only four years earlier, in 1995. There, Sagiryan served as a managing partner, head of its investment banking division and from 2001 the president.

One of Sagiryan's early achievements at Renaissance, he recalled, was the reopening of the fully licensed branch of Crédit Lyonnais in Saint Petersburg (opened in 1878 as the first instance in Russia of a bank operating under its foreign name). Both Anatoly Sobchak and Vladimir Putin were the champions of the bank's return to the northern capital and, Sagiryan claimed, invited him to negotiate with Jean-Yves Haberer, then the bank's president. Today, it operates as Crédit Agricole CIB from the same address at 12 Nevsky Prospekt.

This is a bit of an exaggeration. Sobchak was mayor of St Petersburg with Putin as one of his deputies from 1991–6 and then federal prosecutors launched a criminal investigation against him. In early November 1997, with Putin's help, Sobchak managed to flee to Paris returning in June 1999 shortly before Putin, already Director of the FSB, became Prime Minister of Russia. By the time Sagiryan was transferred to Renaissance, both Sobchak and Putin had been out of business in St Petersburg.

In the mid-1990s, William 'Bill' Browder, an American-born British financial analyst with Russian roots, whose grandfather was the infamous Secretary General of the American Communist Party (CPUSA), began doing business in Russia, bankrolled with $25 million from financier Edmond Safra. William's ancestor, Earl Browder, was known from the KGB and its predecessors' registry files as agent RULEVOY ('Helmsman'). In fact, almost all of Earl's relatives were Stalin's secret agents. For whatever reason, William decided to become a capitalist and do his business in Russia.

In 1995 in Moscow, two naturalized Americans, Boris Jordan and Leonid Rozhetskin, together with a New Zealander named Stephen Jennings, co-founded an investment bank that they called Renaissance Capital. Renaissance, where Sagiryan had been one of the principal decision-makers, would play a very prominent role in the story that cropped up a decade later.

By 1995, Romney was out of Bain & Co. on the way to his political career, but the gears set in motion under his and Willard's leadership continued to turn while the cigarette business had become part of Bain's culture, documents show. 'Bain's Russian deals,' the report notes, 'culminated with some of the firm's most dangerous and effective projects.' It will be remembered that until 1999, Igor Sagiryan was Bain Russia's managing partner.

As soon as Sagiryan had comfortably settled in Renaissance Capital's head office, he invited Yuri Sagaidak to take care of his new company's 'economic security'.

Born in Russia in 1950, retired KGB colonel Yuri Sagaidak was a graduate of the KGB High School in Moscow, the same School 101, later Andropov Institute and the SVR Academy, where all Russian intelligence officers are taught tradecraft skills. On his first foreign posting, Sagaidak served for five years in Indonesia and in 1987 was sent to London posing as a correspondent of *Komsomolskaya Pravda*. This daily Russian tabloid, founded in 1925, does not only proudly display its communist medals on the front page but also preserves its old name verbally translated as 'the Young Communist League's version of the truth', which is ridiculous. While being officially accredited in the British capital, this small, dapper man unsuccessfully tried to 'cultivate' Lady Helen Olga Hay, better known as Olga Maitland, then a columnist for the *Sunday Express* and later chairwoman of Families for Defence. When Sagaigak arrived in London, Olga was a candidate (then unsuccessful) to the British Parliament. He met her at a party conference in Brighton. In 1989, MI5 decided Sagaidak was a risk to national security and declared him *persona non grata*. When the KGB, now FSB/SVR/FSO, restored its positions after the collapse of the Soviet Union, Sagaidak moved to the Interstate Bank as assistant to its president. In 1999, he was invited to work in the Moscow office of Renaissance Nominees Ltd., a Cyprus-registered Renaissance Capital subsidiary. From 2001 to 2005, he was the vice director of Renaissance Capital-Financial Consultant LLC and member of the Board of Directors. Other board members were Yuri Kobaladze from the KGB foreign intelligence directorate, who had also operated in Britain from 1977 to 1984 posing as a TV journalist, Nikolai Itskov from the Soviet Army, and Stephen Jennings, the Renaissance Capital's CEO.

In 2011, Sagaidak registered a company in Lithuania called Consulit with a staff of five people and received a residence permit, which, according to the Lithuanian weekly *Veidas*, was extended once but a further extension was refused in 2013. According to one report, the company's registered address was in one of the apartments owned by Kazimiera Nijole Butkeviciene, the mother of Lithuania's first post-independence defence minister who was later convicted for attempted fraud.[8] Sagaidak's former colleague, another FSB officer by the name of Igor Sushchin also used to work for Renaissance Capital at its Renaissance Broker division, being responsible for 'information security'. The 2017 indictment of the US Justice Department charged Sushchin and three of his accomplices with the massive hack of Yahoo. He was formally fired from the bank on 16 March, the day after US officials announced the charges.

Browder's Hermitage Capital Management Limited is registered at PO Box 95 in St Peter Port, Guernsey. After his Russian business was ruined, as he claims, by fraudulent means, William Browder testified to the US Helsinki Commission about his early activities in Russia. 'I founded Hermitage in 1996 in partnership with the late Edmond Safra as a way for western investors to invest in the Russian stock market,' he said. 'The firm ultimately grew to become the single largest foreign portfolio investor in Russia, with some $4 billion under management [ten years later], a substantial portion of which came from US institutional and individual investors [and primarily the billionaire Ziff brothers]. One of the big reasons for the firm's success was our strategy of investing in the stocks of companies that were out of favour due to bad management, corruption, shareholder rights abuses or outright theft. We would then work to change management, stop fraud and defend the interests of minority shareholders through shareholder activism. If we were successful in improving corporate governance, the market would ultimately recognize this. As the company came back into favour, its stock price would rise, our investors would

---

[8] BNS/TBT Staff, Vilnius, 'Former KGB Spy Given Lithuanian Residence Permit', 2 October 2015.

profit and the Russian economy would be better off for having a more productive, transparent businesses. For several years it was a win-win situation for everyone except corrupt corporate management and their partners in government.'[9] This explanation does not mention Browder's special relations with HSBC bank and his 'grey' market operations with Gazprom papers. Such operations are legitimate in principle yet lead to or facilitate, in the words of shadow banking specialists,[10] 'a semi-legal and unidentified export of capital, opaque ownership structures, tax evasion' and other questionable activities.

On 25 July 1998, two years after Browder and Safra founded Hermitage Capital Management for the purpose of investing in Russia, Vladimir Putin was appointed Director of the FSB, one of the successor agencies of the KGB. In August, about $4.8 billion of the International Monetary Fund (IMF) funds went amiss during the implosion of the Russian financial markets. They were supposed to prop up the banking system and the ailing and sharply devalued ruble. Instead, they ended up on the accounts of private banks and corporations either headed or controlled by FSB collaborators and then vanished into thin air.[11] In September 1998, one of the nation's largest privately owned financial institutions, the SBS-Agro bank, declared it was badly hit by the Russian financial crisis and was later declared bankrupt.[12] During the same year, Safra's Republic National Bank made a report to the FBI that began an investigation into vast money laundering that came to focus on the Bank of New York and ultimately helped break a $6 billion crime ring that was traced to Russia. As one financial expert put it, 'there isn't enough to connect the IMF funds with the money laundering affair that engulfed the Bank of New York a year later to the day [of the IMF $4.8 billion settlement], in August 1999 – although several of the personalities straddled the divide between the bank and its clients.'

Following public charges made by US Treasury Secretary Robert Rubin, as early as March 1999, both Russian and American media delved deeply over the years into

---

[9] Hearing, 'Testimony of William Browder', *Commission on Security & Cooperation in Europe the US Helsinko Commission*, 23 June 2009.

[10] See for example Anastasia Nesvetailova (ed.), *Shadow Banking: Scope, Origins and Theories* (Abingdon, Oxon, and New York, NY: Routledge, 2018), 91.

[11] Quoted from Sam Vaknin, *Crime and Corruption* (Skopje: A Narcissus Publications, 2002).

[12] According to the Agency for Restructuring Credit Organizations, which was created to sort out Russia's troubled banking sector, SBS-Agro had assets of $9.31 million and creditors' claims of $1.47 billion. See 'Russia's SBS-Agro Bank Declared Bankrupt', *Huron Daily Tribune*, 16 February 2003. Alexander Smolensky was the founder and president of the bank. He stayed in Moscow during the crisis while his family lived in a luxury mansion in Vienna, Austria, with his wife Galina acting as his trustee in both Austria and Switzerland. In 1999, Russian prosecutors issued a warrant for his arrest including charges of embezzlement and money laundering. This warrant, however, was later withdrawn, as Galina Smolensky told this writer, 'In exchange for an oath of allegiance to the regime'. Smolensky's net worth in 2003 was estimated at 230 million US dollars. For details about Smolensky, see Hoffman, *The Oligarchs* (2003) and Ian Jeffries, *The New Russia: A Handbook of Economic and Political Developments* (London: RoutledgeCurzon, 2002).

the IMF funds affair. The money trail from the Federal Reserve Bank of New York to Swiss and German subsidiaries of the Russian Central Bank was comprehensively reconstructed. Radio Free Europe/Radio Liberty, based on its own sources and an article in the Russian weekly *Novaya Gazeta*, claimed that half the money was almost instantly diverted to shell companies in Sydney and London. The other half was mostly transferred to the Bank of New York and to Credit Swiss as well as other private Swiss banks. Until 9 August 1999, Putin was at the helm of the FSB and most likely informed in every detail about all its secret financial operations including the above-mentioned transactions.

As mentioned before, in 2001 Sagiryan was promoted to become President of Renaissance Capital. A year later, in 2002, his friend by the name of Vladimir Dzhabarov from the FSB Directorate K (counter-intelligence supervision of the credit and financial system, that is, of all banking operations and investment businesses) advised Sagiryan to hire one Dmitry Klyuev. Directorate K reports to the Chief Directorate of Economic Security (GUEB). At that time General Dzhabarov's boss at the FSB headquarters and the GUEB chief was Colonel General Yuri Zaostrovtsev and they both played a key role in determining the fate and prosperity of all leading Russian businessmen and businesses. And not only Russian.

According to Yuri Sagaidak's testimony at court, Klyuev was hired by Sagiryan to act as a 'tax advisor who had skills in arranging tax refunds through the [Russian] court system.' Sagaidak and Klyuev have known each other since 2002. Then, Sagiryan, Sagaidak's boss at Renaissance, wanted Klyuev to arrange a refund for a company that allegedly belonged to George Soros, a Hungarian–American investor. Whether it was a fully legal operation or not is not possible to establish now but the proceedings were completed within several months. In 2003, Sagaidak and Klyuev jointly founded Aurora Travel LLP (their third partner there was Iliya Shpurov, president of Inpark and vice president of the International Congress of Industrialists and Entrepreneurs in Moscow), which operated for the next six years.

During 2004, all prices for metal and rolled iron jumped 1.5 to 2 times. One of the biggest iron ore production and concentration plants in Russia is Mikhailovsky. Until 2004, the owner of Mikhailovsky was a Russian businessman of Georgian origin named Boris Ivanishvili, born in 1956. Later, he became better known as Bidzina Ivanishvili, returning to his original Georgian name. From October 2012 to November 2013, Ivanishvili served as the Prime Minister of Georgia and leader of the party that won the majority of votes in the parliamentary elections. In 2004, Ivanishvili lived in France (where he was reportedly granted citizenship) and was planning to sell Mikhailovsky and a stake in the metallurgical business TulaCherMet. Among many competitors, he chose his friend Vasili Anisimov (Coalco) and Anisimov's partner, the leading Russian businessman Alisher Usmanov (Ural Steel), who agreed to buy 47% of Mikhailovsky shares (while Usmanov was selling 50% of the Ural Steel metal plant to Mikhailovsky). Both Anisimov and Usmanov had to top up their share offers with cash to cover the valuation difference. Unbeknown to other partners, Anisimov represented the interests of Berezovsky and Patarkatsyshvili in this deal. Berezovsky later claimed that he and Patarkatsyshvili transferred about US$500 million to the accounts of the companies controlled by Anisimov to finance the purchase of Mikhailovsky. Overall, Usmanov and Anisimov acquired 97% of the plant's shares.

It was reported that the deal was worth $1.65 billion. One billion was credited by the VTB, a leading Russian bank headed by Andrei Kostin, from 2002 the chairman of the VTB Group. For 13 years, from 1979 to 1992, Kostin served in the Soviet Foreign Ministry and in 1985 was posted as Second Secretary (a typical KGB slot) to the London Embassy after the expulsion of 25 Soviet diplomats declared PNG following the defection of Gordievsky. Here, one of Kostin's diplomatic colleagues was Alexander Lebedev, then an officer of the Economic Directorate of the KGB, who was posted to London in 1988 operating under the diplomatic cover of Economic Attaché. In 1992, Kostin and Lebedev together founded the Russian Investment Company. Lebedev also owns, among others, the London *Evening Standard*, *The Independent* and the *Independent on Sunday*. Interestingly, *The Independent* was the first newspaper to break the news about the death of Alexander Perepilichny.

In October 2004, during a leisure trip to Austria, Oleg Kiselev, then Chairman of the Renaissance Capital's Board of Directors found himself in the same group as Dmitry Klyuev. The two men had met before. Kiselev is a Russian businessman 'of the first generation' and is co-founder, with Mikhail Friedman, of the cooperatives Alfa-Photo and Alfa-Eco, the first company of what later grew into Alfa Group Consortium. When he and Klyuev were travelling to Austria, Kiselev was heading the Renaissance Capital Investment Group, was also a member of the Presidential Council of the Russian Federation, member of the Board of Directors of Novolipetsk Steel, and member of the Executive Board of the Russian Union of Industrialists and Entrepreneurs – an organization very close to the Kremlin. After several responsible positions at Nanotechnologies State Corporation, from February 2014 Kiselev has been serving as Deputy Chairman of the Executive Board of Rusnano Management Company LLC, which manages the assets of Rusnano. (Rusnano, a government-owned company headed by Anatoly Chubais, was founded in an attempt to create a Russian version of nano-industry.) During the same year Igor Sagiryan, who was then serving as President of Renaissance Capital, founded and headed Ping Pong Limited, initially a UK-only but now an international restaurant business.

No one ever explained what made Kiselev act as he did, but according to the court documents, he asked Klyuev to invent a scheme that would help freeze the Mikhailovsky share transfer. Again, it is unclear why this should have been done before 13 January 2005, as Klyuev had been instructed. According to several press reports, both the FSB and the criminal structures were interested in that deal although in 2005 hardly any mobster in Russia would contemplate acting against Ivanishvili or Usmanov. Anyway, by the time Klyuev's people started to move, the agreed sum had already reached Ivanishvili's bank accounts.

For the commission of $1 million (with a 50% paid up front), Klyuev's assistants invented a simple sham and 96% of Mikhailovsly shares were arrested by the decision of the Arbitrary Court. Naturally, with such powerful players as Usmanov and Anisimov, they were released two weeks later, on 31 January.

It took the officers of the Economic Crime Directorate seven months to investigate. On 10 August the police fraud squad, headed by Senior Lieutenant Anton Golyshev and armed with a search warrant, raided the office of Kiselev. Among other things they found a large envelope marked 'Administration of the President of the Russian Federation'. That is, of Vladimir Putin, then elected to this post for the second time. Inside the envelope, Golyshev found documents relating to the arrest of the Mikhailovsky shares, the court's orders and writs, enforcement proceeding orders, various protocols and the registrar's statement for the shares of the Mikhailovsky plant. There was also a plan of the operation and several passports.

Kiselev wisely refused to tell the investigators how the envelope with the documents appeared in his office. He also managed to quietly leave Russia and settle in London before his Moscow lawyer first heard about the charges. Two years later the case fell apart and Kiselev returned. As already mentioned, he is now at Rusnano, one of the deputies of Anatoly Chubais. Chubais was a political celebrity in Russia who managed to survive presidents Yeltsyn (two terms), Putin (two terms), Medvedev, and Putin again (another two terms). He was Bain Link's best contact in the Yetlsyn's administration during the privatisation that some experts call 'a dark chapter of Russia's economic history, in which nearly all of the superpower's assets were steered into the hands of a few local oligarchs and cutthroat Western corporations'.[13]

It was Klyuev who delivered the envelope to Kiselev. In a few days, Klyuev met his business partner, the former KGB colonel Sagaidak, who informed him that he knew about Klyuev's role. 'Kiselev himself told me,' Sagaidak claimed, asking Klyuev to add 'operational details' only. After hearing Klyuev's version Sagaidak said he would inform Stephen Jennings, the majority shareholder and chairman of the Board of Directors of Renaissance Capital.[14] Sagaidak also warned Klyuev that Renaissance had nothing to do with this affair and that Kiselev acted on his own. Later, during the interrogation, Jennings confirmed that he learned about Kiselev's involvement from Sagaidak. In the meantime, Anton Golyshev, a business crimes specialist from Moscow's Chief Directorate of Internal Affairs (GUVD) visited and interviewed Kiselev in London. Soon the case was closed. Klyuev's associates were sentenced to minimal terms that allowed them to get a prompt release. Klyuev himself was given a suspended sentence of three years.

Some commentators try to present the Mikhailovsky case in a simplified way. 'Klyuev and his lawyer, Andrei Pavlov,' Michael Weiss writes in *World Affairs* (June 2012), 'tried to steal $1.6 billion in shares from the iron ore company Mikhailovsky GOK ['GOK' is a Russian acronym for 'ore production and concentration plant'].

[13] See Cherkis and Carter, 'Mitt Romney's Bain Made Millions on Big Tobacco in US, Russia', *The Huffington Post*, 9 October 2012. According to their report, 'Bain also noted that it was in '"close contact"' with Anatoli Chubais and one of Chubais' deputies, Dimitri Vasiliev. Chubais was, perhaps, the most powerful government figure overseeing the Russian privatisations, serving as Boris Yeltsin's privatisation czar during the early-1990s.'

[14] Originally from New Zealand, UK-based Jennings rebuilt Renaissance Capital – the Moscow-based investment bank he co-founded in 1995 – after the 1998 Russian financial crisis. 'In 2012 he sold his remaining 50 per cent stake in Renaissance, 20 years after he arrived in Russia on a mission to carry out its first privatisation (of a biscuit factory) following the collapse of the Soviet Union,' an Auckland newspaper reported. 'I don't want to gloat because I have a lot of affection for Russia,' Jennings said, 'but yes, I'm lucky I'm not doing business there at the moment.' See Christopher Adams, 'Kiwi multi-millionaire says Africa holds big opportunities for NZ', *The New Zealand Herald*, 16 July 2016.

An investigation was launched by the Interior Ministry department headed by Major Pavel Karpov. According to a version suggested by Browder's lawyers, instead of fulfilling his duty, Major Karpov became an accomplice of his suspect. He and Klyuev went on holiday together to Larnaca, Cyprus, four months before the verdict against the latter was announced.'

In reality, it seems both Kiselev and Karpov were instructed to act as they did by the FSB Directorate 'K'. By that time, President Putin had his people fill all key positions and managed to transfer a former Leningrad KGB chief Alexander Bortnikov to Moscow. On 2 March 2004 Bortnikov succeeded Zaostrovtsev as Dzhabarov's direct boss and head of FSB's Chief Directorate of Economic Security. (Bortnikov was reported to have been implicated in a money-laundering case but as soon as Dmitry Medvedev became the President of Russia, he placed him at the helm of the Russian Security Service.) What plan was behind the seizure of the Mikhailovsky shares is unclear. There could have been some personal reasons, or it was to stop Berezovsky's involvement in the deal. In any case, the operation failed.

One day in 2005, Browder's Hermitage Fund started to deal with Gazprom shares and invest in equity or equity-related securities of other important Russian companies. Three years later, Boris Nemtsov, a well-known Russian liberal politician, together with Vladimir Milov, likewise a popular opposition figure and former deputy energy minister, published an investigative report entitled 'Putin and Gazprom'. They stress that from the first days of Putin's presidency Gazprom has been under his close personal supervision. Only a few weeks after his election as Russian president, Putin replaced Victor Chernomyrdin as Gazprom's Chairman assigning his old pal and associate Dmitry Medvedev to this position. A year later another of Putin's cronies, Alexey Miller, became Deputy Chairman and Gazprom's CEO. At one time, 11 out of 18 top managers of Gazprom were Putin's nominees and former KGB officers, according to Nemtsov and Milov.

Sometime before Browder's investment fund entered the Gazprom share market, about 6.3% of its shares somehow disappeared from the company's balance. Their estimated value was $20 billion. It is the interest only second after what the Russian state itself holds in Gazprom. Nemtsov and Milov estimated the dividends for such interest should be about $170 million a year. Then the company's revenue was $93 billion, that is, 7% of the Russian GDP and twice as much as Russia's defence spending. In 2016, Gazprom's net income, according to the company's website, was $14.9 billion.

Thus, Gazprom shares were very attractive for foreign investors but in 2005, special government permission was required to deal with them. Browder decided to buy Gazprom shares through the Russian companies Kameya (Cameo), Riland (Ryland), Parfenion (Parthenion) and Machaon (Ma-ha-ón). The first belonged to the Cyprus-registered company Zhoda Limited and the last three to Kone Holdings and Glendora Holdings, also registered in Cyprus. Paul Wrench, a Guernsey resident and at the same time: chairman, HSBC Private Bank World Funds plc; managing director, HSBC Management (Guernsey) Limited; and so on, plus non-executive director (since October 2001–present) of Hermitage Capital Management, was also registered as director of two management companies for Kone and Glendora. Funds were allocated on the accounts of these companies and they started to buy Gazprom shares as well as those of Transneft, Surgut Oil'n Gas and other important Russian businesses. This is what Browder calls transparent business schemes.[15]

That would be only half the problem. In his capacity as a financial analyst, Bill Browder and his team from Hermitage Capital Management started to specialise in business investigations and financial analyses, sharing their 'product' with media outlets like *The New York Times*, *Financial Times*, *Wall Street Journal*, *Businessweek* or Reuters. They also used to supply relevant information to Putin's administration. This is how Mr Browder explained his fund's activities to members of the US Helsinki Commission. 'Due to weak courts and legal protections,' he said, 'our biggest leverage was often the bully pulpit of the press. Since 1996 we waged dozens of high-profile public activist campaigns targeting mismanagement and corruption at some of the largest companies in Russia.' These included: Gazprom, the state-controlled natural gas monopoly; Unified Energy Systems, the national electricity utility; Sberbank, the largest bank in Russia; and Surgutneftegas, the fourth-largest oil company in the country, whose ownership, Milov says, is the number one top secret of the Russian oil industry.

Thus, with Browder's intervention, some of the 'grey schemes' employed by leading Russian business players became known. On the one hand, public companies had to improve their performance and, as a result, their market capitalisation became higher. At the same time, those who secretly profited at the expense of the shareholders started to lose money. Bill Browder has immediately turned from 'one of our own people', welcomed by Putin and his administration, into an enemy. After the arrest of Mikhail Khodorkovsky, all Russian oligarchs who wanted to live and carry on making their business went to the Kremlin where 'no terms except an unconditional and immediate surrender were accepted', as Galina, the wife of Smolensky, told me during a lunch in Vienna. Khodorkovsky was a Russian oligarch, with a fortune estimated to be worth $15 billion in 2003. In October of that year, he was arrested and charged with fraud.[16] Browder welcomed the prosecution of Khodorkovsky and cheered his arrest. At the World Economic Summit in Davos in 2005, William Browder was named one of the Global Leaders of Tomorrow.

---

[15] For details, see 'US Senate Judiciary Committee Hearing Transcripts, Exhibits and Correspondence Related to Donald Trump's 2016 Presidential Campaign', 31 May 2016. See also, 'Testimony of Natalia Veselnitskaya Before the United States Senate Committee on Judiciary', Committee Chairman Charles E. Grassley, the Senate of the USA, Committee on the Judiciary, Washington DC, 20 November 2017, 13–21.

[16] Khodorkovsky was granted a pardon and released from prison in late December 2013 having served ten years. On 22 December, two days after his release, Khodorkovsky appeared at a news conference at the private Checkpoint Charlie Museum in Berlin's Friedrichstrasse. On 24 December, he was interviewed by the BBC. In March 2014, Khodorkovsky addressed a meeting on Maidan in Kiev. He also delivered keynote speeches at the World Economic Forum, Chatham House and the Atlantic Council among others. In September, he officially relaunched the Open Russia movement. In October 2014, Khodorkovsky visited the US, delivering the keynote address at Freedom House in Washington, DC, and giving a speech at the Council on Foreign Relations in New York. The Open Russia Club was opened on 10 November 2015 at 16 Hanover Square, Mayfair, London W1.

The theme of that Davos meeting was 'Taking Responsibility for Tough Choices'. Soon, to his surprise, he was banned from entering Russia as a 'threat to the national security'.

In January 2006, Selen Securities LLC and Financial Investments LLC, the local investment holding companies of Renaissance Gaz (RenGaz) registered in Russia, were sold to the Cyprus-registered company Connery Holdings Ltd. Five days later Connery sold them to its parent company registered in the British Virgin Islands. In February, Selen Securities and Financial Investments re-registered their local tax offices to Moscow Tax Inspectorates No. 25 and No. 28. Later in 2006, the former RenGaz subsidiaries were sold to several Russian individuals. Simon Moyse, the Renaissance Capital spokesman, probably had this final step in mind when he declared that the RenGaz subsidiaries 'were sold as shell companies to individuals for purposes of liquidation'. However, a much different fate awaited them.

During the same time, in early 2006, the Austrian Raiffeisen Bank International (RBI) bought the Impexbank from Ivanishvili and his partner for $550 million.

On 5 April 2006, two police officers, Anton Golyshev and Pavel Karpov, travelling first-class through the Sheremetievo-2 International airport's VIP lounge, and Dmitry Klyuev, a tax consultant travelling business class, flew to Larnaca, Cyprus. It was not a holiday trip and not the one undertaken on its participants' own will. Regarding Larnaca and other foreign destinations suitable for secret meetings, the FSB learnt to be very careful in their own country after many scandals involving public figures whose offices and apartments were bugged and filmed. Since at least 2004 – President Putin's first term in office – all important meetings would take place in countries outside Russia.

Soon after Golyshev and Karpov returned, during the same month, arbitration courts in Moscow and Kazan ruled in favour of the three obscure shell companies that filed lawsuits against the two former RenGaz subsidiaries based on fraudulent contracts. According to the court documents, the two subsidiaries had been sued over the alleged non-delivery of Sberbank and Unified Energy Systems shares. Notably, the RenGaz 2005 and 2006 audited financial statements and offering memoranda showed that RenGaz was organised for the sole purpose of owning Gazprom shares for its investors and should never have owned other shares. Altogether, the two former RenGaz subsidiaries were sued for $605 million, but the plaintiffs were awarded $525 million only because one of them failed to appear in court.

If properly investigated, such fraud wouldn't hold water. To begin with, except for one sales and purchase agreement – anyway, not real – signed by the Renaissance-appointed General Director of Financial Investments LLC on 1 November 2005, that is, before the two RenGaz subsidiaries were sold (which implicates Renaissance officials), the RenGaz companies did not sign any such agreements. Secondly, all 'directors' and 'lawyers' representing both plaintiffs and defendants were, in reality, false representatives making false claims. Finally, the sums for which the companies were sued strictly corresponded to their revenues for the fiscal year, which suggested that confidential information was leaked to the perpetrators. Because in each case, the defence counsel for the former RenGaz subsidiaries accepted the claim without objections, the arbitration judge released the plaintiff from the requirement of proving the case.

Some of the audited financial statements that Renaissance Group distributed to its international clients show that RenGaz subsidiaries paid $108.1 million in capital gains taxes in 2006. But according to their filings with Rosstat, the Russian Statistics Committee, the RenGaz subsidiaries only paid $1.2 million in taxes that year. The independent investigation found out that RenGaz subsidiaries had in fact paid the full $108.1 million in 2006 but at the end of the year received a tax refund of $106.9 million leaving only $1.2 million to the Russian Treasury.

While it is comparatively easy to move several hundred thousands, one needs a legal mechanism in place to operate hundreds of millions, especially when funds must be secretly routed from Russia to Western accounts. The operation must involve lawyers, tax officials, police officers from the Economic Crime Department, a small private bank and a number of technical assistants, not to mention FSB and SVR supervision, direction and control. It must also involve a friendly Western bank. In December 2006 and March 2007, the two former RenGaz subsidiaries opened bank accounts at the Universal Savings Bank (USB), abbreviated in Russian as 'UBS' (a parody on the world-famous Swiss UBS), from where the fraudulently received tax refund of $106.9 million was allegedly transferred to Vienna's Raiffeisen Zentralbank Österreich (RZB). RZB is the central institution of the Raiffeisen Banking Group and the sole holder, it was claimed, of the US dollar correspondent account for Universal Savings Bank. The RZB is one of the leading banking institutions in Central and Eastern Europe. It is also a partner of Gazprom and is suspected by some researchers of laundering money for the Russian mafia and Russian secret services. Until 2006, Universal Savings Bank, a small and by now long defunct Moscow bank, belonged to Klyuev but in 2006, he says, he sold it to a man named Sioma Korobeinikov.

Semen Moiseyevich ('Sioma') Korobeinikov was a colourful Jew born in 1951 in Odessa. Before the collapse of the Soviet Union, he was an antique trader in Moscow, along with another no less colourful individual by the name of Semion Mogilevich. Later Korobeinikov moved to Israel, but when his former associate relocated to Hungary soon to become a 'Billion Dollar Don', the mob boss of the Russian organised crime in Europe, Korobeinikov, joined him in Budapest. It is widely reported that Mogilevich has always been a high-value asset of the KGB and later FSB, although no official records have become available. In October 2009, the FBI placed him on The Most Wanted list, but six years later Mogilevich's name was formally removed because by that time he was living in Russia, with whom the United States has no extradition treaty, so there was no reason to bother.

By 2006, Korobeinikov had got involved in the import of leading global fashion brands and later founded a private joint stock company that he called People's Trade Enterprise, closely collaborating with the Moscow government, before he headed the Universal Savings Bank that formerly belonged to Klyuev. After at least two successful tax return operations – one with the former RenGaz subsidiaries and another with three former Hermitage companies – Korobeinikov liquidated the bank and, in September 2008, fell to his death from a balcony on a construction site in one of Moscow's 'elite' commercial districts.

In September 2010, it was reported that Austria's financial watchdog, the Financial Market Authority, found no evidence that the RZB was involved in laundering the proceeds in relation to the Universal Savings Bank affair. The FMA said it had acted on information received from an unnamed source and dispatched a money-laundering task force to RBZ to check relevant transactions. 'We went into the papers and documents and we didn't find any evidence of money-laundering,' the official statement read.

No one in Russia ever investigated the RenGaz subsidiaries affair. Renaissance had provided its companies for testing the scam, it worked, and the Treasury did not claim the loss. Although duly warned, persons in charge seemed not to care. In such countries as Russia, this happens only when higher authorities are involved. As it is, the tax refund scheme turned out to be a much better trick than simply moving large amounts of cash to the accounts of shell companies, as was done with the IMF aid in 1998. It is also much safer because Western banks feel comfortable receiving transfers from tax inspectorates. Once tested on Renaissance's own entities, the scheme could be tried on others.

Reporting the alleged crimes of the 'Klyuev gang' or 'criminal syndicate', the Hermitage lawyers highlighted another episode that happened in 2006. After a closer look, it also seems misinterpreted, as it now stands. 'In August 2006,' Michael Weiss writes in the previously quoted article in *World Affairs*, 'Karpov and his superior at the Interior Ministry, Lieutenant Colonel Artem Kuznetsov, acting at Klyuev's behest, arranged the arrest of Fyodor Mikheyev, a 36-year-old fertilizer executive from Moscow.'[17] In all publications that followed, this episode is presented as a simple kidnap-for-ransom affair carried out by some corrupt police officials.

In reality, it only looked like kidnapping. Quite possibly, it was the result of the 'wind of change' that was blowing in the Directorate 'K', where General Dzhabarov was leaving his powerful office to give place to a new man. General Victor Voronin, who previously served in the Federal Tax Administration in Moscow and in St Petersburg's Inland Revenue Department, moved in as the new Directorate 'K' chief reporting directly to Bortnikov (since then, Voronin was quietly replaced by Ivan Tkachev after a sweeping overhaul of the economic department of the FSB in July 2017). Two years later, in May 2019, it was announced Tkachev was also moving following the arrest of one of his subordinates, FSB Colonel Kirill Cherkalin, on major bribery charges. According to *The Moscow Times*, Russian authorities have seized $185.5 million in cash from Cherkalin in a sting operation, making him the country's richest ex-law enforcement official under investigation for corruption.

In the Tax Administration, Voronin's boss was Anatoly Serdyukov. Serdyukov, who would eventually become Minister of Defence (sacked by Putin in November 2012), is also important to this story.[18] As expected, after formal retirement from the FSB, General Dzhabarov moved to his friend Sagiryan's offices and was appointed First Vice President of Renaissance Capital in charge of relations with state bodies.

---

[17] Michael Weiss, 'Explosive Video Documents Depth of Putin's Mafia State', *World Affairs*, June 2012.

[18] See Michael Weiss, 'Corruption and Cover-Up in the Kremlin: The Anatoly Serdyukov Case', *The Atlantic*, 29 Jan 2013.

In the Russian hierarchy, if the first deputy is major general, his boss must be at least lieutenant general.

The FSB was obliged to know that one of the leading Russian banks recently credited $100 million to the fertiliser company that employed Mikheyev despite almost zero chance of its return. According to the documents, one-fifth of this sum, or $20 million, was spent on purchasing railway wagons for which the credit was granted while the rest was quietly transferred to private accounts. Somebody in Directorate 'K' calculated that another $20 million could perhaps be squeezed out of the company's boss so Mikheyev, one of its employees, was detained and kept in a safe house. Mikheyev's wife upset the apple cart by calling the Counter Terrorism Command. They freed her husband, but no one was arrested for his 'kidnapping' because the case was quickly hushed up by the FSB. Mikheyev later testified that he was told Lieutenant Colonel Kuznetsov and Major Karpov worked for the Presidential Administration.

Starting from 2006, officers from the City of Moscow Police Economic Crime Directorate began showing interest in the activities of three Hermitage companies (Machaon, Parthenion and Ryland), and in the Hermitage partner-company Kameya. All of them were dealing with Gazprom shares. Lieutenant Colonel Kuznetsov, who had been accused by the Hermitage lawyers of kidnapping Mikheyev, was now assigned to work on the Hermitage case.

While all these events were in development, in December 2006 Igor Sagiryan masterminded, founded and headed Renaissance Development (now RCS Development) – a group of investment and development companies – while still remaining, together with his friend General Vladimir Dzhabarov, President and First Vice President of Renaissance Capital respectively. Renaissance Development became a convenient vehicle for large-scale financial operations. Since 2013, Alexander Dzhabarov has been serving as its Financial Director. At the same time, Edward Dzhabarov moved from the office of Renaissance Capital to head a department at Sberbank CIB.

Major Karpov of the Moscow Police and two lawyers, the attractive blonde Yulia Mayorova, and Andrei Pavlov (a husband-and-wife couple who would figure in every tax-refund case pertinent to our narrative), spent the first working week of January 2007 holidaying *à trois* in London. For the next few years, it would become their favourite pastime in different parts of the world. Also in January 2007, Klyuev and his young wife Ekaterina Sokolova went to Dubai to be joined there later by Olga Stepanova and her husband Vladlen Stepanov. This last couple is important because, first of all, until 2010 Stepanova headed Moscow's Tax Inspectorate No. 28, one of the two tax inspectorates that sanctioned various tax refunds that figure in this story, even without obligatory approval by the supervising authorities like the Federal Tax Administration. Secondly, for more than ten years, from 1995 to 2008, Stepanov and Perepilichny were managing a network of offshore shell companies through whose accounts considerable funds were moved. This was not a 'criminal syndicate activity', as claimed in many published accounts but a sophisticated financial operation. In one of the interviews in 2011, Stepanov called Perepilichny 'a financial wizard'.

From Dubai, the group proceeded to Lausanne where Stepanov had opened several bank accounts with Credit Swiss. The available records show that substantial amounts of money had been transferred daily from these accounts to such diversified beneficiaries that it was clear those payments had nothing to do with Stepanov's declared professional activity in Moscow. Also, large sums were regularly credited to his Swiss accounts, which make it clear Mr Stepanov was involved not in his own but in somebody else's financial operations. Except for several payments for real estate in Kempinski Palm Jumeirah, Dubai, which did not exceed several million dollars, the rest was clearly not Stepanov's business. And even those property investments in Kempinski could in fact belong to somebody else.

On 16 January 2007, Klyuev, his wife and the Stepanov couple returned to Moscow from Geneva. Karpov, Mayorova and Pavlov came back from London sometime earlier, on 5 January. On 27 January, at the World Economic Forum Annual Meeting in Davos, William Browder met the Russian prime minister Dmitry Medvedev, asking him to help with his sudden and unexpected visa problem. Medvedev promised to look into the matter. Hermitage lawyers claim that soon after, Lieutenant Colonel Kuznetsov of the Interior Ministry called the Hermitage Moscow offices offering a private meeting to sort things out, which was politely declined.

In April, Klyuev, Sokolova and the police officer Kuznetsov went to Larnaca by private jet while the second group consisting of Mayorova with Karpov and Pavlov arrived there on 30 April. Stepanova and her husband came next, on 8 May. Thus, two police officers, a tax official, a tax refund specialist-turned-private banker and his two lawyers gathered in this cosy and sunny Cyprus resort to discuss business.

Larnaca is good for everything else but not business. For business you should go to Limassol. In Larnaca there are no 5-star hotels, business clubs and private beaches, and the only decent restaurant in town is rather small, expensive and Japanese, which is good because otherwise to get good fish in this small resort with its nice palm-tree seafront, busy port and marina is practically impossible.

After their return, an operational officer of the Directorate 'K' reported to General Voronin that Kameya LLC, controlled by Browder, was actively involved in a criminal offence. Voronin promptly authorised the investigation.

The company in question, Kameya LLC, was originally founded by two different legal entities but from 2006 its sole shareholder was Zhoda Ltd from Cyprus, a client of Hermitage. It was an investment vehicle headed by one Ivan Cherkasov, an employee of Hermitage who at the same time served as Managing Director of Kameya. In 2006, Kameya paid Zhoda $183 million as dividends for the sale of Gazprom shares to Giggs Enterprises, a limited liability company also registered in Cyprus.[19] The investigation initiated by the FSB was carried out by the Interior Ministry. As a result, Cherkasov had to leave Russia and settled in London, while the company was forced to pay a tax of 24% contrary to the Russia-Cyprus Tax Treaty.

On 4 June 2007, Kuznetsov and Karpov led a group of armed police in a raid on the Hermitage Moscow office. According to court documents, police officers

---

[19] For details, see 'Testimony of Natalia Veselnitskaya Before the United States Senate Committee on the Judiciary', 20 November 2017.

removed Hermitage's computer server, virtually all of its computers, and dozens of boxes of confidential financial records. Following a swoop by detectives on the offices of Firestone Duncan, Hermitage's legal and audit advisors, all of the original statutory and financial documents of the Hermitage companies were confiscated. Firestone Duncan's computer server, numerous computers and attorney-client privileged documents relating to all of Firestone Duncan's clients were also taken away. Enough material was seized to fill two vans. The official justification for the raid on two offices was the ongoing investigation of Kameya's business. Records and documents of more than 20 companies unrelated to Kameya were also seized by the officers during the raid.

The 'processing' of all confiscated material was finished in October 2007. On 29 November, a Moscow defence attorney commissioned by Firestone Duncan notified Major Karpov that Hermitage had found serious violations of law in the financial claims brought by the court in its charges filed against the Hermitage companies.

A few hours later, Igor Sagiryan contacted William Browder. Sagiryan explained that he was aware of all of Browder's problems in Russia. In reality, the only people who could have known about the problems at that time were senior executives of Hermitage, its lawyers, and those who had orchestrated the fraud. During his call, Sagiryan suggested a personal meeting. Browder agreed to meet in ten days' time upon his return from a planned business trip abroad.

The meeting was arranged for 11 December 2007 at the Dorchester in London. A day before, Browder received a telephone call from Stephen Jennings, the main shareholder of Renaissance Capital. At that time, he was the CEO of RenCap, an American subsidiary of Renaissance Capital later serving as the CEO of Renaissance Group. The aim of Jennings' call was to encourage Browder to keep an open mind regarding the forthcoming visit.

They met at the Spatisserie and ordered tea. Although, unlike his guest, Browder was at home in London, he was nervous. As he later recalled, the Armenian stated that he was fully aware of the theft from the Hermitage companies and all of the legal problems that Heritage was experiencing in Russia. Sagiryan said Renaissance Capital would quite possibly be able to help and suggested that he could arrange for the stolen Hermitage companies to be liquidated, which in his view should facilitate getting rid of all problems. Sagiryan also said that once a company was liquidated there would be no more records, therefore no more investigations. Browder decided this proposal had little or nothing to do with what was going on and declined.

Within approximately two weeks the tax refund application made on behalf of three former Browder's companies was authorised and the Russian Treasury paid the unprecedented sum of $230 million to the accounts opened especially for this reason at the Moscow Universal Savings Bank and another small Russian financial institution, the Intercommerz bank. According to the Hermitage lawyers, part of that $230 million was channelled through the Austrian correspondent accounts held with two New York banks. The sole holder of US dollar correspondent accounts for both USB (acc. no. 70-55.061.527) and Intercommerz (acc. no. 70-55.079.669), they stated, was Raiffeissen Zentralbank Österreich (RZB) in Vienna.

Later, Moscow police informed the law firm acting on behalf of Firestone Duncan that the documents and seals of Machaon, Parthenion and Ryland, three Russia-registered companies formerly belonging to Hermitage, had never been passed on to anybody.

Hermitage solicitors and after them several Russian journalists managed to find out the following. After it was credited to the accounts in USB and Intercommerz, the sum, which was initially 5.4 billion Russian rubles, after having been exchanged into US dollars was 'layered' with the help of a great number of shell companies and trusts. The so-called 'layering' is an important part of the money-laundering process – it is meant to make the trailing of illegal proceeds difficult for law enforcement agencies to follow. It was discovered that after a series of complex financial transactions, funds were finally parked on several secret accounts in various parts of the world including Britain. During the inquest hearings it became clear that, at least with some of those shell companies, Perepilichny was directly involved. It also turned out that his London financiers, the EFG Private Bank Limited, part of the global private banking group EFG International based in Zurich, were absolutely unaware of many of his business deals in spite of the routine checks. Ironically, this bank is located in Leconfield House on Curzon Street in Mayfair, the headquarters of MI5 from 1945 to 1976.

To launder part of the sum received from the Treasury as a result of the Hermitage companies' affair, a Moscow account of the private commercial bank named Krainiy Sever ('Far North') was also used.[20] Thus, $52 million was transferred to the Moldavian Banca de Economii to two shell limited liability companies – Bunicon-Impex Srl and Elenast-Com Srl between 4 and 13 February 2008. On 5 February more than $3.6 million were further transferred from Bunicon to various offshore companies, out of which $726,000 landed in the accounts of the British Nomirex Trading Ltd. Altogether, during this short period $365 million passed through the accounts of Nomirex. Its most active commercial partners were the Russian Sberbank and VTB – both closely connected with Mr Sagiryan and Russian secret services. On 6 February, Nomirex transferred $1.9 million to the account of Quartell Trading Ltd at Credit Suisse.

Quartell Trading is the company registered in the British Virgin Islands. It is a majority shareholder of Horus Invest Resource. The inquest heard that Perepilichny was the general director of Horus with a one per cent shareholding. It was also discovered that Quartell used to send money to the Cypriot company Arivust Holdings, whose beneficiary was Vladlen Stepanov, the former husband of Olga Stepanova, and Perepilichny's business partner since 1995. It will be remembered that Stepanova, at the time head of Tax Inspectorate No. 28, a Russian version of HM Revenue and Customs, was directly involved in refunding the $230 million that

---

[20] According to the Organized Crime and Corruption Reporting Project (OCCRP) report of 25 June 2015, French authorities have launched an investigation into money laundering and organised crime activities in France, Monaco and Luxembourg. Court records and internal banking documents seen by OCCRP show that the bank (Krainiy Sever) accumulated funds released by Moscow tax inspectorates and then wired them abroad.

became the focal point of the so-called Magnitsky case – part of the US Senate's Judiciary Committee's investigation.

Remarkably, neither the sum of $106.9 million from the RenGaz companies' affair nor $230 million from the Hermitage claims ever surfaced on the Swiss accounts managed by Stepanov. Stepanov's financial transactions exposed by Perepilichny only involved comparatively small sums, with no more than $2 million being transferred to various foreign accounts. His only role seems to have been limited to this simple task. In all probability Stepanov, like Perepilichny, acted as a rather low-level account manager.

Stepanov's other involvement questioned by the Hermitage attorneys dealt with various properties in the Dubai's Kempinski Palm Jumeirah condominium, some of which were purchased in his name. Alas, that doesn't mean anything as estates are often purchased in somebody else's name, which can be a physical person, often a frontman, or an offshore entity.

Before the February money rush, Major Karpov, Yulia Mayorova and her husband Andrei Pavlov – a police investigator and two lawyers working together with Klyuev on the tricky tax refund schemes – decided to follow the tradition and spend the first days of New Year in 2008 à trois abroad. On 1 January they flew to Istanbul returning to Moscow after three nights at the luxury Çırağan Palace Kempinski. According to some reports, Klyuev and the Stepanovs were spending New Year's Day and the following week in Dubai, as they did a year before, where they were joined by Pavlov on 5 January. Mayorova and Karpov remained in Moscow.

As the documents handed over by Perepilichny to the Hermitage lawyers reveal, January and February 2008 were busy months for Stepanov, which seems incompatible with his alleged holiday mood and relaxed lifestyle in Dubai. From the printouts of his account activity for the period it follows that Stepanov was only technically involved with all those transactions that every few minutes passed through his bank accounts. His Credit Swiss account manager with a popular Belorussian name, who resides in the quiet and peaceful municipality of Freienbach on the shores of Lake Zurich, had always been extremely kind to her Moscow client giving as much support as she could.

For example, on 17 January payments were made to a Chinese company dealing with household textiles; a French hotel group; a German firm specialising in aviation foams; and a private individual in Russia who received more than $100,000 for unspecified services. After all those payments the account balance remained at minus more than $200,000. Nevertheless, on the next day, 21 payments were made.

In June, the Universal Savings Bank was liquidated and all its documents were destroyed when the truck carrying them exploded right in the centre of Moscow.

In October 2008, Magnitsky gave an interview to *Businessweek* (now *Bloomberg Businessweek*) presenting his version of recent events by testifying against everyone who had been involved in what he considered a large-scale fraud. The article was published on 5 November and less than a week later the Stepanov couple left for Dubai to be out of reach while waiting for the situation to clear up.

According to the Hermitage legal team, after a series of meetings and telephone calls on secure lines, Sagiryan also flew to Dubai accompanied by his friend General Dzhabarov, formerly of the FSB Directorate K. It was an error because their direct contact with other participants of this operation had, until that moment, not been registered. Dzabarov remained in Dubai for another few days while Sagiryan and the Stepanov couple returned to Moscow on 23 November, passing through customs and passport control at the same time, which is documented. The following morning, the FSB informed a CID investigator that Sergey Magnitsky had a passport valid for travel abroad and that he was applying to the UK Embassy in Moscow for an entry visa. On the same day, police officers detained Magnitsky and confiscated all his documents.

Some time later, confronted with evidence that they were in Dubai together, Sagiryan invented a story that he and General Dzhabarov met by chance at the local Ping Pong dim sum restaurant situated on the lower ground floor of the Dubai Mall. This was another faux pas. While the Dubai Mall was indeed opened on 4 November 2008, slightly over two weeks before the duo arrived at the Emirates, the Ping Pong dim sum, the first non-UK business of the Ping Pong restaurant chain that belongs to Sagiryan, welcomed its first patrons almost a year later.

Ping Pong, the brand launched in 2005, currently has eleven sites in London including Soho, St Christopher's Place/St James Street and Covent Garden, and a number of international ventures in Brazil, the Middle East and the US. Most recent new sites are the Brazil-2, a 100-cover restaurant, and the Washington-2, a 250-cover venture. Ping Pong's London Marketing Manager (now CEO) is Artiom 'Art' Sagiryan, one of Igor's three sons (the other two are fully involved in their father's various business ventures in Russia).

According to the established tradition, on Thursday 1 January 2009, Major Karpov of the Moscow Police, Yulia Mayorova and her husband Pavlov left for Madrid and Barcelona returning to Moscow a week later. Soon they would celebrate Yulia's 30th birthday together.

In the meantime, the Hermitage solicitors – Firestone Duncan in Moscow and Brown Rudnick in London – had a very productive idea that the Hermitage problem may be greatly helped by applying to the US courts for judicial assistance. Neil Micklethwaite of Brown Rudnick filed such an application with the Southern District Court of New York on 27 July 2009. The idea was to convince the court to issue a subpoena on the two New York banks that were clearing US dollar accounts of the Austrian RZB, and on RenCap Securities Inc., a Renaissance US subsidiary. The attorneys believed it could help in finding out what exactly was the role played by the Renaissance officials as well as how defrauded funds were routed and on which accounts that they landed. The application was successful. But Moscow learned about it in advance and was prepared.

During the same month, a deal was struck and a 50% stake in Renaissance Capital was sold to the ONEXIM Group of the pro-Kremlin oligarch Mikhail Prokhorov. Simultaneously, Igor Sagiryan was transferred to Troika Dialogue, a multinational investment banking and asset management firm headquartered in Moscow. Troika's principal owner was an Armenian named Ruben Vardanyan, once called a poster boy of Russian capitalism.[21] Sagiryan was appointed Troika's president while his friend General Dzhabarov remained in Renaissance to oversee the transfer. In September 2009, he joined Sagiryan as First Vice President of Troika.

In the same year, Perepilichny moved to the UK and, with his wife and two children, settled in a rented house in St George's Hill, a private estate in Weybridge, Surrey, surrounded by beautiful old trees and quietly hidden from the outside world, with private lawn tennis and golf clubs.

On 16 November 2009, Magnitsky died in his prison cell after a prison doctor of the Matrosskaya Tishina medical unit, where he had been sent because of a health condition, refused to approve necessary treatment. This prison is a symbolic place. It attained some fame for holding the putsch plotters who protested against President Mikhail Gorbachev's reforms in August 1991. The coup d'état attempt was masterminded and headed by the then KGB chief Vladimir Kryuchkov, who would also serve his term here later becoming Putin's adviser. After Magnitsky's death, the Russian investigation developed very slowly until it ended with charges and then, after a trial, a guilty verdict against the deceased.

When Magnitsky was still alive and in jail, Browder launched an international campaign, meeting US senators and congressmen every few weeks. The Hermitage lawyers compiled a list of those involved in Magnitsky's arrest and the theft of Browder's Russian companies. Finally, Browder found support in the Maryland Democrat senator Benjamin Louis 'Ben' Cardin, chairman of the US Helsinki Commission. The commission invited Browder to the US to testify.

Like Lugovoy, one of the suspects in the Litvinenko assassination, who quickly became an MP, General Dzhabarov was elected to the upper house of the Federal Assembly (Russian Parliament) three months after he left Renaissance and moved to Troika. Now senator and First Deputy Chairman of the International Affairs Committee of Russia's Federation Council (which, as one reporter quipped, is styled as a senate but functions as a claque for the Kremlin), Dzhabarov is one of the 'untouchables'. He is the proud owner of four Moscow apartments, a large piece of land for individual housing construction plus three parking lots for his three cars, which are not domestic brands like Lada, Volga or Niva but rather Audi A6, Lexus

---

[21] According to Bloomberg (Jake Rudnitski, 'Troika Laundering Claims Put Founder Vardanyan's Legacy in Focus', 7 March 2019), state-owned Sberbank paid $1 billion to buy Russia's oldest investment bank from Vardanyan and his partners in 2012, then paid them an extra $400 million the following year. Vardanyan has since built a high profile as a philanthropist in his native Armenia, spending millions of dollars to restore an ancient monastery in the Caucasus country and founding an international school, as well as funding the annual $1 million Aurora Prize for Awakening Humanity. Vardanyan, Bloomberg reports, met with Prince Charles during a 2013 visit to Armenia and the Dilijan International School has links to the British royal's Dumfries House project in Scotland. He hosted film star George Clooney in Armenia's capital, Yerevan, during the inaugural presentation of the Aurora Prize in 2016. Clooney serves on the prize's selection committee along with former French Foreign Minister Bernard Kouchner, ex-US ambassador to the United Nations Samantha Power, and former Irish president Mary Robinson.

LS600 and VW Touareg. In March 2014, the general's name was added to the US Department of the Treasury Specially Designated Nationals and Blocked Persons List (SDN) for his role in rubber-stamping the Russian invasion and annexation of the Crimea. The assets of such individuals and companies, called 'SDNs', are blocked and US citizens are generally prohibited from dealing with them, which, understandably, did not bother him.

After listening to Browder's arguments, Senator Cardin introduced a bill in the US Congress complemented by the list of Magnitsky's offenders, which became known as the Cardin List. At the time it included 60 people and among them doctors, pre-trial detention centre wardens, members of the court service, police and tax officers, and a few petty criminals who were used in this operation as pawns. They are all accused of human rights violations. Maybe they did indeed violate Sergey Magnitsky's human rights, but this story is not about Sergey.

In the spring of 2010, Perepilichny was facing the dilemma of whether to return to Russia where the Magnitsky affair had become a cause célèbre and the subject of countless Russian and international news articles, or to find a way to remain in Britain. At the beginning of the year, he already managed to secure an investor visa for his wife Tatiana by getting a loan of £1 million from his bank (a British branch of a Swiss financial institution). This money plus the sum of more than £100,000 that he had additionally transferred was invested into a gilt – fixed-interest loan securities issued by the UK government. As his former bank manager explained, this had to be worth in excess of £1 million and had to stay above the value of £1 million for the five years that the client held that gilt. By the time he called Browder's office, Perepilichny should have realised that, thanks to the lawyers' efforts, many elements of the financial operation in which Magnitsky was occasionally got involved were gradually becoming known. He also realised that his long-time friend and business companion Stepanov should have been somehow involved because it was Stepanov's wife who single-handedly authorised the refund. And William Browder, Perepilichny knew, was very interested to know as much as possible about this case. So, he decided to change sides and chose the right person to deal with. By that time, Browder was on the way to succeeding Boris Berezovsky as Russia's enemy number one and he really could help. In what seemed a simple deal, some important financial documents changed hands in exchange for Perepilichny's political asylum as a whistleblower. Perepilichny might not have realised that he was signing his own death sentence.

In the summer of 2010, Neil Micklethwaite of Brown Rudnick started to work on a new legal document. This time it was a 'Money Laundering Suspicion Report' addressed to the Attorney General of Switzerland. It was dispatched on 28 January 2011 by e-mail, fax and courier, with copies sent to other interested parties including the Credit Swiss where both Perepilichny and Stepanov had their bank accounts. In April, Stepanov's accounts were frozen and Moscow learned about Perepelichny's treachery.

The man who died at the heart of the most beautiful and prosperous British county, Surrey, at one of its most secure and quiet places, was born on 15 July 1968. In 1991, he graduated with high marks from the elite Moscow Institute for Physics and Technology (MFTI) where he studied at the Faculty of Physicochemical Biology.

According to one of his co-students, Perepilichny was a good student who dreamed of continuing his post-graduate studies in the US. In 1989, two years before his graduation, he started to save money for his trip by selling computers, as many young people did in Russia at that time. In 1990–91, a friend from his youth recalls,[22] Perepilichny headed a small private company named Gefest, which managed to sell a newly developed computer application to the High Military Aviation School in Riga, Latvia. During that time this Baltic republic, still part of the Soviet Union, was going through the period of restoring its independence, which had been declared in May (Latvian de facto independence was restored in August 1991). Soon Perepilichny was trading on the newly opened Moscow Mercantile Exchange and in the mid-1990s became an investment banker of a sort. According to a source who knew him well at the time, in 1996 Perepilichny was boasting of working for the newly established Federal Security Service (FSB). It was, he said, pure business collaboration.

Indeed, the Service needed a lot of talented and well-educated young people to adapt to new conditions in Russia. It had enough operational officers like Litvinenko who could investigate and shoot, but was short of 'volunteer helpers and brains', the term that had been widely used during Soviet times for more subtle operations like money laundering, setting up and management of offshore companies, secure investments and financial transactions that would be difficult to trace. The *siloviki*, former KGB and Soviet Army officers who were gaining power in Russia replacing the Communist Party apparatchiks, could not do such work but the newly cast young Russian *beezinetsmen* would. And they learned very quickly. Vladlen Stepanov, who was six years older than Perepilichny, said that starting from 1995 he and Perepilichny had been partners in some financial operations yielding excellent profits. It seems that at a certain time, they were engaged to make profits not only for themselves but also for somebody else.

That was obviously still the case in January–June 2008, for which period Perepilichny had copies of certain bank records that belonged to Stepanov. In early 2011, the Hermitage lawyers used him as their star witness in the case against what they called the 'Klyuev Gang'. The late US senator John McCain even urged President Obama to use an executive order to sanction the group wholesale as a 'dangerous transnational criminal organization' – a rather simplified approach to what seems a very complicated scheme.

From the documents provided by Perepilichny, which were later used by Brown Rudnick solicitors in their Swiss filing, it is clear that Stepanov and Perepilichny controlled a number of offshore accounts of several shell companies registered both in Britain and in the known tax havens. One can also see that large sums of money were constantly passing through those accounts in what became known in the professional lingo as the aforementioned 'layering', that is, complex financial transactions to camouflage the source and the final destination of funds. In the course of their investigation, Hermitage lawyers learned that several payments were also made from Stepanov's Swiss accounts as instalments for luxury properties in

---

[22] Yuri Panchul's LiveJournal entry of 28 November 2012, 11:29 p.m. https://panchul. livejournal.com/236271.html

his name and in those of his wife's two female deputies. They concluded it was the money stolen from the Treasury by Klyuev's 'gang'. But, unsurprisingly, the Russian Treasury came to a very different conclusion, so no one was convicted or brought to book except for a couple of proxies. On the contrary, some have gone on to receive state honours or job promotions, while their former chief executive suddenly became Russia's Minister of Defence.

Soon after Stepanov learnt that his Swiss accounts were frozen, he launched a public attack on Perepilichny. On 17 May 2011, he published an announcement in the Russian *RBK Daily*: 'Let us now talk about Aleksandr Perepilichny,' Stepanov wrote. 'This man owes me a lot of money. As a matter of fact, not only to me but also to scores of other creditors. He cheated me by pocketing my money and assets. Currently, he is hiding in London. We became acquainted in the mid-nineties. By that time, I was already quite prosperous, taking advantage of my professional skills in the mining business.[23] And that is when this "financial wizard" showed up in my life. Since 1995 Perepilichny had been in charge of my money. In the early 00s, I even notarized a power of attorney that allowed Perepilichny to withdraw money from my personal account in Switzerland. He was multiplying my capital on the stock exchange. Both of us were also involved in investment business by putting money, for example, into lucrative real estate in the United Arab Emirates. However, the "financial wizard" had failed to see the financial bubble burst coming and was responsible for my money and property losses.' This should have been a 'red flag' for Perepilichny, but he could hardly do anything.

Stepanov's wife, who he officially divorced in December 2010, left her Tax Inspectorate in the autumn of that year and together with two former deputies (but not those whose names figured in the documents provided by Perepilichny, those two reportedly left Russia with their families) moved to the MoD's Arms Procurement Agency (APA). For over five years, from February 2007 to early November 2012, the ministry was headed by Anatoly Serdyukov, a former boss of both Stepanova and General Voronin, who succeeded Dzhabarov as head of the FSB's Directorate 'K'. This Directorate, by all estimates, should have been properly informed about the above-mentioned tax refund and the following financial transactions.

Four days before Perepilichny was found dead in Weybridge, President Putin fired Serdyukov, the son-in-law of his close friend, who during his tenure as Defence Minister was involved in several scandals including the embezzlement of funds.

Among his achievements at the head of the MoD, Serdyukov was especially proud of the new arms procurement programme. In March 2012, the Russian news agency RIA Novosti reported: 'The development of weaponry based on new physics principles, direct-energy weapons, geophysical weapons, wave-energy weapons, genetic weapons, psychotronic weapons, etc., is part of the state arms procurement

---

[23] In reality, how Stepanov got his 'money and assets' is unclear. According to one report, he was a low-wage worker who dug mines and laid optical fibre cables for a living, which wouldn't have earned him enough to raise the capital to start a business.

program for 2011–2020.'[24] This is what Serdyukov had said at a meeting with President Putin. For many people, this may sound new and sensational, but not for the experts.

It is of course up to pathologists to explain what led to the death of Alexander Perepilichny near his English home. For the time being, they either seem at a loss or reluctant to disclose their findings. In November 2012, the second post-mortem came back as 'inconclusive'. Among other things, a psychotronic weapon acting from a distance is a possible explanation that, surprisingly, no one wants to consider, including the Surrey Police (who were not even present at the pre-inquest court hearings). Detectives stated there was no proof that Perepilichny was poisoned or assaulted. However, the absence of evidence is in no way evidence of absence. Detectives admitted they had been unable to find the cause of death. Although it was reported that some traces of *Gelsemium elegans* (GE), nicknamed 'heartbreak grass', were allegedly found in Perepilichny's stomach contents, this was probably a good reason for his insurance company to file a lawsuit. It's unlikely that this strong young man died because of GE poisoning since no typical manifestations such as neurological abnormalities and respiratory depression were recorded. Although death after ingestion of a lethal dose occurs quite rapidly, usually within an hour, and Perepilichny died about 25 minutes after he collapsed, there is no place where he could have been poisoned in such a short span of time. Except, of course, at home, but this is unlikely.

Gelsemium, a Latinized form of the Italian *gelsomino*, which means jasmine, is used in the treatment of facial and other neuralgias as a cardiac depressant and in spasmodic affections. In Chinese traditional medicine, *Gelsemium elegans* has been used to treat migraine, neuralgia, sciatica, cancers, and various types of sores. It is also a homoeopathic remedy for feverishness or hyperactivity. In this particular case, if any minuscule traces of GE were really found, *Gelsemium elegans* could have been used at some point as a nervous system relaxant (during the inquest it was reported that in the last two days of his life Perepilichny was under visible stress).

Further tests of the compound found in Perepilichny could not definitively identify it as *Gelsemium*. Professor Monique Simmonds, deputy director of science at Kew Gardens, who conducted the tests, told the inquest she could not say exactly what the compound was.

In April 2018, participants of the inquest spent a considerable amount of time discussing the last two days and nights that Perepilichny had spent in Paris enjoying a romantic holiday with Elmira Medynskaya from Kiev. Elmira had been registered with one of the Ukrainian dating agencies and in March 2012 Perepilichny chose her from the list. In May, they met for the first time and Perepilichny invited Elmira for lunch and then dinner at the Kiev Premier Palace Hotel, a 5-star luxury property at the heart of the city where he was staying. During the next two months they exchanged email and SMS messages (for whatever reason, Perepilichny signed them with the alias 'Sergei Kovalev') before he asked her to meet him again, this time

---

in Nice, France, at the end of July. There they stayed at the famous Negresco on the prestigious Promenade des Anglais. After three days of luxury wining, dining and shopping, she left for Ukraine and he returned to England having agreed to meet again. She described him as a good-looking, strong, healthy and well-educated businessman and he certainly liked her too because their next romantic rendezvous was in the French capital on 8 November.

As before, they wined and dined in several good places, spending two nights at the most excellent, quiet and comfortable Le Bristol, a favourite haunt of my own located on Rue du Faubourg Saint-Honoré. On 9 November, after a light lunch at Le Fouquet's on Champs-Élysées, they opted for a late dinner at the Buddha Bar just a few minutes walk from Le Bristol.

It was about 10:00 p.m., the bar was still full, their small table uncomfortably placed and Perepilichny didn't like what he was served. Six years later Medynskaya was grilled for several hours to recall every detail of that dinner and in particular every single moment after it while the inquest tried to establish – without success – whether Perepilichny could have been poisoned there. Bob Moxon Browne QC, for Legal and General Assurance, said 'It seems likely that Mr Perepilichnyy ate something that disagreed with him on the night before his death. That could have been because someone malignantly put poison in his food.'

To paraphrase Albert Mackey, a masonic scholar, the propositions of Mr Moxon Browne were distinguished for their absolute independence of all authority and for the bold assumptions presented in the place of facts.

There is actually no evidence that Perepilichny had been poisoned at any moment. Although, speaking about their late dinner on that day, Ms Medynskaya admitted that Perepilichny 'was sit and he was not really look at me'. She also stated that when she saw him early next morning, 'He was very in good shape, he smiled, and he invite me for the breakfast … he was having good diet, he was eating eggs and hot chocolate … He was in a good mood.' At about seven o'clock in the morning they departed together to the airport and there he said he wanted to meet her in Switzerland in December. After which they both left: she to Kiev, and he to London. It was 10 November 2012. He collapsed on the same day near his home in Weybridge, Surrey, at about 5:15 p.m. and died less than half an hour after paramedics appeared at the scene.

In August, three months before Perepilichny was found dead, now Lieutenant Colonel Karpov of the Moscow Police filed a libel suit against Browder in the High Court of London. It was announced that to handle his libel action Karpov had retained the services of Andrew Caldecott QC, one of the most expensive libel barristers around, and Geraldine Proudler of the corporate law firm Olswang. Karpov's defence lawyers had little doubt about who was going to win until the day when Mr Justice Simon decided to throw out the claim ruling that the case could not proceed on the grounds that the Russian did not have a prior reputation in England and Wales to defend. Subsequently, Karpov's libel suit against Hermitage was struck out as an abuse of process and the claimant was obliged to pay Hermitage's legal costs, which he failed to do. At one moment, when the High Court ordered him to attend court for questioning about his assets Karpov, rather impetuously, sent a mocking poem to the Hermitage lawyers instead of an appropriate response. As a result, during the May 2017 hearing, Mr Justice Haddon-Cave ordered the bailiffs and constables to arrest Karpov the moment he set foot on British soil for contempt of court and disobedience.

Karpov won his case against Hermitage Capital Management, its CEO William Browder and Jamison Firestone, co-founder of the law firm Firestone Duncan, in Moscow, as reported by *Life*.

In September 2012, Jean-Michel Orieux stepped down as Ping Pong CEO and became CEO of the UK division of the French bakery chain Paul. He grew Ping Pong into an 11-strong operation launching internationally. Paul Sarlas, an Australian, replaced Orieux as head of the Ping Pong restaurant group owned by Igor Sagiryan. After less than a year Sarlas, in turn, stepped down as chief executive giving way to Art Sagiryan, the son of Igor.

On 14 December, President Obama signed the Magnitsky Bill (with Senator Cardin's List) into law, which became formally known as 'Russia and Moldova Jackson-Vanik Repeal and Sergei Magnitsky Rule of Law Accountability Act of 2012'. All those whose names are on the list are prohibited from entering the US and using its banking system. Although Pavel Karpov was on the list, he was not banned from travelling to the UK when the London High Court was deciding on his case.

Soon after, President Putin signed Russia's 'asymmetric response' to the Magnitsky Act. It included the names of 71 Americans who Russia announced *persona non grata*. At the top of the list were officials from the US Department of Justice and those law enforcement officers who prosecuted and convicted the arms smuggler Victor Bout, Russia's infamous 'Merchant of Death'. Then followed some American lawmakers and those who lobbied for the Magnitsky Bill. The list ends with several former members of the President George W. Bush administration and the officers in charge of the secret CIA prisons in Europe.[25]

---

[25] Shortly before this book went to press, I received a copy of 'The Testimony of Natalia Veselnitskaya before the United States Senate Committee on the Judiciary', chaired by Charles E. Grassley, of 20 November 2017. I also managed to watch Andrei Nekrasov's documentary *The Magnitsky Act: Behind the Scenes*. I am not a friend of Russia and, like Andrei, a severe critic of the Kremlin's politics. But I absolutely liked what Veselnitskaya said in her concluding remarks: 'After witnessing in April 2016 the pulling of Nekrasov's film in Brussels, reading in the media press how liberals dragged Nekrasov through the mud and several weeks later analyzing what happened in the hearing in the House Foreign Affairs Committee on May 18, 2016, and then his colleagues used the same words only because he dared (!) to call Browder a conman and his story very questionable, for America to call its laws after an individual whose story can be a fraud, I thought we will probably never be the same. This sickening feeling of injustice and humiliation over the law caused me a desire to come to Congress and testify in person. Anyone who wants to get down objectively to the bottom of this story simply can't but share the dismay at how in the global centre of the freedom of speech – the United States – this freedom has morphed into the most heinous form of abuse that led to the real cold war imposed on all of us.'

As soon as the 2016 US presidential elections were behind him, Donald Trump made a spectacle of his consideration of Mitt Romney for the role of America's chief diplomat. The two met at Trump's golf course and dined on frog legs. The President-elect expressed his admiration of his guest and his achievements, and after the dinner Romney said to the reporters that they had a 'discussion about affairs throughout the world, and these discussions I've had with him have been enlightening and interesting and engaging. I've enjoyed them very, very much.' As *The New York Times* sarcastically put it, 'If you had asked Romney at that moment what he thought about Trump University, he'd probably have announced plans to enrol.' However, shortly afterwards Trump said he was passing over Romney for the post. In March 2018, he dismissed Rex Tillerson, who he had previously appointed, and nominated Mark Pompeo, the Director of the CIA, as his foreign policy chief. In April, the Senate confirmed Pompeo as the United States' 70th Secretary of State. Gina Haspel succeeded him as a new CIA director, the first woman named to the position. She is a career spymaster who once ran a CIA prison in Thailand.

During those April days, the judicial inquiry to ascertain the facts relating to Perepilichny's death continued at the Old Bailey in London in front of Nicholas Hilliard, the coroner. 'There is a strong probability,' Bill Browder told the inquest, 'that Alexander Perepilichny was murdered.' This time he was probably right although Detective Superintendent Ian Pollard of the Surrey Police said the original post-mortem did not find signs of third-party involvement or foul play and the second post-mortem returned inconclusive.

Whatever the final decision of the coroner, it is not going to be objective because in difficult cases it is common practice for the pathologist, when providing a cause of death, to be asked to indicate whether in his or her opinion death was natural or otherwise. However, with regards to the death of Alexander Perepilichny, like in the cases of Litvinenko, Berezovsky and Skripal, the government is refusing to release 'super-sensitive' evidence, which could shed light on the real circumstances surrounding those people. (When this book went to press, Sergei Skripal and his daughter were considered to be legally alive although in hiding.) The former Home Secretary, Amber Rudd, had made an application preventing the disclosure of intelligence files concerning Perepilichny. She had also filed a public interest immunity certificate arguing that disclosure of possible evidence collected by the Security Service MI5 and SIS, their sister agency, might damage national security. According to *The Guardian*, around a hundred Surrey Police documents were also withheld. 'This,' Luke Harding writes, 'included two documents described as especially secret.'

In September 2018 it was announced that Sajid Javid, former managing director at Deutsche Bank appointed Home Secretary,[26] lodged a secrecy application at the inquest citing national security concerns. Sensitive material that could reveal if the Russian was working for or in contact with British intelligence and/or security services before he died will not be made public at his inquest, a coroner has ruled. Andrew O'Connor QC, for the government, said the disclosure of sensitive material

---

[26] Since July 2019, Chancellor of the Exchequer.

raised a 'real risk of serious harm to one or more public interests', *The Guardian* reported.

Like the Litvinenko Inquiry, this inquest has not been without flaws. Thus, Henrietta Hill QC, acting for Hermitage, told the judge considering the Perepilichny case that there were striking parallels between his death and the murder of Alexander Litvinenko, although she knew about the latter case only from official reports and had no way of comparing them based on primary sources. 'What we have here at its highest,' she announced, 'is a reprisal killing on British soil by poisoning of an individual living in the UK whose death has been perpetrated by a Russian crime group with links to the Russian state.' As expected, Ms Hill failed to produce a single bit of proof supporting her claim.

Perepilichny stomach contents were discarded after the autopsy and two post-mortem examinations had failed to find a cause of his death. It took detectives a week to discover his shadowy deals in Russia and with Russian-related businesses elsewhere, despite the fact that Perepilichny featured in the Serious Organised Crime Agency (SOCA) database and that a communication from Interpol in 2010 claimed Perepilichny was suspected of 'fraud, money laundering and abuse of power',[27] the inquest heard.

I did not hesitate in sending this chapter to the publisher before the Perepilichny inquest was over and the verdict announced. I knew there would be nothing in the hearings to contradict or support my version that a psychotronic weapon could have been used in Weybridge, possibly as a test in preparation for a more important operation against Berezovsky. In 2019, I had little doubt that Perepilichny's demise would for a long time remain an unexplained death.

---

[27] 'Russian Alexander Perepilichny had "criminal links",' *BBC News*, 2 June 2016.

СОВ. СЕКРЕТНО

СССР
НАРОДНЫЙ КОМИССАРИАТ
ВНУТРЕННИХ ДЕЛ

"___" марта 1940 г.
№ 794/б

г. МОСКВА

ЦК ВКП(б)

товарищу СТАЛИНУ

В лагерях для военнопленных НКВД СССР и в тюрьмах западных областей Украины и Белоруссии в настоящее время содержится большое количество бывших офицеров польской армии, бывших работников польской полиции и разведывательных органов, членов польских националистических к-р партий, участников вскрытых к-р повстанческих организаций, перебежчиков и пр. Все они являются заклятыми врагами советской власти, преисполненными ненависти к советскому строю.

Военнопленные офицеры и полицейские, находясь в лагерях, пытаются продолжать к-р работу, ведут антисоветскую агитацию. Каждый из них только и ждет освобождения, чтобы иметь возможность активно включиться в борьбу против советской власти.

Органами НКВД в западных областях Украины и Белоруссии вскрыт ряд к-р повстанческих организаций. Во всех этих к-р организациях активную руководящую роль играли бывшие офицеры бывшей польской армии, бывшие полицейские и жандармы.

Среди задержанных перебежчиков и нарушителей гос-

т. Калинин - за
Каганович - за

A letter from the People's Commissariat for Internal Affairs to Stalin, dated March 1940, asking to sanction the execution of thousands of Polish prisoners – an event that later became known as the Katyn massacre.

Appendix II

Special Tasks: Assassination Files

- Fanny Kaplan, a young revolutionary who allegedly tried to assassinate Lenin, was detained by a vigilante (it was not a citizen's arrest), handed over to the VeCheka and later shot by the former sailor Pavel Malkov, the Kremlin commandant, Moscow, 3 September 1918.
- Alexander Ilyich Dutov, Lieutenant General, one of the leaders of the Cossack anti-revolutionary movement, assassinated by a Bolshevik agent in Suidun (now Shuiding), China, 6 February 1921.
- Vladimir Stepanovich Nesterovich (alias 'Mieczysław Jarosławski'), RU resident agent in Vienna, defected to Germany, poisoned in Mainz, Germany, by Comintern agents, brothers Arthur and Gustav Golke, 6 August 1925.
- Ignacy Lugwig-Marian Gintowt-Dziewałtowski (alias 'Yurin', aka Ignaty Leonovich Dzevaltovsky), in 1924 – ICCI representative in Bulgaria, from March to November 1925 – RU resident agent in Lithuania, defected to Poland, poisoned by a female Soviet agent in Warsaw, Poland, December 1925.
- Symon Vasylyovych Petlyura, journalist, writer, politician, nationalist leader, head of the Ukrainian Army and State in February–December 1919, emigrated to France in early 1924, assassinated (shot) by Sholom Schwartzbard, a Ukrainian anarchist of Jewish descent and allegedly a Soviet agent, Paris, 25 May 1926.
- White Guard general Baron Peter Nikolayevich Wrangel, the last commander-in-chief of the Russian Imperial Army, evacuated the remnants of the White forces and the Russian Imperial Navy from the Crimea in 1920, poisoned by his butler's brother, allegedly a Soviet agent, Brussels, 25 April 1928.
- White Guard general Alexander Pavlovich Kutepov, evacuated with his corps from the Crimea in November 1920, moved to Bulgaria then to France in 1924, after the death of General Wrangel appointed commander of the ROVS, kidnapped in Paris by Soviet OGPU agents, 26 January 1930.
- Georg Semmelmann, former OGPU agent and defector, murdered by another OGPU agent, Andreas Piklovič, who shot his victim twice in the head, Vienna, 25 July 1931.
- Hans Wissinger, a Comintern courier, allegedly assassinated by Soviet agents Hugo Marx and George Mink, Hamburg, 22 May 1932.
- Witold Szturm de Sztrem, until 1933 a member of the underground RU spy network in Austria, disappeared without any trace in the vicinity of Vienna, December 1933.
- Valentin Markin, underground RU operative in Germany (1926–9), later OGPU-NKVD head of station in New York, was found in the Luxor Hotel in Manhattan with a severe head wound, subsequently dying in a hospital, 1934.

- Dmitry Sergeyevich Navashin, former banker and freemason, stabbed to death allegedly by NKVD officer of special reserve Panteleimon Takhchiyanov, Paris, 25 January 1937.
- Mark Rein, Trotsky's sympathiser who maintained contact with him in Norway, disappeared in Barcelona, 9 April 1937.
- Juliet Stuart Poyntz, a former agent of the Special Tasks Group in Paris, recruited by the RU in October 1934 and a month later sent to New York, where she disappeared, presumably murdered, 3 June 1937.
- Andrés Nin, a leader of the Spanish revolutionary party POUM, abducted and killed by NKVD agents, Alcalá de Henares near Madrid, 20 June 1937
- Hans Freund (Moulin), former secretary of Trotsky, abducted and murdered in Barcelona, 2 August 1937.
- Ignatz Reiss, an important NKVD defector, shot and murdered by NKVD agents in Lausanne, Switzerland, 4 September 1937.
- Erwin Wolf, former secretary of Trotsky, disappeared in Barcelona, 13 September 1937.
- Karl Landau, former POUM secretary, abducted and murdered in Barcelona, 23 September 1937.
- Nikolai Vladimirovich Skoblin, former general of the Russian Army and an NKVD agent, took part in the abduction of General Miller in Paris, assassinated in Spain by the NKVD agents commanded by Lev Nikolsky (aka 'Alexander Orlov'); Barcelona, late October 1937.
- Ivan Solonevich, editor-in-chief of *The Voice of Russia*, survived an assassination attempt in Sofia, Bulgaria, 3 February 1938.
- Georges Agabekov, an important OGPU defector and later author, who escaped an abduction attempt by Soviet agents in Constanza, Romania, on 11 January 1932, was last seen in Paris in March 1938, murdered by NKVD, most likely in Barcelona, Spain.
- Yevhen Oleksiyovych Konovalets, leader of the Organization of Ukrainian Nationalists (OUN), blown up by NKVD agent Pavel Sudoplatov, Rotterdam, Holland, 23 May 1938.
- Rudolf Klement, former secretary of Trotsky, secretary of the Movement for the IV International, killed in Paris, 13 July 1938. His decapitated and mutilated body was recovered from the Seine at Meulan, about 20 miles from the French capital, at the end of August 1938.
- White Guard General Yevgeny Karlovich Miller, emigrated to Norway in February 1920 and from there to France, abducted by NKVD agents in Paris 22 September 1937, later imprisoned and shot in Moscow, 11 May 1939.
- The Soviet invasion of Poland was a secret Soviet military operation that started without a formal declaration of war on 17 September 1939. In October, the Soviet foreign minister Vyacheslav Molotov reported to the leadership that the Soviets had suffered 737 deaths and 1,862 casualties during the campaign, although Polish specialists claim up to 3,000 deaths and 8,000–10,000 wounded. According to Polish sources, on the Polish side, 3,000–7,000 soldiers died fighting the Red Army, with 230,000–450,000 taken prisoner. Additionally, according to various

sources, the Soviets killed tens of thousands of Polish prisoners-of-war. On 24 September the Soviets killed 42 staff and patients of the Polish military hospital in the village of Grabowiec, near Zamość. More than 20,000 Polish military personnel and civilians perished in the Katyn massacre carried out by the NKVD in April and May 1940 following Stalin's orders approved by the Politburo.

- The Winter War was a military conflict between the Soviet Union and Finland, which began with the Soviet invasion of Finland on 30 November 1939. According to the estimates by Finnish historians (2005), 25,904 persons died or went missing and 43,557 were wounded on the Finnish side during the war. This accounts for a total of around 70,000 casualties. The war ended with the Moscow Peace Treaty on 13 March 1940.

- Trotsky (born Lev Davidovich Bronstein), leader of the Bolshevik revolution and founder of the IV International, survived an armed attack on his home by a group of Soviet agents headed by David Alfaro Siqueiros in Mexico City on 24 May 1940. Three months after the first attack, Trotsky was assassinated in his house by NKVD agent Ramón Mercader, who used an ice axe as a weapon, Mexico City, 20 August 1940. Trotsky was taken to a hospital, operated on but died on the next day.

- Strange and unexplained suicide of the Soviet defector Walter Krivitsky, Washington, DC, 10 February 1941.

- Julius Trossin, a German-born courier of the RU, whose path crossed Soviet espionage operations in Germany, Romania, Finland, Estonia and the United States, came to the attention of the police and was arrested in Hamburg on 6 July 1933. As a result, a large RU network was exposed and links to the station in Britain broken. Trossin was 'turned' by the Gestapo and agreed to return to the USSR as a German agent. There, the OGPU arrested him in November 1933 and he was sentenced to ten years in jail. In September 1941, he was shot near the town of Orel.

- Franz von Papen, a German nobleman, General Staff officer and politician, Chancellor of Germany in 1932 and vice chancellor under Adolf Hitler 1933–4, German ambassador to Vienna, Austria, and later Reich's ambassador to Turkey. His assassination was organised by the NKVD, but the bomb carried out by a 25-year-old Yugoslav Moslem named Omer Tokat, a communist student of the Istanbul University's Law School, prematurely exploded killing no one except the assassin himself, Ankara, Atatürk Boulevard, 24 February 1942.

- Vsevolod Aleksandrovich Blumenthal-Tamarin, Russian and Soviet actor with German roots who, after the Nazi invasion of the Soviet Union, collaborated with the Germans by taking part in several campaigns organised by the Reich Ministry of Public Enlightenment and Propaganda in 1941–45. Blümenthal-Tamarin was assassinated on 10 May 1945 in Münsinger, Switzerland, not far from the German-Swiss border. Allegedly, the assassin was an NKVD agent and one of Blumenthal's distant relatives by the name of Igor Miklashevsky. Although this fact is mentioned in several published sources, including Anthony Beevor's book about Olga Chekhova, this information cannot be verified.

- Raul Gustaf Wallenberg, a Swedish architect, businessman and diplomat, detained by the Soviet SMERSH in January 1945 while serving as his country's special envoy to Budapest, he subsequently disappeared. Wallenberg was later reported to have died in a Moscow NKVD prison on 17 July 1947.

- Jan Masaryk, Czech foreign minister in 1940–1948, according to a police report of 2004, was thrown out of his bathroom window in Prague, 10 March 1948.
- Assassination attempt against Marshal Josip Broz Tito of Yugoslavia by Soviet undercover agent Iosif Grigulevich, Belgrade, 1953.
- Wolfgang Salus, one of Trotsky's former secretaries, poisoned by the MGB agent Otto Freitag in Munich, 13 February 1953, died on 4 March 1953.
- Georgi Okolovich, one of NTS's leaders and anti-Soviet émigré, survived an assassination attempt because the MGB assassin, Nikolai Khokhlov, refused to carry out his assignment to commit murder, Frankfurt am Main, 18 February 1954.
- Alexander Trushnovich, also one of NTS's leaders and anti-Soviet émigré, abducted from West Berlin's British Sector with the help of Stasi agent Heinz Glezke and choked to death on the way to the Soviet Zone on 13 April 1954. He was spirited back from Germany to the Soviet Union and secretly buried.
- Valery Tremmel of the NTS, abducted in Linz, Austria, June 1954.
- Georgy Khrulev, another NTS member, abducted in West Berlin in the autumn of 1954, brought to the Soviet Union and placed in a labour camp.
- Robert Bialek, former General Inspector of the East German Interior Ministry and one of the co-founders of the Stasi, defected to West Germany in 1953. Bialek was forcefully transported to East Berlin on 4 February 1956 and executed in prison.
- The Hungarian Revolution or the Hungarian Uprising of 1956 was a nationwide revolt against the government of the Hungarian People's Republic and its Soviet-imposed policies. On 4 November, Soviet troops invaded Budapest and crushed the revolution. More than 2,500 Hungarians and 700 Soviet troops were killed in the conflict, and 200,000 Hungarians fled as refugees. Mass arrests and denunciations continued for months thereafter. By January 1957, the new Soviet-installed government had suppressed all public opposition. Soviet ambassador Yuri Andropov, his assistant Vladimir Kryuchkov and the KGB chief Ivan Serov played leading behind-the-scenes roles in the operation, codenamed VIHR, to suppress the uprising.
- Nikolai Yevgenyevich Khokhlov, captain of the Soviet MGB who refused to murder Georgy Okolovich in Frankfurt/Main, poisoned by a mixture of unidentified drugs, allegedly containing radioactive isotope Thallium-202, Germany, 15 September 1957.
- Lev Rebet, an important political figure of the OUN, murdered by KGB agent Bogdan Stashinsky with the help of a specially constructed poison gun, Munich, 15 October 1957.
- Géza Losonczy, journalist and politician, Minister of Press and Propaganda in the Imre Nagy government of 1956. Arrested in April 1957. In prison, he went on a hunger strike and died shortly before the trial, Budapest, 21 December 1957.
- Imre Nagy, Hungarian communist politician. Nagy enlisted in the Austro-Hungarian Army during the First World War and served on the Eastern Front

where he was taken prisoner. Changed sides and joined the Russian Communist Party and the Red Army. In 1930 became a Soviet citizen. Nagy had been an active NKVD agent codenamed VOLODYA since January 1933. Appointed the Prime Minister of Hungary, he soon fell out of favour with the Soviet leadership and was sacked. During the anti-Soviet Hungarian Uprising of 1956, became the PM again. Arrested, secretly tried, found guilty of treason and executed by hanging in a Budapest prison, 16 June 1958.

- Pál Maléter, Major General of the Hungarian Army, fought on the Eastern Front in the Second World War with Nazi troops, captured by the Red Army, changed sides, became a communist and was trained by the GRU in sabotage and subversive operations. Later parachuted behind German lines. Returned to Hungary after the war. In 1956 changed sides again, joined the Hungarian Uprising and on 29 October was appointed Minister of Defence in the Imre Nagy government. On 4 November, together with other members of the official Hungarian delegation, arrested by the KGB at the Soviet military base in Tököl as part of Operation VIHR ('Whirlwind'). Later sentenced to death and hanged with Nagy and the Hungarian journalist Miklós Gimes in the courtyard of a Budapest prison, 16 June 1958.

- Miklós Gimes, Hungarian journalist born in 1917. His parents, medical doctors and specialists in psychoanalysis, were active supporters of the Hungarian Soviet Republic of Béla Kun in 1919. A devoted Stalinist, Gimes became a communist journalist reporting from Zurich, Vienna and Paris in 1954. Took an active part in the Hungarian Uprising. Arrested in December 1956, executed with Nagy and Maléter in Budapest, 16 June 1958.

- Stepan Andriyovych Bandera, Ukrainian political activist and leader of the nationalist movement for the independence of Ukraine, murdered by KGB agent Bogdan Stashinsky using a specially constructed gun charged with highly toxic Hydrogen cyanide (HCN) gas, Munich, 12 October 1959.

- An apartment house where NTS families, including children, lived was blown up – miraculously, no victims, Sprendlingen, Germany, July 1958.

- Béla Lapusnyik, the Hungarian AVH defector (AVH – Allamvedelmi Hatosag – was the much feared and hated Hungarian communist secret police), poisoned in a special security prison and died in the Vienna General Hospital (AKH) on 4 June 1962.

- Victor Andreyevich Kravchenko, Soviet foreign trade official, defected to the United States during the Second World War. In 1949, he sued the French Communist Party for libel in what became known as the trial of the century, which he won. Kravchenko was found dead from a gunshot wound to his head in his apartment in Manhattan, New York, 25 February 1966.

- Vladimir Nikolayevich Voinovich, a Soviet dissident writer, poisoned by KGB officers in the Moscow Metropol hotel, 11 May 1975. Voinovich was stripped of his Soviet citizenship and expelled from the country in 1980, lived in exile in Munich, returned to Russia in 1990. Died in Moscow in July 2018.

- Nikolai Fedorovich Artamonov (aka Nicholas Shadrin), Soviet naval officer who defected to the United States in 1959, abducted by KGB agents in Vienna and died on the Austrian-Czech border, 21 December 1975.

- Vladimir Kostov, a Bulgarian defector, shot in the back by a ricin-laced pellet, survived the assassination attempt, Paris, 28 August 1978.
- Georgi Markov, another Bulgarian dissident and a former member of the close circle of the Bulgarian communist leader Todor Zhivkov, poisoned in London by a pellet containing ricin in what became known as 'The Umbrella Murder', 7 September 1978.
- The Soviet-Afghan War began with the Soviet invasion of Afghanistan on 24 December 1979. Arriving in the capital Kabul, the KGB supported by Spetsnaz troops staged a coup killing President Amin and installing Soviet loyalist Barak Karmal. The conflict lasted nine years until February 1989. According to several sources, between 562,000 and 2,000,000 civilians were killed and millions of Afghans fled the country. The final and complete withdrawal of Soviet forces began on 15 May 1988 and ended on 15 February 1989 under President Mikhail Gorbachev.
- Afghan leader Hafizzulah Amin, poisoned by the undercover Soviet operator, Colonel Mitalin Talybov (codenamed SABIR), posing as his cook, and then shot by a Spetsnaz unit in his Tajbeg Palace in Kabul, 27 December 1979.
- Boris Korczak, a CIA operative who was deployed to Denmark as an access agent with some electronics business as his front but managed to get recruited by the KGB in Copenhagen. In November 1979, his cover was blown by the CIA head of station during a reception at the Soviet Embassy. Korczak returned to the US where, like Markov and Kostov, he was shot with a ricin-laced pellet while shopping in a food store in Vienna, Virginia, August 1981. The agent survived.
- Sergey Yuryevich Kholodov, a Russian journalist who investigated corruption in the Soviet Army especially in its units stationed in East Germany. His assassination, aged 27, by a booby-trapped briefcase bomb was the first of many killings of journalists in Russia. Moscow, 17 October 1994.
- Ivan Kharlampievich Kivelidi, a Russian journalist-come-businessman and banker of Greek descent (and a few days later, his secretary) died after both contacted the landline telephone receiver dosed with a powerful toxic substance that had not been publicly identified, almost certainly the nerve agent 'Novichok' (designated A-232), Moscow, 4 August 1995.
- Dzhokhar Dudayev, first president of the Chechen Republic of Ichkeria, assassinated by two laser-guided missiles as a single victim of a covert operation by the Russian special forces, Chechnya, 21 April 1996.
- Vladimir I. Ryashentsev, former general manager of the cooperative ANT, died under unclear circumstances aged 47, Los Angeles, 1 July 1997.
- Galina Vasilievna Starovoitova, a Soviet dissident and later a Russian politician and MP, gunned down while entering her apartment building in St Petersburg, 20 November 1998.
- Gennady Berkovsky (also spelt Berkovski), a former KGB colonel, was shot dead on 24 July 2000 outside his Benowa Waters mansion in the suburb of the Gold Coast, a city in the Australian state of Queensland.
- Vladimir Artyomovich Pasechnik, the head of the Soviet bioweapons programme at the Biopreparat facility, a world-class microbiologist and a high-profile Russian

defector to the UK in 1989, was found dead not far from his British home. He was in good health but died suddenly from a stroke. A nerve agent that mimics a stroke and leaves no traces was believed to be the cause of his death in Wiltshire, England (where Sergei Skripal and his daughter were allegedly poisoned), 23 November 2001.

- Dzhabrail Yamadayev, commander of the Russian GRU Spetsnaz unit Vostok, assassinated by a bomb blast in Dyshne Vedeno, Chechnya, 5 March 2003.
- Sergey Nikolayevich Yushenkov, a liberal Russian politician and an MP since 1989, who together with Boris Berezovsky co-founded a new political party, Liberal Russia, shot dead near his house in Moscow, 17 April 2003.
- Yuri Petrovich Shchekochikhin, an investigative journalist, writer and liberal lawmaker in the Russian Parliament, died suddenly from a mysterious illness just before his scheduled departure to the US where he planned to meet with FBI investigators for the second time to discuss some money-laundering issues. His medical documents have been classified by the Russian authorities. The symptoms of his illness were similar to those of Roman Tsepov and Alexander Litvinenko. Moscow, 3 July 2003.
- Zelimkhan Yandarbiyev, the acting president of Chechnya, blown up in his car by Russian GRU operatives in Doha, Qatar, 13 February 2004.
- Victor Andriyovych Yushchenko, poisoned by FSB/SVR operatives in collaboration with their Ukrainian counterparts by adding a complex 2,3,7,8 TCDD-AFP agent in his food, Kiev, 4–5 September 2004.
- Roman Igorevich Tsepov, founder of the security company Baltik Escort controlled by Victor Zolotov, Putin's personal bodyguard. As one of the most influential figures in the financial and political life of St Petersburg, Tsepov took part in the first presidential inaugural ceremony of Vladimir Putin. On 11 September, several hours after visiting his contacts at the local FSB office where he had a cup of tea, Tsepov collapsed with the same symptoms as Litvinenko and died after suffering severe radiation sickness before he could be taken to a specialist hospital in Germany, 24 September 2004.
- Aslan Maskhadov, third President of the Chechen Republic of Ichkeria, killed in an operation by FSB special forces in Chechnya, Tolstoy-Yurt, 8 March 2005.
- Anatoly Vasilyevich Trofimov, former head of the KGB investigation department and later deputy director of the FSB, assassinated by an unidentified gunman, Moscow, 10 April 2005. He who lived wickedly could hardly die honestly, they say.
- Abdul-Halim Sadulayev, fourth president of the Chechen Republic of Ichkeria, killed in a gun battle with the FSB troops and pro-Moscow militiamen in Argun, Chechnya, 17 June 2006.
- Andrey Andreyevich Kozlov, First Deputy Chairman of the Central Bank of Russia, credited with combating 'grey schemes' of Russian private banks trying to halt their money-laundering operations for corrupt officials in the Russian government (and, unbeknown to him, for the Russian Intelligence Services); shot in the head by two assassins in a parking lot of a football stadium in Moscow, 13 September 2006. Kozlov died early the next day.
- Anna Stepanovna Politkovskaya (née Hanna Mazepa, New York, NY, August 1958), a Russian investigative journalist, writer and human rights activist of international

repute, shot and murdered in her apartment house on Putin's birthday, Moscow, 7 October 2006.

- Alexander Walterovich Litvinenko, Russian defector, assistant to Boris Berezovsky, poisoned on 1 November by a complex substance containing radioactive Polonium-210, died in London, 23 November 2006.
- Yegor Timurovich Gaidar, Soviet and Russian economist and politician, acting Prime Minister of Russia from June to December 1992, unexpectedly died on 16 December 2009 in his country house in the Moscow region. Gaidar was deliberately poisoned by Russian secret services during his visit to Ireland to divert attention from the poisoning of Alexander Litvinenko. Maynooth, Co. Kildare, 24 November 2006.
- Igor Ponomarev, Permanent Representative of the Russian Federation to the International Maritime Organization (IMO), as such, he was a colleague and good acquaintance of Mario Scaramella, who played the role of liaison between Litvinenko and the Mitrokhin Commission of the Italian Parliament. Suddenly and mysteriously, Ponomarev died aged 41 from unknown causes because the Russian Embassy rushed the IMO diplomat's body back to Moscow without an autopsy being conducted in the UK. His death may also be a result of poisoning to divert attention from Litvinenko and cast a shadow on Scaramella. London, 30 October 2006.
- Arkady 'Badri' Patarkatsyshvili, a Russian-Georgian businessman, later one of the wealthiest Georgians worldwide, a long-time friend and business associate of Boris Berezovsky, who contested the 2008 Georgian presidential election finishing third. Badri collapsed at his home, Downside Manor, and died in his own bed in Leatherhead, Surrey, England, on 12 February 2008. Even in this case, assassination cannot be completely ruled out. In October 2018, the government of Georgia accused the former president Mikheil Saakashvili of masterminding the assassination of Badri.
- Alnur Musayev, Kazakhstan's former intelligence chief, survived an attempt to kidnap him by four Russian-speaking gunmen, Vienna, 22 September 2008.
- Ruslan Yamadayev, Chechen military leader and politician, Hero of Russia, assassinated on the way back from a meeting in the Kremlin, Moscow, 24 September 2008.
- Karinna Akopovna Moskalenko, a Russian human rights lawyer and her family were poisoned by mercury found in her car, causing her and her three children to suffer headaches, nausea, vomiting and heart problems, Strasbourg, 13 October 2008.
- Umar Israilov, former bodyguard of the Chechen president Ramzan Kadyrov, who abandoned the pro-Russian Chechen camp and became an outspoken critic of Kadyrov, fatally shot as he walked out of a grocery store, after an attempt to kidnap him failed, Vienna, 6 January 2009.
- Stanislav Yuryevich Markelov, a Russian human rights lawyer, shot to death by a single gunman in broad daylight in central Moscow, 19 January 2009. Anastasiya Baburova, a Ukrainian student of journalism in Moscow, was killed with Markelov.

- Sulim Yamadayev, a de facto commander of the Russian GRU Spetsnaz unit Vostok, shot in the back of the neck in an underground garage by a Russian agent (later Interpol issued arrest warrants for seven Russian citizens of Chechen origin); Dubai, 29 March 2009.
- Natalya Estemirova, a human rights activist and board member of the Russian historical and civil rights society memorial, abducted by unknown persons around 8:30 a.m. near her home in Grozny, Chechnya, 15 July 2009. Presumed dead.
- Sergei Knyazev (aka Serykh), a former GRU military intelligence officer, emigrated with his family to Canada and from there to Great Britain; jumped to his death with his wife and stepson from a block of flats in Scotland used to house asylum seekers, Glasgow, 7 March 2010.
- On 10 April 2010, the Tupolev Tu-154 (NATO reporting name CARELESS) aircraft of the Polish Air Force crashed near the city of Smolensk, Russia, killing all 96 people on board. Among the victims were the President of Poland Lech Kaczyński and his wife Maria, the former President of Poland in exile Ryszard Kaczorowski, the chief of the Polish General Staff and other senior Polish military officers, the president of the National Bank of Poland, Polish government officials, 18 members of the Polish Parliament, senior members of the Polish clergy and relatives of the victims of the Katyn massacre carried out by the Soviet NKVD in April and May 1940. The group was arriving from Warsaw to attend an event commemorating the 70th anniversary of mass executions of Polish nationals that took place not far from Smolensk. In January 2018, the Polish government subcommittee re-investigating the accident claimed that a number of explosions had occurred aboard the airliner. On 11 April 2018, the committee for re-investigation of the crash of TU-154M in Smolensk, Russia, appointed by the Polish government, published a new, preliminary report in which it concluded that the aircraft was 'destroyed in the air as a result of several explosions'. More than eight years after the accident, the report states, the Russian Federation still maintains possession of the plane wreckage, the black boxes with original flight data recordings and other evidentiary material.
- Sergei Olegovich Tretyakov, colonel of the SVR (Russian foreign intelligence), deputy head of station under the diplomatic cover of First Secretary of the Russian UN Mission in New York, spied for the CIA and FBI, defected in October 2000. Ten years after his changing sides, Tretyakov died at his home aged 53 and many suspected and still suspect foul play. However, Pete Earley, the American journalist and writer who interviewed Tretyakov for his book *Comrade J.* (2008), wrote to this author: 'I do not believe his death was in any way related to the SVR and Russia, despite their best efforts to claim credit. The autopsy shows that he choked on chicken, which Helen [his wife] had fixed him. This is consistent with what she told me the day of his death when she was so upset. This is also consistent with what the FBI found and also the local police.' In an official statement, his wife said he had died of a heart attack. Florida, 13 June 2010.
- Ahmed Zakayev, former actor, deputy prime minister and prime minister of the unrecognised Chechen Republic of Ichkeria, as well as foreign minister under presidents Maskhadov and Sadulayev, who took part in military operations against

the Russian forces during two Chechen wars. Since January 2002, Zakayev and his family have been permanently residing in London having been granted political asylum a year later. In his exile, Zakayev had been supported by Boris Berezovsky, Norwegian businessman Ivar Amundsen, and his actress friend Vanessa Redgrave. He also maintained close friendly relations with Litvinenko and Gordievsky. After several assassinations of prominent Chechen personalities that became internationally known, the security service MI5 issued an unprecedented public warning that Zakayev was the target of a murder plot, London, May 2012.

- Alexander Yuryevich Perepilichny, a Russian whistleblower who died under mysterious circumstances, most probably assassinated by Russian agents, Surrey, England, 10 November 2012.

- Boris Abramovich Berezovsky, an academic, member of the Russian Academy of Sciences, business tycoon and politician, probably the most prominent opponent of the Kremlin regime in exile after Trotsky. Berezovsky was found dead in his former wife's home. Although the post-mortem examination found that his death was consistent with hanging, the coroner at the inquest recorded an open verdict. If the body of the dead man was indeed that of Boris Berezovsky, there must be little or no doubt that the Kremlin's enemy number 1 was assassinated, Titness Park, Sunninghill, Berkshire, England, 23 March 2013.

- Rakhat Aliyev, a senior official of the government of Kazakhstan – he was chief of the tax police, deputy chief of the state security service (KNB, the successor to the KGB), first deputy foreign minister and twice ambassador to Austria. Until June 2007, Aliyev was married to Dariga Nazarbayeva, the eldest daughter of the Kazakh president. Charged with kidnapping and murder by the Kazakh authorities, Aliyev was taken into custody in June 2014 and jailed at a Vienna high-security prison pending trial. Found dead in his solitary cell in Josefstadt prison – the second such case in Austria where a foul play is suspected, Vienna, 24 February 2015.

- Boris Yefimovich Nemtsov, a successful politician, former deputy prime minister of Russia, governor of the Nizhny Novgorod region, but also an opposition leader and outspoken critic of Vladimir Putin, assassinated on a bridge near the Kremlin with four shots in his back, Moscow, 27 February 2015.

- Pavel Grigorievich Sheremet, a Byelorussian-born Russian and Ukrainian journalist, assassinated by a car bomb in Kiev on 20 July 2016.

- Denis Nikolayevich Voronenkov, a Russian politician and MP first representing the Unity Party and then the Communist Party in the State Duma, in the 2016 legislative election, he lost his seat and emigrated to Ukraine. There, he became a vocal critic of Vladimir Putin and the Russian politics towards Ukraine, actively collaborating with the Ukrainian authorities. Voronenkov was shot dead by a Ukrainian national, Pavel Parshov, in what was without doubt a contract killing with the assassin hired by the Russian Intelligence Services, Kiev, 23 March 2017.

- Maxim Mikhailovich Shapoval, commanding officer of the Ukrainian Spetsnaz of the Chief Directorate of Intelligence of the Ministry of Defence, recently returned from the combat zone in Donbass. At the time of his death as a result of a car bomb explosion, Colonel Shapoval was investigating Russian aggression in eastern Ukraine, collecting intelligence for The Hague international tribunal on war crimes (the International Criminal Court), Kiev, 27 June 2017.

- Sergei Viktorovich Skripal, former GRU officer, posted to Malta and then Spain, where SIS recruited him as an agent-in-place, betrayed by a Russian mole in the Spanish National Intelligence Centre (CNI) Roberto Flórez García. Allegedly poisoned by a nerve agent together with his daughter in Salisbury, Wiltshire, on 4 March 2018. Fate unknown.

- Three Russian journalists – Kirill Radchenko, Alexander Rastorguyev and Orkhan Dzhemal – went to the Central African Republic (CAR) in July 2018 to investigate the activities of Russian private military contractors. They were shot dead after the vehicle in which they were travelling was attacked on a remote road in the volatile country. Their fate has cast a spotlight on a growing Russian presence in Africa, involving the Kremlin, private companies with ties to the Russian president and large shipments of weapons, CNN reported. New evidence shows that the journalists were victims of a well-planned ambush involving a senior police officer with shadowy Russian connections.

- In June 2017, in an interview with the American writer and filmmaker Oliver Stone for a four-part television series, the President of Russia, Vladimir Putin, said that he has survived five assassination attempts.

Abbreviations and Acronyms

ACA	Alias Cover Address, SIS
AFP	Agence France-Press
APN	Agency Press News, USSR
ARCOS	All-Russian Co-operative Society, joint trade organization
AWE	Atomic Weapons Establishment, UK
BfS	Bundesamt für Strahlenschutz ('Federal Office for Radiation Protection'), Germany
BKA	Bundeskriminalamt ('Federal Criminal Police Office'), Germany
BND	Bundesnachrichtendienst ('Federal Intelligence Service'), Germany
BOB	Berlin Operations Base of the CIA
BRD	Bundesrepublik Deutschland ('Federal Republic of Germany'), West Germany
BVT	Bundesamt für Verfassungsschutz und Terrorismusbekämpfung ('Federal Office for the Protection of the Constitution and Counterterrorism'), Austria
'C'	Chief of Secret Intelligence Service, SIS or MI6
C/CEE	Controller, East European Controllerate, SIS
CCI	Central Computer Index
Centre	HQ of the KGB, their predecessors and their successor SVR, previously Lubyanka, now Yasenevo aka 'The Forest'
CERS	Centre d'Etudes et de Recherches Scientifiques ('Scientific Studies and Research Centre'), Syria
CF	Central Facilities department, SIS
Cheka	Chrezvychainaya Komissiya ('Extraordinary Commission for Combating Counter-revolution and Sabotage')
CIA	Central Intelligence Agency, The Agency, USA
CID	Criminal Investigation Division
CNI	Centro Nacional de Inteligencia ('National Intelligence Centre), Spain
CO	Commanding Officer
COMINT	Communications Intelligence
Comms	Communications
CPGB	Communist Party of Great Britain
Comintern	Communist International
CPL	Continental Petroleum Limited
CPSU	Communist Party of the Soviet Union
CPUSA	Communist Party of the USA
CX	Secret SIS report
DDO	Deputy Director for Operations, CIA (until October 2005)

DDP	Deputy Director of Plans, CIA (until March 1973, then DDO)
DDR	Deutsche Demokratische Republik ('German Democratic Republic'), East Germany
DG	Director-General of MI5
DI	Defence Intelligence (since 2009, formerly Defence Intelligence Staff), UK
Directorate S	KGB Directorate in charge of the 'illegals'
DLB	dead letter box
D/NCS	Director of the National Clandestine Service (from October 2005, previously DDO), CIA
DRG	diversionno–razvedyvatelnaya gruppa ('sabotage and reconnaissance group'), USSR/RF
ECCI	Executive Committee of the Communist International
ELINT	Electronic Intelligence
ESP	Extrasensory perception
FBI	Federal Bureau of Investigations, The Bureau, USA
FCD	First Chief Directorate, KGB's foreign intelligence branch, also known as PGU in Russian
FCO	Foreign & Commonwealth Office, aka the Foreign Office, UK
FO	Foreign Office
FPÖ	Freiheitliche Partei Österreichs ('Freedom Party of Austria')
FSB	Federalnaya Sluzhba Bezopasnosti ('Federal Security Service')
FSK	Federalnaya Sluzhba Kontrrazvedki ('Federal Counterintelligence Service'), predecessor of the FSB, RF
FSKN	Federalnaya Sluzhba po Kontrolyu za Narkotikami (that is, 'po kontrolyu za oborotom narkotikov', 'Federal Drug Control Service'), RF
FSO	Federalnaya Sluzhba Okhrany ('Federal Protective Service'), RF
GC&CS	Government Code and Cipher School, UK
GCHQ	Government Communications Headquarters, UK
GPU	Gosudarstvennoe Politicheskoe Upravlenie ('State Political Directorate'), USSR
G/REP	Printing and forging department, SIS
GRU	Glavnoe Razvedupravlenie, Soviet and Russian Military Intelligence, since 2010 – Main Directorate of the General Staff of the Russian Armed Forces
GUEB	Glavnoe Upravlenie Ekonomicheskoi Bezopasnosti ('Chief Directorate of Economic Security')
GUGB	Glavnoe Upravlenie Gosudarstvennoi Bezopasnosti ('Chief Directorate of State Security'), USSR
GULAG	Glavnoe Upravlenie Lagerei ('Chief Directorate of Corrective Labour Camps'), USSR
HMG	Her Majesty's Government, UK
H/MOS	Head of station, Moscow, SIS
HQ	Headquarters
H/SOV/OPS	Head of Soviet Operations, SIS
HUMINT	Human Intelligence (intelligence obtained from human sources)

H/VIE	Head of Vienna station, SIS
ILS	International Lenin School, USSR
IM	Inoffizielle Mitarbeiter ('Unofficial collaborator'), MfS
IMPULSE	Signals monitoring system of the KGB station
INO	Inostrannyi Otdel ('Foreign Intelligence Department'), Soviet Russia and USSR
INS	Immigration and Naturalization Service, USA
IONEC	Intelligence Officer's New Entry Course, SIS
IONS	Institute of Noetic Sciences in California, USA
IRA	Irish Republican Army
JIC	Joint Intelligence Committee, UK
KGB	Komitet Gosudarstvennoi Bezopasnosti ('Committee for State Security'), USSR
KI	Komitet Informatsyi ('Committee of Information'), Soviet foreign intelligence agency
KIM	Kommunisticheskii International Molodiozhy ('Communist International of Youth')
KPD	Kommunistische Partei Deutschlands ('German Communist Party')
KPÖ	Kommunistische Partei Österreichs ('Austrian Communist Party')
KSČ	Komunistická strana Československa, Czech and Slovak Communist Party
Line EM	Work among the Russian community and émigré, KGB station
Line KR	Counterintelligence and security Line of the KGB station
Line N	Illegals Support Line of the KGB station
Line PR	Political intelligence, black propaganda, disinformation, 'active measures' Line of the KGB station
Line X	Scientific & Technical intelligence Line in the KGB station
LKA	Landeskriminalamt ('State Criminal Police Office')
MfS	Ministerium für Staatssicherheit, aka Stasi, DDR
MGB	Ministerstvo Gosudarstvennoi Bezopasnosti ('Ministry of State Security'), USSR
MI1c	Military Intelligence Service 1c, predecessor of MI6
MI5	British Security Service
MI6	Alternative (old) designation for SIS, Secret Intelligence Service, British overseas intelligence agency
MID	Military Intelligence Division, until March 1942 under the General Staff of the US Army
MLAT	Mutual Legal Assistance Treaty
MPS	Metropolitan Police Service, London
MOS/1	Deputy head of Moscow station, SIS
MVD	Ministerstvo Vnutrennikh Del ('Ministry of Internal Affairs'), USSR
NKGB	Narodnyi Komissariat Gosudarstvennoi Bezopasnosti ('People's Commissariat for State Security'), USSR
NKVD	Narodnyi Komissariat Vnutrennikh Del ('People's Commissariat for Internal Affairs'), USSR
NSA	National Security Agency, USA

NTS	Narodno-Trudovoy Soyuz ('People's Labour Union' often for some reason translated as 'National Alliance of Russian Solidarists')
OGPU	Ob'edinennoe Glavnoe Politicheskoe Upravlenie ('Joined Main Political Directorate'), Soviet intelligence and security service, successor of the VCheKa
OibE	Offiziere im besonderen Einsatz ('Officer in the special employment'), MfS
Okhrana	Tsarist security service, Russian Empire, 1881-1917
OKW	Oberkommando der Wehrmacht, Supreme Command of the German Armed Forces
OMS	Otdel Mezhdunarodnykh Svyazei ('International Liaison Department'), the intelligence branch of the Comintern
OMSBON	Otdelnyi Motostrelkovyi Batalion Osobogo Naznacheniya ('Special Motorized Battalion'), NKVD
OSS	Office of Strategic Services, USA
OTU	Operations and Technical Directorate, KGB
OUN	Organization of Ukrainian Nationalists
OV	Operativ-Vorgang ('Operational Record File'), MfS/KGB
ÖVP	Österreichische Volkspartei ('Austrian People's Party')
PCM	Partido Comunista Mexicano ('Mexican Communist Party')
PET	Politiets Efterretningstjeneste, Nationa Security and Intelligence Service of Denmark
PGU	Pervoe Glavnoe Upravlenie ('First Chief Directorate'), foreign intelligence branch of the KGB
Porton Down	Science Park, home of Defence Science and Technology Laboratory of the MoD; and Public Health England
POUM	Partido Obrero de Unificación Marxista ('Workers' Party of Marxist Unification'), Spain
RAF	Royal Air Force, UK
RF	Russian Federation
RKKA	Raboche-Krestyanskaya Krasnaya Armiya ('The Workers-Peasants Red Army')
ROVS	Rossiisky Obschevoiskovoi Soyuz ('Russian Combined Services Union')
RU	Razvedupr, Soviet military intelligence, later GRU
RYAN	Raketno-yadernoe napadenie ('Nuclear Missile Attack')
SAS	Special Air Service, a special forces unit of the British Army
Sayeret Matkal	General Staff Reconnaissance Unit, a special forces unit of the Israel Defence Forces
SBP	Sluzhba Bezopasnosti Prezidenta ('The Presidential Security Service'), RF
SBO	Security Branch Officer, SIS
SBS	Special Boat Service, UK
SBU	Sluzhba Bezpeky Ukrayiny, the Security Service of Ukraine
SCD	Second Chief Directorate, KGB's internal security branch
SIGINT	Signals Intelligence (derived from interception and analysis of signals, whether from communications between people, abbreviated to COMINT, or between devices – ELINT)

SIS	Secret Intelligence Service, UK
SNIE	Special National Intelligence Estimate, USA
SNK	Sovet Narodnykh Komissarov, Council of People's Commissars
SO15	The Counter Terrorism Command or SO15, a Specialist Operations branch within London's Metropolitan Police Service
SOE	Special Operations Executive, UK
SOV/OPS	Soviet Operations department, SIS
Spetsnaz	Special Forces, USSR/RF
SPHP	Service de Protection des Hautes Personnalités, France
SR	Socialist Revolutionary
SRAC	Short Range Agent Communication
SS	Sluzhba Svyazi ('Communication Service'), predecessor of the OMS
S&T	Scientific & Technical Intelligence, KGB
Stapo	Staatspolizei, Austrian security police
Stasi	Common name for MfS, Ministerium für Staatssicherheit ('Ministry for State Security'), DDR
StB	Czechoslovak security and intelligence service
SVR	Sluzhba Vneshnei Razvedki ('Foreign Intelligence Service of Russia')
SW	Secret Writing, invisible writing technique
TASS	Telegraph Agency of the Soviet Union
TNA	The National Archives, Kew, UK
TOS/AC	Technical & Operations Support/Agent Communications
TOS/CE	Technical & Operations Support/Clandestine Entry
TOS/PH	Technical & Operations Support/Photography
TOS/SW	Technical & Operations Support/Secret Writing
ULTRA	Wartime signals intelligence obtained by breaking high-level encrypted enemy radio and teleprinter communications, GC&CS/UK
Unit 269	Sayeret Matkal, Israel
UPA	Ukraińska Powstańcza Armia ('The Ukrainian Insurgent Army')
VChKa	All-Russian Cheka, the immediate successor of the Cheka and predecessor of the OGPU
VCO	Visiting Case Officer, SIS
YZ	Highly classified telegram, SIS
ZUB	Zentrale Unterstützungsgruppe des Bundes für gravierende Fälle der nuklearspezifischen Gefahrenabwehr ('Central Federal Support Group in Response to Serious Nuclear Threats'), Germany

Bibliography

Archival and Manuscript Collections

Bundesarchive Deutschland, Koblenz, BArch, B 131/1289, Bundeskriminalamt: Ermittlungen gegen [Cudyk Hepner, Abraham Beitner und] Wolfgang Wildprett, 1954–56, Sicherungsgruppe EL II – 103/56 geh. Berlin, 5. Oktober 1956; Fall: Wolfgang Wildprett Mordauftrag z.N. Wladimir Poremsky.

Bundesbeauftragte für die Stasi-Unterlagen (BStU), Berlin, MfS Document: Abteilung I, Aufklärung B, Referat I, 'Plan Operativen Maßnamen zur Liquidierung des Thurow, Rudi'.

Bundesgerichtshof (BGH), Karlsruhe, Court sentence (Urteil) 9StE 4/62 (Stashinsky), 19 October 1962.

Byelorussian Museum of the Great Patriotic War, Minsk: Elena Mazanik Papers, Maria Osipova Papers, Nadezhda Troyan Papers, Valentina Shchutskaya Papers, Tatiana Bauer Papers, Minsk Underground Movement Papers.

CIA, Current Intelligence Weekly Summary, 'Berlin, 17 August 1961'.

CIA/FOIA, 'KGB Exploitation of Heinz Felfe: Successful KGB Penetration of a Western Intelligence Service', 13 April 1977, 159 pages.

Columbia University Libraries, Archival Collections, Rare Book and Manuscript Library, Aleksei Aleksandrovich von Lampe papers, ca. 1777–1969.

Department of the Army, US Army Intelligence and Security Command, FOIA Office, Forte George G. Meade, 'Records on Soviet Defectors', ZF010285w.

DIA, 'Soviet and Czechoslovakian Parapsychology Research (U)', DST-1810S-387-75, September 1975, Part II, 'Psychotronic Generator Research', Part V 'Conclusions', Part VI 'Trends and Forecasts', 8 pages.

Dokumentationsarchiv des österreicheschen Wiederstandes (DÖW), Vienna, Folder 14899 'Josef Hofbauer'.

Duke University Archives, Durham, NC, Dissertation of Nikolai Evgenyevich Khokhlov 'Dimensional Preference and Discriminability in Judgments of Multidimensional Stimuli', 1968.

Hoover Institution Archives, Nikolai Evgen'evich Khokhlov Papers (1956–1992), Collection no. 2011C23, Stanford, California 94305-6010.

Imperial War Museum, London, *Secret Agent's Handbook of Special Devices*.

Manuscript Division, Library of Congress, Washington, DC, Dmitrii Antonovich Volkogonov papers, 1887–1995, ID number MSS83838.

NARA, RG 263 Entry ZZ-19, B 14, Memorandum for the Record, April 22, 1976, Subject: 'Assassination of Stefan Bandera'.

NARA, RG 263, Entry ZZ-18, B 6, Memorandum for Chief, CIA Soviet Russia Division, August 24, 1961, 1–2, Stefan Bandera Name File, vol. 2.

NARA, RG 263, File 'Stefan Bandera', Box 6, Folder 4, 294 pages.

Queensland Courts, Coroners Court, Brisbane, Office of the State Coroner Findings of Investigation, 'non-inquest findings into the death of Noelene Gaye BISCHOFF and Yvana Jean Yuri BISCHOFF', File No. 2014/122 & 2014/123, 30 March 2015.

Records of the US Department of State Relating to the Internal Affairs of Austria, 1950–1954 (NA-RG 59), Wilmington, DE, Scholarly Resources, 1988. The National Archives, Kew,

HS4/334, 'Agreed Record of Discussions between British and Soviet Representatives on the Question of Subversive Activities against Germany and her Allies', copy no. 6.

The Mitrokhin Commission Archive, Rome.

The National Archives, Kew, KV 3/417, 'MI5's D.3 Survey of Russian Espionage in the United Kingdom 1935–1955', SF441-0302-8/VI.

The National Archives, Kew, PREM 19/1647, Prime Minister's office files 1985–UK/Soviet relations: part 4, 3 Jan–25 Oct 1985.

The National Archives, Kew, 'The Litvinenko Inquiry', archived on 13 June 2016.

The Security Service of Ukraine (SBU), Kiev, declassified documents from the Agent File 'Bogdan Stashinsky alias OLEG' No. 10459 and Stashinsky's 'Operational Cultivation File "TARAS"' No. 4, 7 volumes.

US Department of State, Foreign Relations of the United States, 1950–1955, Washington, DC, The Intelligence Community, 1950–1955, Document 209: National Security Council Report.

University of Nebraska-Lincoln, Libraries, Archives and Special Collections, 'Wilhelm Kube', International Military Tribunal Collection, MS 10, series IV, Box 1, Folder 7.

Private Document Collection

Tennent H. Bagley's family: Brussels, Belgium/Washington, DC, USA

Unpublished Typescripts

Efremov, Sergiy, 'Masonstvo na Ukraïni', monograph, 4 chapters, 1918.

Embassy of the Russian Federation to the United Kingdom, 'Salisbury: Unanswered Questions', report, 4 March 2019, 52 pages.

Kernbach, Serge, 'Unconventional Research in USSR and Russia: Short Overview', 2013, 23 printed pages.

Khokhlov, Nikolai, *Pravo na Sovest*, 613 printed pages, 1993, with Khokhlov's handwritten corrections and insertions, author's archive.

Scarlett, John, 'Modern System of Accountability of Security and Intelligence Services', talk at Magdalen College, Oxford, 1 March 2004, twelve printed pages.

Scarlett, John, 'From Intelligence to Intervention: Essentials for Policy Formulation', JIC Chairman's Talk at Wilton Park Conference, 17 January 2004, seven printed pages.

Volodarsky, Boris, 'Soviet Deception Operations', a textbook chapter, author's archive.

Volodarsky, Boris, *Bomba v dele Kube*, 375 typed pages, author's archive.

Wetz, Ulrike, *Geschichte der Wiener Polizeidirektion vom Jahre 1945 bis zum Jahre 1955 mit Berücksichtigung der Zeit vor 1945*, PhD thesis (1970), Vienna University dissertations, 1971.

Williams, Warren W., *British Policy and the Occupation of Austria, 1945–55*, PhD thesis (2004), University of Wales, Cardiff.

Author's Interviews

Boris Berezovsky, former Russian oligarch (interviewed in London, November 2006–December 2009).

Calland F. Carnes, former counterintelligence officer with DIA, FBI, Naval Investigative Service, and Army (interviewed 2017).

Paolo Guzzanti, former Italian senator, former head of the Mitrokhin Commission of the Italian Parliament (interviewed in Surrey, UK, and Rome, Italy, spring 2007–autumn 2009).

Dr Nikolai E. Khokhlov, Soviet defector (interviewed September 2003–February 2004).

Dr Nikolai N. Korpan, The Rudolfinerhaus, Vienna (interviewed December 2004–May 2005 and again January 2018).

James Pavitt, former Deputy Director of Operations (DDO), CIA (interviewed in Europe, 2008–9).

Joseph C. Evans, former senior officer, CIA Counterintelligence Staff (interviewed in August 2005).

Leila Gordievskaya, at the time wife of Oleg Gordievsky (interviewed in London by Seva Novodvortsev for *BBC Sevaoborot*, 14 September 1991 https://www.seva.ru/audio/oborot/1991/s910914vs202as.mp3).

Leila Gordievskaya, former wife of Oleg Gordievsky (interviewed in Moscow by Igor Pomerantsev for *RFE/RL*, October 2014).

Leila, Maria and Anna Gordievskiye, former wife and daughters of Oleg Gordievsky (interviewed in Moscow by Katya Pryannik for *MK*, September 2003).

Markus Wolf, former head of East German Foreign Intelligence, HWA (interviewed in January–December 2004).

Michael Shipster, former head of MI6 station in Washington, DC, (interviewed in London, October 2007).

Nikolai Khokhlov, Soviet defector, former NKVD/KGB officer, Germany (interviewed September 2003–February 2004).

Oleg Gordievsky, Soviet defector (interviewed in Surrey and London every day from 23 November 2006 to 20 December 2007).

Olga Aroseva, actress, Moscow, a daughter of Alexander Yakovlevich Arosev, revolutionary, Chekist, writer and diplomat (interviewed in Vienna, December 2005).

Professor Dr Michael Zimpfer, Zentrum für Medizin und Gesundheit/Vienna Medical Center, Vienna (interviewed August 2017–March 2018 and March 2019).

Raymond Asquith (now Lord Oxford), former head of MI6 station in Moscow (interviewed in London, October 2007).

Stanislav A, Levchenko, Soviet defector, former KGB officer, Japan (interviewed in June 1999).

Tennent H. Bagley, former chief of Soviet bloc counterintelligence, CIA (interviewed in Brussels and Vienna, July 2003–January 2014).

Vladimir Chuguev, former private secretary to Alexander Kerensky (interviewed in Saint-Lô, France, August 2002).

Vladimir Rezun (literary pseudo. 'Victor Suvorov'), Soviet defector, former GRU officer, Geneva (interviewed in London, May 1998–August 2010).

Documentaries And Broadcasts

'Disbelief', director Andrei Nekrasov, 2004.

'El asesinato de Trotsky', director Matias Guelburt, writer Nicolas Guelburt, producer Sebastián Gamba, narrator Julio Bracho, cast Esteban Volkov, 20 August 2007 (Mexico).

'Forbidden History: The Murder Bureau', UKTV, producer Bruce Burgess, with Boris Volodarsky, summer 2017.

'How to Poison a Spy', directors Peter Norrey and John O'Mahony (Blakeway/3BM), presenter Jeremy Vine, reporter John Sweeney, chief consultant Boris Volodarsky, BBC Panorama, BBC One, 22 January 2007.

'Hunting the KGB Killers', director Chris Malone, True Vision Productions, Channel 4, 17 April 2017.

'KGB: The Soviet Secret Police' with Nikolai E. Khokhlov, produced by Mischa Scorer, consultants Edward Crankshaw and Peter Reddaway, BBC One, February 1974.

'Likvidator KGB Khokhlov: Ispoved' predatelya', author Dmitry Minchenok, director Olga Borshch, TVTs, September 2006.

'Meet the Press' (Longines Chronoscope Interviews) with Nikolai Khokhlov interviewed by Larry Lesueur and Kenneth Crawford, *CBS*, November 1954.

'Otsy i deti: Deti Shpionov (2)' with Nikolai Khokhlov and Tatyana Guschina-Okun, author Vladimir Tolz, Radio Liberty, October 2002.

'Poisoned by Polonium: The Litvinenko File', writers Olga Konskaya, Andrey Nekrasov, director Andrey Nekrasov (Dreamscanner), BBC One, 22 January 2007.

'Salisbury Nerve Agent Attack: The Inside Story', reporter Jane Corbin, producer & director Mike Rudin, executive producer Karen Wightman, BBC Panorama (season 27, episode 40), BBC One, 22 November 2018.

'Silenced – Georgi Markov and the Umbrella Murder' (original title: Zum Schweigen Gebracht – Georgi Markov und der Regenschirm Mord), author and director Klaus Dexel, Klaus Dexel TV Filmproduktion in co-production with Mamoko Entertainment and Audiovideo Orpheus in cooperation with ZDF/Arte, Germany, 2013.

'Stepan Bandera – rassekrechennaya zhizn', author and narrator Leonid Mlechin, director Igor Maksimchuk, TVTs, 2010.

'Szadrin: Potrójny Agent', author and director Wojciech Bockenheim, narrator Piotr Borowiec, producer Grzegorz Madej, TVN, Poland, 2006.

'Tainy razvedki: likvidatsyia Stepana Bandery', author Alexander Kolpakov, director Dmitry Dokuchayev, Telecompany Ostankino, 2012.

'The Assassination of Russia', director Jean-Charles Deniau, producer Charles Gazelle, consultants Alexander Litvinenko and Yuri Felshtinsky, Transparencies Productions, 2002, RUSI, London, March 2002.

'The Billion Dollar Don', reporter Tom Mangold, producer Toby Sculthorp, BBC Panorama, BBC One, 6 December 1999.

'The Defector', director and writer Mark Jonathan Harris, producer Andrew Kravchenko, writer and co-producer Paul Wolansky, executive producer James Egan, narrator Isaac Liev Schreiber, American Sterling Productions and Wild at Heart Films, July 2008.

'The Magnitsky Act: Behind the Scenes', author and director Andrei Nekrasov, private viewing, Museum of Journalism, Washington, DC, June 2016.

'The Polonium Plot', CBS News, 21 January 2016.

'The Secret KGB Paranormal Files', Associated Television International, director Jeremy Cole, executive producer David McKenzie, producer Judy Lyness, narrator Roger Moore, USA, 2001.

'The Umbrella Assassin', writer and director Mark Radice, producers Mark Radice and Brian Brunius, narrator Toby Stephens, reporter John 'Jack' Hamilton, produced by Windfall Films production for Channel 13/WNET in association with Five and Discovery Networks Europe, 2006.

'Traitors: Oleg Gordievsky' (rus), narrator Andrey Lugovoy, produced by Viange Production for the channel Zvezda, 2014.

Published Documents

'Polonium-210 poisoning: a first-hand account', Dr Amit C Nathwani, James F. Down, John Goldstone, James Yassin, Paul I. Dargan, Andres Virchis, Nick Gent, David Lloyd, and John D. Harrison, *The Lancet*, 388/10049 (September 2016), 1075–1080.

'Testimony of Nikolai Evgeniyevich Khokhlov, Former MGB Agent', interpreted by Eugene S. Serebrennikov, *Hearing Before the Subcommittee to Investigate the Administration of the Internal Security Act and Other Internal Security Laws of the Committee on the Judiciary*, United States Senate, 83rd Congress, Second Sessions on Activities of Soviet Secret Service, May 21, 1954 (Washington, DC: US GPO, 1954).

'Testimony of Natalia Veselnitskaya' *Before the United States Senate Commission on the Judiciary*, Committee Chairman Charles E. Grassley, November 20, 2017.

'Testimony of Nikolai Khokhlov, Care of International Research Inc., New York, NY', *Hearing Before the Subcommittee to Investigate the Administration of the Internal Security*

Act and Other Internal Security Laws of the Committee on the Judiciary, United States Senate, 85th Congress, First Session on Scope of Soviet Activity in the United States, October 1 and 16, 1957, Part 86 (Washington, DC: US GPO, 1957), 4817-41.

'Testimony of Nikolai Khokhlov: Thought Control in Soviet Art and Literature and the Liberation of Russia', Investigation of Communist Activities in the Los Angeles, Calif., Area', *Hearing Before the Committee of Un-American Activities*, House of Representatives, 84th Congress, First and Second Sessions, 27 June 1955–5 July 1956 (Washington, DC: US GPO, 1955–6), part 8.

'The Litvinenko Inquiry: Report into the Death of Alexander Litvinenko', Chairman Sir Robert Owen, presented to Parliament pursuant to Section 26 of the Inquiries Act 2005 Ordered by the House of Commons to be printed on 21 January 2016 (London: Williams Lea Group on behalf of the Controller of Her Majesty's Stationery Office, 2016).

'The polonium-210 poisoning of Mr Alexander Litvinenko', John Harrison, Tim Fell, Rich Leggett, David Lloyd, Matthew Puncher and Mike Youngman, *Journal of Radiological Protection*, 37/1 (March 2017), 266–78.

CIA Center for the Study of Intelligence, 'Soviet Use of Assassination and Kidnapping', 19/3 (February 1964), 27 pages.

Federal High Court, Karlsruhe, Germany, Verdict in the Stashynsky trial of 19 October 1962–9 StF 4/62.

US Department of State, External Research Paper, 'NTS: The Russian Solidarist Movement', Series 3, No. 76, 10 December 1951 (Washington, DC: US GPO, 1951).

Veselova, O., Lisenko, O., Patrilyak, I. and Sergiychuk, V. (eds.), *OUN v 1941 rotsi: Dokumenty* (Kiev: National Academy of Science/Institute of History, 2006), in 2 parts.

Books and Articles

Albanese, David C.S., '"It takes a Russian to beat a Russian": The National Union of Labor Solidarists, nationalism, and human intelligence operations in the Cold War', *Intelligence and National Security*, 32/6 (February 2017), 782–96.

Albats, Yevgenia, *The State Within a State: The KGB and its Hold on Russia – Past, Present, and Future* (New York, NY: Farrar, Straus and Geroux, 1994).

Alexander, John, 'ESP Wars East & West: An Account of the Military Use of Psychic Espionage as Narrated by the Key Russian and American Players', book review, *Journal of Scientific Exploration*, 30/3 (2016), 453–7.

Alibek, Ken, with Handelman, Stephen, *Biohazard: The Chilling True Story of the Largest Covert Biological Weapons Program in the World – Told from the Inside by the Man Who Ran It* (London: Arrow, 2000).

Anders, Karl (pseudo. Kurt Wilhelm Naumann), *Mord auf Befehl: Der Fall Staschynskij, eine Dokumentation aus den Akten* (Pfaffenhofen/Ilm: Ilmgau-Verlag, 1963).

Anders, Karl, *Murder to Order*, paperback (London: Ampersand Book, 1965).

Andersen, Jakob, med Oleg Gordievsky, *De røde spioner* (Copenhagen: Høst & Søn, 2002).

Andrew, Christopher with Dilks, David, *Missing Dimension: Governments and Intelligence Communities in the Twentieth Century* (London: Macmillan, 1984).

Andrew, Christopher, 'Historical Attention Span Deficit Disorder: Why Intelligence Analysis Needs to Look Back Before Looking Forward', in *New Frontiers of Intelligence Analysis: Papers Presented at the Conference on New Frontiers of Intelligence Analysis – Shared Threats, Diverse Perspectives, New Communities* (Rome, 2005), first published online on *History & Policy* independent forum of academic historians, 01 June 2004.

Andrew, Christopher, 'Intelligence, International Relations and "Under-theorisation"', *Intelligence and National Security*, 19/2 (Summer 2004), 170–84.

Andrew, Christopher, and Gordievsky, Oleg, *KGB: The Inside Story* (London: HarperCollins, 1990).

Andrew, Christopher, and Mitrokhin, Vasili, *The Mitrokhin Archive: The KGB in Europe and the West* (London: Allen Lane/The Penguin Press, 1999).

Andrew, Christopher, and Mitrokhin, Vasili, *The Mitrokhin Archive II: The KGB and the World* (London: Allen Lane/Penguin Books, 2005).

Andrew, Christopher, *For the President's Eyes Only: Secret Intelligence and the American Presidency from Washington to Bush* (London: HarperCollins, 1995).

Andrew, Christopher, *Secret Service: The Making of the British Intelligence Community* (London: Heinemann, 1985).

Andrew, Christopher, *The Defence of the Realm: The Authorized History of MI5* (London: Allen Lane, 2009).

Andrew, Christopher, *The Secret World: A History of Intelligence* (London: Alan Lane/Penguin Books, 2018).

Anonymous, 'Operation Vladimir', *News* [Austria], 23 (4 June 2008), 66–69.

Anonymous, 'Plot that Backfired: A Soviet agent defects and imperils his family' [Nikolai Khokhlov], *Life* (3 May 1954), 52.

APA (Austrian Press Agency), 'Gesetzwidriges Vorgehen amerinakischer Behörden gegen österreichischen Staatsbürger', *Österreichische Zeitung*, Dienstag, 13 April 1954, 2.

Applebaum, Anne, *Red Famine: Stalin's War on Ukraine* (London: Allen Lane, 2017).

Arjakovsky, Antoine, *Voyage de Saint-Pétersbourg à Moscou: Anatomie de l'âme russe* (Paris: Salvator, 2018).

Aroutyunov, Akim A., *Dossier Lenina bez retushi: dokumenty, fakty, svidetelstva* (Moscow: Veche, 1999).

Aroseva, Natalia, *Sled na zemle* (Moscow: Politizdat, 1987).

Aroseva, Olga, *Prozhivshaya dvazhdy* (Moscow: Astrel, 2012).

Ashley, Clarence, *CIA SpyMaster: Kisevalter, the Agency's Top Case Officer Who Handled Penkovsky and Popov* (Gretna, Louisiana, LA: Pelican Publishing, 2004).

Aven, Petr, *Vremya Berezovskogo* (Moscow: AST/Corpus, 2017).

Babacek, Mojmir, 'Psychotronic and Electromagnetic Weapons: Remote Control of the Human Nervous System', *Global Research*, 31 January 2013 and 16 March 2014.

Bader, William B., *Austria Between East and West, 1945–1955* (Stanford, CA: Stanford University Press, 1966).

Bagley, T.H. 'Bane of Counterintelligence: Our Penchant for Self-Deception', *International Journal of Intelligence and Counterintelligence*, 6/1 (Spring 1993), 1–20.

Bagley, Tennent H., 'Ghosts of the Spy Wars: A Personal Reminder to Interested Parties', *International Journal of Intelligence and Counterintelligence*, 28/1 (2015), 1–37.

Bagley, Tennent H., *Spy Wars: Moles, Mysteries and Deadly Games* (New Haven and London: Yale University Press, 2007).

Bagley, Tennent H., *Spymaster: Startling Cold War Revelations of a Soviet KGB Chief as revealed to his ex-CIA agent friend* (New York, NY: Skyhorse Publishing, 2013).

Bakatin, Vadim, *Izbavlenie ot KGB* (Moscow: Novosti, 1992).

Barrass, Gordon S., *The Great Cold War: A Journey Through the Hall of Mirrors* (Stanford, CA: Stanford University Press, 2009).

Batshev, Vladimir, 'Pokhischenie Trushnovicha', *Stolitsa*, 45 (1992).

Baumann, Gerold Gino, *Los voluntarios latinoamericanos en la guerra civil española: en las brigadas internacionales, las milicias, la retaguardia y el Ejército Popular* (San José, Costa Rica: Guayacán, 1997).

Bazhanov (Bajanov), Boris, *Avec Stalin dans le Kremline* (Paris: Les Editions de France, 1930).

Bazhanov, Boris, *Bazhanov and the Damnation of Stalin*, paperback (Athens, OH: Ohio University Press, 1990), translation and commentary by David W. Doyle.

Beale, Neville, 'I Spy lunch', *The Spectator*, letters (23 January 1999), 26.

Bearden, Milt, and Risen, James, *The Main Enemy: The Inside Story of the CIA's Final Countdown with the KGB*, paperback (New York, NY: Ballantine Books, 2003).

Beaune, Daniéle, *L'enlèvement du Général Koutiepoff* (Aix-en-Provence: Publications de l'Université de Provence, 1998).

Becker, Robert O., and Selden, Gary, *The Body Electric: Electromagnetism and the Foundation of Life* (New York, NY: William Morrow & Co., 1985).

Begich, Nicholas J., *Controlling the Human Mind: The Technologies of Political Control or Tools for Peak Performance*, paperback (Eagle River, AK: Earthpulse Press, 2006).

Begoum, F.M. (pseudo. John P. Dimmer), 'Observations of the Double Agent', *Studies in Intelligence*, 6/1 (Winter 1962), 57–72, declassified.

Berdyaev, N.A. *Istoki i smysl russkogo kommunizma* (Paris: YMCA-PRESS, 1955).

Berdyaev, Nikolai A., *The Origin of Russian Communism* (Ann Arbor, MI: University of Michigan Press, 1959).

Bereanu, Vladimir, and Todorov, Kalin, *The Umbrella Murder* (Bury St Edmunds, Suffolk: TEL, 1994).

Berezovsky, B. A., Baryshnikov, Yu. M., and Gnedin, A. V., 'Three Problems of the Theory of Choice on Random Sets', Social Science Working Paper 661 (Pasadena, CA: California Institute of Technology, December 1987).

Berezovsky, Boris, and Felshtinsky, Yuri, *The Art of Impossible* (Falmouth, MA: Terra-USA, 2006), 3 vols.

Bergman, Ronen, *Rise and Kill First: The Secret History of Israel's Targeted Assassinations* (New York, NY: Random House, 2018).

Bethell, Nicholas, 'Bond «enemy» goes to Russia with love', *The Sunday Telegraph*, 24 May 1992.

Bethell, Nicholas, *Spies and Other Stories: Memoirs from the Second Cold War* (London: Viking, 1994).

Bimmerle, George, '"Truth" Drugs in Interrogation', *Studies in Intelligence*, 5/2 (Spring 1961), A1–A19.

Birstein, Vadim J., *The Perversion of Knowledge: The True Story of Soviet Science*, (New York, NY: Westview Press, 2001).

Bittman, Ladislav, *The KGB and Soviet Disinformation* (McLean, VA: Pergamon-Brassey's International Defense Publishers, 1985).

Bonch-Bruyevich, Vladimir D., *Vospominaniya o Lenine* (Moscow: Nauka, 1969).

Bortnevsky, V.G., *Zagadka smerti generala Wrangelya: Neizvestnye materialy po istorii russkoi emigratsyi* (St Petersburg: St Petersburg University Publishing, 1996).

Breitman, Richard, and Goda, Norman J.W., *Hitler's Shadow: Nazi War Criminals, US Intelligence, and the Cold War* (Washington, DC: National Archives, 2012).

Brook-Shepherd, Gordon, *The Austrians: A Thousand-Year Odyssey*, paperback (London: HarperCollins, 1997).

Brook-Shepherd, Gordon, *The Storm Birds: Soviet Post-War Defectors* (London: Weidenfeld & Nicolson, 1988).

Brook-Shepherd, Gordon, *The Storm Petrels: The First Soviet Defectors, 1928–1938* (London: Collins, 1977).

Bubke, Hermann, *Der Einsatz des Stasi- und KGB-Spions Otto Freitag im München der Nachkriegszeit*, paperback (Hamburg: Dr Kovac Verlag, 2004).

Bulgakov, Mikhail, *The Master and Margarita* (London: Collins and Harvill Press, 1967), translated by Michael Glenny.

Burds, Jeffrey, *The Early Cold War in Soviet West Ukraine, 1944–1948*, Carl Beck papers in Russian and East European Studies No. 1505 (Pittsburgh: Center for Russian and East European Studies, 2001).

Burstein, Dan, and De Keijzer, Arne, *Secrets of the Lost Symbol: The Authorized Guide to the Mysteries Behind* The Da Vinci Code *Sequel* (New York, NY: HarperCollins, 2010).

Butkov, Mikhail, *KGB i Norge* (Oslo: Tiden Norsk, 1992).

Calder, Nigel, *Unless Peace Comes: A scientific forecast of new weapons* (New York, NY: Viking Press, 1968).

Campbell, Kurt M., *Soviet Policy Towards South Africa* (Houndmills, Basingstoke, Hampshire, and London: The Macmillan Press, 1986).

Catton, Philip E., *Diem's Final Failure: Prelude to America's War in Vietnam* (Lawrence, KS: University Press of Kansas, 2002).

Chai, Peter R., Hayes, Brian D., Erickson, Timothy B. & Boyer, Edward W., 'Novichok agents: a historical, current, and toxicological perspective', *Toxicology Communications*, 2/1 (2018), 45-8.

Chaikovsky, Danila (ed.), *Moskovs'ki vbivtsi Banderi pered sudom*, zbirka materialiv (Munich: Ukrains'ke vidavnitstvo v Myunkheni, 1965).

Chamberlin, William Henry, *The Russian Revolution 1917–1921* (London: Macmillan, 1935), 2 vols.

Charters, David A., and Tugwell, Maurice A.J. (eds.), *Deception Operations: Studies in the East–West Context* (London: Brassey's, 1990).

Cook, Andrew, *On His Majesty's Secret Service: Sidney Reilly, Code-Name ST1*, paperback (Stroud, Glouchestershire: Tempus Publishing, 2002).

Cookridge, E.H. (pseudo. Edward Spiro), *Gehlen: Spy of the Century* (New York, NY: Random House, 1971).

Corera, Gordon, *The Art of Betrayal: Life and Death in the British Secret Service* (London: Weidenfeld & Nicolson, 2011).

Cormac, Rory, *Disrupt and Deny: Spies, Special Forces, and the Secret Pursuit of British Foreign Policy* (Oxford: Oxford University Press, 2018).

Cotton, Simon, 'Litvinenko poisoning: polonium explained', *The Conversation*, 21 January 2016.

Cotton, Simon, 'Nerve agents: what are they and how do they work?' *The Conversation*, 8 March 2018.

Coudenys, Wim, 'A Life Between Fact and Fiction: The History of Vladimir G. Orlov', *Revolutionary Russia*, 21/2 (December 2008), 179–202.

Cowell, Alan, *The Terminal Spy: The Life and Death of Alexander Litvinenko* (London: Doubleday, 2008).

Cummings, Richard H., *Cold War Radio: The Dangerous History of American Broadcasting in Europe, 1950–1989* (Jefferson, NC, and London: McFarland & Company Inc., Publishers, 2009).

Dawisha, Karen, *Putin's Kleptocracy* (New York, NY: Simon & Schuster, 2015).

Delfino, Reinaldo T., Ribeiro, Tatiana S., and Figueroa-Villar, Jóse D., 'Organophosphorus compounds as chemical warfare agents: review', *Journal of the Brazilian Chemical Society*, 20/3 (March 2009), 407–28.

Deriabin, Peter, and Bagley, T.H., *The KGB: Masters of the Soviet Union* (London: Robson Books, 1990).

Deriabin, Peter, and Gibney, Frank, *The Secret World* (London: Arthur Baker, 1960).

Deriabin, Peter, with Evans, Joseph C., *Inside Stalin's Kremlin: An Eyewitness Account of Brutality, Duplicity and Intrigue* (Washington and London: Brassey's, 1998).

Dewar, Hugo, *Assassins at Large: Being a Fully Documented and Hitherto Unpublished Account of the Executions Outside Russia Ordered by the GPU* (Westport, CT: Hyperion Press, 1981, reprint of the 1952 edition published by Beacon Press, Boston).

'Die Sache mit Skorzeny. Manche geschichte wird nun unerzählt bleiben: zum Tod des Antifaschisten Karl Kleinjung', *Information DRAFD*, Juni 2003.

Dietze, Manfred, 'Auszüge aus Trauerrede zum Ableben von Generalleutnant a.D. Karl Kleinjung anlässlich der Urnenbeisetzung am 06.03.2003 auf dem Zentralfriedhof Berlin-Friedrichafelde', http://www.mfs-insider.de/Abhandlungen/Kleinjung1.htm, 2 May 2017.

Dimitrova, Alexenia, *Otdel za Ubiistva: Tainata istoria na sekretna Sluzhba 7*, paperback (Sofia: 24 chasa, 2010).

Dokuchayev, Mikhail S., *Moskva. Kreml. Okhrana* (Moscow: Business Press, 1995).

Dorril, Stephen, *MI6: Fifty Years of Special Operations*, paperback (London: Fourth Estate, 2001).

Dubrovsky, Nikolai, *Bessmertie podviga* (Minsk: Izdatelstvo Belarus, 2004).

Dulles, Allen (ed.), *Great True Spy Stories* (London: Book Club Associates, 1968).

Dulles, Allen, *Der lautlose Krieg: 39 berühmte Spionagefälle* (Munich: Nimphenburger Verlag, 1968).

Earley, Pete, *Comrade J.: The Untold Secrets of Russia's Master Spy in America After the End of the Cold War* (New York, NY: G.P. Putnam's Sons/Penguin, 2007).

Earley, Pete, *Confessions of a Spy: The Real Story of Aldrich Ames* (New York, NY: G.P. Putnam's Sons, 1997).

Editorial, 'Anhaltung eines Textilchemikers durch die Amerikaner', *Wiener Zeitung*, 85 (3 April 1954), 4.

Editorial, 'Mysteriöse Verhaftung in Döbling', *Neues Österreich*, 2726 (1 April 1954), 1.

Editorial, 'US, Russia Hope to Safeguard Mini-Control Techniques', *Defence News* (January 11–17, 1993), 4, 29.

Ehrenburg, Ilya, 'Konets Vilgelma Kube', *Krasnaya zvezda*, (24 September 1943), 4.

Ehrenburg, Ilya, 'Prestuplenia i nakazanie', *Pravda*, 24 September 1943.

Ellison, D. Hank, *Handbook of Chemical and Biological Warfare Agents*, 2nd ed. (Boca Raton, FL: CRC Press/Taylor & Francis Group, 2008).

Ellman, Michael, 'Stalin and the Soviet Famine of 1932–33, Revisited', *Europe-Asia Studies*, 59/4 (June 2007), 663–93.

Fedorov, Lev, 'Smert zamedlennogo deistviya: Rossiya nakanune khimicheskogo apokalypsisa', *Sovershenno sekretno*, 7 (July 1992), 6–8.

Felshtinsky, Y., *Trotsky Archive: The Communist Opposition in the USSR, 1923–1927*, paperback (Edinburgh: Terra Publishing, 1990), 4 vols.

Felshtinsky, Yuri, and Pribylovsky, Vladimir, *The Age of Assassins: The Rise and Rise of Vladimir Putin* (London: Gibson Square Books, 2007).

Felshtinsky, Yuri, *Byl li Stalin agentom Okhranki*? Sbornik statei, materialov i dokumentov (Moscow: Terra-Knizhnyi Klub, 1999).

Felshtinsky, Yuri, *Lenin and his Comrades: The Bolsheviks Take Over Russia, 1917–1924*, paperback (New York, NY: Enigma Books, 2010).

Felshtinsky, Yuri, *Oglasheniyu podlezhit: SSSR-Germaniya, 1939–1941*, Dokumenty i materialy (Moscow: Moskovskiy rabochiy, 2004).

Felshtinsky, Yuri, *The Corporation: Russia and the KGB in the Age of President Putin* (New York, NY: Encounter Books, 2009).

Fischer, Benjamin B., 'Double Troubles: The CIA and Double Agents during the Cold War', *International Journal of Intelligence and Counterintelligence*, 29/1 (January 2016), 48–74.

Fischer, Benjamin B., 'Stalin's Killing Field (The Katyn Controversy)', *Studies of Intelligence* (CIA), 43/3 (Winter 1999–2000), 61–70.

Fischer, Benjamin B., *A Cold War Conundrum: The 1983 Soviet War Scare*, monograph (Washington, DC: Center for the Study of Intelligence, 1997).

Forsyth, Frederick, *Icon* (London: Bantam Press, 1996).

Forsyth, Frederick, *The Deceiver* (London: Bantam Dell Pub Group, 1991).

Forsyth, Frederick, *The Fist of God* (London: Bantam Dell Pub Group, 1994).

Forsyth, Frederick, *The Fourth Protocol* (London: Viking, 1984).

Forsyth, Frederick, *The Fox* (London: Bantam Press/Penguin Random House, 2018).

Forsyth, Frederick, *The Outsider: My Life in Intrigue* (London: Bantam Press/ Penguin Random House, 2015).

Friis, Thomas Wegener, 'Intelligence and Counterintelligence in Denmark', in Wladyslaw Bulhak and Thomas Wegener Friis (eds.), *Need to Know: Eastern and Western Perspectives*, paperback (Odense: Syddansk Universitetsforlag, 2014), 245–68.

Frolik, Josef, *The Frolik Defection: The Memoirs of an Intelligence Agent* (London: Leo Cooper, 1975).

Gessen, Masha, *The Man Without a Face: The Unlikely Rise of Vladimir Putin* (New York, NY: Riverhead Books, 2012).

Gerber, Burton, *Vaults, Mirrors and Mashes* (Washington, DC: Georgetown University Press, 2009).

Gill, Anton, *A Dance Between Flames: Berlin Between the Wars* (London: John Murray, 1993).

Ginsborg, Paul, *Familie in der Diktatur: Familienpolitik unter Lenin, Stalin, Mussolini, Atatürk, Hitler und Franco* (Hamburg: Hoffmann und Campe, 2014).

Goldfarb, Alex, with Litvinenko, Marina, *Death of a Dissident: The Poisoning of Alexander Litvinenko and the Return of the KGB* (London and New York: Simon & Schuster, 2007).

Gordievsky, Oleg, *Next Stop Execution* (London: Macmillan, 1995).

Grimes, Sandra, and Vertefeuille, Jeanne, *Circle of Treason: A CIA Account of Aldrich Ames and the Men He Betrayed* (Annapolis, MD: Naval Institute Press, 2012).

Grushko, Victor F., *Sud'ba razvedchika: Kniga vospominanii* (Moscow: Mezhdunarodnye Otnosheniya, 1997).

Gupta, Ramesh C. (ed.), *Handbook of Toxicology of Chemical Warfare Agents*, 2nd ed. (Amsterdam. Academic Press, 2015).

Gurevitch, Eric M., 'Thinking with Sylvia Ageloff', *Hypocrite Reader*, 55 (August 2015), 1–14.

Guzzanti, Paolo, 'Moi agent Sasha Litvinenko' (interviewed by Anastasiya Kirilenko), RFE/RL, 23 November 2009.

Guzzanti, Paolo, *Il mio agente Sasha – La Russia di Putin e l'Italia di Berlusconi ai tempi della seconda Guerra fredda* (Rome: Aliberti Editore, 2009).

Hammond, Thomas T. (ed.), *Witnesses to the Origins of the Cold War* (Seattle and London: University of Washington Press, 1982).

Harding, Luke, 'Alexander Litvinenko: the man who solved his own murder', *The Guardian*, 19 January 2016.

Harding, Luke, *A Very Expensive Poison: The Definitive Story of the Murder of Litvinenko and Russia's War with the West*, paperback (London: Guardian Faber Publishing, 2016).

Harding, Stan, *The Underworld of State* (London: George Allen & Unwin Ltd, 1925), with an introduction by Bertrand Russell.

Hay, Alastair, 'Novichok: the deadly story behind the nerve agent', *The Conversation*, 20 March 2018.

Hayman, Andy, with Gilmore, Margaret, *The Terrorist Hunters: On the Frontline of Britain's War Against Terror*, paperback (London: Transworld Publishers, 2010).

Hofman, David E., *The Oligarchs: Wealth and Power in the New Russia*, paperback (New York, NY: Public Affairs, 2002).

Hollingsworth, Mark, *Londongrad: From Russia with Cash – The Inside Story of the Oligarchs*, paperback (London: Fourth Estate, 2010).

Holzman, Michael, *James Jesus Angleton, the CIA and the Craft of Counterintelligence* (Amherst, MASS: University of Massachusetts Press, 2008).

Hood, William, *Mole: The True Story of the First Russian Intelligence Officer Recruited by the CIA* (New York and London: W.W. Norton & Company, 1982).

Hristov, Hristo, *Dvoiniyat zhivot na agent 'Pikadili'* (Sofia: Ikonomedia, 2008).

Hruby, Peter, *Dangerous Dreamers: The Australian Anti-Democratic Left and Czechoslovak Agents* (Bloomington, IN: iUniverse, 2010).

Hurt, Henry, *Shadrin: The Spy Who Never Came Back* (New York, NY: Reader's Digest Press McDraw-Hill Book Company, 1981).

Imberger, Harald, *Nelkenstrauss ruft Praterstern*, paperback (Vienna: Libera Press, 1981).

Ioffe, Emanuil, 'Ot kakoi bomby vzorvalsya Kube?', *Vlast*, 13 (4 April 1997), 5.

Jensen, Bent, *Ulve, får og vogtere – Den Kolde Krig i Danmark 1945–1991* (Copenhagen: Gyldendal, 2014), 2 vols.

Johnson, Loch K. (ed.), *Strategic Intelligence: Understanding the Hidden Side of Government* (Westport, CT, and London: Praeger Security International, 2007), vol. 1.

Jordan, Pamela A., *Stalin's Singing Spy: The Life and Exile of Nadezhda Plevitskaya* (London & New York: Rowman & Littlefield, 2016).

Kalugin, Oleg, *Spymaster: My Thirty-Two Years in Intelligence and Espionage Against the West*, paperback (New York, NY: Basic Books, 2009).

Kandyba, Viktor M., *Tainy psychotronnogo oruzhiya* (St. Petersburg: Nevsky Prospekt, 1998).

Kasenkina, Oksana, *Leap to Freedom* (Philadelphia, PA: J.B. Lippincott, 1949).

Kasten, Len, 'Psychic Discoveries Since the Cold War', *Atlantis Rising*, 14 (Winter 1998).

Kautilya, *The Asthashastra*, edited, rearranged, translated and introduced by L.N. Rangarajan (Gurgaon, Haryana, India: Penguin Books/Penguin Random House, 1992).

Kaznacheev, Aleksandr, *Inside a Soviet Embassy* (London: Hale, 1963).

Kelly, Col. Francis John, *Vietnam Studies: US Army Special Forces 1961–1973* (Washington, DC: Department of the Army, 1981).

Kemper, Erwin, *Verrat an Österreich* (Vienna: Zeitschriftenbuch, 1996).

Khlevniuk, Oleg V., *Master of the House: Stalin and His Inner Circle* (New Haven and London: Yale University Press, 2009).

Khlevniuk, Oleg V., *Stalin: New Biography of a Dictator* (New Haven and London: Yale University Press, 2015).

Khlevniuk, Oleg, *1937: Stalin, NKVD, i sovietskoe obschestvo* (Moscow: Respublika, 1992).

Khmelnitsky, Dmitry, *Ledokol iz "Akvariuma"* (Moscow: Izdatel Bystrov, 2006).

Khohklov, Nikolai, 'Heroism of a Russian Woman', *Possev*, 17 (25 April 1954), 5–6.

Khokhlov (Chochlow), Nikolaj, *Recht auf Gewissen* (Stuttgart: Deutsche Verlags-Anstalt, 1959).

Khokhlov, Nikolai, 'I would not murder for the Soviets', as told to Milton Lehman, *The Saturday Evening Post* (November 20 and 27: parts 1 & 2; December 4 and 11: parts 3 & 4), 1954.

Khokhlov, Nikolai, 'Vstrecha s proshlym', *Novaya Gazeta*, 46 (1 July 2004).

Khokhlov, Nikolai, *In the Name of Conscience: The Testament of a Soviet Secret Agent* (New York, NY: David McKay Company, 1959).

Khokhlov, Nikolai, *Likvidator s Lubyanki: Vypolnyaiya prikazy Pavla Sudoplatova* (Moscow: Algoritm, 2017).

Khokhlov, Nikolai, *Pravo na sovest* (Frankfurt/Main: Possev Verlag, 1957).

Kirpichenko, V.A., *Razvedchiki: litsa i lichnosti* (Moscow: Mezhdunarodnye otnosheniya, 2017).

Klebnikov, Paul, *Godfather of the Kremlin: Boris Berezovsky and the Looting of Russia* (New York and London: Harcourt, 2000).

Knott, Paul, *The Accidental Diplomat: Adventures in the Foreign Office* (Leeds, West Yorkshire: Scratching Shed Publishing Ltd, 2014).

Kohl, Paul, *Schöne Grüße aus Minsk* (Munich: Droemer, 2001).

Korzhakov, Alexander, *Boris Yeltsin: Ot rassveta do zakata*, paperback (Moscow: Interbook, 1997).

Kostov, Vladimir, *The Bulgarian Umbrella: The Soviet Direction and Operations of the Bulgarian Secret Service in Europe* (Houndmills, Basingstoke, Hampshire, and New York: Palgrave Macmillan, 1988).

Kouzminov, Alexander, *Biological Espionage: Special Operations of the Soviet and Russian Foreign Intelligence Services in the West* (London: Greenhill Books, 2005).

Krasnov, Vladislav, *Soviet Defectors: The KGB Wanted List* (Stanford, CA: Hoover Institution Press Stanford University, 1986).

Kronenbitter, Rita T., 'Leon Trotsky, Dupe of the NKVD', *Studies in Intelligence*, 16/1 (Special Edition, 1972), 15–61.

Kryuchkov, Vladimir A., *Lichnoe delo* (Moscow: Exmo, 2003).

Kuzio, Taras, 'Crime, Politics and Business in 1990s Ukraine', *Communist and Post Communist Studies*, 47 (2014), 195–210.

Kuzio, Taras, *Putin's War Against Ukraine: Revolution, Nationalism, and Crime*, paperback (North Charleston, SC: CreateSpace, 2017).

Kuzio, Taras, 'Rise and Fall of the Party of Regions Poiltical Machine', *Problems of Post-Communism*, 64/3 (May 2015), 174–86.

Kuzio, Taras, *Ukraine: Democratization, Corruption, and the New Russian Imperialism* (Santa Barbara, CA: Praeger, 2015).

Leake, Christopher, and Stewart, Will, 'Putin targets foes with "zombie" gun which attack victims' central nervous system', *Daily Mail*, 1 April 2012.

LeVine, Steve, 'Everything you wanted to know about the KGB but were afraid to ask', *Foreign Policy* (6 July 2010), interview with Boris Volodarsky.

LeVine, Steve, *Putin's Labyrinth: Spies, Murder, and the Dark Heart of the New Russia* (New York, NY: Random House, 2008).

Lewis, Jason, and Mangold, Tom, 'Police probe "new KGB poison attack"', *The Mail on Sunday* (April 6, 2008), front page, 6–7.

Limond Hart, John, *The CIA's Russians* (Annapolis, MD: Naval Institute Press, 2003).

Litvinenko, Alexander, *Allegations: Selected Works by Alexander Litvinenko*, paperback (Slough, Berkshire: Aquilion, 2007).

Litvinenko, Alexander, and Felshtinsky, Yuri, *Blowing Up Russia: The Secret Plot to Bring Back KGB Power* (London: Gibson Square Books, 2015).

Litvinenko, Alexander, *Lubyanskaya Prestupnaya Gruppirovka: Ofitser FSB daiot pokazaniya*, paperback (New York, NY: Grani, 2002).

Lopez-Muñoz, Julian, *La mafia rusa: Genésis, desarotto y asentamiento en España* (Madrid: Editorial Dykinsson S.L., 2017).

Lucas, Edward, *Deception: Spies, Lies, and How Russia Dupes the West* (London: Bloomsbury, 2012).

Lucas, Edward, *The New Cold War: How the Kremlin Menaces Both Russia and the West* (London: Bloomsbury, 2008).

Lunev, Stanislav, with Ira Winkler, *Through the Eyes of the Enemy: Russia's highest ranking military defector reveals why Russia is more dangerous than ever* (Washington, DC: Regnery Publishing, 1998).

Lyandres, Semion, 'The 1918 Attempt on the Life of Lenin: A New Look at the Evidence', *Slavic Review*, 48/3 (Fall 1989), 432–48.

Lyandres, Semion, 'The Bolsheviks' "German Gold" Revisited', *The Carl Beck Papers in Russian & East European Studies*, 1106 (February 1995), 1–132.

Macintyre, Ben, 'If Kremlin didn't poison Skripal, who did?' *The Times*, 21 April 2018.

Macintyre, Ben, 'Sergei Skripal – the life of a double agent', *The Times*, 13 March 2018.

Macintyre, Ben, 'Sergei Skripal: "Forthwith" gave MI6 telephone directory of Russian agents', *The Times*, 10 March 2018.

Macintyre, Ben, 'The greatest spy story of the Cold War', *The Times*, 4 July 2015.

Macintyre, Ben, 'The KGB were always masters of fake news', *The Times*, 18 November 2017.

Macintyre, Ben, 'The spy poisoned by the KGB – but who lived to tell the tale', *The Times*, 1 December 2006, 6–7.

Macintyre, Ben, 'This Russian cyberattack would be hilarious were the GRU not so sinister', *The Times*, 5 October 2018.

Macintyre, Ben, *The Spy and the Traitor: The Greatest Espionage Story of the Cold War* (London: Viking, 2018).

Maddrell, Paul, Moran, Christopher, Iordanou, Ioanna & Stout, Mark, *Spy Chiefs: Intelligence Leaders in the United States and United Kingdom* (Washington, DC: Georgetown University Press, 2017), vol. 1. Foreword by Patrick M. Hughes.

Malinovskaya, Muza, and Eitingon, Leonid (daughter and son of Muza Malinovskaya and Leonid Eitingon), *Na predelnoi vysote* (Velikiye Luki: Velikokukskaya Tipografiya, 2009).

Mangold, Tom, *Cold Warrior: James Jesus Angleton – the CIA Master Spy Hunter* (New York, NY: Simon & Schuster, 1991).

Manning, Jeane, and Begich, Nick, *Angels Don't Play this HAARP: Advances in Tesla Technology*, paperback (Eagle River, AK: Earthpulse Press, 1997).

Marcus, Tom, *Soldier Spy: The true story of an MI5 officer risking his life to save yours* (London: Penguin, 2017).

Marenches, Alexandre Count de, and Ockrent, Christine, *The Evil Empire: The Third World War Now – By the Former Head of the French Secret Service* (London: Sidgwick & Jackson, 1986).

May, Edwin C. and Vilenskaya, Larissa, 'Overview of current parapsychology research in the former Soviet Union', *Subtle Energies*, 3/3 (May 1992), 45–67.

May, Edwin C., Rubel, Victor, and Auerbach, Lloyd, *ESP Wars East & West: An Account of the Military Use of Psychic Espionage as Narrated by the Key Russian and American Players* (Palo Alto, CA: Laboratories for Fundamental Research, 2014).

Mazanik, Elena, *Vozmezdie* (Minsk: Mastatskaya Literatura, 1981).

McDonald, Peter, 'The Spy who came into the warm' ('KGB – The Soviet Secret Police', BBC1, Tuesday, 8:30), *Radio Times* (1974), 6–7.

McLoughlin, Barry, and McDermott, Kevin (eds.), *Stalin's Terror: High Politics and Mass Repression in the Soviet Union*, paperback (Houndmills, Basingstoke, Hampshire, and New York: Palgrave Macmillan, 2004).

McMoneagle, Joseph, *The Stargate Chronicles: Memoirs of a Psychic Spy*, paperback (Hertford, NC: Crossroad Press, 2015).

McTaggart, Lynne, *The Field: The Quest for the Secret Force of the Universe* (New York, NY: HarperCollins Publishers, 2002).

McTaggart, Lynne, *The Intention Experiment: Use Your Thought to Change the World* (London: HarperElement, 2007).

Medvedev, Vladimir T., *Chelovek za spinoi* (Moscow: Russlit, 1994).

Melton, H. Keith, *The Ultimate Spy Book* (New York and London: Dorling Kindersley, 1996), with Forewords by William Colby and Oleg Kalugin.

Menzel, Birgit, Hagemeister, Michael, and Rosenthal, Bernice Glatzer (eds.), *The New Age of Russia: Occult and Esoteric Dimensions* (Munich-Berlin: Verlag Otto Sagner, 2012).

Merridale, Catherine, *Lenin on the Train* (London: Allen Lane, 2016).

Merridale, Catherine, *Red Fortress: The Secret Heart of Russia's History* (London: Allen Lane, 2013).

Mezrich, Ben, *Once Upon a Time in Russia: The Rise of the Oligarchs and the Greatest Wealth in History* (London: Arrow Books/Penguin Random House, 2015).

Minchenok, Dmitry, 'Anti-killer No. 1', *Ogonök*, 18 (3–9 May 2004), 60–3.

Mirzayanov, V., Fedorov, L., 'Otravlennaya politika', *Moskovskie novosti*, (20 September 1992).

Mirzayanov, Vil S., *State Secrets: An Insider's Chronicle of the Russian Chemical Weapons Program* (Denver, CO: Outskirts Press, 2008).

Möchel, Kid, *Der geheime Krieg der Agenten: Spionage Drehscheibe Wien* (Hamburg: Rasch und Röhring Verlag, 1997).

Morcillo, Cruz, and Muñoz, Pablo, *Palabra de Vor: Las mafias rusas en España*, paperback (Madrid: Espasa, 2010).

Motyl, Alexander J., *Ukraine, Europe, and Bandera*, Cicero Foundation Great Debate Paper, No. 10/05 (March 2010).

Murphy, David E., Kondrashev, Sergei A., and Bailey, George, *Battleground Berlin: CIA vs KGB in the Cold War* (New Haven and London: Yale University Press, 1997).

Murphy, David E., *What Stalin Knew: The Enigma of Barbarossa*, paperback (New Haven & London: Yale University Press, 2005).

Myers, Steven Lee, *The New Tsar: The Rise and Reign of Vladimir Putin*, paperback (New York, NY: Simon & Schuster, 2016).

Nehring, Christopher, 'Umbrella or Pen? The murder of Georgi Markov. New facts and old questions', *Journal of Intelligence History*, 16/1 (2017), 47–58.

Nemtsov, Boris, *Ispoved buntarya* (Moscow: Partisan, 2007).

Nikitine, Colonel B.V. [Boris Nikitin, chief of Petrograd counterintelligence in 1917], *The Fatal Years: Fresh revelations on a chapter of underground history* (London: William Hodge & Company Limited, 1938), with a preface by Sir Alfred Knox.

Noakes, Jeremy, 'Viceroys of the Reich? Gauleiters 1925–45', in Anthony McElligott and Tim Kirk (eds.), *Working Towards the Führer: Essays in Honour of Sir Ian Kershaw* (Manchester: Manchester University Press, 2004).

Opal, Barbara, 'US, Russia Hope to Safeguard Mind-Control Technology', *Defense News* (January 11–17, 1993), 29.

Ostermann, Christian F., (ed.), *Uprising in East Germany, 1953: The Cold War, the German Question, and the First Major Upheaval Behind the Iron Curtain* (Budapest: Central European University Press, 2001).

Ostrander, Sheila, *Psychic Discoveries Behind the Iron Curtain* (Upper Saddle River, NJ: Prentice Hall, 1984).

Ostrander, Sheila, and Schroeder, Lynn, *Psychic* Discoveries: *The Iron Curtain Lifted* (London: Souvenir Press Ltd, 1997).

Petrov, Nikita, *Die sowjetischen Geheimdienstmitarbeiter in Deutschland: Der leitende Personalbestand der Staatssicherheisorgane der UdSSR in der Sowjetischen Besatzungszone Deutschlands und der DDR von 1945–1954. Biographisches Nachschlagewerk* (Berlin: Metropol, 2010).

Pipes, Richard, *The Russian Revolution* (New York, NY: Alfred A. Knopf, 1990).

Pirogov, Peter, *Why I Escaped: The Story of Peter Pirogov* (New York, NY: Duell, Sloan and Pearce, 1950).

Plokhy, Serhii, 'How a KGB Assassin Used the Death of his Child to Defect', *Politico Magazine* (online edition), 5 January 2017.

Plokhy, Serhii, *The Man with the Poison Gun: A Cold War Spy Story* (New York, NY: Basic Books, 2016).

Polgar, Thomas, *The KGB: An Instrument of Soviet Power*, paperback (Washington, DC: AFIO, 1983).

Politkovskaya, Anna, *A Russian Diary* (London: Harvill Secker, 2007), with a Foreword by Jon Snow.

Politkovskaya, Anna, *Putin's Russia*, paperback (London: Harvill Press, 2004).

Preston, Paul, *We Saw Spain Die: Foreign Correspondents in the Spanish Civil War*, paperback (London: Constable, 2009).

Primakov, Yevgeny, *Russian Crossroads: Toward the New Millennium* (New Haven and London: Yale University Press, 2004).

Rappaport, Helen, *Caught in the Revolution: Petrograd, 1917* (London: Hutchinson, 2016).

Ratnikov, Boris K., and Rogozin, Georgy G., *Kartina mira v predstavlenii spetzsluzhb: Ot mistiki do osmysleniya*, paperback (Moscow: Academiya Upravleniya, 2011).

Rayfield, Donald, *Stalin and His Hangmen: An Authoritative Portrait of a Tyrant and Those Who Served Him* (London: Viking/Penguin Books, 2004).

Reid Jr., Charles, 'Vladimir Putin's Culture of Terror: What is to be Done?' *University of St. Thomas Journal of Law and Public Policy*, 9/2 (Spring 2015), 275–376.

Rhine, J.B., *Parapsychology Today* (New York, NY: The Citadel Press, 1968).

Rimington, Stella, *Open Secret: The Autobiography of the Former Director-General of MI5* (London: Hutchinson, 2001).

Rosmer, Alfred, 'A Fictionized Version of Trotsky's Murder', *Fourth International*, 10/3 (March 1949), 91–4.

Ross, Michael, with Jonathan Kay, *The Volunteer: The Incredible True Story of an Israeli Spy on the Trail of International Terrorists* (New York, NY: Skyhorse Publishing, 2007).

Rossolinsky-Liebe, Grzegorz, *Stepan Bandera: The Life and Afterlife of a Ukrainian Nationalist – Fascism, Genocide, and Cult* (Stuttgart: ibidem-Verlag, 2014).

Roth, Jürgen, *Die roten Bosse: Rußlands Tycoone übernehmen die Macht in Europa* (Munich-Zurich: Piper, 1998).

Roxburgh, Angus, *Moscow Calling: Memoirs of a Foreign Correspondent* (Edinburgh: Birlinn Ltd, 2017).

Rueda, Fernando, *Espías y traidores: Los 25 mejores agentes dobles de la historia*, paperback (Madrid: El Esfera de los Libros, 2012).

Rueda, Fernando, *La Casa: El CESID*: Agentes, *operaciones secretas y actividades de los espías españoles*, paperback (Barcelona: Roca Editorial, 2017).

Rueda, Fernando, *La Casa II: El CNI*: Agentes, *operaciones secretas y acciones inconfesables de los espías españoles*, paperback (Barcelona: Roca Editorial, 2017).

Safire, William, 'Putinism Looms', *The New York Times*, 31 January 2000.

Sánchez, Germán, 'Mujeres españolas al Servicio del KGB', *Cambio 16*, 1250 (6 November 1995).

Sannikov, Georgy, *Bolshaya Okhota: Razgrom Ukrainskoi Povstancheskoi Armii* (Moscow: Olma-Press, 2002).

Satter, David, *Age of Delirium: The Decline and Fall of the Soviet Union* (New York, NY: Alfred A. Knopf, 1996).

Schlitz, Marilyn, and Gruber, Elmar, 'Transcontinental Remote Viewing', *The Journal of Parapsychology*, 44/4 (December 1980), 305–17.

Schmidt, Ulf, 'Cold War at Porton Down: Informed Consent in Britain's Biological and Chemical Warfare Experiments', *Cambridge quarterly of healthcare ethics: CQ: The international journal of healthcare ethics committees*, 15/4 (Fall 2006), 366–80.

Scott, Len, 'Intelligence and the Rise of Nuclear War: *Able Archer*-83 Revisited', *Intelligence and National Security*, 26/6 (December 2011), 759–77.

Serge, Victor, *Vie et mort de Léon Trotsky*, paperback (Paris: La Découverte/Poche, 2003), Preface by Richard Greeman.

Shebarshin, Leonid, *Ruka Moskvy: zapiski nachalnika sovetskoi razvedki* (Moscow: Tsentr-100, 1992).

Sheymov, Victor, *Tiebreaker: Tower of Secrets II*, paperback (Vienna, VA: Cyber Books Publishing, 2013).

Sheymov, Victor, *Tower of Secrets: A Real Life Spy Thriller* (Annapolis, MD: Naval Institute Press, 1993).

Shkadov, I.N. (ed.), *Heroes of the Soviet Union*, short bibliographical dictionary (Moscow: Voenizdat, 1987–1988), 2 vols.

Shore, Tom, *Pilgrim Spy: My Secret War against Putin, the KGB and the Stasi* (London: Coronet, 2018).

Shvets, Yuri B., *Washington Station: My Life as a KGB Spy in America* (New York, NY; Simon and Schuster, 1994).

Sigl, Rupert, *In den Klauen des KGB: Errinnerungen eines Doppelagenten*, paperback (Leoni am Starnbergersee: Druffel-Verlag, 1980).

Silver, Arnold M., 'Questions, Questions, Questions: Memories of Oberursel', *Intelligence and National Security*, 8/2 (April 1993), 199–213.

Siqueiros, David Alfaro, *Menya nazyvali Likhim Polkovnikom: Vospominaniya* (Moscow: Gosudarstvennoe izdatelstvo politicheskoi literatury, 1986).

Sixsmith, Martin, *The Litvinenko File: The true Story of a Death Foretold* (London: Macmillan, 2007).

Smith, Michael, *New Cloak, Old Dagger: How Britain's Spies Came in From the Cold* (London: Weidenfeld & Nicolson, 1996).

Smith, Michael, *The Anatomy of a Traitor: A History of Espionage and Betrayal* (London: Aurum Press Ltd, 2017).

Smithson, Amy E., Mirzayanov, Vil S., Lajoie, Roland, and Krepon, Michael, 'Chemical Weapons Disarmament in Russia: Problems and Prospects', Report No. 17, October 1995 (Washington, DC: Henry L. Stimson Center, 1995).

Snegiryov, Vladimir, 'Ubiistva zakazyvalis v Kremle', *Trud* (24–25 July 1992).

Snepp, Frank, *Decent Interval: An Insider's Account of Saigon's Indecent End Told by the CIA's Chief Strategy Analyst in Vietnam* (New York, NY: Random House, 1977).

Spence, Richard B., *Trust No One: The Secret World of Sidney Reilly* (Los Angeles, CA: Feral House, 2002).

Stafford, David, *Spies Beneath Berlin* (London: John Murray, 2002).

Steele, John L., 'Assassin Disarmed by Love: The Case of a Soviet Spy Who Defected to the West', *Life*, September 7, 1962, 70–2, 77.

Stejskal, James, *Special Forces Berlin: Clandestine Cold War Operations of the US Army's Elite, 1956-1990* (Havertown, PA: Casemate Publishers, 2017).

Stevens, Serita, and Bannon, Anne, *Book of Poisons* (Cincinnati, OH: Writer's Digest Books, 2007).

Stockton, Bayard, *Flawed Patriot: The Rise and Fall of CIA Legend Bill Harvey* (Washington, DC: Potomac Books, 2006).

Sudoplatov, Pavel (signed by pseudonym 'M.L. Topol'), 'Viza na ubiystvo', *Voenno-istorichesky zhurnal*, 11 (1990), 48–62.

Sudoplatov, Pavel, and Sudoplatov, Anatoly, with Schecter, Jerrold L. and Schecter, Lorna P., *Special Tasks: The Memoirs of an Unwanted Witness – A Soviet Spymaster* (London: Little Brown, 1994).

Sudoplatov, Pavel, *Spetzoperatsyi Lubyanka i Kreml, 1930–1950* (Moscow: Olma Press, 2003).

Sulyga, Evgeny, 'Pochemu bezhal na Zapad odin iz organizatorov ubiistva gaulyaitera Kube?', *Sovetskaya Belorussiya*, 93 (Saturday, 24 May 1995).

Suskind, Ron, *The Way of the World: A Story of Truth and Hope in an Age of Extremism* (New York, NY: HarperCollins, 2008).

Suvorov, Victor (pseudo. Vladimir Rezun), *Aquarium: The Career and Defection of a Soviet Military Spy*, translated by D. Floyd (London: Hamish Hamilton, 1985).

Suvorov, Victor (pseudo. Vladimir Rezun), *Inside Soviet Military Intelligence* (London: Macmillan, 1984).

Talbot, David, *The Devil's Chessboard* (London: William Collins, 2015).

Talbott, Strobe, 'The making of Vladimir Putin', *Politico Magazine* (online edition), 19 August 2014.

Thatcher, Margaret, *The Downing Street Years* (London: HarperCollns, 1993).

The New Encyclopædia Britannica, Volume 28, MACROPÆDIA, 15th edition (1995), 980–94.

Thomas, Hugh, *History, Capitalism and Freedom*, paperback (London: Centre for Policy Studies, 1979).

Tokaev, G.A., *Mes mémoires: Le paradis de Stalin* (Paris: Le Colombe, 1957).

Tokaev, G.A., *Soviet Imperialism* (London: Gerald Duckworth & Co., 1954).

Tokaev, Grigori Aleksandrovich, *Betrayal of an Ideal* (Bloomington, IN: Indiana University Press, 1955).

Trotsky, Leon, *Trotsky's Diary in Exile, 1935* (Cambridge, MA: Harvard University Press, 1958).

Tschekhowa, Olga, *Meine Uhren gehen anders: Erinnerungen* (Munich: Herbig Verlagsbuchhandlung, 1973).

Tsygankov, Vladimir D., and Lopatin, Vladimir N., *Psychotronnoe oruzhie i bezopasnost Rossii* (Moscow: Sinteg, 1999).

Tucker, Jonathan B., *War of Nerves: Chemical Warfare from World War I to Al-Qaeda* (New York, NY: Pantheon Books, 2006).

Turonek Jerzy, *Białoruś pod okupacją niemiecką* (Warsaw: Książka i Wiedza, 1993).

Tutaev, David, 'The Man the Russians Tried to Kill', *John Bull*, 11 September 1954, 45; 18 September 1954, 9-11, 38; 25 September 1954, 40–42.

Uglev, Vladimir, 'A mystery of two perfume bottles: Russian chemist about poisoning in Salisbury', interview with Dmitry Volchek (in Russian), RFE/RL Prague, 13 October 2018.

Urban, Mark, *The Skripal Files: The Life and Near Death of a Russian Spy* (London: Macmillan, 2018).

Urban, Mark, *UK Eyes Alpha: Inside Story of British Intelligence* (London: Faber & Faber, 1996).

Vakhaniya, Vladimir, *Lichnaya sekretnaya sluzhba I.V. Stalina*, sbornik dokumentov (Moscow: Svarog, 2004).

van Heijenoort, Jean, *With Trotsky in Exile: From Prinkipo to Coyoacan* (Cambridge, MA: Harvard University Press, 1978).

Van Herpen, Marcel H., *Putin's Propaganda Machine: Soft Power and Russian Foreign Policy* (Lanham, MD: Rowman & Littlefield, 2016).

Vedeneyev, Dmitro, and Lisenko, Oleksandr, 'Organizatsyia Ukrainskih Natsyonalistov i zarubizhni spetssluzhby, 1920–1950', *Ukrainian History Magazine*, 3 (2009), 132–46.

Vinokurov, Igor, and Gurtovoi, Georgy, 'The Media, Government Departments and Psychotronic Weapons', *Aura-Z*, no. 2 (July 1993), 38–43, CIA-FOIA.

Vinokurov, I., and Gurtovoi, G., *Psychotronnaya voina* (Moscow: Misteria, 1993).

Vishnyakov, O., Uglev, V., 'Interview s petlioi na shee', *Novoe vremya*, 6 (1993), 40–41.

Volodarsky, Boris, 'A venomous agent: the true story of Sergei Skripal', *The Times*, 24 March 2018.

Volodarsky, Boris, 'The threat from Russia's spies has only increased since the fall of Communism', *The Spectator*, 325/9701 (2 August 2014), 15–17.

Volodarsky, Boris, 'Years of the Spy', *American Intelligence Journal* (USA), 31/2 (2013), 152–4.

Volodarsky, Boris, *Nikolai Khokhlov, WHISTLER, Self-Esteem with a Halo*, paperback (Vienna and London: Borwall Publishing, 2005), with a Foreword by Oleg Gordievsky.

Volodarsky, Boris, *Stalin's Agent: The Life and Death of Alexander Orlov* (Oxford: Oxford University Press, 2015).

Volodarsky, Boris, *The KGB's Poison Factory: From Lenin to Litvinenko* (Barnsley, S. Yorkshire: Frontline Books/Pen & Sword Books, 2009, 2017).

Related articles by the author: 'Cosí gli 007 di Mosca hanno incastrato Scaramella', *Il Giornale* (Italy), XXXIV/26 (31 January 2007), 1–10 (with Oleg Gordievsky); 'Getting the Reds out of the Orange Revolution', *The Wall Street Journal* (USA), XXIII/184 (14 October 2005), 11; 'La guerra clandestine dei russi', *Il Giornale* (Italy), XXXIV/130 (2 June 2007), 1–14; 'License to Kill', *The Wall Street Journal* (USA), XXIV/228 (20 December 2006), 15; 'Russian Venom', *The Wall Street Journal* (USA), XXIV/208 (22 November 2006), 13; 'Terror's KGB Roots', *The Wall Street Journal* (USA), XXV/208 (23–25 November 2007), 11; 'The KGB's Poison Factory', *The Wall Street Journal* (USA), XXIII/84 (7 April 2005), 13; 'The Ukraine's Tapegate Dilemma', *The Salisbury Review* (UK), 24/2 (Winter 2005), 15–17; 'Untangling the web of deception', *The Spectator* (UK), 303/9327 (19 May 2007), 38–40, (with Oleg Gordievsky); 'The dark arts of the Russian poisoners',

The Times (UK), 72476 (7 March 2018), Times2, 2–3; 'A Venomous Agent', *The Times* (UK), 24 March 2018.

Wark, Wesley, *Twenty-first Century Intelligence* (London: Routledge, 2004).

Weiner, Tim, *Legacy of Ashes: The History of the CIA* (New York, NY: Anchor Books/ Random House, 2008).

Winch, Michael, *Republic for a Day: An Eye-Witness Account of the Carpatho-Ukraine Incident* (London: Robert Hale Ltd., 1939).

Wolf, Markus, *Die Troika* (Berlin: Aufbau-Verlag, 1989).

Wolf, Markus, *Geheimnisse der russischen Küche* (Hamburg: Rotbuch Verlag, 1995).

Wolf, Markus, with McElvoy, Anne, *Man Without a Face: The Autobiography of Communism's Greatest Spymaster* (London: Jonathan Cape, 1997).

Womack, Helen (ed.), *Undercover Lives: Soviet Spies in the Cities of the World* (London: Weidenfeld & Nicolson, 1998).

Wrangel, Peter N., 'Mart 1920', *Beloe Delo*, ed. by Alexei A. von Lampe (Berlin: Mednyi Vsadnik, 1926–8), 1/1 (1926), 61–76.

Wrangel, Peter N., 'Zapiski: Noyabr 1916 – Noyabr 1920', *Beloe Delo* ed. by Alexei A. von Lampe (Berlin: Mednyi Vsadnik, 1926–8), 6/4–6 (1928), 5–242.

Wrangel, Peter N., *Always with Honour* (New York, NY: Robert Speller & Sons, 1957), Foreword by Herbert Hoover.

Wrangel, Peter N., *The Memoirs of General Wrangel, the last commander-in-chief of the Russian National Army*, translated by Sophie Goulston (London: Williams & Norgate, 1929).

Wright, Andy, 'The Russian Spy Who Convinced America to Take ESP Seriously: History's Spookiest Spook' [Khokhlov], *Atlas Obscura*, 13 January 2017.

Yeltsin, Boris, *Midnight Diaries* (London: Weidenfeld & Nicolson, 2000).

Yeltsin, Boris, *The Struggle for Russia* (New York, NY: Macmillan Publishers/Times Books, 1995), translated by Catherine A. Fitzpatrick.

Yushchenko, Victor, *Nederzhavni taemnitsi: Notatki na beregakh pamyati* (Kiev: Folio, 2014).

Zakharov, Nikolai S., *Skvoz gody* (Tula: Grif & Co., 2003).

Zygar, Mikhail, *All the Kremlin's Men: Inside the Court of Vladimir Putin* (New York, NY: PublicAffairs, 2016).

Index